American Indian History

American Indian History

Volume 2

Pavonia Massacre—Zuñi Rebellion
Appendixes
Indexes

edited by

Carole A. Barrett
University of Mary

Salem Press, Inc.
Pasadena, California   Hackensack, New Jersey

∞ The paper used in these volumes conforms to the American National Standard for Permanence of Paper for Printed Library Materials,
Z39.48-1992 (R1997).

Essays originally appeared in *Ready Reference: American Indians*
(1995), *Great Events from History: North American Series, Revised Edition*
(1997), and *Racial and Ethnic Relations in America* (2000). New material
has been added.

Library of Congress Cataloging-in-Publication Data
American Indian history / edited by Carole A. Barrett.
  p. cm. — (Magill's choice)
Includes bibliographical references and index.
  ISBN 1-58765-067-3 (set : alk. paper) — ISBN 1-58765-068-1 (vol. 1 :
alk. paper) — ISBN 1-58765-069-X (vol. 2 : alk. paper)
  1. Indians of North America—History. I. Barrett, Carole A. II. Series.
E77 .A496 2003
970'.00497—dc21

2002007731

First Printing

PRINTED IN THE UNITED STATES OF AMERICA

CONTENTS — VOLUME 2

Contents

Contents

COMPLETE LIST OF CONTENTS

Volume 1

Volume 2

American Indian History

Pavonia Massacre

Date: February 26, 1643
Locale: Pavonia, New Amsterdam (modern New Jersey)
Tribes involved: Hackensack, Wecquaesgeek
Categories: Colonial history, Wars and battles
Significance: This massacre, perpetrated by European settlers on peaceful Indian tribes, led to brutal retaliation by the Indians and the eventual destruction of Pavonia.

Pavonia, a Dutch settlement located in the current Staten Island and Bayonne-Jersey City region, was the terminus of a trail used by Indians to move trading goods. A use tax imposed in 1639 and other incidents so outraged the Hackensack that in 1642 they killed two settlers. In 1643, a number of Wecquaesgeek Indians fled in terror from Mohawk raids—some to Pavonia, near the Hackensack, seeking Dutch protection.

Following a carefully laid-out plot, eighty soldiers launched a brutal surprise attack on the Indian camp shortly after midnight on February 26 to revenge the killing of the settlers. Between 80 and 120 Indians were killed and about thirty prisoners taken. In retaliation for this massacre, regional tribes intermittently terrorized the Dutch over the next decade.

See also: Indian-white relations: Dutch colonial.

Laurence Miller

Paxton Boys' Massacres

Date: December 14-27, 1763
Locale: A Conestoga village near Lancaster, Pennsylvania
Tribes involved: Iroquois Confederacy (Cayuga, Mohawk, Oneida, Onondaga, Seneca, Tuscarora), Lenni Lenape, Shawnee, Susquehannock
Categories: Colonial history, Wars and battles
Significance: Growing tensions between Pennsylvania backcountry settlers and Native Americans reflect western resentment of inequitable representation.

The French and Indian War (1754-1763) was a particularly difficult time for settlers in the Pennsylvania backcountry. By the early 1750's, the harmony that had characterized the relationship between Native Americans and the colony since the time of William Penn had ended. Led by the Six Nations of the Iroquois Confederacy, various Pennsylvania tribes, encompassing numerous Native American villages throughout the region, fought to limit future European expansion onto ancestral lands. The struggle engendered much bloodshed and carnage on both sides.

During the war, the Pennsylvania Assembly, influenced by pacific Quakers, pursued a policy of negotiations rather than resorting to armed confrontation. Despite pleas from embattled backcountry residents for military assistance, provincial leaders steadfastly refused to organize or outfit an official militia. As a result, western residents were left to fend for themselves. By the 1760's, the Quaker policy had produced some minimal results. Pennsylvania authorities were able to reestablish peaceful relations with a few villages. Cooperative tribes were promised land rights, commercial opportunities, and protection from their enemies. However, many villages questioned the sincerity of the offers and remained at war. This put backcountry residents in a particularly difficult situation. It was virtually impossible for them to differentiate between peaceful and hostile natives, a distinction that could become a matter of life or death. Therefore, many homesteaders chose simply to label all of the indigenous population as hostile until all had agreed to a peace.

The Massacres. On the morning of December 14, 1763, the tensions generated the first of two massacres. A band of approximately four dozen angry Pennsylvania backwoodsmen attacked an unsuspecting Conestoga village situated approximately fifty miles northwest of Lancaster. The village was inhabited by fewer than two dozen Susquehannocks. A month earlier, in a petition to Governor John Penn, these same Susquehannocks had promised to maintain the peace that they claimed they had always honored. Nevertheless, the Pennsylvanians, who called themselves the Paxton Boys, complained that villagers were assisting and sheltering Native American warriors. Several of the warriors were believed to have murdered nearby settlers. In the assault, the Paxton Boys struck quickly, burning the village's huts and killing three Susquehannock men, two women, and a child.

Panicked by the raid, fourteen Susquehannock survivors fled to the safety of provincial authorities in Lancaster. Upon their arrival, the refugees were placed under protective custody and held in the town jail. It was there that the Paxton Boys found them on December 27, and it was there that the backwoodsmen committed a second massacre. Enraged that local officials would shelter the natives, a force of about one hundred well-armed Paxton Boys rode up to the jailhouse. They burst into the build-

Two days after Christmas, 1763, about one hundred backwoodsmen who called themselves the Paxton Boys shot and tomahawked defenseless Susquehannocks who had been jailed after the backwoodsmen's earlier attacks. (Library of Congress)

ing, seized the keeper, and then shot and tomahawked the defenseless Susquehannocks. A few minutes later, with their task accomplished, the backwoods raiders rode off to their homes, satisfied that they had taken an important step toward easing the Native American threat within the region.

News of the two attacks created a flurry of activity in Philadelphia. Governor Penn immediately issued a proclamation instructing western magistrates to apprehend those involved in the massacres. Colonial officials, fearing additional assaults, rounded up 125 friendly Native Americans, many of whom had converted to Moravianism, and brought them to Philadelphia. Meanwhile, the colonial Assembly asked New York authorities to provide a sanctuary for the refugees. However, the New York governor denied the request. Instead, a regiment of British regulars was assigned to escort the "Moravian Indians" to a military barracks on a Delaware River island and to defend them against all potential assailants. The Assembly's precautions were not popular in the backcountry. John Elder, a Presbyterian minister and militia colonel who was alleged to be the Paxton Boys' organizer, warned that "the minds of the inhabitants are so exasperated against the Quakers" that western residents were ready to confront the Assembly and take matters into their own hands.

The Paxton Boys Head for Philadelphia. By late January, 1764, reports about an impending attack by the Paxton Boys swirled through Philadelphia. One letter to Governor Penn claimed that fifteen hundred well-armed backwoodsmen, a force three times larger than the British regiment guarding the Native Americans, were planning to march on the city and go door to door until they had found all the Native Americans in Philadelphia. The westerners intended to burn down the houses of those who resisted. The letter ended with a prediction that the backwoodsmen would fight to the death, if necessary.

The rumored march became a reality in early February. Although considerably smaller than most reports had forecast, a force of two hundred backwoods residents, comprising primarily Scotch-Irish Presbyterians from the lower Susquehanna River region, began a hike toward the provincial capital. Armed with muskets, tomahawks, and pistols, they announced that they were coming to Philadelphia to rectify the various abuses directed at them by the Assembly.

Intercepting the westerners at Germantown, five miles northwest of the city, Benjamin Franklin led a delegation appointed by the governor. Matthew Smith and James Gibson, two militia officers, presented Franklin with a petition that identified nine specific grievances. Surprisingly, the primary complaint had nothing to do with the colony's Native American policy. Instead, the Paxton Boys protested that the four western counties had significantly less representation in the Assembly than did the three eastern counties. If this inequity were rectified, the backwoodsmen claimed that the other eight complaints, all of which dealt with policies concerning Native Americans, would be remedied.

While Franklin conferred, other Philadelphians prepared for an attack. Some local residents insisted that the force in Germantown was simply an advance unit of Paxton Boys and that hundreds more would soon arrive. To defend the city against the "Lawless Party of Rioters," the Assembly swiftly enacted emergency legislation. Six companies, each with one hundred volunteers, were hastily organized. Cannons were pulled into defensive positions around the courthouse. Shops were closed. The roads and ferries leading into the city were blockaded. The British regiment guarding the Native American refugees was placed on alert.

Franklin Negotiates. Aided by the city's impressive mobilization, Franklin's deliberations proved fruitful. The westerners agreed that if their petition were promptly delivered to the governor and Assembly, they would return home. In a gesture aimed at compromise, the Philadelphia delegation announced that the Paxton Boys had been misunderstood and were, in fact, "a set of worthy men who laboured under great distress." The delegation then accompanied about thirty backwoodsmen into the city. The following day, one of the visitors was permitted to inspect several Native Americans to determine whether they had been involved in recent attacks upon settlers. They had not. Several days later, the westerners' petition was presented to the legislature.

In July, the Assembly responded legislatively to the Paxton Boys' demands. Pennsylvania formally declared war against the Lenni Lenape and Shawnee tribes. A bounty for Native American scalps, another of the westerners' demands, was enacted. Money also was appropriated for the creation of an official provincial militia, something the Quaker government had steadfastly refused to do, even during the French and Indian War. The colony's search for the Paxton Boys involved in the two massacres had ended months earlier, with no arrests made.

Pennsylvania felt the impact of the Paxton Boys' activities for years to come. Most important, the crisis initiated an ongoing dispute about fair and equitable representation for western counties. It was a contest in which political power eventually shifted away from Philadelphia Quakers and toward a diverse and democratic coalition of political leadership. Ultimately, the crisis surrounding the Paxton Boys' Massacres served as an initial step toward the political divisions that generated an independence movement within the colony.

See also: French and Indian War; Indian-white relations: English colonial; Iroquois Confederacy; Iroquois Confederacy-U.S. Congress meeting; Paxton Boys' Massacres; Proclamation of 1763.

Paul E. Doutrich

Sources for Further Study

Franz, George W. *Paxton: A Study of Community Structure and Mobility in the Colonial Pennsylvania Backcountry.* New York: Garland, 1989. Focuses on political and socioeconomic development of the Paxton community.

Hindle, Brooke. "The March of the Paxton Boys." *William and Mary Quarterly,* 3d ser., 3 (October, 1946): 461-486. Still one of the best narrative accounts of the massacres.

Jacobs, Wilbur R. *The Paxton Riots and the Frontier Theory.* Chicago: Rand McNally, 1967. A brief booklet that includes many primary documents produced during the episode.

Kelley, Joseph J., Jr. *Pennsylvania: The Colonial Years.* Garden City, N.Y.: Doubleday, 1980. Includes a general description of the Paxton Boys episode.

Schwartz, Sally. *"A Mixed Multitude": The Struggle for Toleration in Colonial Pennsylvania.* New York: New York University Press. 1987. A general history that describes the various tensions within colonial Pennsylvania and how the colony dealt with them.

Peach Wars

Date: 1655-1664
Locale: Hudson River Valley, New York
Tribes involved: Esophus, Lenni Lenape
Categories: Colonial history, Wars and battles
Significance: This conflict is regarded as the most significant confrontation between the Dutch and the Indians; the end of the conflict also marked the end of Dutch rule.

Dutch traders depended upon the Indian tribes of the Hudson and Niagara regions for their livelihood. With the development of frontier trading posts in 1620, the Dutch established a permanent presence in the wilderness. Governor-general Willem Kieft began an extensive campaign to intimidate and subjugate Indian tribes after he took office in 1639. In 1655, a Dutch farmer killed a Delaware woman for picking peaches in his orchard. Her tribe quickly retaliated, and ambushes occurred throughout the Hudson Valley, even at New Amsterdam.

Fighting was particularly fierce on the northern reaches of the Hudson, at the settlement of Wiltwyck. The new governor-general, Peter Stuyvesant, arrived with a militia that forced the attacking Esophus tribe into negotiation. The Dutch, however, murdered the Indian delegation. Retaliatory raids resulted in eight Dutch casualties, and warfare continued for five years.

In 1660, Stuyvesant embarked on a new policy: taking Indians as hostages to ensure peace. The Esophus, however, refused all Dutch peace offers until Stuyvesant ordered the hostages sold into slavery. In 1664, after the Mohawks agreed to help the Dutch defeat the Esophus, the English captured New Netherland, ending both the Peach Wars and Dutch rule.

See also: Bacon's Rebellion; Beaver Wars; Fur trade; Iroquois Confederacy; Indian-white relations: Dutch colonial; Manhattan Island purchase; Pavonia Massacre; Peach Wars; Pequot War.

Richard S. Keating

Pequot War

Date: July 20, 1636-July 28, 1637
Locale: Connecticut
Tribes involved: Pequot, Narragansett
Categories: Colonial history, Wars and battles
Significance: The first major conflict between Native Americans and New England settlers.

As suggested by their name (from *pekawatawog*, "the destroyers"), the Pequots were once the most formidable tribe in New England. Part of the Eastern Algonquian language family, the Pequots, by the dawn of the seventeenth century, were well established in what is now Connecticut. Their powerful sachem (principal chief) was the venerable Sassacus, who was born near what is now Groton. In spite of many years of experience, Sassacus faced, in his seventies, the biggest crisis in his people's history. Although the Pequots had a virtual hegemony over their adjacent nations—as the leader of the Mohegans, Uncas was married to the daughter of the Pequot chief—the Pequots had trouble coping with the impact of the European powers in the Connecticut Valley. The Pequots found themselves caught between the Dutch moving eastward from New Netherlands and the English moving westward from the Massachusetts Bay Colony and Connecticut. European competition for control over trade on the Connecticut River proved to be a destabilizing factor in intertribal relationships.

The political climate was ripe for violence. It began when two English traders were killed in Connecticut—John Stone in 1633 and John Oldham on July 20, 1636. It has never been firmly established that the Pequots were responsible for their deaths. When John Gallup, an English merchant, found natives in control of Oldham's ship, anchored off Block Island, he fought with them in July, 1636, for control of it. Captain John Endecott, the first governor of the Massachusetts Bay Colony, with ninety soldiers, conducted a punitive raid on Block Island, killing every male native there. Although most of the casualties were Narragansetts, not Pequots, Endecott

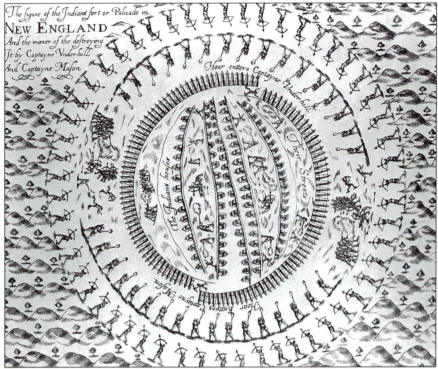

Contemporary engraving of the 1637 defeat of the Pequots at Fort Mystic, their forti-
fied village, from Captain John Underhill's account in Newes from America (1638).
(Library of Congress)

pushed eastward along the Connecticut coast, demanding reparations
from the Pequots, who refused, resisted, and suffered at least one death, as
well as the destruction of several villages.

Siege of Fort Saybrook. Sassacus, outraged, invited the Narragansetts to
join him in war on the English. Their chief, Miantonomo, was favorably
disposed toward the colonists, probably due to the influence of Roger Williams, the founder of Rhode Island. Even without Narragansett support,
Sassacus acted, laying siege to Fort Saybrook, situated on the Connecticut
River, during the winter of 1636-1637 and concurrently attacking several
outlying English settlements, including Wethersfield, where at least nine
settlers were killed.

Puritan retaliation was not long in coming. Captains John Mason and
John Underhill shared command. Born in England, Mason had served as an
army officer in the Netherlands before his arrival in Massachusetts in 1632.
From Hartford, he set forth with a band of eighty, supported by the

Mohegans and Narragansetts. Like Mason, Underhill had been born in England and then was reared in the Netherlands, where his father had fought the Spanish. Since 1630, he had lived in Massachusetts. Mason and Underhill initially went eastward, by ship, along the Connecticut coast, making landfall at Narragansett Bay. Then, with their native allies, they moved westward by land. After crossing the Pawcatuck and Mystic Rivers, they were poised to attack the main Pequot village at sunrise on May 25, 1637. The Puritan forces divided, each half attacking one of the two main gates, located at opposite ends of the stockaded native settlement. The English did not profit as much as expected by their surprise attack; their opening forays were repulsed. Then the colonials set fire to the wigwams, and as the village burned, the Pequots faced horrible alternatives. Some, mostly women and children, remained inside the fort, perishing in the flames. Those who fled, mostly the warriors, were cut down by the English and their Narragansett, Mohegan, and Niantic allies. Between six hundred and one thousand Pequots perished in this massacre. Only two colonials were lost, a mere twenty wounded. Underhill rejoiced in the "mighty victory," comparing his annihilation of the Pequots to David's destruction of his foes in biblical times.

A large group of Pequot refugees sought sanctuary in a swamp near New Haven, only to be discovered and destroyed on July 28, 1637. In the subsequent confusion, Sassacus and a handful of followers fled, seeking asylum in Mohawk territory. Desiring to prove their loyalty to the English, the Mohawks beheaded Sassacus.

Uncas Rises to Power. As a consequence of the Pequot War, Uncas, the son-in-law of Sassacus, seized control of the Mohegan tribe. With English support, Uncas began a career of conquest that made him the most powerful sachem in New England. Miantonomo, sachem of the Narragansetts, was killed by command of Uncas in 1643, perhaps as a political act asked by his English allies. Although Uncas initially prospered as a prominent warrior and ruler, he discovered his English allies to be unpredictable. When he attacked Massasoit in 1661, the Puritans forced him to give up prisoners and plunder; during Metacom's War (1675-1676), Uncas surrendered his sons as hostages to the colonists, who, defeating Metacom (or King Philip) of the Wampanoags, effectively ended Indian resistance to European settlement.

The Pequot War also marked the advent of almost constant conflict between the Puritan settlers and the natives, and its results were ultimately tragic for all the Native Americans. The Pequots, who (together with the Mohegans) had counted perhaps four thousand men when the English arrived at Plymouth Rock in 1620, steadily declined in numbers. An estimate made in 1643 suggested that there were twenty-five hundred men in their group. Following their defeat, many of the Pequots were massacred or enslaved; those enslaved were shared between the Europeans and other natives, some being deported as far from home as Boston or the island of Bermuda. Others were assimilated into other tribes, by being resettled among their former enemies. In 1655, the Pequots were moved to two reservations on the Mystic River. By 1674, there were only three hundred men in this once-proud nation. Pequot place names disappeared: The Pequot River, for example, became the Thomas. Their power had been forfeited, their identity nearly eradicated. In 1990, there were between nine hundred and sixteen hundred Pequots.

See also: Metacom's War; Saybrook, Battle of.

C. George Fry

Sources for Further Study

Cave, Alfred A. *The Pequot War*. Amherst: University of Massachusetts Press, 1996. The first in-depth study of the Pequot War, emphasizing the motives behind the hostilities through archaeological, linguistic, and anthropological analysis.

De Forest, John W. *History of the Indians of Connecticut from the Earliest Known Period to 1850*. Hartford, Conn.: W. J. Hammersley, 1851. Reprint. Hamden, Conn.: Shoestring Press, 1988. A classic study of the native peoples of Connecticut.

Josephy, Alvin M., Jr. *Five Hundred Nations: An Illustrated History of the North American Indians*. New York: Alfred A. Knopf, 1994. This generously illustrated volume is sympathetic to the point of view of the Native Americans. References to the situation in New England are corrective to earlier writings.

Orr, Charles, ed. *History of the Pequot War: The Contemporary Accounts of Mason, Underhill, Vincent, and Gardener*. Cleveland, Ohio: Helman-Taylor, 1897. A valuable anthology of eyewitness reporting on the Pequot War from the Puritan perspective, drawing on the recollections of major English participants.

Peale, Arthur L. *Memorials and Pilgrimages in the Mohegan Country*. Norwich, Conn.: Bulletin Company, 1930. Peale, author of a groundbreaking study of Uncas, was celebrated for his knowledge of the Mohegans and the Pequots. Remarkably readable reflections.

Salisbury, Neal E. *Manitou and Providence: Indians, Europeans, and the Making of New England, 1500-1643*. New York: Oxford University Press, 1982. A thorough, objective study of the contrasting attitudes and values of the

Native Americans and the Europeans during a century and a half of contact and conflict.

Stoutenburgh, John L., Jr. *Dictionary of the American Indian.* New York: Philosophical Library, 1960. A concise resource with excellent brief biographies and summary descriptions of key events in Native American history.

Vaughan, Alden T. *New England Frontier: Puritans and Indians, 1620-1675.* Boston: Little, Brown, 1965. This helpful study of a half-century of relationships between Native Americans and European settlers is a fine starting point for research.

Pima uprisings

Date: 1695, 1751
Locale: Southern Arizona, northwestern Mexico
Tribes involved: Pima
Categories: Colonial history, Wars and battles
Significance: These uprisings, instigated by Spanish mistreatment and possibly by personal ambition, caused significant death and destruction and undermined the formerly cordial relations between the Spanish and Indians.

By the late 1600's the Spanish Jesuits had established a successful system of missions and maintained cordial relations with the Upper Pimas. In Tubutama, however, in 1694 the Spanish unjustly and summarily executed three Pimas for alleged horse stealing and forcibly silenced Pima leaders who were openly critical of the Spaniards and their methods. Christianized Opata Indians who oversaw running the mission herds and lands at Tubutama alienated the Pimas with attitudes of condescension and superiority.

In 1695 an uprising occurred by a disaffected faction of Pimas at Tubutama. Three Opata were killed. Moving southwest and enlisting some allies, they destroyed the presidio at Altar and killed the missionary at Caborca.

The Spanish retaliated immediately. They killed a few women and children and destroyed fields at Caborca as a lesson but were not able to find the instigators of the uprising. The aid of peaceful Pima leaders who were not part of the uprising was enlisted to identify the instigators. The first one identified was instantly beheaded. This set off a frenzy among the Spanish, who killed nearly fifty Pimas, including several peaceful ones.

As soon as the Spanish left, enraged Pimas organized and destroyed Tubutama, Caborca, and churches at Imuris and San Ignacio. Again, Spanish forces, this time aided by friendly Pimas, retaliated by killing a few Pimas and burning their crops, but they were again unable to engage the instigators. A number of Pima headmen who realized they could not oppose the Spanish arranged to surrender the instigators to the Spanish soldiers, who then left. The damage was done, however; much of Pima territory was destroyed. The Pimas were divided into pro- and anti-Spanish factions. Anger and distrust of the Spaniards smoldered among many Pimas.

A second Pima uprising occurred in 1751. The uprising was instigated by Luis Oacpicagigua, who had formerly served the Spanish so well that he was made captain-general of the Pimas. Oacpicagigua claimed that he revolted against the cruelty and oppression of Spanish military and missionary rule and was trying to end their domination over his people. The Spanish claimed that he desired to be chief of all the Pimas. This uprising was isolated rather than general. It began at Saric, near Tubuand. Oacpicagigua and some Western Pimas killed eighteen Spaniards invited to his house, attacked Tubutama, and killed two missionaries at Caborca and Senoita. After the deaths of more than a hundred Spaniards and more than forty Pimas and a loss of support, Oacpicagigua ceased hostilities and was imprisoned.

The Jesuit missions never recovered from this uprising by the time of their expulsion in 1767. Several missions remained in operation but with successively declining success and influence. By the beginning of the nineteenth century, the Pimas had pretty much returned to their former way of life.

See also: Indian-white relations: Spanish colonial; Pueblo Revolt; Zuñi Rebellion.

Laurence Miller

Pine Ridge shootout and Peltier killings

Date: June 25-26, 1975
Locale: Pine Ridge Reservation, South Dakota
Tribes involved: Oglala Sioux
Categories: Protest movements; Twentieth century history

Significance: The Pine Ridge shootout was a turning point for the American Indian Movement (AIM) in their relations with the Bureau of Indian Affairs (BIA).

In 1973, members and supporters of the American Indian Movement (AIM) occupied the town of Wounded Knee, South Dakota, on the Pine Ridge Reservation. The activists were demonstrating against what they considered to be autocratic and sometimes corrupt practices of the Oglala Sioux tribal political leaders, especially Richard Wilson, the tribal chairman. Wilson, an aggressive opponent of AIM, along with local Bureau of Indian Affairs (BIA) officials, requested federal support in removing the activists. The occupation evolved into a state of siege lasting seventy-one days and leaving two native people dead. AIM leaders were indicted, but the case was dismissed after a federal judge accused the Federal Bureau of Investigation (FBI) of gross misconduct.

Discontent and strong opposition to the Pine Ridge Reservation tribal government and the chairman continued. On June 25, 1975, violence erupted again when a BIA policeman killed a young Oglala man. The following day, in an exchange of gunfire, two FBI agents were slain outside a house about fifteen miles from the town of Pine Ridge. Although the occupants of the house fled, two Oglala men were ultimately apprehended and charged with the murders; they were acquitted. Leonard Peltier, another suspect, was arrested in Canada, extradited to the United States, and sent to prison after a controversial trial in which he was sentenced to two consecutive life terms.

Peltier declared himself innocent of the killings and appealed his conviction many times. During the appeals, the court found that the government had acted improperly in arresting and trying him. Federal authorities admitted to falsifying affidavits used to extradite Peltier from Canada. Witnesses in the original trial had been coerced, and evidence supporting Peltier's claims was suppressed. In spite of these irregularities, the courts refused to overturn Peltier's conviction. Peltier's case became known throughout the world. Many people believed that, even if he were guilty, he had not been granted a fair trial. Amnesty International declared him a political prisoner, and important religious leaders spoke out on his behalf. A book and three films were made about the case. In 1992, a "Mr. X" confessed to the killings. Peltier's supporters continued to hope that they could win him a new trial.

Other victims of the 1975 violence included Leonard Crow Dog, an Oglala medicine man and spiritual leader of the movement who was arrested at his home on the neighboring Rosebud Reservation, and AIM supporter Anna Mae Aquash, a Micmac Indian woman, believed by the FBI to be a witness to the killing of the two agents. Aquash was found murdered in 1976.

There was a determined effort to get Peltier pardoned by President Bill Clinton at the end of his term in 2000, but pressure and protests from the FBI persuaded Clinton to refuse the pardon. In April, 2002, Peltier's lawyers filed a lawsuit against former FBI director Louis Freeh, the FBI Agents Association, and numerous past and present FBI officials for spreading lies about Peltier in their attempts to derail a pardon.

See also: American Indian Movement; Bureau of Indian Affairs; Indian-white relations: U.S., 1934-2002; Trail of Broken Treaties; Wounded Knee occupation.

Lucy Ganje and Cynthia A. Bily

Pontiac's Resistance

Date: May 8, 1763-July 24, 1766
Locale: Great Lakes region
Tribes involved: Chippewa, Lenni Lenape, Huron, Illinois, Kickapoo, Miami, Mingo, Ottawa, Potawatomi, Seneca, Shawnee
Categories: Colonial history, Wars and battles
Significance: A pan-Indian uprising presents the greatest threat to British expansion before the American Revolution.

Having signed the Treaty of Paris on February 10, 1763, Great Britain and France concluded the French and Indian War, nearly a decade of battle for empire in North America. Victorious, Great Britain then had to decide how to organize its vast new territories, embracing Canada and the area lying between the Appalachians and the Mississippi River. At issue in these trans-Appalachian lands were the rights, vital interests, profits, and responsibilities of the remaining Frenchmen, fur traders and trappers, British governors and colonials with claims to these territories, land speculators, the British army, and, not least, Native Americans. A plan to separate trans-Appalachia from eastern British colonies and keep out settlers had been recommended by William Petty, earl of Shelburne, then president of Britain's Board of Trade. Shelburne had hoped that his plan would be implemented by 1767, but despite mounting political pressure for Parliament to act on imperial reorganization, nothing was done until Shelburne had left office. What determined his successor's action and his issuance of the Proclamation of 1763 was a native uprising and the siege of the British fort at Detroit by a little-known Ottawa war chief, Pontiac.

A large, imposing figure, Pontiac was born in present-day northern Ohio, the son of an Ottawa father and a Chippewa (Ojibwa) mother. Although he married several times (as was customary), only one of his wives and two sons have been identified. Esteemed for his strategic skills and his intelligence, he had become a war chief by 1755, when he was in his mid-thirties. The Ottawa, like most of their neighbors, were traders who had profited from close relationships with the French and who, therefore, fought with French forces in America during the French and Indian War. Pontiac had fought with the French when they defeated British troops commanded by General Braddock at Fort Pitt in western Pennsylvania.

Indian Grievances. France's defeat, sealed by the Treaty of Paris, proved disastrous to frontier natives, who were constrained thereafter to deal with the British. Contrary to the intent of the Proclamation of 1763, colonial settlers poured across the Appalachians into American Indian territories. In addition, Lord Jeffrey Amherst, commander in chief of British forces, discontinued bestowing on the tribes gifts and supplies, the most import of which was gunpowder. During the war, Amherst had also provided alcohol to the natives, but he refused to dispense it at war's end. Thus, genuine hardship from a lack of gunpowder, which curtailed their hunting and disrupted their fur trade, an unslaked addiction to drink, discomfort due the diminution of other supplies, and increasing white encroachments on their lands furnished many Great Lakes tribes with serious grievances against the British.

PONTIAC.

The Ottawa chief Pontiac, who organized a pan-Indian resistance to English colonists in the 1760's. (Library of Congress)

On April 27, 1763, Pontiac convened a general war council in order to finalize war plans that envisaged a wholesale assault on British forts along the frontier. His call to arms solicited support from Chippewas, Lenni Lenapes (Delawares), Hurons, Illinois, Kickapoos, Miamis, Mingos, Potawatomis, Senecas, and Shawnees. On May 8, 1763, he and three hundred warriors—mostly his own tribesmen, along with Chippewas and Potawatomis—entered Fort Detroit, weapons concealed and ready to strike. Previously alerted to Pontiac's intentions, however, Major Henry Gladwin foiled Pontiac's attack from within and the natives put Gladwin's fort under what became a six-month siege. Within weeks, every British fort west of Niagara was destroyed: Forts Sandusky, St. Joseph, Miami, Quiatenon, Venango, Le Boeuf, Michilimackinac, Edward Augustus, and Presque Isle. Forts in the Monongahela Valley, such as Fort Ligonier, were attacked. Only Fort Pitt and Fort Detroit survived. Before the winter of 1763, the British had suffered costly ambushes such as one outside Detroit at Blood Ridge and counted two thousand casualties overall.

Fearful that their entire frontier would collapse, the British counterattacked. By late fall, tribal resistance had weakened, as the natives were unused to protracted warfare and lacked the measure of aid they had expected from the French. At Fort Pitt, blankets distributed by the fort commander, Captain Simon Ecuyer, infected besieging natives and produced a devastating smallpox epidemic, while another of Amherst's commanders tracked them with English hunting dogs. In late autumn, Pontiac lifted the siege of Detroit, although elsewhere some Indian forces continued fighting throughout 1764. Other tribes, however, had concluded peace treaties with Colonel John Bradstreet at Presque Isle as early as August, 1763. By July, 1765, Pontiac had entered peace negotiations that resulted in a treaty signed with the British at Oswego on July 24, 1766, a treaty under which he was pardoned.

Following his pardon, Pontiac was received with hostility by neighbors in his Maumee River village and he, his family, and a handful of supporters were driven out by tribe members who wanted resistance to continue. While at a trading post in Cahokia (Illinois), Pontiac was murdered in April, 1769, by Black Dog, a Peoria Indian whom the British may have paid in hopes of forestalling future rebellions.

Alteration of British Policy. In the aftermath of Pontiac's resistance, the British, apprehensive about a renewal of Native American resistance, altered their Indian policy. They abandoned their Indian posts everywhere in the West, except at Detroit, Michilimackinac, and Niagara, and cross-mountain trade was placed again in colonial hands. British authorities, seeking to remove yet another cause of native grievances, renewed the practice of favoring tribes with sumptuous gifts. Unable to stem the tide of European settlers into trans-Appalachian tribal lands, as the Proclamation Line of 1763 was intended to do, British representative William Johnson negotiated a new boundary with Iroquois leaders at Fort Stanwix in September, 1768. This line was drawn farther west, in hopes of lessening chances of friction between the natives and the settlers. Britain's concerns over Native American affairs soon gave way to coping with rising resistance among its own colonials.

In retrospect, Pontiac's pan-Indian alliance represented the greatest threat mounted by Native Americans against Great Britain's New World expansion prior to the outbreak of the American Revolution. It dramatically launched Native American resistance to white civilization, resistance that subsequently included uprisings by Little Turtle (1790-1794) and by Tecumseh (1809-1811) and, during the last three decades of the nineteenth century, drew the U.S. military into the lengthiest and most numerous succession of campaigns in its history, ending with the Battle of Wounded Knee in 1890.

See also: French and Indian War; Indian-white relations: English colonial; Indian-white relations: French colonial; Proclamation of 1763.

Mary E. Virginia

Sources for Further Study

Hawke, David. *The Colonial Experience.* Indianapolis: Bobbs-Merrill, 1966. Chapter 13 brilliantly places Pontiac's resistance in the context of Great Britain's halting steps toward imperial reorganization.

Leach, Douglas E. *Arms for Empire: A Military History of the British Colonies in North America, 1607-1763.* New York: Macmillan, 1973. A formidable study that details the increasingly impossible task Great Britain faced in trying to devise an effective military defense for a vast colonial empire against France and Spain, British colonists, and Native Americans. The latter chapters provide excellent background on Pontiac's resistance.

_____. "Colonial Indian Wars." In *History of Indian-White Relations,* edited by Wilcomb B. Washburn. Vol. 4 in *Handbook of North American Indians.* Washington, D.C.: Smithsonian Institution Press, 1988. More specific in its focus than the Leach study, this article combines British and American Indian politics and perspectives in the context of colonial wars.

Nester, William R. *Haughty Conquerors: Amherst and the Great Indian Uprising of 1763.* Greenwood, Conn.: Praeger, 2000. An up-to-date history of Pontiac's resistance.

Parkman, Francis. *The Conspiracy of Pontiac and the Indian War After the Conquest of Canada*. 1874. Reprint. 2 vols. Lincoln: University of Nebraska Press, 1994. Despite minor inaccuracies, this remains the classic study of the subject. Based on original documents and written by one of the greatest of American historians.

Peckham, Howard. *Pontiac and the Indian Uprising*. Princeton, N.J.: Princeton University Press, 1947. Corrects Parkman's inaccuracies, updates the subject, and provides fresh insights into American Indian attitudes.

Sosin, Jack M. *Whitehall and the Wilderness: The Middle West in British Colonial Policy, 1760-1775*. Lincoln: University of Nebraska Press, 1961. Concentrates on the evolution of British policy in trans-Appalachia between 1760 and 1765, including British adjustments to Pontiac's resistance.

Powhatan Confederacy

Date: 1570's-1644

Locale: Eastern Virginia

Tribes involved: Arrohattoc, Appomattoc, Mattapanient, Pamunkey, Youghtanund, Powhatan, Accohannock, Accomac, Chesapeake, Chickahominy, Chiskiack, Cuttatawomen, Kecoughtan, Moraughtacund (Morattico), Nandtaughtacund, Nansemond, Onawmanient, Opiscopank, Paspahegh, Piankatank, Pissaseck, Patawomeck, Quiyoughcohannock, Rappahannock, Sekakawon, Warraskoyack, Weanoc, Werowocomoco, Wiccocomico

Categories: Colonial history, Native government

Significance: Wahunsonacock makes political alliance with native tribes in the Virginia region against encroaching European settlers.

The term "Powhatan" is used in several ways. It was the name given to a group of tribes of Virginia Indians; the name of an Indian village; the "throne name" of a chief; and the name of the man who created the Powhatan Confederacy in eastern Virginia. Geographically, the Powhatan Confederacy extended north to Alexandria along the Potomac River, south to the Neuse River in North Carolina, west along Virginia's fall line, and east to the Atlantic Ocean. Although historians have consistently referred to the chief of the Powhatan Indians and the ruler of the Powhatan Confederacy as Powhatan, his birth name was Wahunsonacock. This discrepancy was caused by the English, who either did not know his birth name or found it more convenient to call him Powhatan because he had so many names.

It has been suggested that Powhatan or his father came from the south. This contention is supported by the fact that Powhatan succeeded his father as chieftain, a practice in opposition to the matriarchal system of succession practiced by the Algonquians of eastern Virginia. Upon his father's death, Powhatan inherited control over six tribes in eastern Virginia: the Arrohattoc (Arrohateck), Appomattoc (Appomattox), Mattapanient (Mattaponi), Pamunkey, Youghtanund, and Powhatan. By the time of Jamestown's founding in 1607, Chief Powhatan's control extended to more than twenty additional

Pocahontas, daughter of Powhatan, married one of the original settlers of Jamestown, John Rolfe, and was instrumental in improving relations between the settlers and the Powhatan Confederacy. After a visit to England, where she was warmly received by the British court, she contracted smallpox and died there in 1617. (Library of Congress)

tribes: the Accohannock, Accomac, Chesapeake, Chickahominy, Chiskiack, Cuttatawomen, Kecoughtan, Moraughtacund (Morattico), Nandtaughtacund, Nansemond, Onawmanient, Opiscopank (Piscataway), Paspahegh, Piankatank, Pissaseck, Patawomeck (Potomac), Quiyoughcohannock, Rappahannock (Tappahannock), Sekakawon (Secacawoni), Warraskoyack, Weanoc (Weyanock), Werowocomoco, and Wiccocomico (Wiccomico).

Most historians agree that the Powhatan Confederacy was forged by Powhatan's treachery, fear, and force. Powhatan allegedly attacked the Piankatank tribe at night and then slaughtered all the captives. When Powhatan invaded the Kecoughtan, he slaughtered all resisters and distributed the captives throughout his domain. He was reputed to have slaughtered the entire Chesapeake tribe because an oracle had divined that Powhatan would be overthrown by a force from the east. He then transplanted his own people to the area formerly occupied by the Chesapeake.

Powhatan consolidated his power by conferring chiefdoms on his relatives, by his own multiple marriages with the daughters of chieftains, and by the intermarriage of his family with the sons and daughters of locally powerful chiefs. The four known brothers of Powhatan all became chiefs: Opitchapam, Powhatan's successor; Opechancanough, the chief of the Pamunkey Indians and a Powhatan successor; Kekataugh, the ruler of the village of Pamunkey; and Japasus (Iopassus), the king of the Potomacs. William Strachey, an English writer who lived in Virginia in the early 1600's, suggested that Powhatan's twelve marriages increased his authority among Virginia's native tribes. A thirteenth wife has been attributed to Powhatan: Oholasc, the regent of the Tappahannocks.

There is no accurate listing of the number of children fathered by Powhatan. At the time of the English arrival in 1607, it was estimated that Powhatan had twenty living sons and twelve living daughters. The better-known Powhatan offspring included Taux-Powhatan, the eldest son and ruler of the Powhatans; Na-mon-tack, who was presented to James I; Pocahontas; Cleopatre; Tohahcoope, chief of the Tappahannocks; Nantaquaus, described by John Smith as the manliest, comeliest, and boldest spirit in a "savage"; Matachanna; and Pochins, chief of the Kecoughtan.

Powhatan's original capital, Werowocomoco, was about ten miles from Jamestown. In 1608, Werowocomoco was abandoned for Orapax on the Chickahominy River to keep Powhatan geographically distant from the English. Powhatan used his retreat to the interior and the threat of the English presence to increase his control over the tribes of the confederacy.

Political and Cultural Organization. The domain over which Powhatan ruled was a collection of villages. There is dispute about the exact number. William Strachey counted thirty-four villages; historians have estimated from thirty to more than one hundred villages. Often a tribe would people more than one village. Regardless of the number, Powhatan ruled about thirty tribes in eastern Virginia with an estimated population of at least 14,300, although this figure is also in dispute. Each village was expected to pay eight-tenths of its rude wealth in tribute to Powhatan. The village was the administrative unit of the Powhatan Confederacy, with power invested in a cockarouse, the weroance or war-leader, the tribal council, and the priest.

The cockarouse was the first person in dignity in the village, a member of the tribal council, and the highest elected civil magistrate, chosen for experience and wisdom. The cockarouse exercised authority only during times of peace, received the first fruits of the harvest, and was in charge of all public and private concerns of the village. The cockarouse presided at tribal councils, was a delegate to Powhatan's council, and held the office for life on condition of good behavior. Although elective, the position of cockarouse might be hereditary in the female line. Women could be cockarouses.

Powhatan appointed the weroance. The weroance was a member of Powhatan's council, the leader in hunting and fishing expeditions, and in charge of all military affairs. The weroance exercised the power of life and death over the members of his tribe, collected the tribute due Powhatan, declared war, maintained a crude ceremonial state, and presided over the village council in the absence of the cockarouse.

The tribal council regulated matters of concern to the whole confederacy. It governed by a sense of right and wrong, by custom, by fashion, by public opinion, and by a sense of honor. It is difficult to determine whether the tribe or the village was the basic political unit of the Powhatan Confederacy, because they were frequently one and the same. Historians generally agree that a king or queen ruled over a tribe. Usually, the king was a weroance. Strachey mentions one queen, Opossunoquonuske of the Mussasran, who was also a weroance. This is probably an exception, because Oholasc was a queen but her son was the weroance.

The highest political authority resided with Powhatan and his council (Matchacomoco). The council was composed of cockarouses, weroances, and the priests of all the subject and allied tribes. The council shared the supreme authority over the Powhatan Confederacy with Powhatan, was convened by the people, and held open meetings. Powhatan presided over this advisory body to declare war or peace, conduct foreign relations, and manage domestic affairs. A unanimous vote of the council was required to implement council decisions, but the personal authority of Powhatan greatly affected council policy.

Powhatan's increasing association with the English may have led to his coronation ceremony, which elevated him both in his own eyes and among his subjects. The Ashmolean Museum in Oxford, England has an object called "Powhatan's Mantle." It measures approximately 233 by 150 centimeters and is made of four pieces of tanned buckskin bearing a design in shell depicting a standing human figure flanked by two quadrupeds and a series of large rosettes. It is unlikely that this particular mantle was Powhatan's coronation cloak, but it is judged to be authentically seventeenth century Virginia Indian.

During Powhatan's lifetime and because of the religious conversion of Pocahontas, his daughter, and her subsequent marriage to John Rolfe, relations between the Powhatan Confederacy and the Jamestown settlement steadily improved. After the deaths of Pocahontas (1617) and Powhatan (1618), Powhatan's successors, particularly his brother Opechancanough, viewed the English as intruders and sought to remove the English from the ancestral native lands. From 1622 until 1676, Native American rebellions occurred intermittently until the eastern Virginia tribes were either defeated or fled westward, leaving the English in firm control of the lands of the Powhatan Confederacy.

See also: Indian-white relations: English colonial; Powhatan Wars.

William A. Paquette

Sources for Further Study

Barbour, Philip L. *Pocahontas and Her World*. Boston: Houghton Mifflin, 1970. A good synthesis of seventeenth century accounts of Jamestown's founding, including much information on Powhatan.

Beverly, Robert. *The History and Present State of Virginia*. Indianapolis: Bobbs-Merrill, 1971. A study of Indian life and customs in the seventeenth century, first published in 1705.

McCary, Ben C. *Indians in Seventeenth Century Virginia*. Williamsburg: Virginia 350th Anniversary Celebration Corporation, 1957. Reviews the history of seventeenth century Native Americans in Virginia.

Rountree, Helen C. *Pocahontas's People: The Powhatan Indians of Virginia Through Four Centuries*. Norman: University of Oklahoma Press, 1990. Written by an ethnohistorian and anthropologist, this is one of the best studies of Jamestown and the settlement's relationship to the Powhatan Confederacy.

_____. *The Powhatan Indians of Virginia: Their Traditional Culture*. Norman: University of Oklahoma, 1989. A comprehensive study of all aspects of life among the Powhatan Confederacy tribes.

Smith, John. *The General History of Virginia, New England, and the Summer Isles*. Philadelphia: Kimber and Conrad, 1812. An account of life in Virginia by the first Englishman to meet Chief Powhatan.

Strachey, William. *The Historie of Travell into Virginia Britania (1612)*. Edited by Louis Wright and Virginia Freund. 1953. Reprint. Nendeln, Liechtenstein: Kraus Reprint, 1967. A contemporaneous account of Virginia's Native Americans.

Powhatan Wars

Date: 1622-1646

Locale: Virginia

Tribes involved: Powhatan Confederacy: Arrohattoc, Appomattoc, Mattapanient, Pamunkey, Youghtanund, Powhatan, Accohannock, Accomac, Chesapeake, Chickahominy, Chiskiack, Cuttatawomen,

Kecoughtan, Moraughtacund (Morattico), Nandtaughtacund, Nansemond, Onawmanient, Opiscopank, Paspahegh, Piankatank, Pissaseck, Patawomeck, Quiyoughcohannock, Rappahannock, Sekakawon, Warraskoyack, Weanoc, Werowocomoco, Wiccocomico

Categories: Colonial history, Wars and battles

Significance: Led by Opechancanough, the Powhatan Confederacy unsuccessfully attempted to drive English settlers from Virginia.

The Powhatan tribes of the Chesapeake Bay region of Virginia had been at peace with the English settlers during the eight years prior to the outbreak of the Powhatan Wars. Powhatan, the chief of this confederacy of about nine thousand, had engaged the English in intermittent warfare from the time of their settlement of Jamestown in 1607. The combination of serious losses of warriors in those conflicts and the 1614 marriage of his daughter Pocahontas to English planter John Rolfe persuaded Powhatan to avoid further hostilities.

A depiction of Powhatan in a longhouse meeting from a German engraving. (Library of Congress)

Upon Powhatan's death in 1618, his brother Opechancanough continued his policy of accommodation. Yet Opechancanough was alarmed at the continued expansion of English settlement on Powhatan land, and he resented the English efforts to assimilate his people into their culture. Consequently, he patiently planned a colony-wide uprising in the hope of driving the English from Virginia.

While often professing to the English his hopes for continued peace, Opechancanough negotiated with the almost thirty tribes in the Powhatan Confederacy to join in his proposed campaign. When the English murdered a highly regarded warrior and prophet named Nemattanow in early March, 1622, on suspicion of killing a white trader, Opechancanough realized that his enemies had presented him with an incident to rally his forces. In two weeks of visits with confederacy tribes, Opechancanough persuaded them to attack simultaneously on March 22.

The devastating strike claimed 347 lives, almost a third of the English population in Virginia. More would have died had not a Pamunkey servant informed his master, who, in turn, warned the main settlements in and around Jamestown, allowing them to prepare for the attack. In response, the English launched a vigorous counterattack, including military expeditions, the destruction of crops, and the burning of villages. This struggle, which took more native lives than English, continued for a decade and ended with a truce in 1632.

Opechancanough ended the truce a dozen years later. Feeble and nearly blind—according to the English sources he was one hundred years old—the Powhatan leader once again persuaded confederation tribes to participate in a coordinated attack on English settlements. Beginning on April 18, 1644, the attack claimed nearly five hundred lives but proved less devastating to the English than the 1622 foray because there were now about eight thousand settlers in Virginia.

The fighting, which lasted for two years, effectively concluded with the English capture of Opechancanough. He was taken to Jamestown, where a guard killed him two weeks later. In October, 1646, the colonial assembly made peace with Opechancanough's successor, Necotowance. The treaty provided for a clear boundary between the two peoples, roughly along the York River. Neither side was to enter the other's territory without the colonial governor's permission.

The English victories in the Powhatan Wars virtually ended native opposition to English expansion in Virginia. The combination of two decades of warfare and disease took a heavy toll not only on the Powhatan Confederacy but also on all Virginia tribes. By 1670, there were only about seven hundred warriors in a total population of barely three thousand. Since the English population had grown to more than forty thousand, further resistance was futile.

See also: Indian-white relations: English colonial; Powhatan Confederacy.

Larry Gragg

Prehistory: Arctic

Date: c. 10,000 B.C.E.-c. 1800 C.E.
Locale: Bering Strait land bridge (Beringia), northern Alaska, northern Canada, the Canadian Archipelago, northern Greenland
Tribes involved: Paleo-Indian predecessors to Aleut, Eskimo, Inuit
Categories: Pre-Columbian history
Significance: The Arctic is the area of North America that has been longest inhabited by Indians.

The Arctic ordinarily is defined as the circumpolar region lying north of the treeline where the warmest temperature is below 10 degrees centigrade; it only roughly approximates the Arctic Circle. In the Western Hemisphere, the prehistoric Arctic culture area included the Bering Strait land bridge (Beringia), northern Alaska and northern Canada, the Canadian Archipelago, and most of Greenland. Next to the Antarctic, it was the last of the global niches in which humans made those adaptations essential to their survival, a process that had begun by 10,000 B.C.E.

   Serious archaeological research into the Western Hemisphere Arctic began in the 1920's with the work of Knud Rasmussen, Kaj Birket-Smith, and Terkel Mathiassen. It bared the outlines of a whale-hunting Eskimo culture named Thule, the origins of which lay in Alaska, where a Paleo-Arctic tra-

Arctic Culture Area

dition dated to 10,000 B.C.E. In 1925, archaeologist Diamond Jenness unearthed evidence of a hitherto unknown Arctic culture, since called Dorset, that predated the Thule tradition. A rapid extension of Arctic research after 1945 by Helge Larsen, Jorgen Meldgaard, J. Louis Giddings, William Taylor, and Elmer Harp, Jr., among others, broadened knowledge of Thule and Dorset cultures. They and other researchers also provided evidence of a pre-Dorset culture that spread across the northern, central, and eastern Arctic during postglacial warming periods and discovered an Arctic Small Tool tradition as well. By the 1990's, the Arctic prehistoric cultural sequence—as defined by archaeological findings—proceeded from Paleo-Arctic (10,000 B.C.E.-6000 B.C.E.), to the Arctic Small Tool tradition (4200 B.C.E.-3100 B.C.E.), to pre-Dorset (4500 B.C.E.-c.1300 B.C.E.) to Dorset (700 B.C.E.-1000 C.E.), to Thule (100-c.1800). Note that there are gaps as well as periods during which traditions overlap. These historically related traditions underlay more recent Aleut and Eskimo cultures and undoubtedly had still more ancient origins in Asia.

See also: Prehistory: California; Prehistory: Great Basin; Prehistory: Northeast; Prehistory: Northwest Coast; Prehistory: Plains; Prehistory: Plateau; Prehistory: Southeast; Prehistory: Southwest; Prehistory: Subarctic.

Clifton K. Yearley

Prehistory: California

Date: c. 8000 B.C.E.-c. 1600 C.E.
Locale: California and northernmost Baja California
Tribes involved: Paleo-Indian precedessors to Achumawi, Atsugewi, Cahuilla, Chemehuevi, Chumash, Costanoan, Cupeño, Diegueño, Esselen, Fernandeño, Gabrielino, Hupa, Juaneño, Kamia, Karok, Luiseño, Maidu, Mattole, Miwok, Patwin, Pomo, Quechan, Salinan, Serrano, Shasta, Tolowa, Tubatulabal, Wailaki, Wappo, Wintun, Wiyot, Yahi, Yokuts, Yuki, Yurok
Categories: Pre-Columbian history
Significance: The prehistory and ethnology of California's Indian societies significantly contribute to understanding the hunting-gathering cultures in rich and varied environments.

Although archaeological findings that are conjectural (and controversial) have placed Paleo-Indian cultures in California as early as 50,000 B.C.E.,

California Culture Area

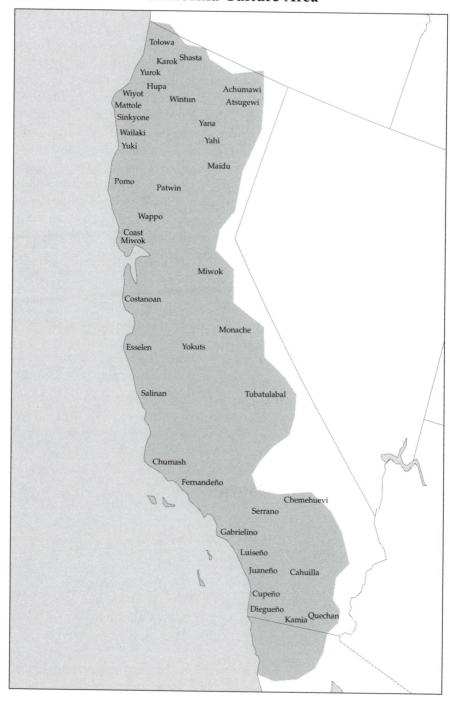

hard evidence confirms their existence there by 8000 B.C.E. Such evidence consists of Clovis points—fluted stone projectile points used in big-game hunting—discovered throughout present-day California in at least eleven archaeological sites, among them Borax Lake, Lake Mojave, Tulare Lake, China Lake, Pinto Basin, Tiefort Basin, and Ebbetts Pass. In addition to Clovis points, other artifacts have been found at many of these digs, including hammer stones; cutting, scraping, chopping, and engraving tools; other projectile points; awls; charms; shell beads; and atlatl (throwing) hooks. At sites in central and Northern California, such artifacts have been located amid the remains of mammoths, giant bison, camels, horses, deer, elk, seal, small land animals, fish, and birds. Cemeteries with human remains in the Sacramento Valley attest the sedentary occupations and lengthy settlements that characterized a number of diverse and complex prehistory communities. Overall, these California communities have been grouped by archaeologists and ethnographers into four broad cultural provinces that roughly coincide with California's major environmental features: Northwest Pacific, Central-trans-Sierran, Southern Coastal, and Southern Desert. Archaeologists estimate the population of prehistoric California at between 300,000 and 350,000 people, comprising nearly five hundred distinct communities and ethnic groups.

See also: Prehistory: Arctic; Prehistory: Great Basin; Prehistory: Northeast; Prehistory: Northwest Coast; Prehistory: Plains; Prehistory: Plateau; Prehistory: Southeast; Prehistory: Southwest; Prehistory: Subarctic.

Clifton K. Yearley

Prehistory: Great Basin

Date: c. 9500 B.C.E.-c. 1800 C.E.

Locale: Central and southern Oregon, eastern California, Nevada, Utah

Tribes involved: Paleo-Indian predecessors to Bannock, Gosiute, Kawaiisu, Mono, Paiute, Shoshone, Ute, Walapai, Washoe

Categories: Pre-Columbian history

Significance: The harsh environment of the Great Basin forced the tribes living there to make significant cultural adaptation for survival.

In the Great Basin, which included portions of present-day central and southern Oregon, eastern California, Nevada, and much of Utah, prehistoric Native Americans confronted the most rigorous environment they encountered anywhere. The region's prehistorical importance, therefore, stems from archaeological evidence that indicates the adaptations made by the ancestors of more than a dozen major tribes to this difficult environment. Archaeological discoveries at Tule Springs, Nevada, suggest that parts of the Great Basin may have been occupied by Pleistocene peoples by 26,000 B.C.E., while other findings in south-central Oregon sug-

Great Basin Culture Area

gest human occupancy by 11,200 B.C.E. These dates are highly controversial, however; uncontroverted evidence places earliest human occupancy of the region at between 9500 B.C.E. and 9000 B.C.E., particularly evidence of the presence of Clovis people, whom archaeologists now believe to have been widespread in the Great Basin as well as the rest of the West by those dates.

Major archaeological discoveries, among a number confirming this, are located at the C. W. Harris site in San Diego, California; Gypsum Cave and Fallon, Nevada; Fort Rock Cave, Oregon; Death Valley, Owens Lake, and Tulare Lake, California; and Danger Cave, Deadman, Promontory, and Black Rock caves in Utah. Throughout most of the Great Basin, early peoples formed small nomadic groups that foraged for lake plants and animals. In environmentally favored sections of the Basin, village life developed and lasted for several millennia. Contacts among regional groups appear to have been frequent, and trade was sophisticated. Artifacts from throughout the Great Basin include a rich variety of projectile points, knives, scrapers, milling stones, coiled basketry, cloths, moccasins, jars, and appliqued pottery.

See also: Prehistory: Arctic; Prehistory: California; Prehistory: Northeast; Prehistory: Northwest Coast; Prehistory: Plains; Prehistory: Plateau; Prehistory: Southeast; Prehistory: Southwest; Prehistory: Subarctic.

Clifton K. Yearley

Prehistory: Northeast

Date: c. 9000 B.C.E.-c. 1600 C.E.

Locale: Northeastern North America

Tribes involved: Paleo-Indian predecessors to Abenaki, Adena, Algonquian, Erie, Fox, Hopewell, Huron, Illinois, Iroquois, Kickapoo, Lenni Lenape, Mahican, Maliseet, Massachusett, Menominee, Miami, Micmac, Mohawk, Nanticoke, Narragansett, Neutral, Old Copper, Ottawa, Owasca, Passamaquoddy, Pequot, Petun, Potawatomi, Sauk, Shawnee, Susquehannock, Tuscarora, Wampanoag, Winnebago, Woodland

Categories: Pre-Columbian history

Significance: The Northeast Woodlands region was the heartland of the forebears of the Algonquian linguistic family. Evidence suggests that Iroquoian speakers have also lived there for thousands of years.

Northeast Culture Area

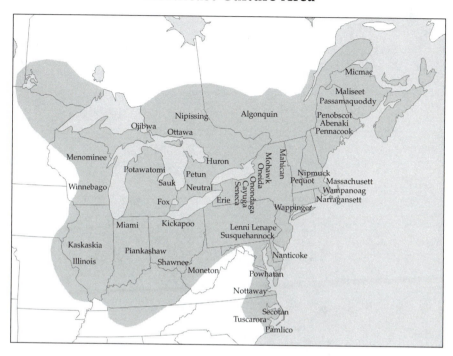

Paleo-Eastern Woodlanders used stone tools and foraged for small game and seasonal plants. Grit-tempered, cord-marked pottery dates from 2500 B.C.E., and fiber-tempered pottery appeared at about 500 B.C.E. Evidence suggests the Adena cultural influence from about 1000 B.C.E. and then Hopewell mound cultural influences from the beginning of the millennium entered the Northeast. After 500 C.E., the region was the recipient of migrations from Caddoan-speaking or Siouan-speaking people of the Mississippian mound cultures. The most important influence on the area two thousand years ago was the agricultural culture associated with Iroquoian-speaking people, who emerged from an archaeological complex called Owasco. It was the Owasco who began to create tribal units and to cultivate crops, returning to agricultural sites year after year simply because certain crops grew well in certain soils and zones.

Native seeds such as squash and bottle gourds have been gathered and planted by paleo-Indians of the Northeast Woodlands for four thousand years. Local economies based on the slash-and-burn agriculture of many native crops had evolved by about 100 C.E. It was only around 800 C.E. that maize (corn) was introduced, probably from the Southwest. It may have been the introduction of corn throughout the continent that lessened the religious influence of the mound-building culture called Hopewell. The cultivation of corn and corn's concomitant mythologies loosened the religious hold Hopewell thought had on the Northeast.

The Northeast Woodlands have long had cultural interchanges with other areas, and this area was the focus of migratory movement from

Mound-Building Cultures and Mound Sites

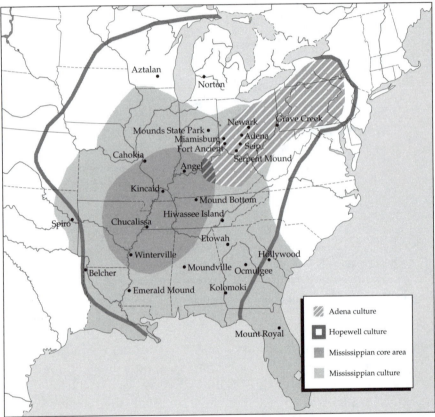

The earliest of the Ohio River Mound Builders, the Adena Indians, are thought to have lived between 700 B.C.E. and 200 C.E. The Adena gave rise to the Hopewell Indian culture, also centered in the valleys of the Ohio River and its tributaries, which is recognized from around 100 B.C.E. until about 400 or 500 C.E. The Hopewell developed vast, nearly continentwide, trading networks. Some researchers posit that Hopewellians were ancestral to the Iroquois. The last North American mound-building culture, the Mississippian, was centered along the Mississippi River, at Cahokia, where East St. Louis, Illinois, now stands. It developed around 700 C.E. and flourished until after 1500. Many scholars believe that the Mississippians were direct ancestors to the Cherokee, Sioux, and other American Indian tribes.

the Great Lakes, the Ohio River Valley, and the Eastern shore routes for thousands of years, setting the stage for the arrival of Europeans in the 1600's.

See also: Prehistory: Arctic; Prehistory: California; Prehistory: Great Basin; Prehistory: Northwest Coast; Prehistory: Plains; Prehistory: Plateau; Prehistory: Southeast; Prehistory: Southwest; Prehistory: Subarctic.

Glenn Schiffman

Sources for Further Study

Jennings, Jesse D. *Prehistory of North America*. New York: McGraw-Hill, 1968.

Newcomb, William. *North American Indians: An Anthropological Perspective*. Pacific Palisades, Calif.: Goodyear, 1974.

Prehistory: Northwest Coast

Date: c. 9500 B.C.E.-c. 1800 C.E.

Locale: From Yakutat Bay in southern Alaska to Cape Mendocino in Northern California

Tribes involved: Paleo-Indian predecessors to Bella Coola, Chehalis, Chinook, Coast Salish, Coos, Haida, Hupa, Karok, Klamath, Klikitat, Kwakiutl, Nootka, Quinault, Takelma, Tillamook, Tlingit, Tsimshian, Wiyot, Yurok

Categories: Pre-Columbian history

Significance: The rugged coastal area of the Northwest provided an environment suited to the development of maritime tribal cultures.

The Northwest Coast culture area extends from the modern regions of Yakutat Bay in southern Alaska south to Cape Mendocino in Northern California. It has a rugged coastline with many deep inlets. In the northern half, mountains rise several thousand feet directly from the edge of salt water. There are numerous small islands offshore, but there are few beaches or low-level areas convenient for village sites.

Natural History. Climatic conditions along this coastal strip are characterized by even temperatures and heavy rainfall (up to one hundred inches a year in many places). The abundant rainfall and moderate temperature of the region produce a distinctive and dense vegetation. Forests extend from

Northwest Coast Culture Area

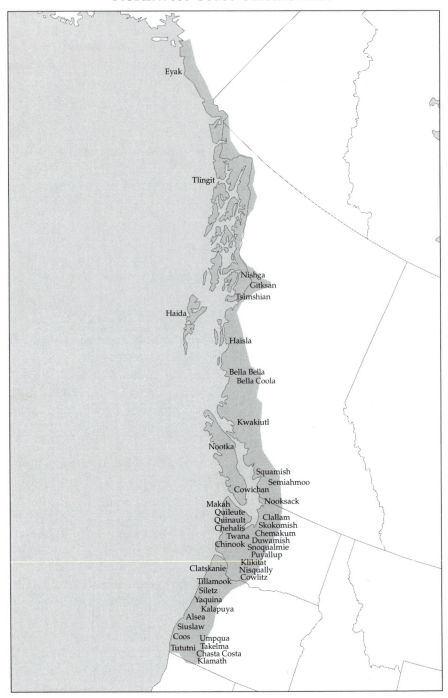

Eyak

Tlingit

Nishga
Gitksan
Tsimshian

Haida

Haisla

Bella Bella
Bella Coola

Kwakiutl

Nootka

Squamish
Semiahmoo
Cowichan
Nooksack
Makah
Quileute Clallam
Quinault Skokomish
Chehalis Chemakum
Twana Duwamish
Chinook Snoqualmie
Puyallup
Klikitat
Clatskanie Nisqually
Cowlitz
Tillamook
Siletz
Yaquina
Kalapuya
Alsea
Siuslaw
Coos Umpqua
Tututni Takelma
Chasta Costa
Klamath

the Pacific shoreline to near the highest ridges of the major river drainage systems, such as the Columbia, Fraser, and Skeena Rivers.

As one goes southward, the terrain changes from towering mountains of raw, naked rock cut by deep canyons gouged out by glacial flow and watercourse turbulence to, around upper Puget Sound and along the Oregon and northwestern California coasts, steep but rounded coastal hills and estuaries resulting from the buildup of sand bars formed at the river mouths.

In prehuman times, wildlife and game of all sorts were unimaginably plentiful. In fact, the extreme abundance of natural resources in this culture area later gave rise to a high degree of civilization without the emergence of agriculture. Maritime, estuarine, and riverine resources were the mainstays that provided an ample foundation for the building of prehistoric human cultures.

The sea and the forests, even today, are the most important providers of sustenance. Fishing and sea mammal hunting required an intricate extraction technology that allowed the first human hunter-gatherers, after their arrival thousands of years ago, to harvest and use the available natural resources to the fullest extent. This required each community to develop the complex tools and skills necessary to ensure their individual success among the many diverse communities that eventually developed in, and occupied, the region.

Archaeological History. Archaeological research has been undertaken in this culture area since the late 1800's. Sites such as those discovered at Port Hammond, Marpole, Vancouver, Yakutat, Graham Island, and the more recent Montague Harbor have revealed numerous peoples, languages, and communities of great biological and cultural diversity.

This culture area is thought to have been inhabited initially by maritime peoples, with highly developed Stone Age technology, and mobile cultures, who could have come from many directions. Athapaskan, Salish, and Penutian speakers were subdivided into more than a hundred communities and dialects, spread from one end of the area to the other, which have provided modern researchers with a wealth of artifacts and information.

Northwest Coast studies entered a new phase with the 1970 discovery of water-saturated "wet" sites, where immersion of material remains below the water table and the lack of oxygen prevents vegetal decay. Sites at Ozette and Prince Rupert are particularly notable for the sophisticated methods of study used in both field and laboratory work.

Radiocarbon dating and other scientific techniques indicate constant occupation of this culture area since at least ten thousand years ago. Localized tribal creation stories suggest that peoples have always existed in their lands. If prehistoric peoples did indeed migrate into the area, linguistic and genetic distribution suggests that they could have come from such diverse places as Siberia (traveling across the Bering Strait land bridge), northeastern China (traversing the exposed continental shelf), or even from Polynesia (boating across the South Pacific) to Mexico or Central America, then as far northward along the coastline as the Columbia River basin.

Various basal cultures have been defined by their remains through a wide variety of descriptive means. Early boreal and protowestern cultures, microblade and pebble tool traditions, and stemmed point and fluted point traditions are all names commonly used to describe these early prehistoric cultures. It is generally thought that the diversity of peoples can best be explained through a combination of migration, diffusion, and adaptation.

See also: Prehistory: Arctic; Prehistory: California; Prehistory: Great Basin; Prehistory: Northeast; Prehistory: Plains; Prehistory: Plateau; Prehistory: Southeast; Prehistory: Southwest; Prehistory: Subarctic.

Michael W. Simpson

Sources for Further Study

Borden, Charles E. *Origins and Development of Early Northwest Coast Culture to About 3000 B.C.* Ottawa: National Museums of Canada, 1975.

Cressman, Luther S. *The Sandal and the Cave: The Indians of Oregon.* Corvallis: Oregon State University Press, 1981.

Drucker, Phillip. *Indians of the Northwest Coast.* Garden City, N.Y.: Natural History Press, 1963.

_____. "Sources of Northwest Coast Culture," In *New Interpretations of Aboriginal American Culture History.* Seventy-fifth anniversary volume of the Anthropological Society of Washington. Seattle: Anthropological Society of Washington, 1955.

Fladmark, Knut R. "The Feasibility of the Northwest as a Migration Route for Early Man." In *Early Man from a Circum-Pacific Perspective,* edited by Alan Bryan. University of Alberta Department of Anthropology Occasional Papers 1. Edmonton, Alberta: Archaeological Researchers International, 1978.

_____. "The Patterns of the Culture." In *Indians of the North Pacific Coast,* edited by Tom McFeat. Seattle: University of Washington Press, 1966.

Prehistory: Plains

Date: c. 9500 B.C.E.-c. 1800 C.E.
Locale: Western Canada and United States
Tribes involved: Paleo-Indian predecessors to Apache of Oklahoma, Arapaho, Arikara, Assiniboine, Atsina, Blackfoot, Caddo, Cheyenne, Comanche, Crow, Hidatsa, Iowa, Kansa (Kaw), Kiowa, Mandan, Missouri, Omaha, Osage, Oto, Pawnee, Ponca, Quapaw, Sarsi, Sioux, Tonkawa, Waco, Wichita
Categories: Pre-Columbian history
Significance: Large herds of mammals in the Great Plains contributed to the development of tribal cultures based on nomadic hunting.

The prehistory of the Great Plains begins with evidence of nomadic Paleo-Indian bands at around 9500 B.C.E. to 9000 B.C.E. These groups arrived before the end of the Pleistocene epoch and took advantage of herds of large mammals, such as mammoth, giant bison, camels, and horses, that have since become extinct (the horse was not reintroduced until the sixteenth century). It ends with the proto-historic period, when Spanish and other European explorers contacted agricultural village peoples and mobile bison hunting groups in the sixteenth through nineteenth centuries.

The earliest Paleo-Indian populations utilized large, bifacial, fluted Clovis points for hunting mammoth. They captured the animals by chasing them into natural traps, such as stream heads or lakes, where females and immature animals were the most likely to be killed. Artifacts such as bifacial scrapers, choppers, worked flakes, and a variety of bone tools were used for butchering and processing hides. Sites of this period, known mainly from the southern and western Plains, include both kill sites and quarries for stone. Examples include Miami (Texas), Blackwater Draw Number 1 (New Mexico), Dent (Colorado), Domebo (Oklahoma), and Colby (Wyoming). No campsites, burials, or remains of dwellings have been discovered for this period.

Around 9000 B.C.E. Clovis points were replaced by unfluted points known as Plainview, shorter fluted points known as Folsom, and other successive styles such as Firstview, Midland, Agate Basin, Hell Gap, Albert, and Cody. The Hell Gap (Wyoming) site provides a long record for bison hunters in the form of a series of temporary campsites that are chronologically transitional between Clovis and Folsom. The hunting of large herds of bison was a Plains tradition for thousands of years, and Folsom culture was based on the nomadic hunting of the giant precursors to modern buffalo, such as *Bison antiquus* and *Bison occidentalis*. These animals were stalked in small groups or killed in large numbers by stampeding herds off cliffs, into ditches, or into traps. Large hunts, which provided abundant supplies of meat, may have required the cooperative efforts of several bands working together. At Olsen-Chubbuck, a site in eastern Colorado, almost two hundred bison were killed and slaughtered. Bones indicate systematic butchering and selective use of choice animal parts. Several sites, such as Lindenmeier (Texas), suggest regular use by nomadic groups from year to year.

The Paleo-Indian way of life, based on large-game hunting, was transformed around 6000 B.C.E. by the end of the Pleistocene and the extinction of species such as *Bison antiquus*. Projectile point styles such as Agate Basin were followed by styles of the Plano tradition, such as Scottsbluff, Milnesand, Portales, and Eden. These were utilized by the last of the big-game hunters until around 5000 B.C.E.

Archaic Period. Between around 5000 B.C.E. and 2500 B.C.E., both human and animal populations in the Plains regions were affected by a period of warmer and drier climates known as the Altithermal period. During this period, reduction of grasslands and water sources resulted in smaller, more highly dispersed human groups. The archaeological evidence of this period is scarce compared with that for earlier and later periods. Sites of this period consist mostly of temporary campsites. When bison were hunted, they belonged to the smaller, modern species *Bison bison*. There is evidence for local experimentation with fiber-tempered pottery in the central Plains around 3000 B.C.E., but this technology does not become important until a much later time.

Among the sites that have provided an understanding of this tradition is Mummy Cave (Wyoming), where thirty-eight distinct cultural levels bore evidence of a hunting-and-gathering lifestyle oriented toward mountain resources between 7300 B.C.E. and 1580 C.E. By 2500 B.C.E., people living in the cave used milling stones, tubular bone pipes, coiled basketry, and fiber cordage. Sites from between 2500 B.C.E. and about 100 C.E. suggest a continuation of the pattern of small groups of nomadic foragers. These groups moved across the landscape in conjunction with the seasonal availability of plant and animal resources, collecting seeds, roots, nuts, and berries when they were in season and doing occasional hunting of bison.

Woodland Period. The Woodland tradition in the Plains begins with the widespread use of pottery. During the Early Woodland period, the eastern Plains were inhabited by semisedentary villages of incipient agricultural-

Plains Culture Area

ists. The year-round occupation of settlements resulted from a combination of increasing sedentism by earlier peoples and the colonization of portions of the central Plains by village cultures from farther east via fertile river valleys.

Although there is no evidence for maize farming until around 500 C.E., by 250 B.C.E. Plains peoples were experimenting with sunflower, chenopodium, squash, and marsh elder. Ceramic styles of eastern Kansas and western Missouri suggest participation in the larger "Hopewell Interaction Sphere," through which maize (corn) may have been introduced during the latter part of this period.

In the vicinity of Kansas City, Hopewellian villages approached 4 hectares (10 acres) in area. Among the new features associated with them were earth-covered burial mounds with stone chambers, usually built on the tops of bluffs. Houses were more substantial, sometimes marked with oblong patterns of postholes. The pottery of this period includes cord-marked and rocker-stamped wares with shapes and decorations similar to Early Woodland styles of the eastern United States. Other Hopewell markers include platform pipes. Maize and beans were cultivated, and large-stemmed or corner-notched projectile points were used for hunting deer and bison.

Burial mounds of the late Plains Woodland and early Plains Village periods are found throughout the eastern Dakotas and in southern Manitoba. Frequently grouped, these were usually situated on bluffs overlooking lakes and valleys. Their forms consisted of low, circular and oblong shapes as well as long, linear embankments. Burials with pottery vessels were placed in timber-covered pits below or within mounds.

In the northwestern and southern Plains, there was a persistence of mobile Archaic patterns. A number of sites indicate the continued practice of communal bison hunts. It is likely that bison hunters were in contact with village farmers, exchanging meat, hides, and other products for cultivated foods.

Plains Village Period. The Late Woodland, beginning around 900 C.E., is marked by an increased reliance on the cultivation of maize in alluvial river valleys. In eastern Kansas there is evidence that suggests contact with Mississippian cultures (probably via canoe along the Missouri River) and the possible existence of trading colonies. Plains Village cultures may have been trading buffalo meat and hides with their neighbors to the east. Among the most characteristic bone artifacts of Plains Village culture is the bison scapula hoe. Ceramics of this period were typically cord-roughened. Some pottery from sites of this period in the vicinity of Kansas City display "sunburst" motifs and other designs reminiscent of the Mississippian culture at the large temple mound village at Cahokia, Illinois.

There was a wide variability in cultures of the Plains at this time. In the central Plains, the best-documented cultures are the Upper Republican, Nebraska, Smoky Hill, and Pomona. Characteristic house types included rectangular earth lodges with four central posts supporting timber roofs covered with soil. Earth lodge villages ranged in size from about fifty to one hundred people. Along the middle Missouri River in the Dakotas, villages of as many as three hundred people were surrounded by ditches and palisades.

Maize was one of the principal cultigens of the Plains Village tradition. A characteristic agricultural implement of this period was the bison scapula hoe. Hunting of bison, deer, and antelope was undertaken with bows and arrows tipped with small, triangular, side-notched points. Fishing in rivers was done with bone hooks and harpoons. Animal products such as hides and bones were intensively utilized by Plains Village peoples. Sites have yielded a wide variety of bone implements, including needles, pins, punches, and flaking tools. Shell ornaments were common. In the Upper Republican and Nebraska phases, fine stone and ceramic pipes, occasionally decorated with human or animal effigies, were among the most important ceremonial items.

Large villages in the east were clearly affected by the contact with complex societies of the eastern Missouri and central Mississippi valleys. In the northwestern and southern Plains, however, ancient patterns of mobile foraging and bison hunting still continued. Nomadic bison hunters traded with both the Plains Village peoples to the east and the Pueblo peoples of northern New Mexico and southern Colorado.

Between 1400 and 1500 c.e., a culture known as the Lower Loup phase appeared along the banks of the Loup and Platte Rivers in eastern Nebraska. Their earthlodge villages were substantially larger than earlier settlements, sometimes covering an area of 100 acres, and often were fortified. In central Kansas, the contemporaneous Great Bend culture was characterized by large agricultural villages that were occupied at the time of the first European incursions, as evidenced by fragments of Spanish armor. In the Middle Missouri region, the proto-historic period is represented by villages with circular house foundations that were probably occupied by the agricultural ancestors of the historic Mandan, Hidatsa, and Arikara peoples. In the far western and northwestern Plains, the mobile bison hunting pattern that had begun at least ten thousand years earlier persisted into the nineteenth century, but it was aided by the introduction of the horse. The historic heirs to this tradition, whose ancestors may never have participated in agricultural Plains Village patterns, are tribes such as the Blackfoot, Arapaho, and Assiniboine.

The first Spanish to arrive in the Great Plains included Francisco Vásquez de Coronado, who in 1541 traveled north in search of a kingdom known to him as Gran Quivira. Reaching central Kansas, he was disappointed to discover settled Great Bend villages with little gold. Nevertheless, it is clear that the indigenous peoples of the Plains share a rich and ancient cultural history.

See also: Prehistory: Arctic; Prehistory: California; Prehistory: Great Basin; Prehistory: Northeast; Prehistory: Northwest Coast; Prehistory: Plateau; Prehistory: Southeast; Prehistory: Southwest; Prehistory: Subarctic.

John Hoopes

Sources for Further Study

Adair, Mary J. *Prehistoric Agriculture in the Central Plains.* University of Kansas Publications in Anthropology 16. Lawrence: University Press of Kansas, 1988.

Bamforth, Douglas B. *Ecology and Human Organization on the Great Plains.* New York: Plenum Press, 1988.

Frison, George C. *Prehistoric Hunters of the High Plains.* 2d ed. San Diego: Academic Press, 1991.

Wedel, Waldo C. *Central Plains Prehistory: Holocene Environments and Culture Change in the Republican River Basin.* Lincoln: University of Nebraska Press, 1986.

_____. "The Prehistoric Plains." In *Ancient North Americans,* edited by Jesse D. Jennings. San Francisco: W. H. Freeman, 1983.

Prehistory: Plateau

Date: c. 9500 B.C.E.-c. 1800 C.E.

Locale: Eastern British Columbia, Oregon, Idaho, Washington

Tribes involved: Paleo-Indian predecessors to Coeur d'Alene, Flathead, Nez Perce, Spokane, Yakima

Categories: Pre-Columbian history

Significance: The native cultures of the Plateau area were among the last to make contact with Europeans and thus maintained their own traditions the longest.

Plateau Culture Area

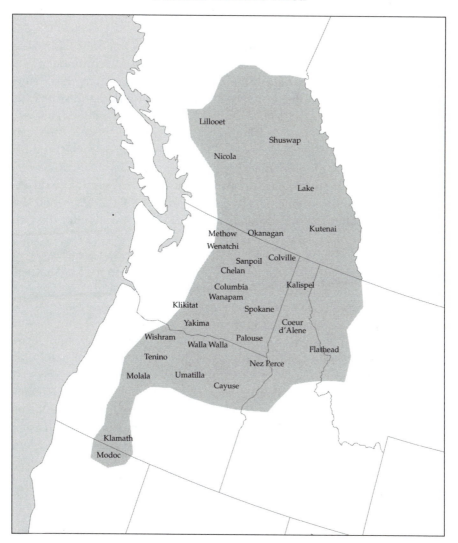

The Plateau culture area is enclosed between the Cascade mountain range to the west and the even higher northern Rockies to the east. The area is very dry; it is closely related to the Great Basin, but its dryness is tempered somewhat by its more northerly location (and therefore cooler temperatures) and the presence of two major river systems, the Columbia and the Fraser.

Alone among all the major regions of the United States, the Plateau does not show any evidence of the fluted Clovis points. Instead, at Lind Coulee in southeastern Washington, non-fluted spear points dated to 9500 B.C.E. have been found. This possibly indicates the hunting of a variety of Ice Age and modern large animals.

Around 9000 B.C.E., life changed at The Dalles in Oregon (a Columbia River site) with the advent of salmon fishing, which would continue to be a major part of the Plateau diet until modern times. Salmon may have supplied as much as half of the food, because it could be dried and stored for long periods. Other items used included birds, mussels, rabbits, beaver, and numerous types of roots and bulbs. This would indicate that the western Archaic form of life, known as the Desert culture farther south, could have begun in this region. Scholars disagree about the similarity of the cultures of the Plateau and the Great Basin. Some have seen very little difference, based on similar tools, moccasins, and folklore. Others feel that the availability of salmon created a much more sedentary lifestyle for the Plateau tribes.

By 5000 B.C.E., Plateau peoples were making grinding stones and living in pit houses, and by 4000 B.C.E., pit house villages existed in the Snake River Valley of Idaho. Well-made, leaf-shaped points were being used to hunt deer, elk, and pronghorn antelope to supplement the river's resources.

Contact with the outside led to changes. Algonquian-speaking peoples appeared about 1000 B.C.E., and with them came the use of ground-stone tools including mauls, pestles, atlatl weights, fish gorges, and tubular pipes, as well as animal sculptures. Contact with the northwestern coastal cultures along the Columbia and Fraser River Valleys led to the final culture phase, called Piqunin. After 1300 C.E., Plateau peoples lived in villages of five to ten earthlodges in the sheltered canyons of the rivers, which often were ten degrees warmer than the surrounding winter countryside. Here they hunted deer and fished for salmon, which they preserved by drying. In the spring and fall, they set up temporary camps in the smaller canyons and uplands to collect canas and kous roots, along with berries, and to hunt larger game.

Plateau peoples were some of the last to come into direct contact with Europeans, with first known encounters being with the Alexander Mackenzie expedition of 1793, along the Fraser River, and the Lewis and Clark expedition, when it reached the Columbia River and its tributaries in 1805.

See also: Prehistory: Arctic; Prehistory: California; Prehistory: Great Basin; Prehistory: Northeast; Prehistory: Northwest Coast; Prehistory: Plains; Prehistory: Southeast; Prehistory: Southwest; Prehistory: Subarctic.

Fred S. Rolater

Prehistory: Southeast

Date: c. 9500 B.C.E.-c. 1600 C.E.
Locale: Southeastern North America
Tribes involved: Paleo-Indian predecessors to Alabama, Atakapa, Biloxi, Caddo, Calusa, Catawba, Cherokee, Chickasaw, Chitimacha, Choctaw, Coushatta, Creek, Hasinai, Hitchiti, Mobile, Natchez, Pensacola, Seminole, Timucua, Tuskegee, Yamasee
Categories: Pre-Columbian history
Significance: The native inhabitants of the Southeast had a long and complex evolution into a number of different types of culture.

The prehistory of the Southeast may be divided into five basic periods: Paleo-Indian, Archaic, Early and Middle Woodland, Mississippian, and Later Woodland Tribal.

The first known inhabitants of the Southeastern region were Clovis culture Paleo-Indians who arrived about 9500 B.C.E. following the herd of mammoths. They were efficient hunters, and by 9000 B.C.E., aided by a warming climate, they had killed all the mammoths. They were replaced by the bighorn bison specialists known as Folsom. Adopting the atlatl (or spearthrower), they moved in smaller bands but still in a nomadic manner. Local variations of nomadic big-game hunters, including the Cumberland, harvested a variety of large animals until approximately 8000 B.C.E. One of the oldest Indian skeletons was found at Little Salt Spring in southern Florida, dated at 9000 B.C.E.

At approximately 8000 B.C.E., a transition was made to the Archaic culture. For 6,500 years, or more than half of the entire period of human occupation, the Archaic peoples dominated the Southeast. Spread over eons of time and a large region, there were many variations of the culture. All showed a mastery of hunting and gathering and effective adaptation to life in the river and stream bottoms of a wet area. They hunted white-tailed deer, buffalo, rabbit, squirrel, and ducks and other birds. They became the first fishers of the area, specializing in catfish in many areas. They also gathered the abundant wild plant matter. From the first, they wandered less, and by 4500 B.C.E. they had settled down to centralized movement based on two homes: one on the stream and one nearby in the hill country. This brought about a population explosion. By 2500 B.C.E., pottery had reached the Savannah River area, from where it slowly spread throughout the Southeast. In 1700 B.C.E., the Poverty Point culture appeared in northern Louisiana; it probably consisted of migrants from

Southeast Culture Area

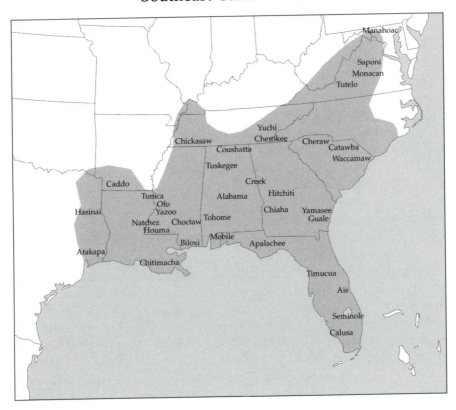

Mexico. They brought elaborate villages, small-scale agriculture, and jade-working.

Combined with influences from the north, Poverty Point led to the Early Woodland phase. The most noticeable factor in Early Woodland is the appearance of a cult of the dead, with its burial mounds filled with grave goods. By 1 C.E., improved agriculture had led to the much more elaborate Middle Woodland period, with hundreds of oval and circular burial mounds. Their grave goods included copper from Lake Superior, obsidian from the Rockies, and soapstone from Minnesota, indicating both a long-range trading system and excellent craftsmanship. After 400 C.E., Middle Woodland declined from overpopulation, too much violence, local goods competing with the imported, and perhaps other causes.

About 800 C.E., the climactic Mississippian culture emerged to dominate most of the Southeast, except Virginia and Florida, until 1600. Based on an elaborate maize, beans, and squash agriculture (with fields often running for miles along river bottoms), they developed city-states such as Moundville, Alabama; Mound Bottom, Tennessee; Etowah and Okmulgee, Georgia; and Natchez, Mississippi, all of which were centered on mound towns. Mound towns were temple mounds on which were built religious and governmental centers and possibly homes for the prominent. They were a highly stratified society led by priest-rulers and a nobility. After 1200, the Southern Death Cult imported from Mexico dominated religion. Art reached its pre-white climax in pottery, statuary, and shell-work.

The Mississippians dominated the Southeast when Hernando de Soto traveled the region from 1539 to 1543, but they had disappeared from everywhere but Natchez by the early 1600's. European diseases are often blamed for their downfall, but it is also known that Moundville split up from overpopulation. The Mississipians were replaced by the Cherokee, Choctaw, Creek, and Chickasaw, as well as many other tribes, by the time of white entry in the early 1600's.

See also: Prehistory: Arctic; Prehistory: California; Prehistory: Great Basin; Prehistory: Northeast; Prehistory: Northwest Coast; Prehistory: Plains; Prehistory: Plateau; Prehistory: Southwest; Prehistory: Subarctic.

Fred S. Rolater

Prehistory: Southwest

Date: c. 10,000 B.C.E.-c. 1540 C.E.
Locale: Southwestern North America
Tribes involved: Paleo-Indians and Anasazi, Hohokam, Mogollon
Categories: Pre-Columbian history
Significance: The tribes of the early Southwest developed sophisticated dwellings and agricultural systems.

Archaeologists have determined that the first people in the Southwest were nomadic hunting and gathering peoples who drifted into the region in small groups in the late Pleistocene period. These people, known in archaeological literature as the Cochise, had minimal tools and equipment, although some of their stone implements were expertly flaked into beautiful spear points and knives. There are several different groups of these "early man points," which are identified by the localities where they were first discovered: Folsom, Sandia, and Clovis.

Near the pueblo of Santa Ana, evidence has been found of a semi-permanent camping ground dating back to the Cochise. Apparently, game was abundant in this area and water was available from several springs. Artifacts found here include a number of stone tools such as knives, scrapers, drills, choppers, points, and grinding implements. These grinding tools, which indicate that the Cochise supplemented their meat diet with seeds and wild grains, consisted of a large, irregular stone with a shallow, concave area in which seeds or grains were placed and a smaller, rounded stone with which the grinding was done. These crude grinding stones ultimately developed into the metate-mano combination which allowed the later agriculturists in the region to prepare corn.

Development of Agriculture. Over a period of centuries, the Cochise evolved from a nomadic society into several different cultures that were

Southwest Culture Area

Prehistoric pictographs on rocks at Adamana, Arizona, 1903. (National Archives)

primarily agricultural and sedentary. The major stimulus for this change was the introduction of corn into the region. Corn had been grown in Mexico since about 7000 B.C.E., and over time new genetic strains more resistant to cold and drought were developed, which made it a viable crop for the Southwest. By about 300 B.C.E., the Cochise had settled down to farming and village life, and by circa 300 C.E., three major agricultural groups had materialized: Hohokam, Mogollon, and Anasazi. All three of these cultures depended on the "sacred triad" of corn, beans, and squash for their subsistence. They practiced simple farming methods, with the digging and planting stick as their principal tool. Agriculture and an accompanying interest in the weather eventually led the three cultures to the development of religious and ceremonial practices by which they hoped to influence nature in their favor.

With the possible exception of the Hohokam, who appeared in southern Arizona along the Gila River in the third century B.C.E., the agriculturalists of the Southwest were indigenous. It was a situation of a people adopting new ideas and developing a new way of life rather than of migrants coming into the area with a new, ready-made culture. Many scholars believe that the Hohokam came from Mexico, although no geographical area of origin has been identified. If, on the other hand, the Hohokam evolved from the Cochise, as did the Mogollon and Anasazi, it is certain that they were an important conduit for influences from the cultures in Mexico to come into the Southwest.

Of the three prehistoric groups, the Mogollon in the mountains of southern New Mexico were the first to cultivate corn and the first to have the bow and arrow, probably having acquired both from cultures in Mexico. The Mogollon were never a cohesive society, perhaps because of the rugged terrain along the Little Colorado River where they lived. Their culture consisted of scattered groups of small villages which, while sharing certain basic traits, were characterized nevertheless by many regional differences.

The Hohokam are generally divided into two main groups: the Desert and the Riverine. The Desert Hohokam, the smaller group, did not settle near streams and so were less successful agriculturally. The Riverine Hohokam built villages along rivers and developed an extensive irrigation system consisting of many miles of canals constructed with rudimentary hand tools. The building of these canals, each of which served several villages, required a high degree of social and political organization as well as effective intercommunity cooperation.

The Anasazi, who lived in the high plateau country of the Four Corners area, apparently acquired corn from the Mogollon. Their first farming methods were extremely crude compared to the other two cultures, but they were such a vigorous, dynamic, and creative people that they soon surpassed their neighbors to the south and were farming the mesa tops as well as the valleys, using irrigation systems of their own design.

Housing. Early in their development, all three prehistoric cultures constructed permanent dwellings known as pit houses. Generally, this was simply a shallow pit dug into the ground, lined with rocks or logs to prevent the sides from collapsing inward, and then covered with a roof made of slim branches and twigs with several inches of mud on top.

The Mogollon pit house was circular, with a single center post to support a conical roof and a short, sloping ramp on one side which served as an entryway. A hole in the center of the roof provided a vent for the fire pit.

The Hohokam pit house was a rectangular hole about 30 feet long with an entire structure built inside it, using the "wattle-and-daub" method, which consisted of small posts set into the ground a few inches apart, interlaced with brush and packed with mud. It was topped by a double-pitched roof and entered by a sloping ramp on one side.

Although the earliest Anasazi lived in caves, by about 500 C.E. they had developed a circular pit house, approximately 5 feet deep and up to 25 feet in diameter. The structure had a flat roof, with entry by ladder through the smoke hole. By about 700, the Anasazi had developed stone architecture and were building aboveground pueblos. As their culture spread through the Southwest, they gradually absorbed most of the other two groups.

Crafts. One of the benefits that results from social organization and specialization is leisure time that can be devoted to the development of arts and crafts. As the Mogollon, Hohokam, and Anasazi began to make utilitarian objects such as pottery, baskets, sandals, robes, and mats, they decorated them according to their own rapidly developing aesthetic tastes. From the beginning, all three groups made jewelry from shells, bone, and minerals such as turquoise. A careful study of all these things reveals the emergence of a rich artistic tradition which was related to other aspects of these prehistoric cultures and which constitutes the artistic heritage of the modern Puebloan artist.

See also: Prehistory: Arctic; Prehistory: California; Prehistory: Great Basin; Prehistory: Northeast; Prehistory: Northwest Coast; Prehistory: Plains; Prehistory: Plateau; Prehistory: Southeast; Prehistory: Subarctic.

LouAnn Faris Culley

Sources for Further Study

Amsden, Charles A. *Prehistoric Southwesterners from Basketmaker to Pueblo.* Los Angeles: Southwest Museum, 1949.

Cordell, Linda S. *Prehistory of the Southwest.* Orlando, Fla.: Academic Press, 1984.

Cummings, Byron. *The First Inhabitants of Arizona and the Southwest.* Tucson, Ariz.: Cummings Publication Council, 1953.

Gummerman, George J., ed. *Exploring the Hohokam: Prehistoric Desert Peoples of the American Southwest.* Dragoon, Ariz.: Amerind Foundation, 1991.

Muench, David. *Anasazi, Ancient People of the Rock.* Palo Alto, Calif.: American West, 1975.

Noble, David G., ed. *The Hohokam: Ancient People of the Desert.* Santa Fe, N.Mex.: School of American Research Press, 1991.

Prehistory: Subarctic

Date: c. 25,000 B.C.E.-c. 1700 C.E.
Locale: Alaska, Canada, Greenland
Tribes involved: Paleo-Indian predecessors to Aleut, Athapaskan, Eskimo (Inuit), Haida, Tlingit, Tsimshian

Categories: Pre-Columbian history
Significance: Linguistic evidence suggests that the native tribes of the Subarctic region are closely related to those of Siberia.

Determination of the lifeways and approximate dates of prehistoric cultures can be accomplished only through examination of archaeological sites and artifacts. Precisely dating the prehistory of the Subarctic is impossible. Considering the fact that many of the languages spoken in this area are related to those spoken in Siberia, however, it is generally believed that early Subarctic dwellers entered North America over the land bridge that connected Siberia and Alaska, where the Bering Strait is now located, during the last Ice Age. There were at least two separate migrations, and probably three, during a period between 25,000 and 10,000 years ago.

The earliest migration probably involved the Athapaskans, as their language group is by far the most widespread and has apparently changed the most over time. The Athapaskan languages spoken in Alaska and Subarctic Canada are related to the Navajo and Apache languages of the American Southwest. Eskimo groups, on the other hand, have languages so similar that a native of Alaska can easily communicate with one of Greenland. A

Subarctic Culture Area

third group, completely unrelated to the other two, is the Northwest Coast Indians.

In a real sense, the prehistory of the Subarctic extends as late as the late nineteenth century, when whites were first attracted into Alaska and Yukon by the gold rush. Unfortunately, the cultures in the region were changed by the impact of white culture before they were thoroughly studied. Some of the more remote regions were never seen by white people until the mid-twentieth century, when air travel made it easier to visit any place on earth. Before this time, transport was primarily by boat in the summer and dog sled in the winter.

Prehistoric Eskimos and Aleuts lived in igloos, made of packed snow. The Athapaskans lived in log cabins quite similar to those built by others much farther south. There were a great number of tribal rituals, some of which are still practiced, but details are difficult to determine, because in most instances outsiders are barred from these rituals; moreover, they are held in native languages that few outsiders understand.

See also: Bering Strait migrations; Prehistory: Arctic; Prehistory: California; Prehistory: Great Basin; Prehistory: Northeast; Prehistory: Northwest Coast; Prehistory: Plains; Prehistory: Plateau; Prehistory: Southeast; Prehistory: Southwest.

Marc Goldstein

Proclamation of 1763

Date: October 7, 1763
Locale: North America
Tribes involved: Pantribal
Categories: Colonial history, National government and legislation
Significance: The British draw a frontier line between Native Americans and colonists, hoping to avoid more costly conflicts.

How would Great Britain, victorious in the French and Indian War against France and its allies, control the vast domain between the Appalachian Mountains and the Mississippi River after 1763? The answer to that question interested not only Native Americans, French Canadians, and British colonial administrators but also American fur traders, merchants, and land speculators. The trans-Appalachian West had increasingly occupied the attention of British and colonial officials since the Albany Congress of 1754.

During the ensuing war, the Crown appointed superintendents to coordinate Native American affairs—Sir William Johnson for the Northern Department and Edmund Atkin (replaced by John Stuart in 1762) for the Southern Department—but exigencies of the moment made the new arrangement inadequate. In the eyes of Whitehall officials, the old policy of leaving control of the frontier to the individual colonies had been chaotic and ruinous. The line of European American agricultural settlement had steadily edged westward, with scant regard for Native American land claims or indigenous culture. Royal governors, superintendents for Native American affairs, and British military men repeatedly had complained that the colonists disregarded Native American treaties and made fraudulent land purchases, and that European American traders mistreated the tribal peoples.

Pontiac's Resistance. The necessity of reaching an accord with the Native Americans seemed even more urgent with Pontiac's Resistance, which had begun in the spring of 1763. The indigenous population, already uneasy over the defeat of their French allies, encountered repeated insults from the British commander in chief, General Jeffrey Amherst, who refused to present them with guns, ammunition, and other gifts, as had been the French custom. Striking first in the remoter sections of the West, such as at Fort Michilimackinac, and later on the Pennsylvania frontier, roving parties of Ottawas, Chippewas, Lenni Lenapes (Delawares), and Senecas overran one British-occupied post after another; by the end of June, only Forts Detroit, Pitt, and Niagara still held out against the warriors. Amherst, near recall from the home government, dispatched relief expeditions to his remaining garrisons, and several colonies raised troops to repel the indigenous combatants. The prospect of fire and sword, the diplomatic skills of William Johnson, Pontiac's calling off the sieges, and the breakup of the coalition of tribes—which never was united on ultimate objectives—explain the demise of the rebellion and restoration of peace in 1764. Anxious to bring an end to hostilities and avoid another outbreak, the British exacted little retribution from the western tribes.

During the uprising, the government announced its new policy for the West, one that had evolved from British experience in the French and Indian War. It was the work of no single minister or subminister, although Charles Wyndham (the earl of Egremont and secretary of state for the Southern Department, 1761-1763), William Petty (the earl of Shelburne, president of the Board of Trade in 1763 and later secretary of state for the Southern Department), and Wills Hill (the earl of Hillsborough, president of the Board of Trade from 1763 to 1765 and later secretary of state for the colonies) were keenly interested in the matter.

Proclamation Line of 1763

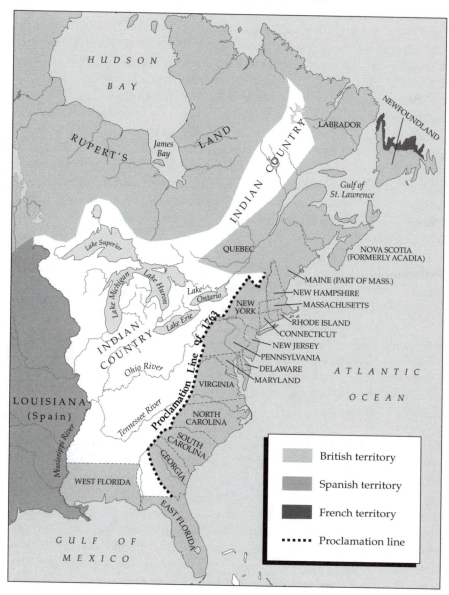

On October 7, 1763, King George III signed the edict now known as the Proclamation of 1763. By its terms, the recently acquired territories of Canada and East and West Florida became Crown colonies, and their inhabitants became entitled to the same rights as the English at home. The proclamation nullified all colonial claims to territories west of the crest of the

Appalachians and set those lands aside for Native Americans "for the present, and until our further Pleasure be known." Wishing to monopolize the substantial and lucrative fur trade of the area, Whitehall hardly wanted colonial farmers crowding out the furbearers' habitat and local traders competing for the business. The trade with the tribal peoples would be "free and open," although traders would have to obtain a license and obey any pertinent regulations. As the Proclamation of 1763 contained no provision for law enforcement in the area beyond provincial boundaries, an ad hoc system of confining trade to a few forts under superintendent and military supervision developed. The Crown expected that the colonials would obey the edict out of allegiance to England. Moreover, the royal government hoped that restless colonists would move northward into the thinly settled districts of Maine, Nova Scotia, and New Brunswick to offset the Catholic French Canadian population there and in Quebec, or relocate southward into Georgia to bolster that buffer province against the Spaniards.

Indian Reaction. Native Americans in the region heard about the Proclamation Line and watched some of the actual surveying with distrust and bemusement. The document promised that

> the several Nations or Tribes of Indians with whom We are connected, and who live under Our Protection should not be molested or disturbed in the Possession of such Parts of our Dominions and Territories as, not having been ceded to, or purchased by Us, are reserved to them, or any of them, as their Hunting Grounds.

British general Thomas Gage rushed copies westward, because he imagined that "these Arrangements must be very satisfactory to the Indians." The tribes, however, had witnessed earlier attempts at boundary treaties, such as at Easton and Lancaster, Pennsylvania, in 1758 and 1760 respectively, and in South Carolina in 1761, crumble as squatters leapfrogged the line.

In the long run, Great Britain's "western policy" failed. Land-hungry settlers spilled over into the trans-Appalachia area in defiance of the Proclamation of 1763. British troops could not guard every mountain gap, nor could they and royal superintendents force traders to patronize specific posts. Several ambitious Virginia speculators, some of whom later joined the patriot cause in the revolution, had claims across the divide. Faced with the prospect of worthless holdings, they pressed for repeal of the order. The maintenance of western garrisons was expensive, especially when American revenues for the army's upkeep failed to materialize, and when the troops did not accomplish their mission. In 1768, the British government, beset with these problems and colonial rebelliousness in the eastern regions, adopted a policy of retrenchment in the West. Control of the trade with Native Americans reverted to the individual colonies, and British troops received orders to abandon all the interior posts except Niagara, Detroit, and Michilimackinac. Almost simultaneously, the government bowed to pressure to push the Native American boundary westward. The Treaty of Fort Stanwix (1768) with the Iroquois Confederacy and the Treaties of Hard Labor (1768) and Lochaber (1770) with the Cherokee signified this change. No longer did the trans-Appalachian West loom uppermost in British imperial policy.

See also: Albany Congress; French and Indian War; Fur trade; Indian-white relations: English colonial; Indian-white relations: French colonial; Iroquois Confederacy; Northwest Ordinance; Pontiac's Resistance.

R. Don Higginbotham, updated by Thomas L. Altherr

Sources for Further Study

Jennings, Francis. *Empires of Fortune: Crowns, Colonies, and Tribes in the Seven Years War in America*. New York: W. W. Norton, 1988. Contains a short discussion of the Proclamation of 1763 and the Native American response.

Martin, James Kirby. *In the Course of Human Events: An Interpretive Exploration of the American Revolution*. Arlington Heights, Ill.: Harlan Davidson, 1979. Links the Proclamation of 1763 with other British decisions to control the colonies, such as stationing ships in American waters.

"Proclamation of 1763: Governor Henry Ellis' Plan May 5, 1763." In *The American Revolution, 1763-1783: A Bicentennial Collection*, edited by Richard B. Morris. Columbia: University of South Carolina Press, 1970. Demonstrates the thinking by one colonial official that prompted the Proclamation of 1763.

Sosin, Jack M. *Whitehall and the Wilderness: The Middle West in British Colonial Policy, 1760-1775*. Lincoln: University of Nebraska Press, 1961. Detailed examination of royal decisions leading to the Proclamation of 1763.

Stagg, Jack. *Anglo-Indian Relations in North America to 1763 and an Analysis of the Royal Proclamation of 7 October 1763*. Ottawa: Research Branch, Indian and Northern Affairs Canada, 1981. Provides a detailed interpretation of the text of the Proclamation of 1763 and the Crown's motives.

Steele, Ian K. *Warpaths: Invasions of North America*. New York: Oxford University Press, 1994. Places the decisions for the Proclamation of 1763 within the context of the military actions of the recent war and earlier treaties.

Prophetstown

Date: Established April, 1808

Locale: Northwestern Indiana

Tribes involved: Chippewa, Iroquois, Lenni Lenape, Miami, Ottawa, Potawatomi, Shawnee, Wyandot (Huron)

Categories: Nineteenth century history, Organizations, Protest movements, Religion and missionary activities

Significance: A Shawnee spiritual leader establishes the headquarters of Native Americans' renewed resistance to Anglo-American expansion.

At least since the 1730's, some native leaders west of the Appalachian Mountains advocated an alliance of tribes to resist the expanding British settlements and the powerful Iroquois Confederacy. Prophets preached a radical idea, beginning a new movement: All native peoples, despite their diverse languages and cultures and ancient tribal rivalries, were really one people, separate and distinct from the Europeans, and never meant to live with the Europeans or to adopt their ways.

By 1795, disagreements over strategy, factional strife within tribes, failing support from European allies, and military defeats disrupted the nativist movement. Tribal leaders willing to accept compromise signed treaties with the new United States government, surrendering millions of acres of land. In return, the U.S. government supported these so-called government chiefs, hoping that through them it could control the tribes and prevent organized resistance east of the Mississippi. Native people now faced a desperate struggle for survival.

Frontiersmen settling old grudges freely hunted and raided on tribal lands. Indians could not testify in U.S. courts and had no protection under U.S. law. Native people took their own form of revenge, escalating the violence. Anglo-American squatters crowded onto tribal lands, openly violating treaties. Displaced refugees fled to the remaining tribal lands, exhausting the already depleted game supply and farmlands. Most tribesmen had become dependent on the fur trade for the necessities of life. Cheap liquor was another basic fur trade commodity. By 1800, alcoholism had reached epidemic proportions among the northwestern tribes. European diseases, against which the native peoples had neither biological immunity nor medical remedies, ravaged tribes. For native peoples throughout the trans-Appalachian West, it was a time of despair, starvation, and social chaos.

Lalawethika Returns from the Dead. In a Shawnee village, in April, 1805, an aging alcoholic called Lalawethika ("Rattle" or "Noisemaker" for his bragging and belligerent behavior) collapsed, apparently dead. Although of no use as a hunter or warrior, Lalawethika had studied with the noted doctor Penagashea. His teacher had died in 1804, however, and working alone, Lalawethika had failed to stop an epidemic that struck his village in early 1805. Now he too, it seemed, was dead.

Before Lalawethika's funeral could take place, he suddenly returned to life. He told his amazed neighbors that he was sent back from the spirit world with a mission. The alcoholic braggart was dead; he had been born again as Tenskwatawa, the "Open Door," to lead his people in a spiritual renewal. The use of alcohol and other vices must stop. Violence between neighbors and the greedy accumulation of material wealth must stop. The people must restore traditional communal values, living in peace with all other tribes. Native people were children of the Master of Life, but Europeans came from the Great Serpent, the Destroyer, and corrupted all they touched. The people must have nothing more to do with them or their goods. If the people purified themselves and faithfully performed the new rituals given in Tenkswatawa's visions, they would restore the spiritual power of the tribes, the earth would be renewed, and the white invaders would disappear forever.

News of the Shawnee prophet spread among the tribes of the region. His message was believable, not only because Tenskwatawa seemed infused with magnetism and power but also because three generations of prophets among the tribes had reported similar visions. Followers gathered around Tenskwatawa in 1805, hoping that he might be able to make the promise of spiritual renewal finally a reality. In the summer of 1805, he established a new village at Greenville, Ohio, on the United States' side of a boundary line set by the 1795 Treaty of Greenville. The new site was not associated with any specific tribe; therefore, it would be easier to establish his great village of all tribes there. This new, independent village would not be controlled by any of the government chiefs, and its location openly defied the hated treaty.

Through the fall and winter of 1805, Tenskwatawa met delegations from many tribes and cultivated alliances with Native American leaders throughout the region. Seven treaties signed by the government chiefs between 1804 and 1807 ceded millions of acres of tribal land to the United States and sent many angry, disillusioned tribesmen into Tenskwatawa's camp. Disciples and allied prophets carried his message throughout the Great Lakes region and to the tribes of the South. The powerful Potawatomi shaman and war chief Main Poc, probably the most influential native leader in the region, journeyed to Greenville in the fall of 1807 to confer with Tenskwatawa. Main Poc was in favor of the movement, although he planned a regional confederacy rather than a union of all native peoples. He firmly refused to give up his old blood feud with the Osage or his fondness for alcohol. On other crucial points, however, he and Tenkswatawa agreed and joined as allies.

Tecumseh. Hundreds of people from a dozen tribes gathered at Greenville. Tenskwatawa, increasingly occupied with his duties as spiritual leader, delegated diplomatic missions to his older brother Tecumseh. Tecumseh was a gifted orator with a wide network of contacts among leaders of both northern and southern tribes. He was, moreover, a respected war chief and a confirmed nativist. Of intertribal heritage himself (his mother was Creek, his father Shawnee), Tecumseh had traveled widely among the tribes and knew their common problems and the need for a common solution. He opposed U.S. expansion; treaty land cessions in which he had no voice had cost him his home. His father and two brothers died fighting the European Americans, and he made his reputation as a warrior in battle against that same enemy.

By 1807, Tecumseh had become his brother's adviser and representative abroad, while Tenskwatawa concentrated on the problems at Greenville. Relations with Shawnee government chief Black Hoof and his followers deteriorated rapidly, and a violent clash seemed likely. The small cornfields and depleted game around Greenville could not feed the village. The site was far from the northwestern tribes, now Tenskwatawa's strongest supporters. U.S. frontiersmen were alarmed by the rapidly growing village so near their settlements, and ugly incidents between individuals or small parties of natives and U.S. settlers escalated. Rumors spread of an impending military campaign against the village.

Main Poc urged Tenskwatawa to move the village to Potawatomi territory. The people would find better hunting and more land for their gardens. They would be farther from enemies and closer to friends. In January, 1808, Tenskwatawa agreed. Through February and March, his followers gathered supplies and prepared for the move. In the first week of April, they burned their old village and started west. Miami government chief Little Turtle, who claimed authority over the region to which Tenskwatawa was moving, attempted to prevent establishment of the new village. Tenskwatawa informed Little Turtle that the Master of Life had chosen the place. There, a great union of all native peoples would guard the boundary between Indian and U.S. lands and prevent further U.S. expansion.

Prophetstown Is Built. While Tecumseh visited Canada to get supplies of food and ammunition from the British, Tenskwatawa supervised the construction of the new village. Called Prophetstown by the U.S. settlers, the village was situated on the northwest bank of the Wabash River, just below the mouth of the Tippecanoe River, in northwestern Indiana. The site quickly became a focal point for the nativist movement. With a population of more than four hundred in June, and more arriving daily, food and other supplies remained a pressing problem. While Tecumseh was persuading the British to help, Tenskwatawa tricked Indiana governor William Henry Harrison into supplying corn. The overconfident Harrison now believed he could control Tenskwatawa and his followers. The winter of 1808-1809 was unusually hard, and Prophetstown suffered severely from food shortages and a devastating epidemic. Many people went back to their old villages, bitterly disillusioned with Tenskwatawa. By summer, Harrison believed that the influence of the Prophet, as Tenskwatawa had become known, was broken and thought he could push another land cession on the tribes of the region. At the Treaty of Fort Wayne, September 30, 1809, government chiefs of the Miami, Potawatomi, and Lenni Lenape signed away millions of acres of land for about two cents an acre.

Members of Tenskwatawa's movement were outraged by the treaty. The widespread anger revitalized the movement, and people flocked again to Prophetstown. While Tenskwatawa remained the spiritual leader of the movement, Tecumseh emerged as the political and military leader. When Tecumseh traveled south to confer with the Creek, Choctaw, Chickasaw, and others, Harrison decided the time to strike had come. He burned Prophetstown after the Battle of Tippecanoe, November 7-8, 1811.

See also: Creek War; Fort Wayne Treaty; Indian-white relations: U.S., 1775-1830; Little Turtle's War; Pontiac's Resistance; Tecumseh's Rebellion; Thames, Battle of the; Tippecanoe, Battle of.

Mary Ellen Rowe

Sources for Further Study

Allen, Robert S. *His Majesty's Indian Allies*. Toronto: Dundurn Press, 1992. Presents material from British sources neglected by U.S. historians.

Dowd, Gregory Evans. *A Spirited Resistance*. Baltimore: The Johns Hopkins University Press, 1992. Traces the nativist movement from the 1730's, providing the ideological and historical context for Prophetstown.

Drake, Benjamin. *Life of Tecumseh*. 1858. Reprint. New York: Arno Press, 1969. Biography using primary documents and interviews with individuals who knew Tecumseh.

Edmunds, R. David. *The Shawnee Prophet*. Lincoln: University of Nebraska Press, 1983. Carefully researched and objective biography of Tenskwatawa.

_____. *Tecumseh and the Quest for Indian Leadership*. Boston: Little, Brown, 1984. Thorough research separates fact from fiction in this biography.

Public Law 280

Date: August 15, 1953
Locale: United States
Tribes involved: Pantribal in the United States
Categories: National government and legislation, Native government, Twentieth century history
Significance: This law limited tribal sovereignty by allowing courts in some states to have jurisdiction over Indian reservations.

During the early 1950's, federal Indian policy returned to the goal of promoting the assimilation of Indians into American society. Tribes were considered to be major barriers to this end, and a number of policies were developed to reduce their influence. One of these measures was Public Law 280, which sought to place tribal Indians under the jurisdiction of the laws of the states in which they resided. This marked a significant change in the legal status of Native Americans, for while Indians had long been subject to federal law, they had usually been considered to be subject to their own tribal courts when on reservations. Like other measures of the 1950's, Public Law 280 sought to undermine those aspects of Indians' legal status that set them apart from other Americans.

Passed by Congress in August, 1953, Public Law 280 authorized state courts to assume civil and criminal jurisdiction of all Indian lands in the states of California, Minnesota, Nebraska, Oregon, and Wisconsin. (Three reservations were excluded by name in the act.) Furthermore, other states were allowed to extend jurisdiction over reservations if they desired by making the necessary changes in their laws or constitutions. A few limits were placed on state powers: States could not levy property taxes on reservations or exercise jurisdiction with regard to Indian water rights. By 1968 nine additional states had extended jurisdiction over Indian lands within their borders.

Public Law 280 was very unpopular with American Indians, who saw it as a drastic limitation on the tribal right of self-government that had been enacted without their consent. (President Dwight D. Eisenhower had objected to the lack of a provision for tribal consent but had signed the act when Congress refused to amend it.)

Indian resentment of the act helped to persuade Congress to amend its provisions in the changed atmosphere of later years. The Indian Civil Rights Act of 1968 included provisions (known collectively as the Indian Bill of Rights) that were intended to safeguard Native American rights. One section altered Public Law 280 to require Indian consent before future extensions of state jurisdiction. States were also allowed to return jurisdiction to tribes. Public Law 280 was further limited in its impact by the Indian Child Welfare Act (1978), which gave tribal courts exclusive jurisdiction over child custody cases on reservations.

Though initially regarded as a major threat to tribal self-government, modification of Public Law 280 lessened its potential for restricting tribal authority. Some states found that they preferred to avoid the expense involved in extending legal jurisdiction, while some tribes found it useful to ask the states to provide law and order. By the late twentieth century, the law was being used in a somewhat more cooperative manner that took Indian opinions into account.

See also: Indian Child Welfare Act; Indian Civil Rights Act; Reservation system of the United States; Termination Resolution; Tribal courts.

William C. Lowe

Pueblo Revolt

Date: August 10, 1680
Locale: Rio Grande River Valley
Tribes involved: Navajo, Pueblo peoples
Categories: Colonial history, Wars and battles
Significance: The most successful uprising against European colonial authority, ensuring the survival of Puebloans as a distinct people.

The first permanent European colony in Pueblo territory was established by Juan de Oñate in 1598. The jewels and gold of the fabled Seven Cities of Cíbola had proven to be a myth, but the Spanish still intended to settle the land. Franciscan friars came to seek converts to Catholicism, the civilian authorities and settlers to seek their fortunes in mining, trading, and ranching. The entire Spanish system was based on the need for American Indian labor. In order to get it, the Spanish imposed the *encomienda* system, which gave large land grants to holders, known as *encomanderos*. The part of this program known as *repartimiento* bestowed upon the *encomanderos* the right to the labor of any nearby natives. Annual taxes also were collected from the natives in the form of produce, textiles, or other resources.

The Spanish were able to impose these measures by access to guns and horses and frequent displays of force. Harsh physical punishments were meted out for even slight infractions. The Franciscans—who recognized no belief system except their own and thus felt justified in exterminating Pueblo religion—saved the most extreme measures for natives practicing their traditional beliefs. Father Salvador de Guerra, in 1655, had an "idolator" at Oraibi whipped, doused with turpentine, and burned to death. Even missing the daily Mass could bring a public flogging.

Causes of the Revolt. This unrelenting assault on native beliefs and practices was the single greatest cause of the Pueblo Revolt. The people believed that harmony within the community and with the environment was maintained through their relationships with a host of spirit figures called kachinas. They communicated with the kachinas at public dances and in ceremonies conducted in their circular churches, called kivas. It seemed no coincidence to the natives that when priests stopped these practices, things began to go wrong.

Severe droughts, famine, Apache raids, and epidemics of European diseases reduced a population of fifty thousand in Oñate's time to seventeen thousand by the 1670's. Three thousand were lost to measles in 1640 alone. At times between 1667 and 1672, people were reduced to boiling hides and leather cart straps for food. The abuse of women and sale of slaves south to work the silver mines of Mexico made it seem that the moral as well as the physical universe was collapsing. Calls were made to return to the old ways.

Popé Plans Retribution. In 1675, forty-seven Puebloans were arrested for practicing their religion. All were whipped, three were hanged, and one committed suicide. One deeply resentful survivor was a Tewa medicine man for San Juan Pueblo named Popé. Incensed by this oppression, he began planning retribution, but his task was formidable.

The Spanish label "Pueblo" obscured the fact that these people were not of one tribe, but members of a collection of autonomous villages that cherished their independence and rarely acted in unison. Although they shared many cultural features, three major language families were represented in the Rio Grande area alone: Zuñi, Keresan, and Tanoan. The latter had three distinct dialects of its own: Tiwa, Tewa, and Towa. Hopi villages of Uto-Aztecan speech lay farther west. Previous revolts had been localized affairs and were suppressed quickly.

In hiding at Taos Pueblo, fifty miles north of the Spanish capital at Santa Fe, Popé began building a multilingual coalition. He enlisted the great Picuris leader Luis Tupatú, a Tiwa speaker who was influential in the northern Rio Grande pueblos; Antonio Malacate, a Keresan spokesman from pueblos to the south; the Tewa war leader Francisco ElOllita of San Ildefonso; and many others. His role becoming more messianic, Popé claimed inspiration from spirit contacts. Gradually, a plan emerged to expel the Spanish from Pueblo territory entirely.

The time came in August of 1680. Runners were sent out bearing knotted maguey cords, each knot representing one day. The uprising was to begin the day the last knot was untied. Governor Antonio de Otermín was told by informants that that day was August 13, but Popé had advanced it to August 10 and the Spanish were caught completely by surprise. Just nine miles north of Santa Fe, the citizens of Tesuque killed Padre Juan Pio early that morning as he came to gather them up for Mass, and upheaval soon swept the countryside as eighty years of frustration came to a boil.

Siege of Santa Fe. Lieutenant Governor Don Alonso Garcia led soldiers on a sweep to the south of the capital and encountered such destruction that he organized the survivors for evacuation south. They left for El Paso del Norte (now Juarez) on August 14. The next day, Governor Otermín found himself besieged in Santa Fe by five hundred Puebloans who demanded that he free any slaves and leave the territory. He responded by attacking, but when the opposition increased to more than two thousand warriors and Otermín's water supply had been cut, he abandoned the capital. On August 21, Otermín led more than a thousand settlers south, meeting Garcia's group on September 13, and the whole bedraggled column reached El Paso on September 29.

Four hundred civilians and twenty-one of thirty-three priests had been killed. To undo their conversions, baptized Puebloans had their heads washed in yucca suds. A new kachina entered the pantheon of Pueblo spirit figures known among the Hopi as Yo-we, or "Priest-killer." In the years following the revolt, the coalition began to unravel, as drought, disease, and Apache raids continued to plague the tribes. Popé, who had become something of a tyrant himself, died in 1688. In 1692, Spain reconquered the area, and the new governor, Don Diego José de Vargas, entered Santa Fe on September 13.

The Pueblo Revolt did much more than dispel the stereotype that Puebloans were unassertive and peaceful farmers who could not unify. It also was much more than a twelve-year respite from colonial oppression. It catalyzed transformations in Native American cultures in many directions. Large numbers of Spanish sheep came into the hands of the Navajo, forming the core of a new herding lifestyle. Weaving skills, possibly passed along by Puebloans fleeing Spanish reprisals, soon turned the wool into some of the world's finest textiles. Previously forbidden horses, now freed by the hundreds, became widely traded. Within a century, tribes such as the Nez Perce, Cayuse, and Palouse to the northwest, Plains Cree to the north, and Sioux, Cheyenne, and others to the east became mounted. With the mobility to access the great bison herds of the Plains, the economic complex that became the popular image of the Native American evolved.

The continued importance of the Pueblo Revolt to all Native Americans was demonstrated during the tricentennial of 1980. Cultural events celebrating the "First American Revolution" were held all across the United States. The revolt was seen as a symbol of independence and religious freedom. It was also recognized that some Puebloans who chose to settle with Otermín at El Paso in 1680 subsequently had lost most of their language, arts, and customs. After three centuries, the Puebloans see their ancestors' revolt as a key reason for their survival as a distinct people.

See also: Acoma, Battle of; Indian-white relations: Spanish colonial; Zuñi Rebellion.

Gary A. Olson

Sources for Further Study

Hackett, Charles W. *Revolt of the Pueblo Indians of New Mexico and Otermín's Attempted Reconquest, 1680-1682*. Translated by Charmion Shelby. 2 vols. Albuquerque: University of New Mexico Press, 1942. The definitive report on the subject to date.

Hait, Pam. "The Hopi Tricentennial: The Great Pueblo Revolt Revisited." *Arizona Highways* 56, no. 9 (September, 1980): 2-6. The entire issue is a beautifully illustrated exploration of Hopi culture, the persistence of which is a tribute to the Pueblo Revolt.

Hill, Joseph. "The Pueblo Revolt." *New Mexico Magazine* 58 (June, 1980): 38. An overview of the subject, with nine illustrations.

Josephy, Alvin M., Jr. *The Patriot Chiefs: A Chronicle of American Indian Resistance*. Rev. ed. New York: Penguin Books, 1993. Gives an account of the precursors to the revolt, but presents no consideration of the aftermath.

Knaut, Andrew L. *The Pueblo Revolt of 1680: Conquest and Resistance in Seventeenth Century New Mexico*. Norman: University of Oklahoma Press, 1997. Explores the mutual interaction between Native Americans and Europeans in the years surrounding the Pueblo Revolt.

Page, James K., Jr. "Rebellious Pueblos Outwitted Spain Three Centuries Ago." *Smithsonian* 11 (October, 1980): 221. Tells the story through Padre Pio's last day. Good observations on the revolt's modern significance.

Preucel, Robert, ed. *Archaeologies of the Pueblo Revolt: Identity, Meaning, and Renewal in the Pueblo World*. Albuquerque: University of New Mexico Press, 2002. A collection of essays exploring the light archaeology and material culture can shed on the historical understanding of the Pueblo Revolt.

Sando, Joe S. "The Pueblo Revolt." In *Handbook of North American Indians*. Vol. 9, edited by Alfonso Ortiz. Washington, D.C.: Government Printing Office, 1979. A brief article that gives details on the planning of the revolt.

Silverberg, Robert. *The Pueblo Revolt*. Introduction by Marc Simmons. Lincoln: University of Nebraska Press, 1994. An account based mainly on Hackett's earlier work. Introduction considers the revolt's legacy three centuries later.

Red River Raids

Date: June, 1815-August, 1817
Locale: Red River Colony, Manitoba, Canada
Tribes involved: Metis
Categories: Nineteenth century history, Wars and battles
Significance: A series of battles between native peoples and European settlers for the fur trade.

In 1811, Thomas Douglas, fifth earl of Selkirk, bought a large number of shares in the Hudson's Bay Company, England's largest fur-trading company. In return, he received 116,000 square miles of land in the Red River Valley in what is now southern Manitoba, just north of the Dakota Territory of the United States. In this huge territory, he planned to build a community called Assiniboia. Colonists would grow food, mainly potatoes, for Hudson's Bay Company trappers but would not be allowed to trap or trade in furs. Selkirk hoped to recruit farmers suffering from an agricultural depression in his native Scotland to settle the land. He sent an advance party, led by Miles Macdonell, a retired army officer from Scotland, to establish an initial base. Selkirk appointed Macdonell the colony's first governor. Macdonell's party of thirty-six Scottish and Irish farmers arrived on August 29, 1812. They settled near the junction of the Red and Assiniboine Rivers, in what is now Winnipeg. The settlement, called Point Douglas, was only a few miles from a North West Company post known as Fort Gibraltor.

Selkirk's original settlement had great difficulty surviving its first years on the prairie. Only help from fur traders and métis working for the North West Company, the Hudson's Bay Company's major rival for furs in the region, enabled Macdonell's group to survive. A French word meaning "mixed," métis was used to describe people of French-Indian, or English-Indian descent. (Sometimes these people were called the Bois Brulés.) Written with a small *m*, the word refers to all persons of mixed blood, but with a capital *M*, it signifies a distinct cultural and ethnic group living in the region of southern Manitoba. These Metis were descended from marriages between native women and European fishermen on Canada's Atlantic coast in the early 1600's. By 1810, the Metis had moved into buffalo (bison) country on the northern Great Plains. Many were employed as buffalo hunters by the North West Company to supply provisions for its trappers.

The second year, a group of eighty more immigrants arrived, which greatly increased the colony's chance for survival. They started growing wheat, barley, oats, and corn, although potatoes remained the principal crop. Some of the settlers also had brought sheep with them. Settlement took place during the War of 1812 with the United States, while another English army was engaging Napoleon's forces in Europe.

Macdonell Versus Trappers and Metis. Macdonell proved to be an arrogant and unpopular governor, and engaged in major conflicts with North West Company trappers and Native Americans. With the population of his colony increasing to more than two hundred Europeans by 1814, he sought to prevent food shortages by prohibiting the export of pemmican from his lands. Buffalo hunters made pemmican—a key food source for trappers and métis—from dried strips of buffalo meat that they pounded into a powder, mixed with melted fat, and stored in buffalo skin bags. The governor angered local trappers and métis by prohibiting the export of pemmican from Assiniboia after January 8, 1814. This order made it difficult for employees of the North West Company to get food, since U.S. troops had recently recaptured the company's key trading post of Detroit, from which food supplies for trappers had been sent west. Now both sources of provisions, Assiniboia and Detroit, were cut off. The trappers for the North West Company saw the Pemmican Proclamation as part of a Hudson's Bay Company plot to destroy their business.

At a meeting in August, North West Company trappers decided to destroy the Red River colony and take back control of the region. To accomplish this goal, the company needed the support of the métis population of the upper Assiniboine River Valley.

Macdonell angered the Metis by prohibiting them from killing buffalo in his colony. The North West Company recognized the Metis as a new nation and accepted their title to lands occupied by Selkirk's colonists. Thus, the North West Company and the Metis came together to drive out the Assiniboia settlers. In 1815, agents of the North West Company arrested Governor Macdonell and brought him to Montreal for trial. He was charged with interfering with Native American rights in what the North West Company claimed was Indian Territory. While the governor stood trial in the east, the Metis attacked the colonists along the Red River, drove them from their homes, and burned their fields.

Only one colonist remained in the community after the attack, but he managed to save some of the wheat crop. When a few settlers, under the leadership of Colin Robertson, returned in the fall, they harvested enough grain to assure survival. A few weeks later, a relief party sent out by Lord Selkirk made it to the Red River. Led by the newly appointed governor, Robert Semple, the settlement began to rebuild. When news of this development reached the headquarters of the North West Company, orders were sent out to destroy the village again. Violence spread into the area again in the spring of 1816. Robertson led a force that took control of the North West Company's Fort Gibraltor in May, giving Assiniboians control of the river.

On June 1, Metis set out on the Assiniboine River in three boats filled with pemmican. When Robertson heard this news, he ordered the abandonment of Fort Gibraltor and left the colony for England. The Metis continued their journey and reached the Red River at Frog Plain, below the Hudson's Bay Company settlement. On June 19, Governor Semple set out with twenty-five colonists to intercept the Metis. At a point in the woods called Seven Oaks, the Metis confronted Semple's band. A Metis named Boucher rode out to talk with Semple, but after they exchanged a few words, a fight broke out between the two and a shot rang out. Firing began from all sides, but the colonists quickly were surrounded by a much larger force and twenty men, including Semple, were killed. The remaining six men escaped into the woods. Only one Metis was killed. The Seven Oaks Massacre gave the North West Company control of the Red River territory once again.

Selkirk's Treaty. Lord Selkirk did not give up on his colony, however, but hired a band of mercenaries to recapture control. Selkirk led the force himself and in June of 1817 returned to Assiniboia after destroying a North West Company outpost. He quickly signed a treaty with local Metis allowing resettlement of the region. Fields were restored, seeds were planted, and settlers brought in a small crop before winter arrived. New colonists from the Orkney Islands came in, along with a small group of French Canadians. Selkirk provided money for a school and a church, and Catholic and Presbyterian missionaries began work among the Cree and Assiniboin Indians living along the Red River. The colony seemed to be at peace at last.

The next summer brought further disaster, however. In August, a vast swarm of locusts attacked Assiniboia. Most of the potato crop was killed, forcing many farmers to abandon their land. Locusts came again in 1819 and devastated the entire prairie. No food or seed remained in the entire valley. Settlers had to send a party all the way into the Wisconsin Territory to buy seeds for a new potato crop. Lord Selkirk's death in 1820 was another major setback for the community, and it would be several years before farmers grew enough to feed the local population. Buffalo herds continued to provide subsistence during hard times. The Metis hunted the buffalo and sold their hides and meat to the farmers. Gradually, however, the native peoples and the new settlers learned to live together and end their hostilities.

While the Red River colony was becoming a permanent part of the landscape, the right for control of the fur trade was waged in the courts. Shortages of fur-bearing animals east of the Rocky Mountains brought economic problems to both companies. In 1821, the companies merged and ended their fighting. The Seven Oaks Massacre was the worst single incident in the great battle for control of Canada's fur trade.

See also: Fur trade; Indian-white relations: Canadian; Riel Rebellions.

Leslie V. Tischauser

Sources for Further Study

Brown, Jennifer S. *Strangers in Blood: Fur Trade Families in Indian Country.* Vancouver: University of British Columbia Press, 1980. Discusses the development of the Metis people in eastern Canada and the Great Plains from the 1600's to the twentieth century. Illustrations and index.

Davidson, Gordon Charles. *The North West Company.* New York: Russell & Russell, 1967. A history of the development and expansion of the second largest fur company in North America. Maps, illustrations, and index.

Morton, W. L. *Manitoba: A History.* Toronto: University of Toronto Press, 1967. One chapter is devoted to the importance of the Red River colony.

Presents a decidedly old-fashioned view of the métis, referring to them as "halfbreeds" and "savages." Maps, illustrations, and index.

Pritchett, John Perry. *Red River Valley, 1811-1849: A Regional Study.* New Haven, Conn.: Yale University Press, 1942. Contains an almost minute-by-minute account of the Seven Oaks Massacre.

Red River War

Date: June, 1874-June, 1875
Locale: Texas Panhandle, western Indian Territory (Oklahoma), and northwestern Kansas
Tribes involved: Arapaho, Cheyenne, Comanche, Kiowa
Categories: Nineteenth century history, Wars and battles
Significance: The U.S. Army defeats three of the West's most formidable Indian tribes, opening large areas of the Southwest to settlement.

Despite good intentions expressed in the 1867 Medicine Lodge Creek Treaty, the southern Great Plains remained a hotbed of hostile Indian activity, lawlessness, and punitive military action. Kiowa and Comanche bands continued to raid into Texas and Mexico, while southern Cheyenne and Arapaho braves still threatened parts of Kansas, often returning to the protection of reservations. The Army, frustrated by restrictions imposed under President Ulysses S. Grant's Quaker Peace Policy, labored to control the volatile situation.

By 1874, the inadequacies of the reservation system and other outside influences combined to trigger a major tribal uprising. For most members of plains tribes, reservation life and the imposition of Anglo-American values threatened the most basic tenets of their existence, depriving them of freedom, mobility, and dignity. This proved especially problematic for young men, whose status largely depended on demonstrations of bravery in war or prowess on the hunt. Reservation Indians suffered poor food; frequently, promised rations were never delivered. Whiskey traders and horse thieves preyed on reservations with relative impunity. Most grievous to the American Indians was the wholesale slaughter of the buffalo, or bison, by hide-hunters and sportsmen who were killing the beasts by the hundreds of thousands, leaving stripped carcasses to litter the prairie. With the arrival of spring, the South Plains erupted in violence, as American Indians left their reservations in large numbers.

Bison meat dries on a line at an Arapaho camp near Fort Dodge, Kansas, 1870. The bison, which roamed the Plains in large herds, formed the basis for the economy of many indigenous peoples of the Plains until white settlers, aided by the railroad, slaughtered most of them during the 1870's. (National Archives)

On June 27, 1874, several hundred Cheyenne and Comanche warriors attacked a group of twenty-eight buffalo hunters at an old trading post in the Texas Panhandle known as Adobe Walls. Prominent among the attackers was Quanah Parker, the son of an influential Comanche chief and his captured wife, Cynthia Ann Parker. Despite overwhelming odds, the well-protected buffalo hunters devastated the attackers with high-powered rifles. Although never confirmed, American Indian casualties probably exceeded seventy.

The attack at Adobe Walls signaled the beginning of the Red River War. In July, Lone Wolf's Kiowas assailed a Texas Ranger detachment, Cheyenne warriors struck travel routes in Kansas, and Comanches menaced Texas ranches. As hostile action intensified, the Army received permission to pursue raiders onto previously protected reservations and take offensive action to end the uprising. On July 20, 1874, Commanding General William T. Sherman issued orders initiating a state of war, the prosecution of which fell to Lieutenant General Philip Sheridan, whose massive jurisdiction included the South Plains. Sheridan, like Sherman an advocate of total war, quickly devised the most ambitious campaign yet mounted by the Army against American Indians in the West.

Sheridan's Campaign. Sheridan's plan called for five independent columns to converge on American Indian camps in the Texas Panhandle, surround them, and punish the Indians to such an extent as to discourage future uprisings. Accordingly, Colonel Nelson Miles marched from Fort Dodge, Kansas, with a large force of cavalry and infantry; Colonel R. S. Mackenzie, with eight companies of cavalry and five infantry companies, moved northward from Fort Concho, Texas; Major William R. Price led a squadron of cavalry eastward from New Mexico; and Lieutenant Colonels John W. Davidson and George P. Buell prepared their commands, comprising several companies of Buffalo Soldiers (African American troopers from the Ninth and Tenth Cavalries), to strike westward from Indian Territory. The total force numbered more than two thousand soldiers and Indian scouts.

In August, Army units moved onto reservations to separate peaceful Indians from the hostile. While almost all Arapahos enrolled as friendly, most Cheyennes refused to submit. Troubles at the Fort Sill agency triggered a confrontation between Davidson's cavalry and a band of Comanches supported by Lone Wolf's Kiowas. Most of these Indians escaped to join hostile factions on the Staked Plains. The Army listed almost five thousand Indians as hostile; of these, roughly twelve hundred were warriors.

A severe drought made water scarce, and late August temperatures reached 110 degrees as Colonel Miles eagerly pushed his men southward. On August 30, near Palo Duro Canyon, the column clashed with Cheyenne warriors, who were soon joined by Kiowas and Comanches. The soldiers prevailed, driving the warriors onto the plains. Miles could not exploit the opportunity, however; supply shortages forced him to retire in search of provisions. The drought gave way to torrential rains and dropping temperatures as Miles linked with Price's column on September 7. Two days later, a band of Kiowas and Comanches assailed a supply train en route to Miles. Following a three-day siege, the American Indians abandoned the effort unrewarded, but the incident complicated the supply crisis.

With Miles temporarily out of action, Mackenzie and his crack Fourth Cavalry Regiment took up the fight. After stockpiling supplies, Mackenzie moved, in miserable conditions, to the rugged canyons of the Caprock escarpment. On September 26, Mackenzie thwarted a Comanche attempt to stampede his horses. Two days later, the crowning achievement of the campaign came as Mackenzie struck a large encampment in Palo Duro Canyon. Following a harrowing descent, wave after wave of cavalry swept across the canyon floor. The soldiers inflicted few casualties but laid waste to the village, burning lodges, badly needed food stocks, and equipment. Mackenzie's troopers completed the devastation by capturing fifteen hundred of the tribe's ponies, a thousand of which the colonel ordered destroyed to prevent their recapture.

Over the next three months, Army units scoured the Texas Panhandle, despite freezing temperatures and intense storms. In November, a detachment from Miles's command destroyed Gray Wolf's Cheyenne camp, recovering Adelaide and Julia German, two of four sisters seized in a Kansas raid. Catherine and Sophia German were released the following spring.

Indian Resistance Fails. Hungry and demoralized, Indians began to trickle into the reservation by October, but most remained defiant until harsh weather and constant military pressure finally broke their resistance. In late February, 1875, five hundred Kiowas, including Lone Wolf, surrendered. On March 6, eight hundred Cheyennes, among them the elusive Gray Beard, capitulated. In April, sixty Cheyennes bolted from their reservation in an effort to join the Northern Cheyennes; twenty-seven of these, including women and children, were killed by a cavalry detachment at Sappa Creek in northwestern Kansas. On June 2, Quanah Parker and four hundred Comanches—the last organized band—surrendered to Mackenzie at Fort Sill.

After a dubious selection process, seventy-four Indians, ostensibly the leading troublemakers, including Gray Beard and Lone Wolf, were shipped to prison in Florida. Gray Beard was later killed trying to escape, others perished in captivity, but some accepted the benevolent supervision and educational efforts of Lieutenant Richard Pratt. Several Red River War veterans remained with Pratt after their release to assist him in establishing the Carlisle Indian School in 1879.

The Red River War was among the most successful campaigns ever conducted against American Indians. It brought almost complete subjugation to three of the most powerful and revered tribes in North America. It also provided a model for future Army campaigns and boldly confirmed the doctrine of total war. Now less concerned with inflicting casualties, the Army would focus on destroying the American Indians' means and will to resist. Combined with the annihilation of the buffalo, this campaign of eradication made it impossible for American Indians to exist in large numbers outside the reservation. Finally, the campaign's successful completion opened vast areas to white settlement and ranching.

See also: Adobe Walls, Battles of; Bison Slaughter; Carlisle Indian School; Indian-white relations: U.S., 1871-1933; Medicine Lodge Creek Treaty.

David Coffey

Sources for Further Study

Chalfant, William Y. *Cheyennes at Dark Water Creek: The Last Fight of the Red River War*. Norman: University of Oklahoma Press, 1997. A thorough study of the final encounter of the Red River War and the circumstances leading up to it.

Haley, James L. *The Buffalo War: The History of the Red River Indian Uprising of 1874*. Garden City, N.Y.: Doubleday, 1976. Provides substantial background information and military analysis. Maps, illustrations, notes, bibliography, and index.

Hutton, Paul Andrew. *Phil Sheridan and His Army*. Lincoln: University of Nebraska Press, 1985. An expansive study of Sheridan's post-Civil War career, including his role as the Red River War's chief architect. Maps, illustrations, notes, bibliography, and index.

Leckie, William H. *The Buffalo Soldiers: A Narrative of the Negro Cavalry in the West*. Norman: University of Oklahoma Press, 1967. Discusses the considerable role played by African Americans in the frontier Army, devoting an entire chapter to the Red River War. Maps, illustrations, notes, bibliography, and index.

Robinson, Charles M. *Bad Hand: A Biography of General Ranald S. Mackenzie*. Austin, Tex.: State House Press, 1993. A comprehensive study that treats Mackenzie's pivotal role in the Red River War in suitable detail. Maps, illustrations, notes, bibliography, and index.

Utley, Robert M. *Frontier Regulars: The United States Army and the Indian, 1866-1891*. Lincoln: University of Nebraska Press, 1984. An essential study of the frontier Army and the Indian Wars. Includes a chapter on the Red River War and a wealth of other pertinent information. Maps, illustrations, notes, bibliography, and index.

_____. *The Indian Frontier of the American West, 1846-1890*. Albuquerque: University of New Mexico Press, 1984. This authoritative treatment of cultures in conflict includes a discussion of the causes and effects of the Red River War. Maps, illustrations, notes, bibliography, and index.

Wooster, Robert. *Nelson A. Miles and the Twilight of the Frontier Army*. Lincoln: University of Nebraska Press, 1993. Includes a chapter on the controversial soldier's extensive Red River War operations.

Reservation system of the United States

Date: Nineteenth century-present
Locale: United States
Tribes involved: Pantribal in the United States
Categories: National government and legislation, Native government, Nineteenth century history, Twentieth century history
Significance: As the United States expanded and increasing numbers of white Americans moved westward, the confinement of American Indians to reservations was deemed the most efficient way to separate Indians and whites while allowing whites access to the greatest amount of land.

In colonial times and the earliest years of the United States, there was little thought given to the need for a permanent answer to the competition for land between Europeans and Native Americans. Because there were vast uncharted areas of wilderness to the west, it was generally thought that the Indian population could be pushed westward—eventually, across the Mississippi—whenever problems arose. This was the main policy of the pre-Civil war era, as eastern tribes were "removed" westward, many to land in present-day Oklahoma.

The movement to place all Indians on reservations began in earnest after the Civil War ended (1865) during the presidency of Ulysses S. Grant. The policy came about because of the failure of previous programs and the desire of white Americans to open more western land for white settlement. From the end of the American Revolution to 1830, Indian tribes had been treated as if they were foreign nations within the United States. The federal government sent ambassadors to negotiate treaties with the tribes, and many groups such as the Cherokees in northern Georgia, had established their own governments and states within the United States. Others had traded territory in the East for land farther west. Trouble began in Georgia after the discovery of gold on Indian land. Eventually, Congress passed a law, supported by Andrew Jackson, offering territory west of the Mississippi River to tribes willing to relinquish their lands in the East. All Indians would have to accept this trade or face forced removal. Several wars and the infamous Trail of Tears, which saw the deaths of thousands of Native Americans, followed the imposition of this removal policy.

Early Reservation Policy. Most of the new Indian lands were in the Plains region—or the "Great American Desert," as whites, who at first believed that it was too hot and dry for farming, called it. In the 1840's, thousands of white settlers began crossing this "desert" on their way to California and Oregon. Travel through Indian Territory could be dangerous and difficult because of Indian attacks, so travelers and settlers called for a safe corridor to be maintained by the army. From this proposal a concentration policy developed, under which Indians would be driven into southern and northern colonies with a wide, safe passageway to the Pacific in the middle. These Indian enclaves, it was said, would be safe from white settlement. In the early 1860's, these Indian lands were closed to all whites except those on official business. In 1869 Congress created a Board of Indian Affairs within the Department of the Interior to control the reservations, and two years later ended the policy of treating Indians as residents of foreign states within the United States. On March 3, 1871, the Indian Appropriation Act declared that tribal affairs would be managed by the U.S. government without consent of the tribes.

Indians were supposed to have enough land on their reservations so that they could continue to hunt, but this idea lasted only briefly as land hunger among white farmers and ranchers after the Civil War led to demands for greatly reducing the size of Indian Territory. If Indians learned to farm rather than hunt, Indian affairs commissioners and congressmen (and most whites) believed, more land could be put to productive use, and the natives would give up their "wild" ways and enjoy the fruits of civilization. Indians were given a choice: Either they could relocate, or volunteer armies would be recruited to force them to move. On the reservations, Indians were to get education for their children, rations from the government until they knew how to grow their own crops, and certain other benefits. By 1877 more than 100,000 Indians had received rations on reservations.

Reservation education programs did not work quickly enough to satisfy many in Congress; additionally, some claimed, they cost too much money. Maintaining a large army in the West to keep Indians within their boundaries also proved expensive. The notion that Indians would become farmers proved false. Congress reacted to these problems by reducing rations, which caused terrible suffering and malnutrition among Indians, and by reducing the number of reservations as more tribes were moved into Indian Territory (Oklahoma). The federal government mandated that all Indian males receiving rations would have to work, but since few jobs existed on Indian lands this policy proved a miserable failure. To improve education and help Indians become more like whites, Congress commanded that all instruction take place in English and that the teaching of Indian religions be banned.

General Allotment Act. In 1887 Congress changed Indian policy by passing the General Allotment Act (Dawes Severalty Act). Designed by Senator Henry Dawes of Massachusetts, who considered himself a friend of the Indians, the new policy provided for an eventual end to the reservation system and the abolition of tribal organizations. In the future, Indians would be treated as individuals, not as members of tribes. Each head of a family would be allotted 160 acres of reservation land, and each adult single person would get 80 acres. The government would keep this land in trust for twenty-five years, and at the end of that period Indians would get title to the land and full citizenship rights. Land on reservations not distributed to Indians would be declared surplus land and could be sold to the highest bidder.

When the bill was passed, there were about 138 million acres of land on reservations. Between 1887 and 1900, Indians had been allotted only 3,285,000 of those acres, while almost 30 million acres were declared surplus and ceded to whites. In addition, of the 32,800 Indian families and individuals getting allotments, fewer than one-third managed to remain on their land for the required twenty-five years to attain full ownership. The program was never applied among the Indians of the Southwest, and these were the tribes most successful in retaining their traditional cultures. In 1891 Indians received the right to lease their lands for agriculture, grazing cattle, and mining. The pressure for leases from cattle ranchers and mining companies was enormous, and hundreds of thousands of acres found their way to white control through leasing provisions that took advantage of Indian poverty. Many reformers and politicians denounced leasing, but only because it made Indians who lived off their leases idle—not because it took advantage of them and made them poor.

Between 1900 and 1921 Congress made it easier for Indians to dispose of their allotments. A 1907 law, for example, gave Indians considered too old, sick, or "incompetent" to work on their land permission to sell their land to whomever they wished. White reservation agents decided questions of competency. Under this program millions more acres were lost as impoverished Indians sold their property at very low prices just to survive. This policy was speeded up in 1917 under the "New Policy" of Indian Commissioner Cato Sells, who declared that all adults one-half or less Indian were "competent," as were all graduates of Indian schools once they reached twenty-one years of age. Under this policy more than twenty-one thousand Indians gained control of their lands but then quickly lost them because they could not afford to pay state property taxes or went bankrupt. This policy was reversed in 1921, but Indians faced new problems as the federal government in the 1920's moved to end all responsibility over Indians.

In 1923, John Collier, a white reformer, became executive secretary of the American Indian Defense Association, the major lobby defending Native American interests before Congress. Collier believed Indian civilization, especially Pueblo culture, to be superior in many ways to the materialistic, violent society found in the United States and Europe. For the first time, under Collier's leadership, Indians presented a program to Congress aimed at preserving their traditional values and way of life. Reservations, it was argued, had to be retained to save these old ways but needed economic assistance to survive. Collier's program called for civil liberties for Indians, including religious freedom and tribal self-government.

The "Indian New Deal." In 1928 the Bureau of Indian Affairs (BIA) issued an influential report by Lewis Meriam, a student of Indian culture. In *The Problem of Indian Administration*, Meriam criticized American policy, condemned the General Allotment Act, and concluded that the BIA showed little interest in retaining Indian culture. The report advocated spending more money for economic assistance and suggested that the aid go directly to local tribal councils. The councils, rather than BIA officials, should decide how to spend the funds. Meriam called for a policy of cultural pluralism: Native Americans should be allowed to live by their old customs and values if they chose.

The Great Depression hit Indian reservations, particularly the poorest in South Dakota, Oklahoma, Arizona, and New Mexico, very hard. By 1933 thousands of Indians faced starvation, according to reports from the Emergency Relief Administration. President Franklin D. Roosevelt appointed John Collier to lead the Bureau of Indian Affairs and deal with the crisis. Collier, with the president's help, pushed the Indian Reorganization Act through Congress in 1934. This law radically changed Indian-white relations and gave Native Americans control of their lands; it was nicknamed the Indian New Deal. The law ended the allotment system, gave local councils authority to spend relief money, and allowed Indians to practice traditional religions and customs. Congress increased appropriations for reservations from twelve million dollars to an average of forty-eight million dollars while Collier held his post. The commissioner had his critics, mainly advocates of assimilation and western senators and congressmen fearful of Indian self-rule. In 1944 the House Indian Affairs Committee criticized Collier's policy and called for a return to the old idea of making Indians into Americans. The next year Collier resigned, and many of his programs ended.

Policy Since World War II. Creation of the Indian Claims Commission in 1946, which was empowered by Congress to settle all Indian land claims against the government, resulted in victories for some tribes. Between 1946 and 1960 the commission awarded more than 300 million dollars to Indian tribes wrongfully deprived of their lands, but Congress saw this as an excuse to end other assistance to reservations. Some BIA officials foresaw the abolition of the reservation system. In the 1950's relocation became a popular idea. More than sixty thousand Indians were moved to cities such as Denver, Chicago, and Houston. To save money and hasten the end of separate development for Native Americans, Commissioner Dillon S. Meyer took away powers of tribal councils and returned decisions concerning spending to BIA headquarters.

In 1953 Congress approved the Termination Resolution, which terminated federal control over Indians living on reservations in California, Florida, Iowa, New York, and Texas. The states now had criminal and legal jurisdiction over the tribes. Results proved disastrous, especially after removal of federal liquor control laws. Unemployment and poverty increased under the termination program. The BIA tried to resolve the unemployment problem by expanding the relocation program, hoping that jobless Indians would find work in cities, but by 1958 more than half of the relocated workers had returned to the reservations.

In the 1960's Congress reversed direction yet again and revoked the termination policy. During the federal government's War on Poverty, it increased tribal funds for education, health care, and job training. Expanded federal aid greatly improved living conditions for Indians, and reservation population increased from 367,000 in 1962 to 452,000 in 1968. Life expectancy improved from a dismal 51 years (1940) to 63.5 (1968), not yet up to white American levels but a great improvement nevertheless. In 1975 the Indian Self-Determination and Education Assistance Act gave tribes control over school funds and returned most important economic decision-making powers to locally elected councils. Three years later Congress established a community college system on reservations in which native languages, religions, and cultures were taught.

The American Indian Religious Freedom Act (1978) protected traditional practices, and the Supreme Court advanced Indian self-determination by authorizing tribal courts to try and punish even non-Indians for violations of the law committed on Indian territory. In a key ruling in 1978 the Court said that tribes could be governed by traditional laws even if they conflicted with state and federal laws. In the 1980's such ideas of separate development continued to dominate reservation policy, and the Reagan administration followed a policy of "government-to-government relationships" among the states, the federal government, and the tribes. In many ways this "new" policy greatly resembled ideas first enunciated by George

Washington in 1794, when Americans also doubted the possibility of assimilation and opted for a policy of pluralism and cultural separation. Although a few reservations have become quite rich because of the lease or sale of mineral rights, and recently because of revenues from gaming concerns, most remain very poor. When a Bureau of the Census study of poverty in the United States in the 1980's listed the ten poorest counties in the union, eight of them were on reservations. Cultural self-determination, improved education, and increased financial assistance had not yet improved economic conditions for many Native Americans. Reservations in South Dakota and New Mexico were the poorest; they also had the highest levels of alcoholism, divorce, and drug addiction found anywhere in the United States.

See also: Allotment system; American Indian Defense Association; American Indian Religious Freedom Act; Bureau of Indian Affairs; General Allotment Act; Indian Claims Commission; Indian New Deal; Indian Self-Determination and Education Assistance Act; Meriam Report; Reserve system of Canada; Termination Resolution; Trail of Tears; Treaties and agreements in the United States.

Leslie V. Tischauser

Sources for Further Study

Brandon, William. *The Indian in American Culture.* New York: Harper & Row, 1974. A massive volume covering Indian-white relations since the beginning; includes an interesting discussion of reservation policy. Includes a good index.

Frantz, Klaus. *Indian Reservations in the United States: Territory, Sovereignty, and Socioeconomic Change.* Chicago: University of Chicago Press, 1999. A thorough, detailed cultural-geographic study of life on American Indian reservations.

Frazier, Ian. *On the Rez.* New York: Picador, 2001. A depiction of contemporary Ogalala Sioux life on the Pine Ridge reservation. Written by an Anglo, somewhat controversial among American Indians.

Fritz, Henry E. *The Movement for Indian Assimilation, 1860-1890.* Philadelphia: University of Pennsylvania Press, 1963. A comprehensive analysis of government policy in the critical period when assimilation policy was the order of the day.

Priest, Benson. *Uncle Sam's Stepchildren: The Reformation of United States Indian Policy, 1885-1887.* New Brunswick, N.J.: Rutgers University Press, 1942. An old but still useful discussion of the origins of the General Allotment Act (Dawes Act).

Washburn, Wilcomb E., ed. *History of Indian-White Relations.* Vol. 4 in *Handbook of North American Indians.* Washington, D.C.: Smithsonian Institution Press, 1988. Contains several useful essays on past and current reservation policy, including William T. Hagan's "United States Indian Policies, 1860-1900" and Lawrence C. Kelly's "United States Indian Policies, 1900-1988." Excellent index, detailed bibliography.

_____. *The Indian in America*. New York: Harper & Row, 1975. Arguably the best one-volume survey of the Indian experience in North America, with many useful insights and comments concerning the reservation system. Contains an extensive bibliography and comprehensive index.

Reserve system of Canada

Date: Nineteenth century-present
Locale: Canada
Tribes involved: Pantribal in Canada
Categories: National government and legislation, Native government, Nineteenth century history, Twentieth century history
Significance: Until well into the twentieth century, Canada's Indian reserve system assumed that lands not specifically defined "surrendered" to white settlement were for traditional Indian use; reactions to abuses in "surrender" arrangements brought more protective self-government and ownership provisions in the 1990's.

By the early 1990's the percentage of land reserved by law for the specific use of Canadian Indian tribes varied considerably from province to province. In eastern provinces such as Newfoundland, reserves were largely symbolic, amounting to about 0.06 percent of all land. To the west, percentages were somewhat higher (2 percent in Alberta, for example), while in the Northwest Territories and the Yukon, a full third of what Canada calls the "traditional lands" remain reserved for the aboriginal tribes, referred to in Canadian law as "bands."

The situation of Indian self-government on reserve lands is a relatively recent development that must be viewed in the light of key legislation passed between 1930 and 1990. One can say, however, that the Canadian federal government has tried, since the 1930's, to ease strains created by unfortunate reversals of what long appeared to be a relatively enlightened history of protecting the lands (if not tribal governing autonomy) of Canadian Indians.

Ideal and Reality of Traditional Reserve Policy. The history of Indian reserves in Canada began at the end of the French and Indian War (1754-1763), when French claims on Canada were abandoned to British imperial control. A British royal proclamation in 1763 forbade governors of both the Canadian and the American colonies from issuing any land grants to colonists unless it was clear that the land in question was not "traditionally occupied" by Indians. This act began the so-called policy of protection, which stipulated that only the Crown held ultimate responsibility for protecting or acquiring traditional Indian lands. Such acquisition, or "surrendering over," was to be with the consent of tribes; what was not "surrendered" to the Crown was presumed to remain Indian property.

When the American Revolution ended in 1783, the influx of Loyalists into Canada caused pressures for colonial land grants to rise. In response, the Crown initiated a series of treaties and purchase agreements, particularly with tribes in Ontario. What was not turned over by sale or treaty agreement would from that date be called Indian "reserves." What appeared to be benevolent recognition of the Indians' traditional lands, however, was not always that generous. In a few extreme cases, such as the Chippewa (Ojibwa) agreement to surrender their Chenail Ecarte and St. Clair lands, only a very small portion was left for exclusive tribal use (in this case, some 23,000 acres out of a total of 2.7 million acres).

For a number of years there was no specific definition of what responsibilities the British might accept with respect to Indian rights within their reserves. This changed by the 1830's, when it became obvious that Indians even farther west were going to be affected by expanding white settlements and that, as their traditional way of life would no longer be possible in areas left as reserves, government assistance would have to be part of the land surrender process. Thus, an agreement concerning the Manitoulin Islands near the north shore of Lake Huron became, in 1836, part of a "new" attitude toward reserves: Indians there were to receive, free from "the encroachments of the whites . . . proper houses . . . and assistance . . . to become civilized and to cultivate land."

At the same time, it became increasingly apparent that the "traditional" reserve system would have to involve higher degrees of Indian dependence on Crown authorities to intercede between them and aggressive settler communities anxious to gain access to the natural resources on Indian land. In 1850, a decade and a half before Canada's federal/provincial arrangement (the Constitutional Act) placed the authority of the Crown across the entire width of the Atlantic, troubles broke out over settler access to minerals in the Lake Superior area. William Robinson was appointed treaty commissioner in order to define how Indian hunting and fishing rights could be preserved while sale and development of mining rights on the same land passed to outside bidders.

With the coming of Canada's independent status after 1867, it became apparent that a specific Indian act would be necessary and somehow should be binding on all provinces of the federal system. Neither the first Canadian Indian Act of 1876 nor later acts, however, provided for the establishment of new reserves. The object of all Canadian Indian acts (into and through the twentieth century) was supposed to be to improve the management and developmental prospects of reserves that already existed. Nevertheless, the traditional but in many ways manipulated concept of what constituted a reserve in Canada continued, for nearly a century, to allow for "surrender" of lands considered to be in excess of tribal needs. Thus, in Quebec Province, some 45,000 choice acres considered Indian reserves in 1851 would be given over to white settlement between 1867 and 1904. The most spectacular case of additional surrenders occurred in Saskatchewan, the source for almost half of the nearly 785,000 acres of Indian lands taken in the early twentieth century. In addition to formal acts of surrender, amendments in 1895 and 1918 to the Indian Act allowed the superintendent-general of Indian affairs to recognize private leases of reserve land that was not being exploited economically by the tribes.

Perhaps the most striking example of consequences that could come from application of these and other amendments occurred in the 1924 Canada-Ontario Indian Reserve Lands Agreement which would stand, despite challenges, into the 1990's. The 1924 agreement essentially acknowledged Indian rights to exploit *non*-precious minerals on their land, but provided for separate conditions to govern (external) exploitation of, and revenues from, precious mineral mines in Ontario (and by extension, elsewhere in Canada).

Post-1930 Trends Toward Self-Government on Reserves. The year 1930 was a watershed, for after that year, federal, or Dominion, approval for surrenders would become the exception rather than the rule. In the same year, the Dominion transferred public land control rights in the Prairie provinces to the provincial governments of Saskatchewan, Alberta, and Manitoba, with the express condition that existing Indian reserves would be maintained unchanged under federal control. The 1930 agreements nevertheless recognized the applicability of the 1924 precious metals "exception" (the Canada-Ontario Reserve Agreement noted previously) to any Indian reserves in the Plains provinces.

Rising governmental and public attention to Indian affairs came in the early 1960's, partially in the wake of the government's *Report on Reserve Allotments* (published in 1959) and partly following publication of a major study by Jean Lagasse on native populations in Manitoba. Lagasse's findings brought the beginnings of community development programs on Indian reserve lands, but they remained limited mainly to Manitoba itself. By 1975, a specific scheme for self-management and community government was legislated in the James Bay Agreement for northeastern Quebec, but this again had limited geographical scope.

Substantial change in conditions affecting life on reserve lands across Canada would not come until the late 1980's, and then specifically with passage of the 1989 Indian Act. A good portion of the local legislative precedents that formed the bases for the Indian Act of 1989 can be seen to have been drawn from key decisions ranging from the James Bay Agreement through the Municipal Grants Act of 1980 and the much broader 1986 Sechelt Indian Band Self-Government Act. When legislators extended such precedents to define the status of the totality of Canada's Indian population, the government in Ottawa granted for the first time several essential principles of self-government to tribes throughout the country. They now included the right to hold full title to property formerly considered their "reserves" (but ultimately controlled by Dominion authorities) and to dispose of that property legally as they might see fit (through sales, leases, or rentals), through procedures they would determine via the autonomous channels of their own councils.

See also: Aboriginal Action Plan; Declaration of First Nations; *Delgamuukw v. British Columbia*; Department of Indian Affairs and Northern Development; French and Indian War; Indian Act of 1876; Indian Act of 1951; Indian Act of 1989; Indian-white relations: Canadian; International Indian Treaty Council; Meech Lake Accord; Nisga'a Agreement in Principle; Nunavut Territory; Oka crisis; Riel Rebellions; Royal Commission on Aboriginal Peoples; Treaties and agreements in Canada; White Paper of Canada.

Byron D. Cannon

Sources for Further Study

Bartlett, Richard H. *Indian Reserves and Aboriginal Lands in Canada*. Saskatoon, Canada: University of Saskatchewan, Native Law Center, 1990.

Frideres, James. *Canada's Indians: Contemporary Conflicts*. Scarborough, Ontario: Prentice Hall of Canada, 1974.

Hawley, Donna L. *The Annotated 1990 Indian Act*. 3d ed. Toronto: Carswell, 1990.

Indian-Eskimo Association of Canada. *Native Rights in Canada*. Calgary: Author, 1970.

Nagler, Mark. *Natives Without a Home*. Don Mills, Ontario, Canada: Longman, 1975.

Riel Rebellions

Date: 1869-1870, 1885
Locale: Manitoba and Saskatchewan, Canada
Tribes involved: Assiniboine, Cree, Metis
Categories: Nineteenth century history, Wars and battles
Significance: Two separate revolts against the government of Canada led to the dispersal and marginalization of the once thriving Metis.

Canadian policies that threatened both the Metis and Indian ways of life were at the heart of two separate revolts in Canada's newly acquired prairie region. (Metis people are of mixed Indian and European descent.) In 1869 the Hudson's Bay Company relinquished its claim over Rupert's Land and the Northwest to the recently confederated nation of Canada. Prime Minister John A. Macdonald set out to build a great nation joined from the Atlantic to the Pacific by a rail line. Although the government negotiated treaties that established Indian reserves, it offered the Metis, whom it did not regard as legally Indian, no such consideration. This contributed significantly to the erosion of the Metis economic and social life.

Red River Rebellion, 1869-1870. Preparing to take over the new territories in the fall of 1869, Canada sent survey parties into the Red River region. The Metis of the region had for many years occupied long, narrow farmsteads along the riverbank. Contrary to this practice, the surveyors delineated square township lots. Both fearing the imminent arrival of large numbers of English-speaking Protestants and fearing that their long-established land tenure would be ignored once Canada asserted control over the area, the Metis and a few of the original white settlers declared a provisional government in early November, 1869. Prairie-born but Montreal-educated Louis Riel, Jr., was elected secretary and, within a few weeks, president of the government of Assiniboia.

The Red River Rebellion actually involved very few military skirmishes. On November 2, 1869, the Metis seized Upper Fort Garry and arrested fifty

Canadians including a militant Orangeman named Thomas Scott. Scott escaped from custody twice but was recaptured each time. He was tried, convicted of treason against the Metis government, and executed in March, 1870. Scott's execution became a rallying point in English Canada against the mainly French Catholic Metis. Riel, who was president of Assiniboia at the time, was held responsible. He was forced into exile for much of the next fifteen years.

The Metis of Assiniboia had no intention of remaining independent of Canada and issued a declaration of their desire to join the Confederation of Canada as a new province with full representation in Parliament. According to their declaration, the new province would have both English and French as its official languages, control of public lands would remain with the local legislature, and the citizens would retain the property rights they held prior to entering confederation.

In May, 1870, after several months of negotiation between Ottawa and the Metis, the Canadian Parliament passed the Manitoba Act. While the establishment of the new province should have met many of the Metis demands, in practice it did not. The province was limited to 100,000 square miles, Parliament rather than the Manitoba Legislature retained control of the public lands, and the conveyance of the Metis' land titles was delayed so long that many Metis sold their rights to land speculators and moved farther west.

The Riel Rebellions, 1869 and 1885

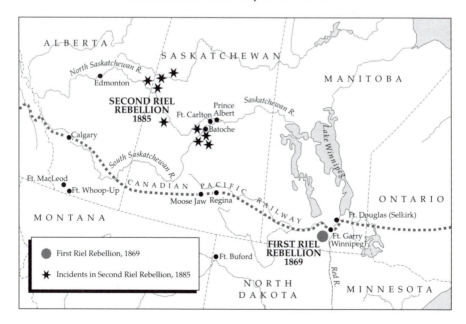

Northwest Uprising, 1885. Many of the same economic concerns that caused the 1869-1870 Red River Rebellion fueled the Northwest Uprising of 1885. This second revolt, however, included Cree and Assiniboine Indians as well as the Metis. Ottawa, fearing a general Indian uprising on the prairies, responded with swift military action rather than negotiation.

Faced with the near extinction of the buffalo and once again with the fear of being uprooted by new settlers, the Metis around Batoche on the Saskatchewan River invited Riel to return from exile to argue their claims with Ottawa. Riel, however, had changed greatly in the intervening decade and a half. He had spent several years in insane asylums in Montreal before settling on a farm in Montana. He was obsessed with the idea that it was his divine mission to establish a French Catholic state in the northwest. He viewed the arrival of four Metis emissaries on June 4, 1884, as divine intervention and returned to Canada to fulfill his mission.

Riel spent much of his time drafting petitions to Ottawa outlining the Metis' grievances. Finally, reminiscent of events in 1869, the Metis, led by Riel and Gabriel Dumont, seized the parish church at Batoche and declared a provisional government. The army and the Northwest Mounted Police responded promptly, and the entire revolt was crushed within two months. The Metis and the Indians, however, did inflict casualties. The first skirmish occurred near Duck Lake when the Mounted Police arrived to assert Canadian authority. The Metis, joined by a few Indians, killed ten of the police and forced the remainder to retreat.

The Indians, starving as a result of the loss of the buffalo and then Ottawa's withholding of treaty rations, were encouraged by the Metis victory at Duck Lake. The Cree and Assiniboine were easily persuaded to join the revolt. Several hundred hungry Indians under the leadership of Poundmaker attacked the fort at Battleford, burning the homes and looting the stores. Other Cree, led by Big Bear, killed nine people, including the Indian agent and two priests in what became known as the Frog Lake Massacre. Three others were spared by Big Bear.

The Canadian military response was swift. Eight thousand well-armed troops were dispatched to the region, and the revolt was summarily crushed. Among the leaders of the revolt, Dumont escaped to the United States, where he performed for a time with Buffalo Bill Cody's Wild West Show. Big Bear and Poundmaker each received three years in prison. Riel, who used his trial as a forum for his cause, was found guilty of treason and hanged on November 16, 1885. Many of the Metis and Cree fled to Montana. Others dispersed to the north. Fearing additional Indian uprisings, the Canadian government rushed to complete the Canadian Pacific Railroad and promptly began to settle the West.

See also: Declaration of First Nations; Department of Indian Affairs and Northern Development; Indian Act of 1876; Indian Act of 1951; Indian Act of 1989; Indian-white relations: Canadian; Red River Raids; Treaties and agreements in Canada.

Richard G. Condon and Pamela R. Stern

Sources for Further Study

Beal, Bob, and Rod Macleod. *Prairie Fire: The 1885 North-West Rebellion.* Edmonton: Hurtig, 1984. Emphasizes the Native Canadian perspective.

Bowsfield, Hartfield. *Louis Riel: The Rebel and the Hero.* Toronto: Oxford University Press, 1971. A good introductory book.

Dempsey, Hugh A. *Big Bear: The End of Freedom.* Vancouver: Douglas & McIntyre, 1984.

Flanagan, Thomas. *Riel and the Rebellion: 1885 Reconsidered.* 2d ed. Toronto: University of Toronto Press, 2000. Provides a revisionist perspective.

Giraud, Marcel. *The Metis in the Canadian West.* Translated by George Woodcock. 2 vols. Lincoln: University of Nebraska Press, 1986. A primary source on the Metis, originally published in French in 1945. Volume 2 deals with the period of the rebellion. Some of the language suggests racial determinism.

McDougall, John. *In the Days of the Red River Rebellion.* Edmonton: University of Alberta Press, 1983. Memoir of a Methodist missionary during the time of the rebellion.

Miller, J. R. *Skyscrapers Hide the Heavens: A History of Indian-White Relations in Canada.* Rev. ed. Toronto: University of Toronto Press, 1991. Chapter 9 deals with the rebellion.

Owram, Doug. *Promise of Eden: The Canadian Expansionist Movement and the Idea of the West, 1856-1900.* Toronto: University of Toronto Press, 1980. Chapter 4 discusses the politics of the Canadian response to the rebellion.

Purich, Donald. *The Metis.* Toronto: James Lorimer, 1988. Highly readable treatment of the Metis. Chapters 3, 4, and 5 deal with the 1869 and 1885 rebellions and their outcomes.

Riel, Louis. *The Collected Writings of Louis Riel.* Edited by George F. G. Stanley. Edmonton: University of Alberta Press, 1985. Shows that Riel was a thinker as well as a political leader.

Siggins, Maggie. *Riel: A Life of Revolution.* Toronto: HarperCollins, 1994. Readable, lively narrative account.

Stanley, George F. G. *The Birth of Western Canada: History of the Riel Rebellions.* Toronto: University of Toronto Press, 1960. Argues that the rebellions were the defining event in western Canadian history.

Rosebud Creek, Battle of

Date: June 17, 1876
Locale: Montana
Tribes involved: Arapaho, Cheyenne, Sioux
Categories: Nineteenth century history, Wars and battles
Significance: This battle was preliminary to the Little Bighorn fight; it neutralized General George Crook's northbound column of the 1876 Sioux campaign, bolstered the Indians' confidence, and opened the door for the Custer defeat.

On January 31, 1876, the U.S. government issued an ultimatum that all Indians must reside on reservations or be deemed "hostiles." This declaration ultimately led to the army's 1876 summer campaign against the northern Plains Indians.

The campaign was a three-pronged pincer tactic designed to surround, push, and engage the "hostile" bands in present northcentral Wyoming and south-central Montana, with Colonel John Gibbon coming from the west, General Alfred Terry and Colonel George Armstrong Custer from the east, and General George Crook from the south. Embarking from Fort Fetterman, Wyoming, on May 29, Crook marched up the Bozeman Trail with

A depiction of the Battle of Rosebud Creek from the August 12, 1876, issue of Frank Leslie's Illustrated Newspaper. (Library of Congress)

more than a thousand troopers and established a base camp at present-day Sheridan, Wyoming. He was joined by more than two hundred Crow and Shoshone allies on June 14.

Mid-June was also when the Hunkpapa Sioux held their Sun Dance in which Sitting Bull experienced his famous vision of many soldiers falling into camp. The Indians knew of Crook's forces and were eager to fulfill Sitting Bull's vision. By June 16, Crook's troops had moved on to the Rosebud River. The next morning, while his forces were relaxing, Crazy Horse's warriors struck.

After the Sioux's initial charge the soldiers were able to regroup enough to take command of the high ground on the valley's northern bluffs. From there, Crook orchestrated his troop's movements. The Rosebud Valley is long, however, and the terrain broken with hills, ravines, and ridges. These created a disjointed battle with scattered pockets of fierce action stretching three miles along the valley. During the fight, Crook mistakenly believed that Crazy Horse's village lay northward and ordered Captain Anson Mills's detachment to find and seize it. The battle intensified, and Crook's Crow and Shoshone allies proved their worth throughout. In one instance they rescued an officer from the Sioux in a hand-to-hand struggle. Meanwhile, Mills, finding no village, returned to the fight, coming to the rear of the Sioux and Cheyenne. This eventually caused the Indians to disengage and abandon the battlefield.

The battle lasted six hours and was filled with intense fighting. Crook proclaimed victory on the notion that he possessed the battlefield in the end. In truth, Crook's troops were bested by Crazy Horse's warriors, and had it not been for the valiant efforts of his Crow and Shoshone allies, Crook would have suffered greater casualties than his twenty-eight dead and fifty-six wounded. The Sioux and Cheyenne suffered comparable casualties but in the end forced Crook to retreat south with his dead and wounded, thus neutralizing his forces at the most critical juncture in the campaign. In Crook's defense, he faced (on onerous terrain) an unexpectedly unified force whose tenacious fighting was unparalleled— a combination Custer would face a week later with more disastrous results.

See also: Bozeman Trail War; Fort Laramie Treaty of 1868; Indian-white relations: U.S., 1871-1933; Little Bighorn, Battle of the; Wounded Knee Massacre.

S. Matthew Despain

Royal Commission on Aboriginal Peoples

Date: 1991-1996

Locale: Canada

Tribes involved: Pantribal in Canada

Categories: National government and legislation, Twentieth century history

Significance: In April, 1991, the government of Canada, in response to aboriginal leaders' concerns, established the Royal Commission on Aboriginal Peoples to review the role and place of aboriginal people in contemporary Canada. The final report, published in November, 1996, made 440 recommendations in response to problems that have long plagued the relationship between aboriginal peoples, the Canadian government, and Canadian society as a whole.

In April, 1991, the government of Canada set forth a sixteen-point mandate for the seven commissioners (four aboriginal, three nonaboriginal) of the newly constituted Royal Commission on Aboriginal Peoples. Amid much upheaval, uncertainty, and in some cases violence, the commissioners held 178 days of public hearings, conducted public hearings in ninety-six communities, listened to dozens of expert witnesses and testimony, and engaged in additional research. Acknowledging that the colonial policy of the federal government for the last 150 years had been wrong, the commission attempted to determine the "foundations of a fair and honorable relationship between the aboriginal and nonaboriginal people of Canada." The commissioners sought to examine this relationship as a central facet of Canada's heritage, describe how the relationship became distorted, and examine the terrible consequences for aboriginal people in the loss of lands, power, and self-respect. The commissioners hoped that the report would repair the damaged relationship and provide a new footing for mutual recognition and respect, sharing, and responsibility. Consisting of five volumes of several thousand pages each, the final report provided a comprehensive answer to the guiding question and related questions and problems.

A History of Mistakes. "Aboriginal peoples" refers to organic and cultural entities stemming from the original peoples of North America, not to collections of individuals united by "racial" characteristics. The commissioners traced the relationship of aboriginal and nonaboriginal peoples through four stages. The first stage was before 1500, when no contact had been made between North American aboriginals and Europeans. The second stage started in the 1500's and was marked by initial mutual curiosity and then increasing trust, trade, exchange of goods, intermarriage, and military and trade alliances that created bonds between and among nations. This stage was crowned by the Royal Proclamation of 1763, which governed the relations between nations on the question of land rights. The third stage began in the 1800's as increasing numbers of Europeans immigrated to Canada. Respect gave way to domination. The new policy of "assimilation" proved, in time, to be a form of cultural genocide. The solution to the problems left by the assimilation policy, the report stated, is in recognizing that "aboriginal peoples are nations." This affirmation is not to say that these peoples are nation-states seeking independence from Canada but rather collectivities with a long, shared history, a right to govern themselves, and a strong desire to do so in partnership with Canada. The fourth stage, the report concluded, was just beginning. The report hoped to assist the process of "renewal and renegotiation" well into the twenty-first century.

The mistakes that characterize the relationship with aboriginal peoples have been serious, often deadly. On average, the life expectancy of aboriginals is lower than that of nonaboriginals; illnesses such as alcoholism and diabetes are more prevalent; families are more often broken or marred by violence, abuse, and criminality, leading to a disproportionately high number of aboriginals in jail; and educational failure and dropout for children is common. The commission argued that these problems had reached the point where aboriginal peoples had become tired of waiting for handouts from governments. It found that these people wanted control over their lives instead of the well-meaning but ruinous paternalism of past Canadian governments. They needed their lands, resources, and self-chosen governments in order to reconstruct social, economic, and political order. They needed time, space, and respect from nonaboriginals to heal their spirits and revitalize their cultures.

Renewing and Restructuring the Relationship. Four principles formed the basis for renewed relationships between aboriginals and nonaboriginals: *recognition* by nonaboriginals of the principle that aboriginals were the original caretakers of the land along with the recognition that non-aboriginals now share, and have a right to, the land; *respect* between peoples for their rights and a resistance to any future forms of domination; *sharing* of benefits in "fair measure"; and *responsibility*, the hallmark of a "mature relationship," which includes accountability for promises made, for behaving honorably, and for the effect of one's actions on the well-being of others. The needs and problems of all groups in their diversity cannot be addressed piecemeal. The renewed relationship entails a fundamental structural component that is centered on reclaiming aboriginal peoples as "nations." These nations, however, are not to be formed by every single aboriginal community in Canada. The commission concluded that the right of self-government cannot reasonably be exercised by small, separate communities, whether First Nations, Inuit, or Metis. It should be exercised by groups of a certain size—groups with a claim to the term "nation." The commission went on to suggest a process for doing this, beginning with a royal proclamation, issued by the monarch as Canada's head of state and guardian of the rights of aboriginal peoples. Such a move would dramatically signal a new day for aboriginal people, setting out the principles, laws, and institutions necessary to turn these into reality. This new royal proclamation would not supplant, but instead support and modernize the Royal Proclamation of 1763, or so-called Aboriginal Peoples' Magna Carta.

The commission recommended that the proclamation contain the following elements: a reaffirmation of Canada's respect for aboriginal peoples as distinct nations; acknowledgment of harmful actions by past governments, which deprived aboriginal peoples of their lands and resources and interfered with family life, spiritual practices, and governance structures; a statement placing the relationship on a footing of respect, recognition, sharing, and mutual responsibility, thus ending the cycle of blame and guilt and freeing aboriginal and nonaboriginal peoples to embrace a shared future; affirmation of the right of aboriginal peoples to fashion their own lives and control their own governments and lands—not as a grant from other Canadian governments but as a right inherent in their status as peoples who have occupied these lands from time immemorial; and acknowledgment that justice and fair play are essential for reconciliation between aboriginal and nonaboriginal peoples and a commitment by Canada to create institutions and processes to strive for justice.

Such a proclamation would be followed by the enactment of companion legislation by the Parliament of Canada. The legislation would create the new laws and institutions needed to implement the "renewed relationship" with a view to providing both the authority and the tools needed for aboriginal peoples to structure their own political, social, and economic future.

Governance and Polity. The most dramatic and sweeping proposal made by the commission was the creation of a parallel parliament for aboriginal peoples. The commission suggested that after the royal proclamation, the

Canadian government draft and pass an act that would establish a body to represent aboriginal peoples within federal governing institutions and advise Parliament on matters affecting aboriginal peoples. A constitutional amendment would create a "house of first peoples" that would become part of Parliament along with the House of Commons and the Senate.

Other recommendations included restructuring the federal government to allow the Department of Indian Affairs and Northern Development (DIAND) and the ministerial position that goes with it to be replaced by a senior cabinet position, the "minister for aboriginal relations," and a new "department of aboriginal relations." In addition, the commission recommended establishing a minister and department of Indian and Inuit services to deliver the gradually diminishing services coming from the federal level.

It recommended three models of self-government: *national* government, to be exercised among aboriginal peoples with a strong sense of shared identity and an exclusive territorial base inside which national governments would exercise a wide range of powers and authority; *public* government, in which all residents would participate equally in the functions of government regardless of their heritage; and *community of interest* government, to be exercised primarily in urban centers where aboriginal persons form a minority of the population but nonetheless want a measure of self-government in relation to education, health care, economic development, and protection of culture. The latter would operate effectively within municipal boundaries, with voluntary membership and powers delegated from aboriginal nation governments and/or provincial governments.

Land Rights and Claims. The commission stated that the land claims process is "deeply flawed" and recommended that it be replaced by a fairer and more balanced system in which the federal government does not act as both defender of the Crown's interests and judge and jury on claims. The commission further stated that this process is not open to Metis claims, thereby leaving Metis people without a land and resource base and with no mechanisms for settling grievances. It also categorized as unfair the governmental demands that aboriginals "extinguish" their general land rights in favor of specific terms laid down in claim settlements and recommended a new process that would result in three categories of allocation: lands selected from traditional territories that would belong exclusively to aboriginal nations and be under their sole control; other lands in their traditional territories that would belong jointly to aboriginal and nonaboriginal governments and be the object of shared management arrangements; and land that would belong to and remain under the control of the Crown but to which aboriginal peoples would have special rights, such as a right of access to sacred and historical sites.

In support, the commission recommended establishing regional treaty commissions and an aboriginal lands and treaties tribunal that would facilitate and support treaty negotiations. Also, the commission called on the federal government to allocate to aboriginal nations "all land promised to them in existing treaties," "to return to First Nations all land it has expropriated or bought, then left unused," and "to establish a fund to help aboriginal people purchase land on the open market." The commission recommended one major piece of companion legislation, namely an aboriginal treaties implementation act that would seek to establish a process for "recognized aboriginal nations to renew existing treaties or negotiate new ones." The act would also "set out processes and principles to guide negotiation, include a commitment to implement existing treaties according to their spirit and intent, and . . . renegotiate treaty terms on which there was no meeting of minds when they were originally set down" and would "establish regional treaty commissions to convene and manage the negotiation process, with advice from the aboriginal lands and treaties tribunal on certain issues."

Other Measures Proposed. Other recommendations included measures to overcome epidemic health problems, child abuse, welfare and economic dependency, and related socioeconomic problems, including poor housing and a lack of overall infrastructure in aboriginal communities. In recommending aboriginal control of education, the commission noted that aboriginal peoples are simply asking for no more than what other communities already have—the chance to say what kind of people their children will become. Aboriginal peoples want schools to help children, youth, and adults learn the skills they need to participate fully in the economy, develop as citizens of aboriginal nations, and retain their languages and the traditions necessary for cultural continuity. The commission also recommended that aboriginal peoples be given control over youth and adult education, including not only education in aboriginal culture, customs, and traditions but also that which will assist in overcoming the massive problems of unemployment in aboriginal communities.

The report of the Royal Commission on Aboriginal Peoples challenged aboriginal and nonaboriginal relationships. It documented the myriad problems of the past century and offered a considered and considerable number of recommendations for change. However, these recommendations, detailed and numerous though they were, are probably not enough to bring about change. As the commissioners noted, "It will take an act of national intention—a major, symbolic statement of intent, accompanied by the laws necessary to turn intentions into action."

See also: Aboriginal Action Plan; Declaration of First Nations; *Delgamuukw v. British Columbia*; Department of Indian Affairs and Northern Development; Fifteen Principles; Indian Act of 1989; Indian-white relations: Canadian; Meech Lake Accord; Nisga'a Agreement in Principle; Nunavut Territory; Reserve system of Canada; Treaties and agreements in Canada; White Paper of Canada.

Gregory Walters

Sources for Further Study

Looking Forward, Looking Back; Restructuring the Relationship; Gathering Strength; Perspectives and Realities; and *Renewal: A Twenty Year Commitment.* 5 vols. Ottawa: Canada Communication Group, 1996. The final report of the Royal Commission on Aboriginal Peoples.

Long, J. Anthony, and Menno Boldt, eds., in association with Leroy Little Bear. *Governments in Conflict? Provinces and Indian Nations in Canada.* Toronto: University of Toronto Press, 1988. Addresses aboriginal-provincial relations focusing on self-government, provincial jurisdiction, land claims, and financial responsibility.

_____. *The Quest for Justice: Aboriginal Peoples and Aboriginal Rights.* Toronto: University of Toronto Press, 1985. Presents a broad cross section of tribal, geographic, and organizational perspectives. The authors discuss constitutional questions such as land rights, concerns of Metis, nonstatus Indians and Inuit, and historical, legal/constitutional, political, regional, and international rights issues.

Miller, J. R. *Sweet Promises: A Reader on Indian-White Relations in Canada.* Toronto: University of Toronto Press, 1991. Contains key, previously published articles concerned with regional developments from the days of New France to the present.

Morrison, Andrea P., with Irwin Cotler, eds. *Justice for Natives Searching for Common Ground.* Montreal: McGill-Queen's University Press, 1997. A volume that came together around the Oka crisis between aboriginal people in Quebec and the government. Its thirty-five essays and stories provide helpful discussions on native women and the struggle for justice, self-determination, title and land claims, the Oka crisis, and legal relations and models for change.

Morse, Bradforse W. *Aboriginal Peoples and the Law: Indian, Metis and Inuit Rights in Canada.* Rev. ed. Ottawa: Carleton University Press, 1989. Provides a basic resource for cases and materials on the original inhabitants of Canada.

Sand Creek Massacre

Date: November 29, 1864
Locale: Sand Creek, southeastern Colorado
Tribes involved: Cheyenne
Categories: Nineteenth century history, Wars and battles
Significance: The slaughter of Cheyenne women and children by Colorado militia regulars presages the subjugation of Great Plains Indians for the next three decades.

Against the backdrop of the American Civil War (1861-1865), on August 17, 1862, the beleaguered Santee Sioux in Minnesota began an uprising against the continuing encroachment of white settlers. This bloody fighting touched off general warfare the length and breadth of the Great Plains and frightened gold seekers in the new mining settlements of Colorado. Governor John Evans of the new Colorado Territory tried to get Cheyennes and Arapahos to give up their hunting ranges for reservations, but they did not want to leave. In the meantime, white settlers' devastation of the buffalo (bison) herds was limiting the tribes' hunting ranges, and regular army troops had moved out to support the Union as a new influx of settlers swept across the plains, seeking fortune and avoiding Civil War service.

Sporadic raids by American Indians made travelers along the California and Santa Fe Trails nervous. White migration and the settlers' practice of decimating buffalo herds merely for their tallow and hides caused concern among the natives, who were further hampered by intertribal warfare, a diminishing food supply, and the scourge of smallpox. On November 10, 1863, Robert North, an illiterate white man of dubious credibility who had lived with the Arapahos, gave a statement to Governor John Evans, saying that the Comanches, Apaches, Kiowas, Northern Arapahos, Sioux, and all Cheyennes had pledged to one another to go to war with the settlers in the spring of 1864.

On December 14, 1863, Evans wrote to Secretary of War Edwin Stanton asking for military aid and authority to call out the state militia. The situation remained relatively quiet in the early spring. Cheyennes and Arapahos were fighting the Utes, the Arapahos were feuding with the Kiowas, and the Sioux bided their time. By April, Colonel John M. Chivington's command had begun an aggressive military campaign against American Indians in general and Cheyennes in particular. This campaign provoked a war that lasted well into 1865 and cost the government thirty million dollars.

Chivington's Campaign. Chivington, the military commander of Colorado Territory, had had a minor success against Confederate forces in New Mexico in 1862. He was a former Methodist minister who was dubbed the Fighting Parson. Zealous and unscrupulous, he harbored political ambitions. Encouraged by Governor Evans, Chivington used scattered incidents to declare that the Cheyennes were at war, and he sent out soldiers to "burn villages and kill Cheyennes wherever and whenever found." Ominously, he declared that he believed in killing American Indians "little and big."

The tribes struck back. By the summer of 1864, fighting and atrocities on both sides plagued western Kansas and eastern Colorado. In June, Evans, trying to separate peaceful tribes from warlike bands, urged friendly Kiowas and Comanches to report to Fort Larned on the Arkansas River in Kansas and Southern Cheyennes and Arapahos to report to Fort Lyon, 250 miles up the same stream in southeastern Colorado. He ordered the friendly tribes to submit to military authority. A skirmish at Fort Larned rendered this strategy useless, and by August Evans had issued a proclamation calling for indiscriminate killing of American Indians. The natives retaliated by closing the road to Denver, which stopped the mail and caused prices of staples to skyrocket. White settlers mobilized for war.

The Cheyenne chief Black Kettle urgently wanted peace. Accordingly, he and other Cheyenne and Arapaho leaders met with Evans and Chivington at Camp Weld near Denver on September 28, 1864. The talks were confusing, because Evans made the distinction between surrender to the military authorities and securing peace by treaty. The tribal leaders did not understand, and they received no clear promise of peace. Clearly, the settlers were spoiling for a fight. In fact, Chivington had recruited enlistees for his Third Colorado Volunteer Regiment from among mining camp toughs and bums with a promise that they would kill American Indians. The stage was set for a tragedy.

After submitting themselves to military authorities at Fort Lyon in early November, Black Kettle's band of approximately six hundred Indians were sent to make camp to hunt buffalo in the broad, barren valley of Sand Creek, a tributary of the Arkansas River in southeastern Colorado about forty miles north of Fort Lyon. Because the younger braves had drifted north to listen to the war drums at a council on the Smoky Hill River, Black Kettle's group mainly consisted of old men, women, and children. They were mostly Cheyennes, with a few dozen Arapahos. They believed they were safe.

Chivington's views were unequivocal. He would take no prisoners and "damn any man that was in sympathy with the Indians." After a bitter night march over rolling prairie, Chivington deployed approximately seven hundred men and four howitzers around Black Kettle's village at daybreak on November 29, 1864. In addition to his Third Colorado Volunteer Regiment, Chivington had 175 soldiers of the First Colorado Cavalry and a small contingent of New Mexico infantry.

Massacre of Cheyennes. Mounted troops and foot soldiers swept across the dry creekbed into the Cheyenne camp. Black Kettle ran up a U.S. flag and a white surrender flag over his teepee at the center of the camp. The flags were ignored. Panic ensued as the natives were butchered where they stood. One of the first killed was White Antelope, a seventy-five-year-old man. The Arapaho chief Left Hand fell quickly. Small groups of Cheyennes fought from sand pits, but most fled in panic. Black Kettle miraculously escaped. Atrocities followed the slaughter.

Eyewitness testimony later recalled,

> They [the Indians] were scalped, their brains knocked out; the men used their knives, ripped open women, clubbed little children, knocked them in the head with their guns, beat their brains out, mutilated their bodies in every sense of the word.

A Lieutenant Richmond of the notorious Third Colorado shot and scalped three women and five children as they screamed for mercy. The final tally of American Indian dead ranged from 150 to 500. Three-quarters of those killed were women and children. Chivington's report said of his troops, "All did nobly."

Chivington returned to Denver in triumph, his men brandishing a hundred American Indian scalps. The triumph would be short-lived. A letter from Indian agent S. G. Colley printed in the *Missouri Intelligencer* on January 6, 1865, mentioned the atrocities and stirred public opinion in the states. General Halleck, the Army chief of staff, ordered Chivington investigated, and the district commander, General Curtis, attempted to have him court-martialed. Instead, Chivington mustered out of the service.

Indian Retaliation. Following the massacre, Cheyennes, Arapahos, and Sioux ravaged the South Platte River Valley. They killed approximately fifty whites, burned stage stations, destroyed telegraph lines, and twice sacked the town of Julesburg in northeast Colorado. With the Civil War drawing to a close, on March 3, 1865, a joint resolution of Congress created a joint committee to study the "Indian problem." A shifty and temporary treaty in October, 1865, made peace on the plains but inexplicably contradicted itself and forbade some tribes any legal home. On January 26, 1867, the final report of the joint committee released testimony about the Sand

Creek Massacre and traced many American Indian wars to "lawless white men always to be found upon the frontier or boundary lines between savage and civilized life."

The American Indian wars lasted until the closing of the frontier. The incessant pressure of whites moving westward across North America had produced constant conflict with the Native Americans. Special circumstances surrounding the Civil War, the Colorado gold rush, and the decline of the buffalo herds led to the tragedy of Sand Creek. The pent-up forces of expansion released in the aftermath of these events ensured that this tragedy would not be an isolated one. Who was "savage" and who "civilized" remains a large historical question.

See also: Bear River Campaign; Indian-white relations: U.S., 1831-1870; Medicine Lodge Creek Treaty; Navajo War; Sioux War; Washita River Massacre.

Brian G. Tobin

Sources for Further Study

Grinnell, George Bird. *The Fighting Cheyennes*. New York: Charles Scribner's Sons, 1915. Drawing heavily on primary documentation and such venerable authorities as Hubert Howe Bancroft, this detailed account of the Sand Creek events evokes Cheyenne sympathies.

Hoig, Stan. *The Peace Chiefs of the Cheyennes*. Norman: University of Oklahoma Press, 1980. This short work paints the Cheyenne in general, and Black Kettle in particular, as men of peace. Includes many interesting photographs.

Josephy, Alvin M., Jr. *The Indian Heritage of America*. Rev. ed. Boston: Houghton Mifflin, 1991. Examines the clash of cultures in words and illustrations.

Lavender, David. *The Great West*. Boston: Houghton Mifflin, 1985. Suggests that Black Kettle may have been more interested in handouts than in peace.

Utley, Robert M., and Wilcomb B. Washburn. *The Indian Wars*. Boston: Houghton Mifflin, 1985. Puts the Sand Creek Massacre in the context of the times.

Santa Clara Pueblo v. Martinez

Date: 1978
Locale: New Mexico
Tribes involved: Santa Clara Pueblo, Navajo

Categories: Civil rights, Court cases, Twentieth century history

Significance: A U.S. Supreme Court decision deepens the concept of tribal sovereignty and reinforces the sanctity of tribal customs in determining tribal membership.

The Santa Clara Pueblo (New Mexico) passed an ordinance stating that if a male member of the tribe married a woman who was not a member of the tribe, their children would be eligible for membership in the tribe. However, children born of a woman from the tribe who married a nonmember man were not eligible for enrollment in the tribe.

When the tribe refused to enroll her daughter, Julia Martinez, an enrolled member of the Santa Clara Pueblo married to a Navajo, brought suit against her tribe on behalf of her daughter. Martinez charged that the tribal law violated her daughter's rights to equal protection under the Indian Civil Rights Act (1968), and further, Martinez contended that the law discriminated against her based on her sex. The tribe argued that its rules for membership were culturally based on a traditional patrilineal system that predated the United States and its laws. The tribe also asserted its sovereign right to determine who is a tribal member without federal government involvement.

In deciding the case in 1978, the U.S. Supreme Court declined to interfere with the tribe's conception of membership. The Court also stressed that the Indian Civil Rights Act did protect the civil rights of individuals from unjust acts of tribal governments, but its overriding purpose was to promote tribal self-government and self-determination rather than impose the dominant society's standards of equal protection. This case deepened the concept of tribal sovereignty and reinforced the sanctity of tribal customs.

See also: American Indian Religious Freedom Act; Federally recognized tribes; Indian Civil Rights Act; Indian Claims Commission.

Carole A. Barrett

Saybrook, Battle of

Date: September, 1636-May, 1637
Locale: Saybrook, Connecticut
Tribes involved: Pequot
Categories: Colonial history, Wars and battles

Significance: Defeat in this battle, actually a nine-month siege of Fort Saybrook, led to the destruction of the Pequots as a power in the Northeast.

The roots of the Battle of Saybrook are found in the 1634 treaty between the Pequots and Massachusetts Bay. The treaty granted the Pequots trade with Massachusetts and peace with the Narragansetts. In exchange the Pequots were required to deliver a specified amount of wampum to Massachusetts. When the Pequot wampum delivery did not meet expectations, Massachusetts officials viewed the wampum delivery as proof of the Pequots' subordinate status. John Winthrop, Sr., former and future governor of Massachusetts, said that the Pequots relinquished their right to Connecticut to Massachusetts in 1635. This claim provided the justification necessary for Massachusetts to involve itself in the settlement of the Connecticut Valley, a region beyond the boundary of the Massachusetts royal charter. Working in conjunction with the Saybrook Company, Massachusetts officials built Fort Saybrook at the mouth of the Connecticut River.

In July, 1636, John Winthrop, Jr., nominal governor of Fort Saybrook, met with the Pequots and issued an ultimatum. Winthrop demanded that the Pequots meet English expectations regarding wampum demands and hand over the killers of Captain John Stone. Winthrop knew that Western Niantics had killed Stone a few years earlier; his demands were not meant to be accepted. To avoid trouble, the Pequot sachem Sassacus placed the Pequot territory under Massachusetts's domain. Shortly thereafter, events occurred that produced the First Pequot War. Block Island Narragansetts killed Captain John Oldham in July, 1636. In August, 1636, colonial militiamen sailed to Block Island and looted and burned empty villages. Colonists then turned their attention to the Pequots. They wanted the Pequots' land, and they used Oldham's murder to justify an expedition against the Pequots. The expedition failed to subdue the Pequots, and the Indians saw the expedition as an injustice.

In September the Pequots took up arms, and by November, 1636, they had isolated Fort Saybrook. The Pequots chose not to attack more northerly communities such as Hartford. The militiamen stationed at Saybrook spent the next nine months cut off from the rest of the colonies, begging for help; none was forthcoming. The Pequots could isolate the fort for that long because the sponsor of the post, the Massachusetts Bay Colony, was distracted by an internal matter concerning the antinomian crisis.

Then in April, 1637, everything changed. In that month colonists drove the Connecticut Valley sachem Sequin and his followers off their land. This ran contrary to the agreements Sequin and the colonists had reached concerning the land. Sequin then appealed to the Pequots, to whom he paid tribute, to aid him. The Pequots did and on April 23, 1637, the Pequots attacked Wethersfield. Connecticut then used the Pequot attack on Wethersfield to justify an offensive war against the Pequots on May 1, 1637. The Pequots hoped their rivals the Narragansetts would support them in their war against Connecticut Valley settlers. The Narragansetts almost did, but Roger Williams secured a Narragansett-Massachusetts alliance that isolated the Pequots. This alliance allowed Connecticut soldiers to attack the Pequots at Mystic in late May, 1637. The predawn attack killed between three hundred and seven hundred Pequots and destroyed the remaining Pequots' will to continue the war. The peace treaty that followed, the Treaty of Hartford (1638), declared the Pequot Nation dissolved.

See also: Pequot War.

Michael J. Mullin

Seminole Wars

Date: November 21, 1817-March 27, 1858
Locale: Florida
Tribes involved: Seminole
Categories: Nineteenth century history, Wars and battles
Significance: A continuation of the U.S. policy of containment and relocation of Native Americans east of the Mississippi.

The conflicts known as the First, Second, and Third Seminole Wars were never declared wars on the part of the U.S. government. The Seminole Wars were a continuation of U.S. policy to contain Native American populations east of the Mississippi and remove them to reservations west of the Mississippi, a policy that resulted in the Indian Removal Act of 1830. They also might be seen as early battles fought over the jurisdiction of runaway slaves that would eventually escalate into the Civil War.

First Seminole War. The First Seminole War was preceded by years of disputes along the Florida-Georgia border, climaxing in the destruction of Fort Negro on the Apalachicola River. Built by the British in 1815 and turned over to a band of runaway slaves on the British departure from Florida, Fort Negro proved an obstacle in the supply route to Fort Scott in Georgia. When a U.S. vessel was fired upon from the fort, Andrew Jackson ordered General Edmund Gaines to destroy the fort. A hot cannonball, fired from the expedition led by Lieutenant Colonel Duncan Clinch, landed in a powder magazine, blowing up the fort and killing 270 of its 344 occupants. Neamathla, village chief of Fowltown, reacted by warning General Gaines that if U.S. soldiers tried to cross the border into Florida, they would be annihilated. A gunfight between U.S. soldiers and Neamathla's Seminoles on November 21, 1817, is considered the opening salvo of the First Seminole War. This conflict, ending with Andrew Jackson's occupation of the city of Pensacola in May, 1818, led to the Adams-Onís Treaty of 1819, in which Spain ceded the territory of Florida to the United States.

The 1823 Moultrie Creek Treaty restricted Seminole settlements to a reservation of four million acres north of Charlotte Harbor and six small reservations for north Florida chiefs. The Seminoles agreed not to make the reservations a haven for escaped slaves. The 1830 enactment of the Indian Removal Act mandated that all Indians be encouraged to trade their eastern land for western land. If they failed to do so, they would lose the protection of the federal government.

In May, 1832, U.S. commissioner James Gadsden convened a meeting with the Seminole chiefs at Payne's Landing. What transpired at the meeting has been the subject of much political and scholarly controversy. All that is certain is that a treaty was signed on May 9, 1832, in which the chiefs agreed that a delegation would travel to inspect the lands in Oklahoma, and, if the lands were satisfactory, the Seminoles would agree to move west as a part of the Creek allocation. The ambiguity of who "they" were—the chiefs or their tribal councils—and the peculiar stipulation that the Seminoles would be absorbed by their longtime enemies, the Creeks, put the validity of the treaty into question. There have been allegations that bribery and coercion were used to get the Seminoles to sign the treaty. All of the chiefs whose names were on the treaty later repudiated it.

An exploratory party left for Oklahoma in October, 1832, and returned to Fort Gibson, Arkansas, in March, 1833, where they entered into a series of negotiations. Again, there have been allegations of coercion and forged marks on the Fort Gibson Treaty, by which the chiefs agreed that the Seminoles would move west within three years.

Second Seminole War. In October, 1834, Indian agent Wiley Thompson brought the chiefs together to discuss plans for a spring removal. The Seminoles gathered in their own council after Thompson's initial meeting, and strong opposition to migration emerged, especially from the Seminole war leader Osceola. Relations deteriorated and skirmishes increased between

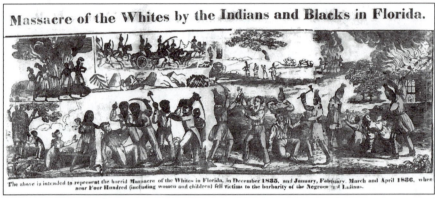

This engraving, portraying the Second Seminole War from the white perspective of the time, appeared in 1836. (Library of Congress)

the government and Seminoles throughout 1835, culminating in the outbreak of war in December. The two most notable incidents occurred on December 28. Ote-emathla, also known as Jumper, and a warrior known as Alligator led 180 warriors in ambushing a relief column under the command of Major Francis Dade. Only 3 of the 108 soldiers escaped slaughter in the fierce battle that followed. Meanwhile, Osceola led sixty warriors in an attack on Fort King with the express purpose of killing Wiley Thompson, who had imprisoned Osceola in chains earlier in the year.

The army was in disarray during most of 1836. General Winfield Scott immediately began to feud with General Gaines. General Call was put in charge of the troops until November, when General Thomas S. Jesup arrived in Florida and assumed the command until 1839. Jesup's command in Florida was crucial for the outcome of the Seminole Wars. The general had persuaded a large number of chiefs and their tribes to emigrate on the condition that they would be accompanied by their African American allies and slaves. When opposition arose among landowners claiming that the Seminoles harbored runaway slaves, a compromise was reached: Only those blacks who had lived with the Seminoles before the outbreak of the war would be permitted to go. More than seven hundred Seminoles had gathered at Fort Brooke north of Tampa by the end of May, 1837. On the night of June 2, Osceola and the Mikasuki shaman Arpeika surrounded the camp with two hundred warriors and spirited away nearly the entire population.

The defection caused a drastic shift in Jesup's tactics; no longer did he feel any compunction about using trickery to gain his ends. In September, General Joseph Hernandez captured King Philip, Yuchi Billy, Coacoochee, and Blue Snake in the vicinity of St. Augustine and imprisoned them at Fort

Marion. When Osceola and Coa Hadjo sent word to Hernandez that they were willing to negotiate, he set up a conference near Fort Peyton. Jesup ordered him to violate the truce and capture the Indians. News of Osceola's capture spread through the nation, and when he was transferred to Fort Moultrie in Georgia, George Catlin visited him and painted his portrait. His death on January 30, 1838, enshrined him as a martyr to the Indian cause.

Coacoochee, having escaped from Fort Marion on November 29, 1837, headed south to join bands led by Jumper, Arpeika, and Alligator. The largest and last pitched battle of the war was fought on the banks of Lake Okeechobee on December 25. Colonel Zachary Taylor commanded eleven hundred men against approximately four hundred Indians. The Indians finally retreated from the two-and-a-half-hour battle, leaving 26 killed and 112 wounded and having sustained 11 killed and 14 wounded.

In February, 1838, further treachery at Fort Jupiter netted more than five hundred Seminoles. Persuasion and mopping-up operations sent many of the remaining Seminole leaders, including Micanopy, the chief, on the westward migration. Jesup's tenure in Florida, which had resulted in the capture, migration, or death of more than twenty-four hundred Indians, ended in May, 1838, when Taylor took over command of the Florida forces. Taylor remained in Florida for another two years, during which time operations were carried out against scattered bands of natives throughout the peninsula.

General Alexander MacComb, commanding general of the army, came to Florida in April, 1839, and declared the war over when he concluded an agreement with the Seminoles, who agreed to withdraw south of the Peace River by July 15, 1839, and remain there until further arrangements were made. Although a guarded trading post was set up on the Caloosahatchee River, the Indians learned that they were not to be allowed to stay in Florida. Chekika, chief of the Spanish Indians, led an attack and destroyed the post in July. After he led a raid on Indian Key in August, 1840, Chekika was surprised in the Everglades and executed.

The commands of General Walker K. Armistead and General William J. Worth saw the final years of the Second Seminole War. Following the successful policy of deceiving chiefs who came to negotiate, most notably Coacoochee, and through continuing guerrilla warfare, the army managed to remove all but about six hundred of Florida's Indians, who were restricted to a temporary reservation south of the Peace River because Congress refused to continue to fund any further campaigns in 1842. The Second Seminole War was more costly than all the other Indian wars combined. Still, new settlers came to the interior of Florida, which had been made accessible by the mapping, exploration, and road-building required by the wars. The military had gained skill in guerrilla warfare and an understanding of the need for interservice cooperation, and the federal government learned to exercise its power to convert economic power into military strength.

Third Seminole War. Between 1842 and the outbreak of the Third Seminole War in 1855, the Seminoles kept to the reservation and followed the dictates of regulations imposed upon them. They remained adamant in their opposition to removal until Secretary of War Jefferson Davis declared that, if they did not leave voluntarily, the military would remove them by force.

In December, 1855, a patrol investigating Seminole settlements in the Big Cypress Swamp was attacked by a band of forty Seminoles led by Billy Bowlegs and Oscen Tustenuggee, marking the first skirmish of the war that was dubbed Billy Bowlegs' War. It was a war of skirmishes, raids, and harassment against small settlements, both white and Seminole. A treaty signed on August 7, 1856, that granted the Seminoles more than two million acres in Indian Territory separate from the Creek allotment, along with a generous financial settlement, was the catalyst to the end of the conflict in Florida. A government offer of money in return for removal was accepted on March 27, 1858. Bowlegs and his band left Florida in May, and two other bands left the following February. Only the Muskogee band led by Chipco, hidden north of Lake Okeechobee, and Arpeika's Mikasuki band, buried deep in the Everglades, a remnant of one hundred to three hundred persons, remained in relative peace in Florida, the ancestors of twentieth century Seminoles.

See also: Civil War; Indian Removal Act; Prehistory: Southeast; Trail of Tears.

Jane Anderson Jones

Sources for Further Study

Covington, James W. *The Seminoles of Florida*. Gainesville: University Press of Florida, 1993. The most thorough history of the Seminoles in Florida; devotes six chapters to the Seminole Wars.

Mahon, John K. *History of the Second Seminole War, 1835-1842*. Rev. ed. Gainesville: University Presses of Florida, 1985. Describes the battles and leaders, the problems of military organization and ordnance, and Seminole culture and history in the period of the Second Seminole War.

Tebeau, Charlton W. "The Wars of Indian Removal." In *A History of Florida*. Rev. ed. Coral Gables, Fla.: University of Miami Press, 1980. This chapter in a standard Florida history covers the Seminole Wars.

Wickman, Patricia R. *Osceola's Legacy*. Tuscaloosa: University of Alabama Press, 1991. A study of the life and myth of Osceola, based on a survey of artifacts and documents.

Wright, J. Leitch. *Creeks and Seminoles: The Destruction and Regeneration of the Muscogulge People*. Lincoln: University of Nebraska Press, 1986. An examination of the culture of the Creeks and Seminoles, and their Spanish, British, and African connections.

Sioux War

Date: Beginning August 17, 1862
Locale: Southern Minnesota
Tribes involved: Sioux
Categories: Nineteenth century history, Wars and battles
Significance: Minnesota Sioux lose their tribal lands to encroaching white settlers in one of the largest mass slaughters in U.S. history.

On August 17, 1862, four Santee Sioux men, returning from a fruitless search for food beyond the boundaries of their southern Minnesota reservation, attacked and killed five white settlers near Acton, in Meeker County. Ordinarily, the culprits would have been surrendered to white authorities, but these were no ordinary times. The Sioux of Minnesota were starving. Long-promised annuities were slow in coming, as usual, and doubts about the ability of a nation divided by civil war to fulfill its obligations to an isolated frontier led traders at the Redwood Agency to refuse to open their warehouses until payment in gold arrived from Washington, D.C. Trader Andrew Myrick had advised the starving population to "go home and eat grass, or their own dung." On August 18, a large war party attacked and looted the Redwood Agency and wiped out most of a military expedition from Fort Snelling. Myrick, among the first to fall, was found with his mouth symbolically stuffed with grass. As politicians argued over payment of annuities in paper money or in gold, the Great Sioux War began.

Prelude to War. Although the outbreak of hostilities appeared to be local, its causes must be viewed in a national context. The Fort Snelling reserve, established in 1819 near present-day St. Paul, was, until 1851, the only land in Minnesota Territory that did not belong to Native Americans. Nevertheless, thousands of white settlers, in the familiar pattern of national expansion, occupied most of southern Minnesota. In 1851, the Minnesota Sioux negotiated away most of their best hunting grounds in the treaties of Traverse de Sioux and Mendota, and were tricked into signing away most of the promised compensation to pay debts, real and imagined, to traders there. The remaining annuities were slow in coming and insufficient to support the Sioux, and there was no promise of permanent occupancy of the Minnesota reservation. Furthermore, there was no consistent policy regarding American Indians in the United States during the period. Native Americans had no legal recourse against white depredations. Appeals for protection from soldier and civilian alike fell on deaf ears. The quality and abilities of American Indian agents declined as the nation moved toward the Civil War. Resentment smoldered, but several hundred of the approximately seven thousand Sioux in Minnesota cut their hair, donned "white men's" clothes, and took up farming following the 1851 treaties. These "farmer" Sioux received most of the annuities, and a rift developed between them and the traditional, or "blanket," Sioux.

Despite the influx of settlers, the Minnesota frontier had been generally peaceful. The occasional murder of a settler by a native resulted in the miscreant being turned over to white authorities for punishment. In 1857, a group of renegade blanket Sioux slaughtered thirty settlers in northern Iowa and southern Minnesota, causing momentary panic in the area. Led by Chief Little Crow, the Sioux denied responsibility for the outlaws and formed a party to pursue them into Dakota Territory. The effort proved futile but apparently satisfied white authorities. No punishment for the Spirit Lake Massacre was forthcoming. Annuities were paid on time, and the prestige of the United States declined among the image-conscious Sioux. By 1862, most of Minnesota's white male settlers had left to fight in the Civil War, and the Sioux, confined to a narrow strip of land along the Minnesota River, were facing starvation.

Little Crow's Reluctance. Chief Shakopee and his followers knew the Acton murders would be avenged. Although Chief Little Crow, long a spokesman for the Sioux, had lost prestige when he cut his hair and began farming, he remained the person most able to unify the Sioux. He was reluctant and argued against war. Accused of cowardice, he replied,

> The white men are like the locusts when they fly so thick the sky is like a snowstorm. Yes, they fight among themselves, but if you strike one of them, they all will turn upon you and devour your women and little children . . . you will die like the rabbits when the hungry wolves hunt them in the hard moon.

Sioux leaders of the Red Cloud delegation, c. 1876 (left to right): Red Dog, Little Wound, interpreter John Bridgeman, Red Cloud, American Horse, and Red Shirt. (National Archives)

Nevertheless, he led the Sioux, forlornly hoping to regain his prestige.

The Sioux were inefficient attackers. Most of the inhabitants of the Redwood Agency escaped to spread the alarm at Fort Ridgely. During the first week, far more whites were spared than were killed, many taken prisoner by Little Crow and protected from harm in his camp. Attacks on New Ulm and settlers in Brown and Renville Counties convinced the Sioux that success was imminent. Little Crow knew that Fort Ridgely, which protected the Minnesota River Valley, would have to fall. Meanwhile, panic spread across the Midwest, as politicians from Iowa, Wisconsin, Nebraska, and Dakota Territory petitioned the federal government for troops and leadership. Minnesota governor Alexander Ramsey, who had negotiated the fateful 1851 treaties, appointed his old political rival, former governor Henry H. Sibley, to lead the Minnesota Militia against the Sioux. General John Pope, in disgrace because of his defeat at the Second Battle of Bull Run in Virginia, was assigned to head the new Northwest Department. His policy of pursue and confine would dominate American Indian policy in the trans-Mississippi West for years to come. He directed the Minnesota war from St. Paul.

On August 20 and again on August 22, before Sibley reached Fort Ridgely with a motley crew of raw recruits, Little Crow and Chief Mankato attacked. The fort's cannon was used to devastating effect; only three of the fort's defenders were killed, and both attacks were repelled. The Sioux attacked New Ulm the second time on August 23, but again failed. Several other settlements suffered attacks, but the fate of the now demoralized Sioux was sealed.

Sibley's Triumph. By the middle of September, Sibley had formed his sixteen hundred troops into a fighting unit and moved north. On September 23, Sibley defeated several hundred warriors under Chief Mankato, who was killed. As most of the combatants slipped away, Sibley rounded up 400 Sioux, conducted trials, and sentenced 306 to death. President Abraham Lincoln reviewed the records and, refusing to "countenance lynching, within the forms of martial law," commuted most of the sentences. On December 28, 1863, thirty-eight Sioux were hanged on a single scaffold at Mankato, the largest mass execution in U.S. history.

The war was not over. Little Crow was murdered near Hutchinson in 1863; Shakopee was kidnapped in Canada and hanged at Fort Snelling in 1865. The U.S. Army, following General Pope's orders, pursued the Sioux west. Such occasional engagements as the Battle of White Hill, Dakota, in 1863, and the Battle of the Little Bighorn, in Montana Territory in 1876, kept the Sioux moving.

The Great Sioux War cost the lives of 413 white civilians, 77 soldiers, and 71 American Indians, counting those 38 hanged at Mankato. There was no treaty, no negotiation to end the war. All Sioux, blanket and farmer, were condemned to lose all but a minuscule piece of their tribal lands in Minnesota, and ultimately, their way of life. The 1890 Battle of Wounded Knee, in which U.S. troops killed almost two hundred Sioux, was the last battle in the American Indian wars.

See also: Indian-white relations: U.S., 1831-1870; Indian-white relations: U.S., 1871-1933; Little Bighorn, Battle of the; Minnesota Uprising; Wounded Knee Massacre.

Stephen G. Sylvester

Sources for Further Study

Anderson, Gary Clayton. *Little Crow: Spokesman for the Sioux*. St. Paul: Minnesota Historical Society Press, 1986. A carefully researched and documented biography of the most important Native American war leader; sympathetic to both Little Crow and the Santee Sioux. Provides a detailed description of the war.

Anderson, Gary Clayton, and Alan R. Woolworth, eds. *Through Dakota Eyes: Narrative Accounts of the Minnesota Indian War of 1862*. St. Paul: Minnesota Historical Press, 1988. Carefully edited, readable first-person accounts of the war, some sympathetic to the blanket Sioux, some to the farmer Sioux who opposed the war.

Blegen, Theodore C. *Minnesota: A History of the State*. St. Paul: University of Minnesota Press, 1975. The standard history of Minnesota. Its chapter on the Sioux War is solid and balanced.

Ellis, Richard N. *General Pope and U.S. Indian Policy*. Albuquerque: University of New Mexico Press, 1970. Ellis's detailed account provides insight into the policy of punishment and containment that grew out of the war.

Green, Jerome A., ed. *Lakota and Cheyenne: Indian Views of the Great Sioux War, 1876-1877*. Norman: University of Oklahoma Press, 2000. Collects first-hand accounts from Indians at the Battle of Little Big Horn.

Hedren, Paul. *Fort Laramie and the Great Sioux War*. Norman: University of Oklahoma Press, 1998. Focuses on the events of 1876 at Fort Laramie.

Lass, William E. *Minnesota: A History*. New York: W. W. Norton, 1977. Chapter 5 is a concise but insightful statement of the war's effect on Minnesota.

Utley, Robert M. *The Indian Frontier of the American West: 1846-1890*. Albuquerque: University of New Mexico Press, 1984. Although the description of the war is brief and simplistic, it places the war in the context of Western policy toward the American Indians.

Snake War

Date: 1866-July, 1868
Locale: Southeastern Oregon, southwestern Idaho
Tribes involved: Northern Paiute (especially the Yahuskin and Walpapi bands),
Categories: Nineteenth century history, Wars and battles
Significance: After two years of guerrilla warfare, peace talks between Brevet Major General George Crook and Snake leader Old Weawea effectively pacified most Snake bands.

The Snakes (named Gens du Serpent by early French explorers) were ancient inhabitants of the Great Basin along upper reaches of the Missouri River southward to the Sweetwater River. From the seventeenth century onward, they invariably had been described as a very poor, largely itinerant people whose chief preoccupation was scrounging food from hard country.

After the failure of Oregon and Nevada volunteers to end Snake attacks on miners during Civil War years, the U.S. Army's First Cavalry and Fourteenth Infantry under General George Crook assumed responsibility for operations in 1866. Thereafter, in a remorseless campaign of forty-eight battles, resulting in five hundred Indian casualties and the death of Chief Pauline, Crook suppressed the Snakes' guerrilla war by exhausting them. Eight hundred Snakes were led to Fort Harney, Oregon, in July, 1868, by Old Weawea, signaling peace. Most Snake survivors retired to the Klamath and Malheur River reservations.

See also: Bannock War; Bozeman Trail War; Indian-white relations: U.S., 1871-1933.

Clifton K. Yearley

Society of American Indians

Date: 1911-1924
Locale: United States
Tribes involved: Pantribal in the United States
Categories: Organizations, Twentieth century history
Significance: Headed by educated Native American professionals, the SAI advocated native educational and social advancement, true historical representation, native franchise, and legal assistance.

On October 12, 1911, more than fifty Native American delegates met in Columbus, Ohio, at the Society of American Indians' (SAI) founding conference. The date, Columbus Day, was significant: This gathering marked a reclaiming of indigenous voices, a rediscovering of native pride.

The "father" of this organization was a non-Native American sociologist from Ohio State University, Fayette A. McKenzie. Six months prior to the October conference, McKenzie had met with Dr. Charles A. Eastman (Sioux), Dr. Carlos Montezuma (Apache), attorney Thomas L. Sloan (Omaha), Laura Cornelius (Oneida), and Henry Standing Bear (Sioux). Coming from different backgrounds, these educated professionals united to form a native-run association. Already assimilated into the dominant society, they sought to retain their Native American identity. Calling themselves the American Indian Association, the group rallied around pan-Indian reforms, especially in the educational arena.

At the October convention, the historical, legal, and cultural bonds connecting all natives were emphasized. The delegates drafted a constitution that advocated native advancement, true historical presentation, native citizenship, and legal assistance. To assert that this was a native movement and not a "white-run" organization, delegates changed the name to the Society of American Indians. National meetings were to be held annually, and Washington, D.C., was designated as the society's headquarters.

The SAI's publication, the *Quarterly Journal*, was first issued on April 15, 1913. The masthead was framed with the society's emblem, the American eagle, on one side and a lighted torch on the other. Below this was the SAI's motto: "The honor of the race and the good of the country shall be paramount."

The journal's editor, Arthur C. Parker (Seneca), was the SAI's most intellectual influence. With his anthropological background, Parker sought to design the SAI after Tecumseh's historical visions. Parker ardently fought for educational reforms, for an American Indian Day, and for visible Native American role models.

As a peacekeeper, Parker often tempered the rising factionalism in the SAI. In 1913 the SAI was at its membership height with more than two hundred active (native) members and more than four hundred associate (nonnative) members. Friction in the following years sharply eroded membership numbers, however; lacking resources for assisting tribes with legal aid and for affecting the structure of the Bureau of Indian Affairs (BIA), members began to air their frustrations internally. Conflicts involved arguments over the abolition of the BIA, the denouncement of peyote religion, and the responsibility of individual tribal complaints. The SAI officially rejected peyote religion, but no consensus was reached on the BIA question, an issue that eventually splintered the SAI.

A change in focus was attempted by renaming the society's publication *The American Indian Magazine*. One of its editors, Zitkala-Sa (Gertrude Bonnin), a Yankton Sioux, became involved in the SAI by opening an educational center among the Utes. Even with Zitkala-Sa's strong contributions, however, the SAI's status remained precarious.

In the early 1920's, a sense of despair clouded the SAI's visions. Pan-Indian unification attempts had failed, BIA abolition was hopeless, political clout was slight (many members were not franchised), and individual interests were detracting from pantribal ones. On June 2, 1924, the Indian Citizenship Act was signed, marking the success of one of the SAI's hardest fought battles. By this time, however, the group was almost completely defunct, and symbolically, this date marks the end of the SAI.

See also: Bureau of Indian Affairs; Indian Citizenship Act; Indian-white relations: U.S., 1934-2002; National Council of American Indians.

Tanya M. Backinger

Sports mascot controversies

Date: Beginning 1970's
Locale: Canada, United States
Tribes involved: Pantribal
Categories: Twentieth century history
Significance: Native American objections to the use of "Indian" and "Indian warrior" mascots for professional, high school, and college sports teams reflects a growing sensitivity to negative stereotyping but also set the stage for a backlash against "political correctness."

The rise in Native American political activism in the 1960's and 1970's, coupled with a general interest in the cultural representation of all minorities, including African Americans, women, and individuals with physical and mental disabilities, led to increasing discomfort with the widespread practice of using "Indian" mascots for sports teams. Common team names, such as "Redskins," "Braves," or "the Fighting [tribal name]," were represented by a person, invariably not of Native American descent, dressed in stereotypical Indian warrior costume as seen in the standard Hollywood western: loincloth, a headband and feathers or full war bonnet, "war paint" streaked on the face, and a bow and arrows or spear in tow. This mascot would enter the playing field, sometimes on horseback, and perform an equally Hollywood-inspired "war dance," using ritually aggressive body language to indicate that the team was going to "massacre" its opponents in the upcoming game. The mascot was often given an appropriate local Indian name, whether that of a historical figure or a suitable invention—the University of Florida mascot is "Chief Osceola," an early nineteenth century Seminole leader, while the former San Diego State University mascot was "Monty Montezuma," reflecting the city's proximity to the ancient Mexican Aztec empire.

The trend toward giving sport teams "Indian" names only began in the early twentieth century. It is probably no coincidence that this fashion began with the closing of the American frontier and the end of outright hostilities between Native Americans and the U.S. government. The reduction of the actual threat posed by Native Americans allowed them to become romantic figures whose virtues could now be idealized.

Although more than six hundred teams have changed their names since the first wave of political sensitivity in the 1970's, the issue of racially charged sports mascots reached another peak in the 1990's. In a large part, this was due to the resistance of remaining Indian-themed teams to changing their names, on the grounds that such names were, in fact, complimentary, referring to Native American bravery, physical prowess, and overall martial virtues. Furthermore, the backers of Indian team names and mascots claimed that words such as "redskin" no longer carried the kind of cultural baggage that had made them pejoratives in the nineteenth century. In twentieth century America, they argued, the primary association of such words was with sports themselves: "Redskins" was first and foremost the name of the Washington, D.C., football team, and the "Braves" play baseball in Atlanta, Georgia. Such arguments were fueled by the conservative backlash against political correctness, perceived as the imposition of the will of overly sensitive minorities on the majority culture.

A Harris poll of 743 sports fans, 217 Native Americans living on reservations, and 134 Native Americans living off reservations, conducted by *Sports Illustrated* magazine in February, 2002, revealed that not only most white Americans (79 percent) but also most Native Americans (83 percent) did not believe that sports teams should stop using Indian nicknames, mascots, or symbols. Surprisingly, the gap in opinion was larger between Native Americans on reservations (67 percent in favor of Indian mascots) and off reservations (89 percent in favor) than between Native Americans as a whole and whites. However, the more significant result of the poll was probably the finding that, while Native Americans might not disapprove of the simple use of even pejorative words such as "redskin," they did object to derogatory representations of Native Americans through the mascots' on-field antics.

Anthropologists Charles Springwood and Richard King, who coedited a collection of essays, *Team Spirits: The Native American Mascots Controversy* (2001), reported that the negative stereotyping of Native Americans as the result of Indian names and mascots tends to come, not from the teams themselves, who regard their names as symbols of strength and power, but from their opponents, who draw upon the vast cultural repertoire of images of Indians as savage, primitive, incompetent, and vanquished to promote their own team spirit. The danger of Indian mascots, Springwood and King argue, is that they provide a cultural arena for the perpetuation of these negative stereotypes that is, ironically, completely irrelevant to the history of actual Native Americans.

Some Native Americans, however, have decided that equal opportunity stereotyping is the best way to get their message across. In 2002, a Native American intramural basketball team at the University of Northern Colorado named themselves the "Fightin' Whites." Their mascot is a 1950's style white male, complete with tie, dimples, and tidy hair. His slogan: "Every thang's going to be all white."

Leslie Ellen Jones

See also: American Indian; Amerind; Native American; Tribe.

Standing Bear v. Crook

Date: 1879
Locale: Nebraska
Tribes involved: Ponca
Categories: Court cases, Nineteenth century history
Significance: A United States district court finds that "an Indian is a 'person' within the meaning of the laws of the United States."

In 1865, the Ponca, a small tribe, were guaranteed a ninety-six-thousand-acre reservation along the Missouri River in northern Nebraska. Three years later, the United States gave the entire Ponca Reservation to the Sioux without consulting the Poncas. The government's solution was to remove the Poncas to Indian Territory (Oklahoma). Despite Ponca protests, in 1879 federal troops escorted the whole tribe south to Indian Territory.

Hardships caused by the journey and the radical change in climate caused many deaths among the Ponca. The people longed to return to their homeland, and in January, 1879, one chief, Standing Bear, set out for home with a small group of followers. After the people reached Nebraska, federal troops arrested the runaways in order to return them to Indian Territory.

The plight of Standing Bear captured national attention, and prominent lawyers in Omaha drew up a writ of *habeas corpus* to prevent the people's return to Indian Territory. On April 30, 1879, when the matter came before the United States district court in Omaha, Judge Elmer S. Dundy ruled "an Indian is a 'person' within the meaning of the laws of the United States" and determined that Standing Bear and his followers had been illegally detained by the federal government. The Ponca affair got national attention and inspired the formation of organizations to fight for Indian rights.

See also: Indian-white relations: U.S., 1871-1933.

Carole A. Barrett

Taos Rebellion

Date: January 19, 1847
Locale: Taos, New Mexico
Tribes involved: Apache, Comanche, Taos
Categories: Nineteenth century history, Wars and battles
Significance: Resistance by Hispanics and Indians in New Mexico leads to the first revolt against new U.S. authority.

In the twenty years prior to the outbreak of the Mexican-American War (1846-1848), the northern borderlands frontier of Mexico had undergone profound changes. A breakdown in relations with Native Americans, particularly the Apaches and the Comanches, resulted in such an increase in Native American raids that whole sections of the frontier were depopulated of settlers. Unable to institute effective pacification measures, the national government in Mexico City largely abdicated responsibility for frontier defense to the northern Mexican states and territories, a task few had the resources to implement or maintain. At the same time, U.S. influence in the borderlands was growing. In the province of New Mexico, the opening of the Santa Fe Trail in 1821 increasingly drew north-central Mexico into the economic sphere of the United States; while in Mexican Texas, large-scale U.S. immigration led that area to declare its independence from Mexico in 1835-1836. When the United States annexed Texas in 1845, precipitating the crisis that would lead to war with Mexico, the northern borderlands frontier of Mexico seemed acutely vulnerable to a U.S. takeover.

Kearney and the Army of the West. In Missouri, Colonel Stephen Watts Kearny recruited the so-called Army of the West among enthusiastic frontier supporters of manifest destiny and Missouri merchants eager to expand their Mexican markets. Following the Santa Fe Trail, Kearny and sixteen hundred troops set out first for Bent's Fort, a trading establishment just north of the Arkansas River, then the United States-Mexico border. Charles and William Bent, with their partner Ceran St. Vrain, had established the post in 1833. From it, they had quickly monopolized the fur and American Indian trades of the southern Rockies and Great Plains. They also had expanded into the Santa Fe trade, operating a mercantile outlet in Taos, New Mexico, where Charles Bent had taken up residence after marrying into a prominent New Mexican family. From Bent's Fort, Kearny's forces left for New Mexico, preceded by James Wiley Magoffin, a

Santa Fe trader acting as President James Polk's emissary. Arriving in Santa Fe, Magoffin secretly met with New Mexico governor Manuel Armijo and persuaded him that resistance was futile. After making a show of defending the province, Armijo fled southward, allowing U.S. troops to occupy New Mexico. On August 18, 1846, Kearny's forces entered Santa Fe, the capital.

Kearny quickly reassured the sixty thousand inhabitants of New Mexico that U.S. rule would not threaten their persons or possessions. The Kearny Code, in conjunction with the United States Constitution, codified these promises and provided a legal framework for the conquered province. Kearny established a new civil government, naming Charles Bent as governor and Donaciano Vigil of Santa Fe as secretary or lieutenant governor. Soon after, Kearny departed for California to continue the conquest of northern Mexico. Colonel Sterling Price, newly arrived from Missouri with additional troops to garrison the province, took military command.

Kearny's governmental appointments had excluded many of the New Mexico *ricos*, or upper classes, who had formerly controlled the province. Several of his appointees, many of whom had traded for years in New Mexico, held land grants or interests in land grants that had been issued earlier by former governor Armijo. Their new positions of authority gave these appointees the opportunity to expand their New Mexico holdings at the ex-

A photograph of Taos Pueblo recorded by the Library of Congress in 1878, approximately three decades after the rebellion. (Library of Congress)

pense of the *ricos*, or so many *ricos* believed. Rumors began circulating throughout the province that the U.S. occupiers wished to register land titles, in preparation for the seizure of the *ricos'* property, and to exact heavy taxes (as a territory of Mexico, New Mexico was exempt from paying national taxes). Moreover, Taos Indians believed that Charles Bent also wished to acquire lands of the Pueblo de Taos. As a result, Tomás Ortiz, Diego Archuleta (formerly Armijo's second-in-command), and possibly Padre Antonio José Martínez of Taos, along with other prominent native New Mexicans, began to conspire against U.S. rule, planning an uprising. Lieutenant Governor Vigil, learning of the conspiracy, quickly suppressed it, but not before news of the planned insurrection had spread to towns and communities in northern New Mexico.

Bent Is Ambushed. On January 14, 1847, Governor Bent left for Taos (also called Don Fernando de Taos, to differentiate it from the pueblo of the same name, only two miles north of the village), ignoring warnings from Vigil that such a journey might be dangerous in the volatile climate following the suppression of the conspiracy. Bent felt reasonably secure, not only because he had long resided in Taos but also because news of U.S. victories farther south in Chihuahua seemed to preclude the possibility of aid reaching New Mexico from that quarter. On January 19, 1847, however, Taos Indians, led by one Tomasito, joined insurrectionists in the village, led by Pablo Montoya. They destroyed U.S. settlers' homes and attacked the residence of Charles Bent. Bent himself was killed and scalped, as were other Americans and Mexican supporters of the new regime. The insurrectionists then burned a nearby distillery at Arroyo Hondo, also operated by a U.S. citizen. Similar uprisings occurred at other northern communities, most notably at Mora, where seven more U.S. settlers, many of them Santa Fe traders, were killed.

When news of these events reached Santa Fe, Colonel Price immediately set out for Taos with 480 men and four artillery pieces, while Vigil took over as provisional governor and issued a proclamation denouncing the rebels. The insurgents, numbering almost two thousand, met Price's forces on January 29, 1847, at the village of Cañada, twenty-five miles north of Santa Fe. The U.S. settlers drove the rebels toward the Pueblo de Taos, where they made their stand in the fortress-like church. On February 3, 1847, the battle resumed. Turning their artillery on the church, the U.S. forces breached the walls, forcing the insurgents out. After more fighting, the Taos Indians and their Hispanic allies eventually surrendered, having suffered losses of 150 persons. U.S. losses were seven killed and forty-seven wounded.

Fate of the Conspirators. While in custody awaiting trial, Tomasito, believed to have been responsible for Bent's murder, was shot and killed by a U.S. soldier. Pablo Montoya and fourteen others were tried by court-martial and sentenced to death. The New Mexico civil court indicted other conspirators, who were subsequently tried for treason against the United States and executed. President Polk and Secretary of War William L. Marcy later pointed out that the conspirators could not actually have been guilty of treason against the United States, as the United States and Mexico were still at war. Nevertheless, they supported the measures taken to end the uprising and the execution of its principal leaders. Diego Archuleta fled New Mexico before he could be apprehended but later returned, took the oath of allegiance to the United States, and became active in territorial politics. Padre Martínez, against whom nothing was ever proven definitely, also escaped indictment and continued his leadership role in northern New Mexico until his death in 1867.

Although peace returned to New Mexico following the uprising, four years of military rule followed. In 1850, the Territory of New Mexico was finally established. Although Anglo-Americans tended to dominate federally appointed positions, the New Mexico *ricos* established firm control over the legislative assembly, largely securing their place in the new order. Other native New Mexicans, however, lost their lands to unscrupulous Anglo-American lawyers who used their knowledge of U.S. law and their political connections to undermine land guarantees given in the Treaty of Guadalupe Hidalgo, which ended the Mexican War. The Taos Indians lost much of their former territory during the period of U.S. rule over New Mexico.

See also: Apache Wars; Gadsden Purchase; Guadalupe Hidalgo, Treaty of; Navajo War.

Joseph C. Jastrzembski

Sources for Further Study

Crutchfield, James Andrew. *Tragedy at Taos: The Revolt of 1847.* Plano, Tex.: Republic of Texas Press, 1995. First comprehensive narrative of the events at Taos. Contains valuable appendices concerning the participants, a chronology of events, casualty figures, and other items of interest.

Keleher, William A. *Turmoil in New Mexico, 1846-1868.* Santa Fe, N.Mex.: Rydal Press, 1952. Details the events leading up to the U.S. invasion of New Mexico and the subsequent occupation of the province.

Simmons, Marc. *New Mexico: An Interpretive History.* Albuquerque: University of New Mexico Press, 1988. Chapter 4 covers the events of the occupation of New Mexico and briefly discusses the Taos Rebellion.

Twitchell, Ralph Emerson. *The History of the Military Occupation of the Territory of New Mexico from 1846 to 1851 by the Government of the United States.* 1909. Reprint. Chicago: Rio Grande Press, 1963. Quotes extensively from government documents; provides biographical sketches of the principal participants.

Weber, David J. *The Mexican Frontier, 1821-1846: The American Southwest Under Mexico.* Albuquerque: University of New Mexico Press, 1982. A comprehensive overview of the Mexican borderlands before the Mexican War. Discusses the economic impact of the Santa Fe Trade, American Indian relations, the church, society, and culture.

Tecumseh's Rebellion

Date: 1809-1811
Locale: Old Northwest (Great Lakes region)
Tribes involved: Chippewa, Iroquois, Lenni Lenape, Miami, Ottawa, Potawatomi, Shawnee, Wyandot (Huron)
Categories: Nineteenth century history, Wars and battles
Significance: Tecumseh, a powerful advocate of united Indian resistance to American encroachments onto Indian lands east of the Mississippi River, led what many believe was the last great hope for effective Indian opposition to the advance of the European American frontier in the eastern portion of the United States.

Soon after the conclusion of the Treaty of Fort Greenville in 1795, frontiersmen, land speculators, and settlers surged into the newly opened lands and beyond into Indian country, thereby exacerbating tensions with the tribes. As pressure mounted for further expansion beyond the line delimited under the terms of the Treaty of Fort Greenville, the governor of the new Indiana Territory, William Henry Harrison, inaugurated a policy designed to acquire additional territory from the Indians incrementally. Hence, between 1802 and 1809, Harrison and Governor William Hull of the Michigan Territory concluded a series of treaties under the terms of which a significant portion of the area between the Great Lakes, the Ohio River, and the Mississippi River were opened for settlement. As the white settlers pressed against the Indians from the south and east, the tribes north of the Ohio Valley were simultaneously pressed from the west by the expansive Chippewa and Sioux in the upper Mississippi region. Hence, under

A portrait of the most influential pantribal leader of the early eighteenth century, Tecumseh, painted by Mathias Noheimer. (Library of Congress)

vicelike pressure from several directions, the tribes increasingly concluded that they would have to coordinate their policies and be prepared to fight or perish.

Indian Resistance. Tecumseh and his brother, the Shawnee Prophet Tenskwatawa, emerged determined to preserve the identity and territorial integrity of the tribes and their lands in the region between the Great Lakes and the Ohio River Valley. Tecumseh maintained that the Americans had been successful in depriving the Indians of their lands because the tribes had consistently failed to stand unified against external encroachments. Hence, he argued that the tribes must create a meaningful confederation and agree not to cede additional lands to the United States without the concurrence of all the tribes in the union. Only in this way could the tribes negotiate with the Americans from a position of strength. Moreover, Tecumseh and his brother called upon the Indians to purge themselves of corrupting influences, such as alcohol, and return to traditional ways. Finally, notwithstanding the Indian disillusionment with the British as a result of Britain's abandonment of the Indians in 1794, Tecumseh again looked to Great Britain for political and material support in his effort to coalesce effective resistance to the Americans. Indeed, because of escalating Anglo-American tensions as a result of the Chesapeake Affair of 1807, the British were more willing to extend the support sought by Tecumseh. Consequently, Tecumseh and his brother made considerable progress toward the establishment of an Indian Confederation and the renewal of Indian society.

In 1808, as momentum gathered behind Tecumseh and his new confederation, he and his brother founded Prophetstown, located near the confluence of Tippecanoe Creek and the Wabash River. The Indian leaders hoped that Prophetstown would serve as a center of the confederation movement and that from it Tecumseh and his brother could influence the policies of the tribes throughout the region bounded by the Great Lakes, the Mississippi River, and the Ohio Valley. In addition, in 1808 Tecumseh visited the British at Fort Malden, across the U.S.-Canadian border near Detroit. On this occasion, the British assured Tecumseh of their full support of the tribes' combined efforts to form a confederation and to resist further American encroachments upon their lands. The British authorities, however, urged the Indian leaders not to be the ones to initiate hostilities along the frontier.

As a result of continued efforts by American authorities to detach additional Indian lands (culminating in the Treaty of Fort Wayne in 1809), American intransigence concerning the implementation of the various treaties negotiated since the Treaty of Fort Greenville, and, finally, continued encroachment by American frontiersmen into Indian territory, hostilities again erupted along the frontier in 1810. Both Tecumseh and the British attempted to ameliorate the crisis, but radical elements among the tribes pressed for more aggressive military action against the Americans.

During the summer of 1811, Tecumseh traveled south of the Ohio River in an effort to enlist the support of the Creek, Cherokee, and Choctaw tribes. The Creeks expressed support for Tecumseh, but Cherokee and Choctaw leaders were reluctant to take actions that might provoke open warfare with the United States government.

Tippecanoe. With Tecumseh absent from his center of power north of the Ohio, Harrison decided to avail himself of the opportunity and attack the geographic heart of the confederation movement—Prophetstown. By November 6, 1811, Harrison's force had moved to a position less than a mile from Prophetstown. The following day, on November 7, as Harrison had hoped, the Indians, unrestrained because of Tecumseh's absence, attacked the American force and were severely defeated amid heavy fighting. Following this costly victory at the Battle of Tippecanoe, Harrison's force destroyed Prophetstown before returning to their base of operations at Vincennes.

Following the Tippecanoe campaign, the frontier war continued; eventually it was submerged in the context of the greater struggle between the United States and Great Britain in the War of 1812. Tecumseh was killed at the Battle of the Thames on October 5, 1813. In many respects, the death of this great Indian leader marked the end of the last real hope of effective Indian resistance to American settlement east of the Mississippi and the extinction of the traditional Indian culture in the eastern portion of the United States.

See also: Fort Wayne Treaty; Indian-white relations: U.S., 1775-1830; Prophetstown; Thames, Battle of the; Tippecanoe, Battle of.

Howard M. Hensel

Sources for Further Study
Billington, Ray Allen. *Westward Expansion*. New York: Macmillan, 1949.
Philbrick, Francis S. *The Rise of the West, 1754-1830*. New York: Harper & Row, 1965.
Prucha, Francis Paul. *The Sword of the Republic*. New York: Macmillan, 1969.
Tucker, Glenn. *Tecumseh: Vision of Glory*. Indianapolis: Bobbs-Merrill, 1956.

Termination Resolution

Date: Beginning August 1, 1953
Locale: United States
Tribes involved: Pantribal in the United States
Categories: National government and legislation, Twentieth century history
Significance: Congress ends its policy of special treatment of American Indians.

Termination was viewed by its advocates as freeing American Indians from special laws and regulations, making them equal to other citizens, and by opponents as precipitously withdrawing federal responsibility and programs. The term used for the federal policy came to be applied to the people themselves: "terminated" tribes. Termination actions included repealing laws setting American Indians apart, ending Bureau of Indian Affairs (BIA) services by transferring them to other federal agencies or to the states, and terminating recognition of the sovereign status of specific tribes.

Termination, many have observed, did not deviate from the norm of federal policy. Its emphasis on breaking up American Indian land holdings is often compared to the General Allotment Act of 1887 (the Dawes Act). The latter required the allocation of a certain number of acres to each person and, during its forty-seven years in force, reduced tribal lands by nearly ninety-one million acres.

In public debate, opponents of termination argued that the United States had a special obligation to American Indians because they had been conquered and deprived of their customary way of life. All people in the United States, opponents said, have the right to be different and to live in the groupings they prefer. Any changes in federal supervision of American Indians should be implemented slowly and with the involvement of the affected tribes; rather than dissolving tribal communities, federal policy should continue meeting tribes' special needs until those needs no longer exist. Opponents also pointed to American Indian culture, tribal lands, and tribal government—their form of community—as their source of strength.

Advocates of termination asserted that all U.S. citizens should be similar, and there should be no communities with special legal rights. Dissolving separate American Indian communities would expedite the integration of these people into the mainstream. American Indians, according to Senator Arthur V. Wakens, would be freed from wardship or federal restrictions and would become self-reliant, with no diminution of their tribal culture. Wakens saw termination as liberation of American Indians and compared it to the Emancipation Proclamation. Non-natives objected to the Indian Reorganization Act (IRA) of 1934, the prior federal policy, and were swayed toward termination by several arguments: American Indian communal property ownership and their form of government resembled communism; the IRA's promotion of American Indian traditions amounted to condoning heathenism; developers wanted tribal lands made available; and Congress perceived that the resignation of Indian Commissioner John Collier (the IRA's chief advocate) and severe BIA budget cuts had diminished its effectiveness, necessitating a stepped-up program of assimilation.

Zimmerman's Formula. After Collier's resignation, Senator William Langer asked Acting Commissioner William Zimmerman for a formula for evaluating tribal readiness for termination. On February 8, 1947, Zimmerman presented, in a congressional hearing, three categories of tribes—those who could be terminated immediately, those who could function with little federal supervision within ten years, and those who needed more than ten years to prepare. He discussed the four criteria used in his lists and presented three specimen termination bills. This testimony was embraced by termination supporters and, Zimmerman believed, frequently misquoted.

In 1950, Dillon Myer, a staunch advocate of immediate termination, became Commissioner of Indian Affairs. Although he claimed to be streamlining the BIA, it seemed to some that he was moving to dissolve both the bureau and all IRA programs. Myer was asked to write a legislative proposal for expeditious termination of federal supervision of American Indians. The result was House Concurrent Resolution 108 (August 1, 1953), which passed with little debate. The resolution directed Congress to make American Indians subject to the same laws, privileges, and responsibilities as other citizens; to end their wardship status; and to free specific tribes from federal control as soon as possible. Once the named tribes were terminated, the BIA offices serving them would be abolished.

PL 83-280 (August 15, 1953) also advanced termination. It transferred to the states, without tribal consent, jurisdiction over civil and criminal offenses on reservations in California, Minnesota, Nebraska, Oregon, and Wisconsin. It provided that, by legislative action, any other state could assume similar jurisdiction.

Termination Bills of 1954. A rush of termination bills was introduced in 1954. As problems with the termination process became known and the membership of congressional committees changed (after 1956), legislation slowed. These acts caused several changes: Tribal lands were either appraised or put under a corporation's management; the federal government no longer protected the land for the tribe; state legislative and judicial authority replaced tribal government; tribe members no longer received a state tax exemption; and tribes lost the benefits of special federal health, education, and other social programs.

Fifteen termination acts were passed between 1954 and 1962, affecting 110 tribes or bands in eight states: the Menominee, Klamath, Western Oregon (sixty-one tribes and bands), Alabama-Coushatta, Mixed-Blood Ute, Southern Paiute, Lower Lake Rancheria, Wyandotte, Peoria, Ottawa, Coyote Valley Ranch, California Rancheria (37 rancherias), Catawba, and Ponca.

Termination of the Menominee of Wisconsin received the most attention. The tribe was specifically targeted in House Concurrent Resolution 108, and their termination act was passed on June 17, 1954. They appeared to be the healthiest tribe economically, as a result of their lumbering and forestry operations, but were not as ready for termination as they seemed. In 1951, the Menominee won a fifteen-year legal battle against the federal government, awarding them $8.5 million in damages for mismanagement of their tribal forest. They could not obtain the award, however, until Congress passed an act appropriating it. The tribe asked that part of the money be released—amounting to fifteen hundred dollars per capita. Senator Wakens's Subcommittee on Indian Affairs told the tribe that if they could manage fifteen hundred dollars per person, they were ready for freedom from federal wardship. Termination, he suggested, was inevitable, and the tribe would not receive the money unless they moved to accept a termination amendment to the per-capita payment bill. The election was not a true tribal referendum, as only 174 members voted; many of these later said that they had not understood what they were voting for.

Final termination of the Menominee did not go into effect until 1961. The tribe had to decide how to set up municipalities, establish a tax system, provide law and order, and sell their tribal assets. There were complications concerning the payment of estimated taxes on Menominee forests. Federal officials saw the tribe's reluctance as procrastination. State agencies could provide only limited assistance, because the tribe was still under federal control.

As a result of these experiences and others, both American Indians and non-Indians became critical of termination. BIA expenditures spiraled in the late 1950's. Many terminated tribe members felt uncomfortable living in the mainstream and often were not accepted socially by non-Indians. Relocated Indians often suffered poverty in the cities and often became dependent on social programs. Some terminated tribes later applied for federal recognition. During its short span (the last act was passed in 1962), termination affected 13,263 of a total population of 400,000, or 3 percent of the federally recognized American Indians. The acts withdrew 1,365,801 acres of trust land, or 3 percent of the approximately 43,000,000 acres held in 1953. The end of federal endorsement of the termination policy was seen in 1969, when President Richard Nixon, in a message to Congress, called for promotion of self-determination and the strengthening of American Indian autonomy without threatening community.

See also: Allotment system; Bureau of Indian Affairs; General Allotment Act; Indian Reorganization Act; Indian-white relations: U.S., 1934-2002.

Glenn Ellen Starr

Sources for Further Study

Fixico, Donald L. *Termination and Relocation: Federal Indian Policy, 1945-1960.* Albuquerque: University of New Mexico Press, 1986. Detailed discussion, from World War II through 1981. Discusses the Menominee and Klamath, as well as smaller tribes. Useful analysis of Dillon Myer and PL 83-280.

La Farge, Oliver. "Termination of Federal Supervision: Disintegration and the American Indians." *Annals of the American Academy of Political and Social Science* 311 (May, 1957): 41-46. Summarizes arguments against termination, except when tribes request it and members are ready to handle their own affairs.

Philp, Kenneth R. *Termination Revisited: American Indians on the Trail to Self-Determination, 1933-1953.* Lincoln: University of Nebraska Press, 1999. A history of termination policy, with useful emphasis on the ambivalent attitudes of Native Americans themselves towards U.S. policy.

Prucha, Francis Paul. *The Great Father: The United States Government and the American Indian.* Vol. 2. Lincoln: University of Nebraska Press, 1984. Portions of chapters 40 and 41 provide a succinct, balanced account of the aims of termination; its articulation in Congress, the popular press, and American Indian publications; congressional and federal actions to bring it about; and its impact.

Stefon, Frederick J. "The Irony of Termination: 1943-1958." *The Indian Historian* 11, no. 3 (Summer, 1978): 3-14. A thorough chronological review that begins with 1887 and ends in 1968. Copiously documented, with many quotations from congressional documents and policymakers.

Walch, Michael C. "Terminating the Indian Termination Policy." *Stanford Law Review* 35, no. 6 (July, 1983): 1181-1215. Well-documented survey of the rise of termination, its effects, and the impact of the fact that Congress did not repeal the termination acts.

Thames, Battle of the

Date: October 5, 1813
Locale: Ontario, Canada
Tribes involved: Shawnee, Sac, Fox, Ottawa, Ojibwa, Wyandot, Potawatomi, Winnebago, Lenni Lenape, Kickapoo
Categories: Nineteenth century history, Wars and battles
Significance: U.S. victory in the Northwestern theater of the War of 1812 also sees the death of Tecumseh and the decline of his multitribal alliance.

The Battle of the Thames was an important United States victory in the Northwestern theater during the War of 1812 with Great Britain. The battle took place on the northern bank of the Thames River near Moraviantown in Upper Canada (southern Ontario Province). In the Battle of Put-In Bay (September 10, 1813), U.S. naval forces won control of Lake Erie. This prevented reinforcement and resupply of the British army at the lake's western end, in the vicinity of Detroit and Fort Malden.

When a superior U.S. force under William Henry Harrison crossed the lake on September 27, the British commander in Upper Canada, Major General Henry Procter, began withdrawing toward the east along the

The Shawnee chief Tecumseh, leader of a confederation of Indian tribes and supporter of the British during the Battle of the Thames, lost his life to the Americans in that confrontation. With his death came the decline of the multitribal alllliance that Tecumseh had fashioned and brilliantly led, dissolution of native support for the British, and victory for the colonists in the Northwestern theater of the War of 1812. (Library of Congress)

Thames River. Procter's native allies, who made up the bulk of his forces, angrily protested the abandonment of their homelands in Michigan. The Shawnee chief Tecumseh, leader of an alliance of warriors from many tribes, was reassured by Procter that a stand soon would be made against Harrison's advancing army. Procter's retreat up the Thames was mismanaged and slow, and most of his spare ammunition and other supplies were lost. Harrison's faster-moving army overtook the British on October 5, forcing Procter to turn and fight before he had reached a defensive position being prepared at Moraviantown.

Tecumseh's Alliance. The British force included five hundred warriors of Tecumseh's alliance. Besides Tecumseh's fellow Shawnees (then dwelling principally in Indiana), there were warriors from the Sac, Fox, Ottawa, Ojibwa, Wyandot, Potawatomi, Winnebago, Lenni Lenape, and Kickapoo nations, all from the Northwest Territory, and a small band of Creeks from the South. Their women and children accompanied the still-loyal warriors.

Approximately a thousand of Tecumseh's followers, angered by Procter's retreat from Michigan, had abandoned the British. Procter's forces totaled more than a thousand, including 450 regulars of the Forty-first Regiment of Foot and a scattering of Canadian militia.

The U.S. army under Harrison numbered about three thousand troops. One hundred twenty of these were infantrymen from the regular army; the rest, Kentucky mounted militia volunteers. A thousand-soldier mounted militia regiment commanded by Colonel Richard Mentor Johnson played a decisive part in the battle. There were also 260 American Indians in Harrison's force, including about 40 Shawnees.

Procter's British and American Indian force, outnumbered three-to-one by the U.S. troops, took a position across a road that ran along the north bank of the Thames River. With the river protecting his left flank and a wooded swamp his right, Procter placed his British regulars in two parallel lines a hundred yards apart. On his left, commanding the road, Procter positioned his one cannon, a six-pounder. Tecumseh's warriors were placed in the swamp on the British right flank. The swamp slanted away at an angle that would enable the natives to fire into the left flank of U.S. troops advancing toward the British infantrymen. Because Procter expected Harrison to send his mounted units, as usual, against the Native Americans, he dispersed the two lines of British soldiers thinly, sheltering behind scattered trees in open order, several feet apart. Only when infantry were positioned almost shoulder-to-shoulder, however, could they effectively repel a cavalry charge. When Harrison noticed this inviting disposition, he sent Colonel Johnson's mounted regiment to attack the British infantry, while his other forces, dismounted as infantry, marched against the natives on the American left. The small force of regular U.S. infantry was assigned to rush the single British cannon.

Colonel Johnson's well-drilled mounted regiment, organized in columns, galloped through the two lines of thinly spread British infantry to their rear. The militiamen then dismounted and began to fire. The British, demoralized and hungry after not having eaten in more than fifty hours, surrendered. Each line of British soldiers seems to have fired a single volley and panicked. The crew of Procter's one cannon fled without even firing it. This part of the battle lasted less than five minutes.

The infantry units on the U.S. troops' left were having much less success against Tecumseh's warriors in the swamp. The poorly disciplined militia infantry, now on foot, were initially repulsed and driven back by the natives. The collapse of the main British position enabled Johnson to swing part of his regiment leftward to attack the Indians' flank. At this point, where his warriors joined the right of the British soldiers, Tecumseh and the Shawnees had taken their position. Led by Johnson and a small, select group that called itself the Forlorn Hope, Johnson's regiment dismounted and pushed into the woods. Heavy firing erupted, and most of the twenty men in the Forlorn Hope were killed or wounded. Colonel Johnson was hit by five bullets, his horse by seven. Early in this intense action, Tecumseh fell, killed by a shot near his heart.

With the death of their leader, the warriors in this part of the swamp (the natives' left) began to fall back. Demoralization spread, and this, coupled with the continuing advance of the U.S. forces, brought an end to the fighting. Although Procter, the British commander, had fled after a brief effort to rally his troops, Tecumseh had stood his ground and died fighting, as he had sworn to do. The native warriors had fought on for more than thirty minutes after the British regulars had given up, but now they slipped away through the woods to find their families. The victory of Harrison's army was complete.

Aftermath. Because of mismanagement of the retreat and his poor handling of the battle, Major General Procter was court-martialed and publicly reprimanded. Harrison became a national hero, as did Colonel Johnson, widely credited with having shot Tecumseh. Of the British troops 12 were killed, 22 wounded, and 601 captured. Harrison reported a count of thirty-three warriors' bodies on the field. Contradictory records suggest that on the U.S. side, as many as twenty-five were killed or mortally injured, and thirty to fifty wounded.

The Battle of the Thames enabled the United States to regain control of territory in the Detroit area that had been lost in earlier defeats, ended any British threat at the western end of Lake Erie, and greatly reduced the danger of tribal raids in the Northwest. An important result of the battle was the decline of the multitribal alliance that Tecumseh had fashioned and brilliantly led. Natives continued to take the field in support of British operations, but now this support was sporadic and ineffective. Tecumseh's strategy of protecting tribal lands through military cooperation with Great Britain had failed. On the northern shore of Lake Erie, the Canadian right flank, a stalemate developed. Harrison's army disintegrated as the enlistment of his militiamen expired, and they returned to Kentucky. The weakened U.S. troops were unable to advance eastward toward Burlington and York, or to threaten British-held Michilimackinac to the north. However, U.S. naval control of Lake Erie prevented fresh initiatives in the area by the British.

See also: Creek War; Fort Wayne Treaty; Indian-white relations: U.S., 1775-1830; Little Turtle's War; Pontiac's Resistance; Prophetstown; Tecumseh's Rebellion; Tippecanoe, Battle of.

Bert M. Mutersbaugh

Sources for Further Study

Dowd, Gregory Evans. *A Spirited Resistance: The North American Indian Struggle for Unity, 1745-1815*. Baltimore: The Johns Hopkins University Press, 1992. Explains the Shawnee leaders' struggles as part of a larger pattern of cultural revitalization and military resistance. Maps, illustrations, and index.

Edmunds, R. David. *The Shawnee Prophet*. Lincoln: University of Nebraska Press, 1983. An insightful study of the Shawnee society that produced Tecumseh and his alliance. Argues that Tecumseh's brother, Tenskwatawa, the Prophet, originated the alliance, which Tecumseh took over as Tenskwatawa's influence faded. Maps, illustrations, and index.

_____. *Tecumseh and the Quest for Indian Leadership*. Boston: Little, Brown, 1984. A brief treatment that concentrates on the warrior brother. Map, illustrations, and index.

Gilpin, Alec R. *The War of 1812 in the Old Northwest*. East Lansing: Michigan State University Press, 1958. A scholarly, well-written study that puts Harrison's 1813 campaign and the Battle of the Thames into context of the entire war in the Northwestern theater. Maps, illustrations, and index.

Sugden, John. *Tecumseh's Last Stand*. Norman: University of Oklahoma Press, 1985. Detailed analysis of the battle and the campaign that preceded it. Examines the question of who killed Tecumseh. Maps, illustrations, and index.

Tippecanoe, Battle of

Date: November 7, 1811
Locale: Indiana
Tribes involved: Kickapoo, Lenni Lenape, Miami, Potawatomi, Shawnee, Winnebago, Wyandot (Huron)
Categories: Nineteenth century history, Wars and battles
Significance: The destruction of Prophetstown by an American army broke the religious power of Tenskwatawa (the Shawnee Prophet) but failed to demoralize the Indian movement led by his brother Tecumseh.

During the early nineteenth century Tenskwatawa began to preach a new religious message among the tribes of the Old Northwest. At the heart of his message was a rejection of European American influence. Aided by his brother Tecumseh, an intertribal Indian movement took hold which threatened the ability of U.S. Indian agents to force land cessions on the tribes of the Old Northwest.

In the spring of 1808, Tenskwatawa and Tecumseh led their followers to the banks of the Wabash River and began to construct a capital for their movement which came to be known as Prophetstown. Working from this base of operations, the two brothers proselytized among the Indian villages of the Great Lakes and the Ohio River Valley. Thousands of warriors from numerous tribes flocked to Prophetstown, causing alarm among American settlers in the region. Tensions increased after Indiana Governor William Henry Harrison concluded the Treaty of Fort Wayne (1809), which provided for a land cession of three million acres of Indian land.

Convinced that Tecumseh was plotting to kill him, Harrison raised an army of a thousand men and prepared a campaign to destroy Prophetstown. When Tecumseh journeyed to the south to bring his message to the Choctaw and the Creek, Harrison saw his opportunity. On November 6, 1811, the American army was on the west bank of the Wabash, within a mile of Prophetstown.

The Battle of Tippecanoe ended Tenskwatawa's spiritual influence but not his brother Tecumseh's resistance efforts. (Library of Congress)

In the absence of his brother, Tenskwatawa had little control over the warriors in his village. The Shawnee Prophet sent a delegation to meet with Harrison on the afternoon of November 6, seeking to assure the governor that they did not have hostile intentions toward Americans. Unimpressed by these words, Harrison planned to attack the Indian village the following day. During the night, Tenskwatawa exhorted his Indian warriors to attack the enemy before dawn. He assured them that his magic would confuse the American soldiers. He also instructed them to kill Harrison.

The Indians struck Harrison's camp two hours before sunrise. Alert sentries fired warning shots in time to wake the Americans. A few warriors managed to penetrate the interior of the American camp, but Harrison managed to escape and rally his troops. Fierce fighting bent the American line on several occasions, but Harrison was able to shift troops skillfully in time.

At dawn, the Indian warriors began to retreat, and Harrison ordered his troops to charge. The American advance forced Tenskwatawa to abandon Prophetstown. During the fighting, Tenskwatawa prayed to the Master of Life for victory. Unfortunately, his spiritual powers failed. Tenskwatawa was discredited by the Battle of Tippecanoe. Many angry warriors confronted the Prophet after the defeat. He blamed the failure of his magic on his wife's unclean state.

Harrison's victory was far from overwhelming. Of the estimated seven hundred warriors who attacked his camp, about fifty were killed and eighty were wounded. The larger American force sustained 188 casualties. Harrison burned Prophetstown, but he failed to end hostilities. The defeated warriors returned to their villages and led further attacks against frontier settlements throughout the Old Northwest.

See also: Creek War; Fort Wayne Treaty; Indian-white relations: U.S., 1775-1830; Little Turtle's War; Pontiac's Resistance; Prophetstown; Tecumseh's Rebellion; Thames, Battle of the.

Thomas D. Matijasic

Trade and Intercourse Acts

Date: 1790-1834
Locale: United States
Tribes involved: Pantribal in the United States
Categories: Eighteenth century history, National government and legislation, Nineteenth century history

Significance: These acts were efforts by the U.S. government to restrain private settlement and enterprise by European Americans in Indian territory; the restrictions eroded as a part of the market revolution of the nineteenth century.

In the late eighteenth and early nineteenth centuries, the United States government feared that rapacious private traders and land-grabbing settlers were creating resentment among Indians that could lead to war on the frontier of white settlement. Therefore, the government sought to prevent the wholesale migration of white settlers westward to lands controlled by Indians, regulate the trade in furs between Indians and European Americans, and acculturate Indians to Euro-American norms. The government hoped that these efforts would preserve peace between Indians and European Americans. The vehicles for these goals were the successive Indian Trade and Intercourse Acts. The first Trade and Intercourse Act was passed in 1790 and was scheduled to expire at the end of the congressional session of 1793. Before expiration, a new Trade and Intercourse Act was passed in 1793. Further laws were enacted in 1796, 1799, and 1802. The 1802 act was made permanent; it stood until 1834.

The Trade and Intercourse Acts built upon precedents established by the Continental Congress in an ordinance of August 7, 1786. The Ordinance of 1786 empowered the federal government to issue licenses to United States citizens allowing them to reside among or trade with Indians. Like the later Trade and Intercourse Acts, the ordinance was an assertion of federal over state power in the regulation of Indian affairs.

The Trade and Intercourse Act of 1790 provided for the licensing of private traders and outlined the penalties for trading without a license. The act of 1790 also detailed the punishments for crimes committed by whites against Indians. The act of 1793 reiterated the provisions of the 1790 act in stronger terms and further authorized the distribution of goods to Indians to promote acculturation to Euro-American mores. In response to the continuing influx of white settlers, the act of 1796 delineated the boundaries of territories belonging to Indians, the first such delineation by the federal government. The acts of 1799 and 1802 were substantially similar to the act of 1796.

In 1834, the federal government for the last time passed an Indian Trade and Intercourse Act. The 1834 act defined Indian territory as all lands west of the Mississippi River excluding the states of Missouri and Louisiana and the territory of Arkansas. The 1834 act banned liquor from the trade and outlawed white fur trappers from operating in Indian territory. Unlike any of the previous acts, however, the 1834 law empowered the federal government to use force to stop intertribal wars in order to protect the interests of fur trade companies. Ironically, a series of acts that began in 1790 by reining in white traders in order to preserve peace ended in 1834 by policing Indians in order to protect traders.

See also: Albany Congress; Fur trade; Indian-white relations: U.S., 1775-1830.

Andrew C. Isenberg

Trail of Broken Treaties

Date: October 6-November 8, 1972
Locale: From Seattle to San Francisco to Los Angeles to Oklahoma City to Washington, D.C.
Tribes involved: Pantribal in the United States
Categories: Protest movements, Twentieth century history
Significance: Militant American Indians take over the Bureau of Indian Affairs to protest U.S. government treaty policies.

Against the backdrop of political activism in 1969, the rise of Red Power began with the occupation of Alcatraz Island, which became a symbol of American Indian unity. New tribal alliances were formed around a common purpose: to bring attention to continuing failures in the bureaucratic administration of American Indian affairs. During the summer gathering at Rosebud Sioux Reservation, residents and members of the American Indian Movement (AIM) began plans for a caravan to Washington, D.C., just prior to election day.

Eight American Indian organizations planned the event, and four national groups endorsed its concept. The new alliance, including tribes from Canada and Latin America, was known as the Trail of Broken Treaties and Pan American Native Quest for Justice. Planning for the possibility of 150,000 participants, cochairs Reuben Snake, a Winnebago, and Robert Burnette, a Lakota, organized eleven committees, including media, medical, congressional contact, emergency legal needs, and participant accreditation.

The spiritual foundation of the caravan was declared in a public statement inviting "all Indians, spiritual leaders of the Western Hemisphere, and Indian interest groups to participate," but excluding all persons who would cause civil disorder, block traffic, burn flags, destroy property, or shout obscenities in the street. . . . Each trail would be led by spiritual leaders who carried the Sacred Peace Pipe and Drum . . . and every pipe smoked was to remind America of the manner in which the treaties were signed.

Burnette emphasized the serious purpose of the caravan:

We should be on our finest behavior . . . ban all alcohol and drugs, with expulsions guaranteed to violators. The Caravan must be our finest hour.

The Trail to Washington. Departing for Washington, D.C., on October 6, caravans passed through historic sites, stopping to offer prayer. Requests had been made for a police escort into Washington, adequate housing, permission to conduct honoring ceremonies at Arlington, and presentation of the Twenty Points. The Twenty Points to be presented formally to the administration covered treaty reform, reform of the Bureau of Indian Affairs (BIA), new land policies, improved cultural and economic conditions, and criminal jurisdiction over non-Indians on reservations.

Even as the caravan traveled, obstructions were being planned in Washington, D.C. In a memorandum to BIA commissioner Louis Bruce, dated October 11, Harrison Loesch of the Bureau of Land Management (BLM) stated, "This is to give you very specific instructions that the Bureau is not to provide any assistance or funding, either directly or indirectly" to the AIM demonstration in early November.

The caravan of the first five hundred participants arrived in Washington, D.C., at 4:00 A.M. on November 2. Denied the official recognition of a police escort, they proceeded through downtown blowing horns and stopping traffic. At 6:00 A.M., they paused in front of the White House to drum and sing a victory song, after which their police escort arrived. The early caravanners faced more barriers when the Army denied permission for Arlington ceremonies, and housing arrangements revealed a building full of rats. They headed for their only home, the BIA, where they were permitted to await accommodations.

Hostilities Escalate. With no solution by afternoon, confusion and hostility escalated. When the shifts changed at 4:00 P.M., the new guards were unaware of the agreement, and in trying to clear the area, began to remove the American Indians forcibly, attacking several with clubs. The misunderstanding escalated into panic as the injured Indians alerted others of impending attacks. Riot police surrounded the building, while Indians inside barricaded doorways with desks and chairs. They broke off table legs for

At the end of the Trail of Broken Treaties caravan, protestors occupied the Bureau of Indian Affairs building for six days after security guards tried to remove them. (Library of Congress)

clubs and stacked typewriters upstairs to drop out the windows on intruders. The Twenty Points and the significant spiritual purpose of the caravans were disregarded in the conflict over housing and food.

The likelihood of gaining public support for their cause was hindered by media attention to the unplanned takeover. Still, the presentation of the Twenty Points was attempted. Appeals for help were telegraphed to the United Nations and the Vatican, as negotiations with government officials were delayed or postponed daily. During the six-day occupation, BIA offices were ransacked, American Indian artifacts taken, files seized, and much damage done to the building.

AIM leaders claimed that federal agents had infiltrated the occupation and had done much of the damage. Some American Indians who had occupied the building and went on official tours of the site weeks later asserted that there was extensive damage in rooms where they were certain there had been no damage before. Slogans, names, and addresses covered walls where there had been no marks at the time of their departure.

American Indians received unexpected support from several people.

Presidential candidate Dr. Benjamin Spock and African American activist Stokely Carmichael appeared at the scene. Representative Shirley Chisholm telegraphed support, and Judge John Pratt delayed holding a show-cause hearing demanded by the federal government to determine if American Indians were in contempt of his order to leave the building. LaDonna Harris, a Comanche and wife of Oklahoma senator Fred Harris, and Louis Bruce stayed the first night in the BIA; as a result of his support for the cause, Bruce was suspended from his post as BIA commissioner.

End of the Protest. The protest ended on November 8. After several attempts at getting a response from White House officials and a series of court actions, demonstrators agreed to leave the BIA building. On behalf of the White House, Leonard Garment, White House minority affairs adviser, Frank Carlucci, director of the Office of Management and Budget, and Bradley Patterson, Garment's assistant, signed documents granting immunity for protesters, funding their transportation home, and committing to respond to the Twenty Points within sixty days.

The number of participants was estimated to have been five thousand. Although Secretary of the Interior Rogers Morton asserted that they were mostly urban activists, more than 80 percent of those who had made the journey were traditional reservation Indians. Among the elders were Frank Fools Crow and Charlie Red Cloud, both chiefs at Pine Ridge, and Tuscarora medicine man Mad Bear Anderson, also a leader at the Alcatraz occupation. Early estimates of damage ranged from half a million dollars to more than two million dollars; however, the final estimate was set at a quarter million dollars, because most artifacts and documents were returned.

The crisis had ended, but nothing had been resolved. Public reaction showed that much of the previous support for the American Indians' cause had been lost. Before winter had passed, echoes of the same demands were heard amid the gunfire during the occupation of Wounded Knee.

Six years later, in July, 1978, several hundred American Indians marched again into Washington, D.C., at the end of the Longest Walk from San Francisco. The event was intended to reveal continuing problems faced by American Indians and expose the backlash movement against treaty rights. Unlike earlier conflicts, it was a peaceful event. Red Power had come full circle—from lively Alcatraz days, through times of violent confrontation, to the spiritual unity celebrated at the end of the Longest Walk.

See also: Alcatraz Island occupation; American Indian Movement; Indian-white relations: U.S., 1934-2002; Longest Walk; Wounded Knee occupation.

Gale M. Thompson

Sources for Further Study

DeLoria, Vine, Jr. *Behind the Trail of Broken Treaties: An Indian Declaration of Independence*. 2d ed. Norman: University of Oklahoma, 1987. Lawyer-theologian DeLoria discusses the doctrine of discovery, treaty-making, civil rights, American Indian activism, sovereignty, and the Trail and Wounded Knee occupations.

Harvey, Karen D., and Lisa D. Harjo. *Indian Country: A History of Native People in America*. Discusses ten culture areas, historical perspectives, contemporary issues, and ceremonies. Presents timelines (50,000 B.C.E. to twentieth century), summaries, lesson plans, and resources. Appendices and index.

Trail of Broken Treaties: BIA, I'm Not Your Indian Anymore. Rooseveltown, N.Y.: Akwesasne Notes, 1973. Contains articles published during and after the Trail events; text of the Twenty Points; the White House response; replies suggested by Trail leadership; and an update on the BIA one year later.

Waldman, Carl. *Atlas of the North American Indian*. New York: Facts on File, 1985. Comprehensive coverage of history and culture, land cessions, wars, and contemporary issues. Maps, illustrations, and appendices.

Trail of Tears

Date: May 28, 1830-1842
Locale: Southeastern United States
Tribes involved: Choctaw, Creek, Chickasaw, Cherokee, Seminole
Categories: Nineteenth century history, Reservations and relocation
Significance: The removal to the western Indian Territory of the Five Civilized Tribes is one of the most tragic events of U.S. history.

Soon after 1783, when the Treaty of Paris ended the American Revolution, demands began for the removal of all Native Americans from the southeastern part of the new United States. After a brief renewal of violent resistance, led by warriors like Dragging Canoe of the Cherokees and Alexander McGillivray of the Creeks, most tribes were peaceful but firm in their efforts to remain in their ancestral lands. The exception was the Seminoles in Florida.

Many early treaties were negotiated to persuade these tribes to move west voluntarily. When the desired result was not achieved, Congress

Trails of Tears:
Routes of Indian Removal to the West After 1830

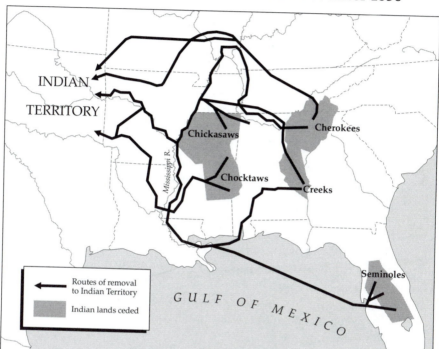

passed the Indian Removal Act in 1830, paving the way for forced removal. President Andrew Jackson, an old foe of the southeastern tribes, signed the bill; it became law on May 28, 1830.

Choctaw Relocation. The first of these tribes to experience forced removal was the Choctaw of southeastern Mississippi. Preliminary treaties with the Choctaws, whose population was about twenty-three thousand, began with the Treaty of Mount Dexter in 1805. Individual Choctaws had been encouraged to incur debts at government trading posts that were beyond their ability to pay. At Mount Dexter, Choctaw leaders were forced to cede four million acres of their land in return for the cancellation of those debts.

The first exchange of Choctaw land for land in the Indian Territory west of the Mississippi River was approved by the Treaty of Doak's Stand in 1820. Pushmataha, the principal chief and able diplomat of the Choctaws, negotiated this treaty with General Andrew Jackson. However, since white settlers already occupied much of the new Choctaw land, the treaty had little effect.

The Treaty of Dancing Rabbit Creek, signed on September 27, 1830, was the first negotiated under the Indian Removal Act. It provided for the exchange of all Choctaw land for land in the Indian Territory. Choctaw acceptance of this treaty was facilitated by intratribal conflicts and by the duplicity of their self-proclaimed spokesperson, Greenwood LeFlore. By the end of 1832, about two-thirds of the Choctaws had emigrated to their new homes. Most others migrated over the next twenty years. A few, including Greenwood LeFlore, remained in Mississippi.

The Choctaw removal became a pattern for the removal of the remaining tribes in the Southeast. The next to experience the process were the twenty-three thousand Creeks of eastern Alabama. Led by such chiefs as Menewa, the Creeks bitterly resisted removal. In 1825, Menewa carried out the execution for treason of William McIntosh, a half-breed chief who favored removal.

Creek Resistance. By 1831, chiefs such as Eneah Micco, although vigorously protesting the invasion of their land by white squatters, realized that only removal could save the Creeks from total destruction. The Treaty of Washington, signed on March 24, 1832, provided for complete removal to the Indian Territory. Although the generous provisions of this treaty soon were ignored, conditions in the Creek Nation became intolerable and they began their sad trek to the west.

Creek migration was interrupted in May, 1836, by reprisal raids against white settlements. This action brought in the U.S. Army, with orders to forcibly remove all Creeks from Alabama. By 1838, the removal was complete. An ironic footnote is that during the course of their removal, several hundred Creek men were impressed into the army for service against their Seminole cousins in Florida.

Chickasaw Removal. The least controversial of the Trail of Tears removal was that of the five thousand Chickasaws from the northern parts of Mississippi and Alabama. For thirty years, the government worked to transform the Chickasaws from a hunting society into an agricultural society that would require less land. By 1830, the process seemed complete, but the result had been widespread poverty. It also produced friction between the full-bloods who resisted the process and the part-bloods who favored it.

The Chickasaw removal process was initiated by the Treaty of Pontotoc Creek in 1832. It was agreed that the Chickasaws would move west when suitable land could be obtained. Finding such land was difficult, with the best possibility being part of the Choctaw domain already established. Levi Colbert, the most prominent of several Chickasaw chiefs, was ill and not present when the Treaty of Pontotoc Creek was signed. He protested the use of coercion by General John Coffee, the leading government negotiator, to get the other chiefs to sign. However, he cooperated with the removal process in order to secure the best possible land and to ease the burden on his people.

Chickasaw removal followed the signing of the Treaty of Doaksville in January, 1837. Land was secured and most of the tribe moved that year. Unlike other tribes, they were able to take most of their possessions with them, and very few died along the way. However, after arrival in the Indian Territory, they faced the typical problems of intertribal conflicts, substandard food, and a smallpox epidemic.

Cherokee Trail of Tears. By 1830, about sixteen thousand Cherokees remained on their ancestral lands, by then mostly in northern Georgia and southeastern Tennessee. Their removal, first called the "trail where they cried," is the source of the name Trail of Tears.

The movement to remove the Cherokees began with the signing of the Georgia Compact in 1802, when President Thomas Jefferson agreed to seek reasonable terms for that removal in a peaceful manner. In 1828, when gold was discovered on Cherokee land in Georgia, the process was facilitated, but not on the reasonable terms stipulated by Jefferson. The state of Georgia nullified Cherokee laws and incorporated a large portion of the Cherokee Nation. The Cherokee defense was led by their democratically elected principal chief, John Ross, who took their case to federal court. Although a decision by Chief Justice John Marshall favored the Cherokees, President Jackson refused to enforce it.

A small group of proremoval Cherokees, led by Major Ridge, signed the New Echota Treaty in December, 1835. Following ratification by the U.S. Senate in May, 1836, the entire tribe had two years to move to the Indian Territory. John Ross and the majority protested the treaty and refused to move. Forced removal began in June, 1838. When the journey ended in March, 1839, there were four thousand unmarked graves along the way. About one thousand Cherokees escaped removal by fleeing into the southern Appalachian Mountains. The final tragedy of Cherokee removal was the murder in the Indian Territory of the proremoval leaders who had signed the treaty.

Seminole Removal. The Seminoles of central Florida, descendants of Creeks who had moved there to escape harassment in the eighteenth century, provide the last chapter in the Trail of Tears. Their population of about six thousand included many African Americans, both freemen and runaway slaves from the Southern states. The desire to cut off that escape route for slaves was part of the incentive for Jackson's invasion and the resulting acquisition of Florida from Spain in 1819 under the Adams-Onís Treaty. The demand to move the Seminoles to the Indian Territory soon followed.

In 1832, an unauthorized group of Seminoles signed the Treaty of Payne's Landing, declaring that all would give up their land and move west. Opposition to the treaty was led by Osceola and Coacoochee (Wildcat). The result was the Second Seminole War, in 1835. Seminoles captured during that war were immediately deported to the Indian Territory. By 1842, the war was over and the remaining Seminoles slowly migrated west. By 1856, the only Seminoles left in Florida were those in the inaccessible swamps of the Everglades.

The Trail of Tears removals rank among the most tragic episodes in United States history. The policies of three American leaders reveal the changing attitudes on how to best accomplish the removals. After Thomas Jefferson's peaceful persuasion and reasonable terms failed, John C. Calhoun, as secretary of war under President James Monroe, favored educating Native Americans to accept the need for removal. In the end, it was Andrew Jackson's policy of forced removal that completed the distasteful task.

See also: Cherokee legal cases; Dancing Rabbit Creek, Treaty of; Indian Removal Act; Indian-white relations: U.S., 1775-1830; Indian-white relations: U.S., 1831-1870; Seminole Wars; Treaties and agreements in the United States.

Glenn L. Swygart

Sources for Further Study

DeRosier, Arthur. *The Removal of the Choctaw Indians.* Knoxville: University of Tennessee Press, 1970. Discusses removal circumstances. Includes maps and portraits.

Ehle, John. *Trail of Tears: The Rise and Fall of the Cherokee Nation.* New York: Doubleday, 1988. Covers Cherokee history from 1770 to 1840. Details the intratribal conflicts relating to removal policy.

Foreman, Grant. *Indian Removal: The Emigration of the Five Civilized Tribes of Indians.* Norman: University of Oklahoma Press, 1932. Surveys the treaties and leaders of removal. Maps and illustrations.

Gibson, Arrell. *The Chickasaws.* Norman: University of Oklahoma Press, 1971. Puts removal in context with Chickasaw history from the eighteenth century to 1907.

Hoig, Stanley. *Night of the Cruel Moon: Cherokee Removal and the Trail of Tears.* New York: Facts on File, 1996. An account of Cherokee removal relying on first-person accounts.

Williams, Jeanne. "The Cherokees." In *Trails of Tears: American Indians Driven from Their Lands*. Dallas: Hendrick-Long, 1992. Puts Cherokee removal in the context of the similar experiences of the Comanche, Cheyenne, Apache, and Navajo.

Wright, J. Leitch. *Creeks and Seminoles: The Destruction and Regeneration of the Muscogulge People*. Lincoln: University of Nebraska Press, 1986. Discusses removal and resettlement in the West. Extensive bibliography.

Treaties and agreements in Canada

Date: 1760-2001
Locale: Canada
Tribes involved: Pantribal in Canada
Categories: Colonial history, National government and legislation, Native government, Nineteenth century history, Treaties, Twentieth century history
Significance: The character of treaties between the Canadian government and Canada's Indian peoples has varied as Indians have lost and partially regained power.

The capture of Quebec from the French in the Seven Years' War in 1760 allowed Britain to consolidate its holdings in North America. In order to establish colonial governments in the newly obtained Quebec and Florida, King George III issued what has become known as the Royal Proclamation of 1763. A provision of the proclamation reserved for the Indians all lands to the west of Upper Canada and provided a mechanism for the Crown to purchase these and other lands from the Indians. Since the French had never recognized aboriginal title in their colonies, however, Quebec and those portions of the Maritimes captured from the French were exempted from this provision of the proclamation.

The early Indian treaties reflected the strong military position of the Indians, and the stated purpose of most treaties was simply peace and friendship. The Indians were important in military rivalries, first between the French and the British and later between the British and the Americans. There were relatively few Europeans compared with Indians, so land cessions were relatively small and were accomplished with onetime payments (usually in the form of trade goods).

After 1812, the Indians were no longer militarily significant, and the character of treaties changed. In recognition of their weaker position, Indians began to make greater demands for relinquishing their lands. European needs for agricultural lands increased at the same time as a result of increased emigration from Europe. In an effort to save money, the Europeans began the practice of issuing annuities rather than onetime payments. In 1817, a land cession treaty was signed with the Saulteaux and Cree to permit the establishment of the Red River Colony of Thomas Douglas, earl of Selkirk. This was the first treaty that entirely ceded native title to lands west of Upper Canada.

In 1850, Special Commissioner W. B. Robinson concluded two treaties with the Ojibwa living along the northern shores of Lakes Huron and Superior. Known as the Robinson-Huron and Robinson-Superior treaties, they were signed after the Ojibwa requested that the Europeans purchase the land before mining it. These two treaties set the precedent of permitting Indians to continue hunting and fishing on their ceded territory.

The Situation at Confederation. Canada was created as a nation in 1867 with the confederation of Nova Scotia, New Brunswick, Quebec, and Ottawa into the Dominion of Canada. The British North America Act, which created Canada, charged the Dominion with discharging the Crown's duties toward the Indians. In 1870, much of the remainder of present-day Canada was transferred from the Hudson's Bay Company to the new nation. This transfer illustrates a paradox in the history of relations between natives and whites in Canada. While the Royal Proclamation of 1763 preserved native title to this transferred territory and established the Crown as the only legitimate purchaser of Indian lands, the sale of Rupert's Land by the Hudson's Bay Company indicated disregard of aboriginal title. Furthermore, in order to facilitate white settlement in the new territory and to connect, via railroad, the settlements in eastern Canada with the colony of British Columbia, the Crown moved to extinguish any remaining native title to that region. Seven treaties, covering much of present-day Canada, were concluded between 1871 and 1877. The provisions of the treaties varied only slightly and were similar to the two Robinson treaties.

The Numbered Treaties. Treaties 1 and 2, negotiated in 1871, were virtually identical and covered lands held by the Swampy Cree and Chippewa (Ojibwa) in southern Manitoba and southeastern Saskatchewan. In exchange for relinquishing title to 52,400 square miles, the Cree and Chippewa were promised 160 acres of reserved land for each family of five, a school, farm implements, a gift of three dollars for each person, and an annuity of three dollars per person. Chiefs and headmen were awarded additional payments. The area covered by Treaty 1 included the Red River farmsteads of the Metis.

With the signing of Treaty 3, known also as the North-West Angle Treaty, in 1873 by the Saulteaux, the initial payment was raised to twelve dollars and the annuity was increased to five dollars per person. Larger reserves (one square mile per family) were also granted, as well as the continued rights to hunt and fish on unoccupied lands. This provision to allow traditional subsistence activities on the ceded territories appears in the remainder of the numbered treaties. As the prairie provinces were established, however, most of the Crown's lands were transferred to the provinces. Increasingly, the courts have ruled that native Canadians are subject to provincial game laws.

Treaty 4, signed in 1874 by the Saulteaux and Cree, encompassed southern Saskatchewan and small portions of Alberta and Manitoba. Treaty 5 was made in 1875 with the Saulteaux and Cree of central Manitoba and extended to northern Manitoba in 1908. The Blackfeet, Blood, Piegan, Sarcee (Sarsi), and Assiniboine tribes of southern Alberta agreed to Treaty 7 in 1877.

Treaty 6 was made in 1876 with Poundmaker's and Crowfoot's Plains and Wood Cree bands in central Alberta and Saskatchewan; however, the bands led by Big Bear refused to sign until 1884 and succeeded in obtaining somewhat greater concessions. The failure of the government to meet the obligations to which it agreed in the treaty are among the factors that contributed to the Riel Rebellion of 1885. Treaty 6 is interesting also in that it is the only one of the numbered treaties that mentions medical care for Indians. It provides that the Indian agent on each reserve maintain a "medicine chest" for the benefit of the Indians. It is likely that medical care was verbally promised during negotiation for other treaties but was not written into the final documents.

Twenty-two years passed between the signing of Treaty 7 and the next set of treaty negotiations. The last four numbered treaties were made in order to make way for northern resource development rather than to permit white settlement. Treaty 8, signed in 1899 with the Beaver, Cree, and Chipewyan, covers portions of Saskatchewan, Alberta, the Northwest Territories, and British Columbia. It was the only treaty covering the Indians of British Columbia. Several small treaties had been negotiated between coastal tribes of British Columbia and the Hudson's Bay Company in the 1850's, but because the Hudson's Bay Company had no authority to negotiate for the Crown, these treaties were not considered valid. After British Columbia entered Confederation in 1871, an attempt was made to have that province negotiate treaties; other than granting several small reserves, the province refused to acknowledge aboriginal title.

Ontario joined with the federal government in the making of Treaty 9 with the Ojibwa and Cree of north central Ontario in 1905 and 1929. The Cree and other Indian groups ceded their remaining territory in northern Saskatchewan with Treaty 10 in 1906.

Treaty 11 was signed in 1922 with the Dene (Slave, Dogrib, Loucheux, and Hare) Indians who occupy the Mackenzie River region between the sixtieth parallel and the Arctic coast. The impetus for this treaty was the discovery of oil a year earlier at Norman Wells.

The numbered treaties presumably settled all land claims based on aboriginal title for Indians living in the prairie and western Subarctic regions, but several court cases have thrown that issue into question. In one of the most important of these cases, *Re Paulette et al. and the Registrar of Titles* (1974), the court held that the Indians covered by Treaties 8 and 11 had not, in fact, extinguished their aboriginal titles to the land.

Modern Land Claims Agreements. The court decisions, coupled with the politicization of Native Canadians, led the federal government to rethink its position on the issue of aboriginal title. The government's desire to develop the natural and mineral resources in its northernmost territories created the conditions necessary for comprehensive land claims settlements. Between 1975 and 1992, five major land claims agreements were concluded. Varying levels of progress were made on several others.

The first of these modern land claims agreements, known as the James Bay and Northern Quebec Agreement, was signed in 1975 by Inuit and Cree of northern and northwestern Quebec, the federal government, and the Province of Quebec. The agreement cleared the way for Quebec to begin hydroelectric development in James Bay. The Northeastern Quebec Agreement, concluded in 1978 with the Naskapi, was for the same purpose.

The James Bay and Northern Quebec Agreement provided $225 million, divided proportionally between the Inuit and the Cree for the lands (excluding mineral rights) in the immediate vicinities of their communities. The natives were allowed to retain exclusive hunting and fishing rights over a much larger area; however, the flooding caused by the hydroelectric development has caused major disruptions of wildlife.

The Inuit chose to form public municipal-type village governments with powers over zoning, taxation, public health, housing, and education. The Cree made their communities into reserves. Representatives of both groups serve on environmental and economic development boards meant to monitor the development of the region.

National native organizations have been highly critical of the James Bay land claims agreements largely because of the clauses that extinguish aboriginal rights. Because the term "aboriginal rights" was not defined, future understandings of its scope have also been negotiated away. In addition, the vague language of the agreement has allowed both the Quebec and federal governments to shirk their obligations.

Far more generous than the James Bay Agreements are the two land claims settlements achieved by the Inuit of the Northwest Territories. The Inuvialuit Final Agreement, which was signed in June, 1984, settled the claim of the twenty-five hundred Inuit living between the Yukon border and central Victoria Island. Under the agreement, the Inuvialuit (or western Inuit) retained title to 91,000 square kilometers but mineral rights to only one-seventh of that land. The Inuvialuit surrendered land covering 344,000 square kilometers. In exchange for the land cessions the Inuvialuit received $152 million to be paid over a thirteen-year period. In an arrangement similar to that established by the Alaska Native Claims Settlement Act, the money has been paid to the Inuvialuit Regional Corporation, which was chartered to invest the proceeds and to manage the land retained by the Inuvialuit. In contrast to the provisions of the numbered treaties, all income earned by the Inuvialuit Regional Corporation from either its lands or investments is subject to taxation.

The Eastern Arctic Claim was negotiated between the federal government and the Tungavik Federation of Natives. Signed in 1992, it settled the claim of seventeen thousand Inuit living in the area of the Northwest Territories between Coppermine and Baffin Island. The claim established Inuit title to 352,000 square kilometers (9.9 percent of the total land and offshore area), making the Eastern Arctic Inuit the single largest landholder in Canada. Unlike other land claims agreements, the Eastern Arctic Agreement includes offshore areas, which continue to be vital food sources. In exchange for relinquishing claim to the remaining territory, the Inuit are to receive $580 million as well as resource royalties earned from their lands. Perhaps the most substantial concession made by the federal government was to allow the Inuit to govern themselves through the formation of a new territory to be known as Nunavut.

Negotiations between the governments of Newfoundland and Canada and the thirty-five hundred Inuit of Labrador proceeded slowly. In 1988, agreements in principle were signed between the federal government and the Yukon Council of Indians and with the Dene-Metis Association of the Mackenzie River region. Neither agreement was concluded. At their annual meeting in July, 1990, the Dene Assembly failed to ratify the accord because of divisions within the organization over the "extinguishment" of the still undefined aboriginal rights. After the failure of the Dene-Metis Land Claims Agreement, the federal government agreed to settle the claim on a region-by-region basis. The communities situated along the lower Mackenzie River signed the Gwich'in Final Agreement a year later, which provided resource royalties and $75 million cash in exchange for relinquishing aboriginal rights and title to most of the region. The Gwich'in (Delta area) natives retained title to slightly more than 21,000 square kilometers. They also retained the subsurface mineral rights to about one-fourth of that land. Like the Eastern Arctic Agreement, the Gwich'in Final Agreement established a framework for self-government.

See also: Aboriginal Action Plan; Declaration of First Nations; *Delgamuukw v. British Columbia*; Department of Indian Affairs and Northern Development; Fifteen Principles; Indian Act of 1876; Indian Act of 1951; Indian Act of 1989; Indian-white relations: Canadian; Indian-white relations: English colonial; Indian-white relations: French colonial; Nunavut Territory; Red River Raids; Reserve system of Canada; Riel Rebellions; Royal Commission on Aboriginal Peoples; White Paper of Canada.

Pamela R. Stern

Sources for Further Study

Dickerson, Mark O. *Whose North? Political Change, Political Development, and Self-Government in the Northwest Territories*. Vancouver: University of British Columbia Press, 1992. Discusses the contemporary political issues facing the Dene, Metis, Inuit, and non-native residents of northern Canada.

Getty, A. L., and Antoine S. Lussier, eds. *As Long as the Sun Shines and the Water Flows: A Reader in Canadian Native Studies*. Vancouver: University of British Columbia Press, 1983. A collection of articles covering relations between the Indians and the Canadian government from the time of the Royal Proclamation of 1763 to the constitutional crisis of the 1980's.

Morris, Alexander. *The Treaties of Canada with the Indians of Manitoba and the North-west Territories*. Toronto: Belfords, Clark & Co., 1880. Reprint. Toronto: Coles, 1971. An account by one of the negotiators of Treaties 3 through 6.

Morse, Bradford W., ed. *Aboriginal Peoples and the Law: Indian, Metis, and Inuit Rights in Canada*. Ottawa: Carleton University Press, 1985. A thorough discussion of all aspects of Canadian law (including treaties) as they apply to native peoples.

Purich, Donald J. *The Inuit and Their Land: The Story of Nunavut*. Toronto: James Lorimer, 1992. Contains a thorough discussion of each of the Inuit land claims agreements, paying special attention to the Eastern Arctic Agreement and the preparations for native self-government in the proposed New Nunavut Territory.

St. Germain, Jill. *Indian Treaty-Making Policy in the United States and Canada, 1867-1877.* Lincoln: University of Nebraska Press, 2001. Explores and contrasts the "civilizing" efforts of the United States and Canada through their Indian treaty policies.

Treaties and agreements in the United States

Date: 1787-2002
Locale: United States
Tribes involved: Pantribal in the United States
Categories: Eighteenth century history; National government and legislation; Native government; Nineteenth century history; Treaties; Twentieth century history
Significance: Native Americans generally look upon their treaties as permanent and inviolate compacts between two sovereign nations. European Americans, in contrast, have tended to consider the treaties to be temporary arrangements subject to alteration and renegotiation. This difference in perspective has been a source of much misunderstanding and bitterness.

Following the American Revolution (1775-1783), the U.S. government continued the European tradition of treating Indian tribes as independent foreign nations, which meant negotiating formal treaties for establishing peace, exchanging land, and recognizing mutual obligations. The government also negotiated agreements or accords, which were less formal and usually dealt with fewer issues. In 1871, Congress passed the Indian Appropriation Act, stating that the American Indians no longer belonged to their own sovereign nations, and treaty making ended. The existing treaties remained valid, unless explicitly abrogated or changed by a law of Congress. Until the twentieth century, the U.S. government often did not look upon Indian treaties as important commitments. Since World War II, however, Native Americans have become increasingly effective in using the federal courts to obtain broad interpretations of treaty rights.

An 1891 council of Sioux leaders settles the Indian wars at Pine Ridge, South Dakota, soon after the Battle of Wounded Knee. In 1893, historian Frederick Jackson Turner would claim that the frontier had been "closed" as an outcome of that battle. (National Archives)

Nature of the Treaties. The U.S. Constitution authorizes the president to negotiate treaties with foreign nations, and these treaties become legally binding after approval by a two-thirds vote in the Senate. Because they are recognized as part of the "supreme law of the land," treaties have the same legal standing as laws passed by Congress. The concept of "supreme law" also means that treaty rights are a matter of federal jurisdiction, and that state governments must follow legal decisions made in federal courts. This is significant, because state governments, reflecting local opinion, often oppose treaty provisions such as the right to hunt and fish off reservation lands.

From 1787 until 1871, the U.S. government negotiated about 800 formal treaties with various Native American tribes and bands, and the Senate ratified some 367 of these into law. The Secretary of War was responsible for negotiating treaties until 1849, when the Office of Indian Affairs was transferred to the Department of the Interior. In 1871, the Indian Appropriation Act, which declared that tribes were not independent nations, ended the practice of contracting by treaty, but the act left the existing treaties in place unless explicitly modified by Congress. Thereafter, the U.S. government continued to enter into agreements with the tribes, but Congress increasingly directed Indian policy by statute. Although Congress passed a statute recognizing all Indians as citizens in 1924, the tribes retained attributes of sovereignty necessary to negotiate agreements and assert treaty rights.

Except for the early period, the U.S. government was generally in a position of dominance when it negotiated treaties with Native American tribes. Following armed conflicts, the government tended to be especially harsh in its demands. Even in the best of conditions, the treaties were written in English, and the Indians frequently did not clearly understand what was written. Basic assumptions, such as the very idea of land ownership, were often foreign to Native American cultures. In addition, the government frequently chose to negotiate with cooperative individuals who were not recognized as legitimate negotiators by tribal majorities. In some cases, as with the Cherokee treaty of removal in 1835, the Senate ratified treaties that had been repudiated by the American Indians.

Indian treaties are especially important for the determination of land claims. About 230 of the treaties included a delineation of boundaries based on a cession of land from the tribe to the U.S. government, with reserved lands (called reservations) for the use of the tribe. Many of the treaties also recognized the retention of hunting and fishing rights in the ceded territories. The treaties usually stated that the tribe would acknowledge the authority of the United States, and the U.S. government promised to provide food and services for the tribe. The treaties generally were silent or unclear concerning whether various provisions were to be permanent or temporary.

Interpretations of Treaties. Because treaties are legal documents, the U.S. Supreme Court has the final authority in determining their meanings. When the language of a treaty is clear, it is applied as written. Because the language is often very unclear, however, the Supreme Court has gradually developed "rules of construction" for resolving disputes. As compensation for the disadvantages of the tribes during the treaty-making process, ambiguities are normally resolved in favor of the Indian perspective, and federal courts attempt to interpret the language as it would have been reasonably understood by the tribal leaders responsible for the negotiations.

In the 1960's and 1970's, for example, some of the most controversial interpretations involved the meanings of treaties in regard to the rights of Native Americans to fish and hunt with traditional methods in the lands ceded to the government. The treaties tended to use vague language such as "at the pleasure of the president," but Indian negotiators were frequently led to believe that hunting-fishing rights would continue as long as the Indians were peaceful. Since 1968, federal courts have ruled again and again that these rights remain valid unless they have been clearly and explicitly abrogated by an act of Congress. In a major case in 1974, a U.S. District Court of Washington State ruled that Indian tribes had the right to one-half of the salmon harvest, and in subsequent years, there were similar rulings in several states, including Wisconsin and Minnesota. Many non-Indian sports fishers and hunters bitterly resented these decisions, resulting in anti-Indian demonstrations and even threats of violence.

Abrogation of Treaties. If there is an inconsistency between the terms of a treaty and a congressional statute, the more recent of the two is legally binding. Based on this principle, the Supreme Court in *Lone Wolf v. Hitchcock* (1903) reaffirmed that Congress has the full authority to abrogate or modify any treaty. The Endangered Species Act of 1973, for instance, overruled those treaties that included the right to hunt eagles on reservations. If Congress wishes to make changes in a treaty, however, this intent must be clear and explicit in a statute. If there is any doubt about the meaning of a statute, the Supreme Court interprets it in ways that uphold relevant treaties.

In contrast to treaties made with foreign countries, treaties with Native Americans often establish property rights. The Fifth Amendment guarantees that there be "just compensation" for any property that is "taken" for public use. The power of Congress to abrogate treaties, therefore, does not release it from the duty of providing fair payment for any taking of land or other property. Frequently in the past, of course, the federal government did take property without compensation. In 1946, Congress passed the Indian Claims Commission Act to allow tribes to seek indemnities for their lost property.

During the 1950's, powerful members of Congress wanted to put an end to Indian treaties. Their long-term goal was to promote assimilation, which they argued would produce greater opportunities and equality. As a first step, they pursued "termination" of the political relationship existing between the federal government and the tribes. Based on the termination law of 1954, numerous small tribes lost most of their claims to sovereignty and many of their treaty privileges. In *Menominee Tribe v. United States* (1968), however, the Supreme Court ruled that Indians retained those treaty rights that were not explicitly mentioned in the termination law, including the right to hunt and fish. President Richard M. Nixon repudiated the termination policy in 1970, and gradually most tribes regained their pre-termination status.

In 1972, the Trail of Broken Treaties protest called for the recognition of greater tribal sovereignty and the return of the treaty-making process. Although the protest did not obtain its announced goals, the resulting publicity appeared to produce a greater public respect for the treaties. By that date, the termination policy found relatively few supporters, and a firm majority of Congress appeared to accept the idea that respect for treaty rights, as interpreted by the courts, is a question of national honor. The general trend of court cases throughout the last quarter of the twentieth century recognized these principles.

See also: Dancing Rabbit Creek, Treaty of; Federally recognized tribes; Fort Atkinson Treaty; Fort Greenville Treaty; Fort Laramie Treaty of 1868; Fort Laramie Treaty of 1851; Fort Stanwix Treaty; Fort Wayne Treaty; Guadalupe Hidalgo, Treaty of; Horseshoe Bend Treaty; Indian Appropriation Act; Indian Citizenship Act; Indian Claims Commission; Indian New Deal; Indian preference; Indian-white relations: U.S., 1775-1830; Indian-white relations: U.S., 1831-1870; Indian-white relations: U.S., 1871-1933; Indian-white relations: U.S., 1934-2002. Iroquois Confederacy-U.S. Congress meeting; *Lone Wolf v. Hitchcock*; Medicine Lodge Creek Treaty; Reservation system of the United States; Termination Resolution; Trail of Broken Treaties; Trail of Tears.

Thomas T. Lewis

Sources for Further Study

Burt, Larry. *Tribalism in Crisis: Federal Indian Policy.* Albuquerque: University of New Mexico Press, 1982. Good coverage of termination policy.

Canby, William. *American Indian Law.* St. Paul: West, 1983. Chapter 6 gives a concise and useful legal analysis of the treaties.

Deloria, Vine, Jr. *American Indian Policy in the Twentieth Century.* Norman: University of Oklahoma Press, 1985. One of many interesting books written and edited from a strong Native American perspective.

Kappler, Charles, ed. *Indian Treaties, 1778-1883.* New York: Interland, 1972. Provides the texts of most of the actual treaties.

Prucha. Francis. *American Indian Treaties: The History of a Political Anomaly.* San Jose: University of California Press, 1995. Views U.S. policy as one of failed paternalism.

St. Germain, Jill. *Indian Treaty-Making Policy in the United States and Canada, 1867-1877.* Lincoln: University of Nebraska Press, 2001. Explores and contrasts the "civilizing" efforts of the United States and Canada through their Indian treaty policies.

Satz, Ronald. *Indian Treaty Rights.* Madison, Wis.: Wisconsin Academy, 1991. Provides a fascinating pro-Indian account of the fishing-rights controversy in Wisconsin and elsewhere.

Washburn, Wilcomb. *Red Man's Land/White Man's Law.* New York: Charles Scribner's Sons, 1971. An older but still useful account.

Wunder, John. *"Retained by the People": A History of the American Indians and the Bill of Rights*. New York: Oxford University Press, 1994. Provides a broad historical account from the Indian point of view, with an excellent bibliography.

Tribal courts

Date: Established 1883
Locale: United States
Tribes involved: Pantribal in the United States
Categories: Native government, Nineteenth century history, Twentieth century history
Significance: U.S. law allows Native American governments to retain their traditional mechanisms for settling legal disputes.

Prior to European contact, all American Indian tribes and bands had institutional mechanisms for settling disputes. The mechanisms varied from Eskimo song duels and Yurok mediation to Cheyenne and Pueblo councils. Under U.S. law, tribal governments have the right to retain or modify adjudication procedures unless Congress limits that right.

For example, in the nineteenth century the Cherokee legal system went through a series of changes from a clan- and council-based system to a system based on an Anglo-American model. In the late nineteenth century Congress expanded federal court jurisdiction in Cherokee territory and finally passed the Curtis Act (1898), which abolished Cherokee tribal courts.

Pueblo adjudicatory systems have been influenced by Spanish and U.S. institutions and policies but were never abolished by federal edict and continue to develop. For example, many Keresan pueblos have a council which decides cases. Many disputes are settled before a partial council or single official acting as a mediator. Important cases are decided by the full council; the presiding officer may act as both prosecutor and a judge. Litigants may be advised by kinsmen or ceremonial group members. In a modification of this system, Laguna Pueblo has a full-time judge while retaining the council as an appellate court.

In the mid-nineteenth century a number of tribes were confined to reservations, creating new problems of social order. In 1883 the Department of the Interior established Courts of Indian Offenses. The judges, tribal members appointed by reservation superintendents, enforced administrative rules established by the Department of the Interior. The superintendent had appellate power over the judges' decisions. In 1888, Congress implicitly recognized the legitimacy of these courts by appropriating funds for judges' salaries.

By 1900, Courts of Indian Offenses had been established on about two-thirds of the reservations. These courts were even established in some pueblos, where they competed with indigenous legal systems. Courts of Indian Offenses have an enduring legacy as a model for the procedures and codes of many contemporary tribal judicial systems.

In 1935, substantive law administered by the Courts of Indian Offenses was revised. Moreover, the Indian Reorganization Act (1934) made it easier for tribes to establish court systems less dominated by the Interior Department. Insufficient tribal economic growth slowed replacement of the Courts of Indian Offenses. By the close of the twentieth century, however, few remained. By contrast, there were more than one hundred tribal courts.

Tribal courts vary in size, procedure, and other matters. The Navajo nation, for example, now has an independent judicial branch which processed more than eighty-five thousand cases in 1992. There are seven judicial districts and fourteen district court judges. The practice of law before these courts is regulated. Appeals may be taken to the high court. Appellate decisions of note are published. In addition, there are local "peacemaker" courts with 227 peacemakers who act generally as mediators.

See also: Indian Offenses Act; Indian Reorganization Act; Indian-white relations: U.S., 1871-1933.

Eric Henderson

Tribe

Date: 1492-present
Locale: The Americas and West Indies
Tribes involved: Pantribal
Categories: Terminology
Significance: The terminology used to describe American Indian social organization has implications for the subjective value placed on that organization by European Americans.

The word "tribe" has deep roots in Indo-European languages and cultures. In Indo-European the word *tre* refers to trees and the way they branch. This later became the word *tri*, meaning one-third, or division into three parts. The word *bus* refers to "bush," or branching plant. In Latin, *tribus* was used in reference to the three groups—Latin, Sabine, and Etruscan—who united to form Rome. The original term comes from the Etruscans. It has come into modern usage through French and Middle English derivations and was carried into North America by colonial peoples.

Definitions. This term describes various human social groups who share a common name, territory, ancestry, and feeling of community. Peoples with similar customs and cultural, linguistic, and religious homogeneity are thought by Western Europeans and European Americans to be tribes. In some areas populated by groups considered tribes, people traveled in nomadic groups loosely bound by family ties. In others they settled and established their tribes on a clan basis; in still other regions the power structure was based on a village or community system.

Some social scientists consider a tribe to be an organized band or group of bands who have shared means of resolving disputes and making communal decisions and possess a written language. A tribe is also thought to be a self-sufficient group of people living and working together but producing little or no surplus goods or services.

A tribe is larger than a family or a band yet smaller than a chiefdom, kingdom, or empire. Some scholars say the term refers to early stages in the development of human political systems and nation-states. This assumes that a tribe lacks a state apparatus, civil government, and the complex political organization commonly associated with the more easily recognized governmental forms of chiefdoms, kingdoms, and empires.

Unfortunately the word "tribe" is often used to refer to any group of people considered "primitive" by others—groups who live a "simple" life of traveling, hunting, migrating, marrying, and meeting for ceremonies and who share a common dialect, customs, culture, and worldview. Such peoples are generally lacking in advanced technology and are organized in ways considered "uncivilized" by citizens of nation-states.

Some of the things that bind any human community together include family and kinship ties; shared beliefs about self, group, and their origins; and the best ways to care for and relate to the environment. The variety of types of social, political, and religious organization regulated through ritualistic, governmental, and other institutional forms are numerous and diverse. Any people who share a language, social structure, worldview, and territory can be assumed to qualify as a tribe.

Tribes and the American Experience. Some indigenous American tribes were so loosely organized that no tribal unit is said to have existed. Their lives were thought to "border on anarchy." They were nomadic or migratory. They had no secret societies, tradition of hereditary nobility, complex clan structures, or settled places of constant habitation. They were small groups, often called "bands," who shared a common identity because of their common presence and activities.

Some assembled into duly constituted independent states when they gathered all their numbers together, while other groups entered into an even higher organic state by confederating with neighboring tribes (a level of organization that could qualify them as nations). Others forced many smaller tribes to take part in the formation and maintenance of an empire, as among the Aztecs, Mayas, and Incas.

Tribe, in its European denotation, signifies only a political unit, whereas the actual diversity among American Indian peoples of organizational forms indicates a wide variety of complex social expressions of the communal uniting of personal and environmental conceptions. Social relations depended on the self-evident order of nature and a people's place in it.

American Indian peoples traditionally had no commonly agreed-upon concept of "tribe." They were generally animists, meaning that they believed everything to be alive and related; all things were defined by their relationship to all other things. They had many varieties of kinship groups, clans, lineage systems, and social structures. Each group had a name for itself in its own language, most often a word that meant "the people" or "human beings." For example, the Tsalagi (Cherokee) word *Junwiya*, the Navajo word *Diné*, and the Nez Perce word *Nimipuu* all mean "the people."

Colonial Europeans often thought of all peoples unlike themselves as primitives and therefore as "tribes." It was their tendency, because of the categorical and reductionist strains of their thinking and languages, to reduce the diversity of indigenous American peoples to a general category of "primitives" or "tribes." They did not recognize or understand the communities and peoples they encountered in their drive to colonize the Americas and to develop new sources of raw materials, generate income for the European monarchies, and procure converts to Christian churches. They generally looked upon native peoples in the Americas as savage, barbaric, uncivilized, primitive, and worthy only of extermination or exploitation.

As the United States developed into a nation, these abstract generalizations were projected onto all indigenous peoples who organized themselves in ways not recognizable to Anglo-Europeans. Indigenous tribal peoples in Hawaii and the Philippines, for example, were viewed as primitives who needed to be controlled or exterminated either by force of arms or by coercive cultural assimilation.

Each tribal community in the Americas is the product of distinctive conditions, circumstances, and experiences from which the community derives the shape of its culture and the form of its identity. There were originally thousands of unique peoples in the Americas before contact with Europeans. Only after contact with Europeans did it eventually become a legal necessity to define oneself in terms of tribal affiliation.

Modern, Legal and Political Considerations. Many indigenous peoples consider the term "tribe" to be offensive, seeing its use as a typical European attempt to justify "civilizing," forcibly assimilating, or exterminating them. Yet they also realize that they must struggle today to receive and maintain recognition as "federally recognized tribes" in order to receive protections under the law and fulfillment of treaty rights and benefits.

Alternative terms such as "ethnicity," "minority group," and "identity group" have been suggested, but any such redefinition involves political (and economic) issues. "Tribe" is a term with distinct political connotations in the United States. American Indian peoples have a constitutionally mandated relationship with the government as defined by treaties and other agreements between recognized Indian nations and their enrolled citizens. This is called the federal-Indian trust relationship and is carried out through various intra- and intergovernmental contacts and institutions. Tribes' inherent, although limited, sovereignty and inalienable right to self-determination is thereby supposed to be assured. At the same time, the federal government's duties and obligations to modern tribes are spelled out.

For these reasons federally recognized Indian tribes traditionally did not seek civil rights. They believed, and many still believe today, that the U.S. government and Indian peoples are best served through the fulfillment of treaties rather than the passage of laws in the interest of immigrant minority groups. There is considerable money and power at stake; thus, what tribe a person is enrolled in and what factors determine membership in an Indian tribal nation become matters of great political and social import. In the United States one cannot receive benefits as a beneficiary in the federal-Indian trust relationship unless one is "an enrolled member of a federally recognized tribe." In other words, an individual must be a citizen of a legally and politically defined "Indian nation" with rights under federal law.

Exactly what defines membership in a federally recognized tribe varies from one group to another. Ancestry, blood quantum, and acclamation are all legally sound bases used to support claims to tribal membership. These bases go against traditional methods of identification such as language, clan membership, and religion. The process of imposing Western political and legal standards tends to erode traditional forms of organization.

Legal definitions are of great import today. Tribes are not states but "dependent" nations with limited sovereignty and an inherent right to self-determination and self-government, even if the specific governmental forms are imposed from without. Many tribal groups maintain their traditional forms of governing themselves, while creating federally recognized nation-state frameworks that allow them to participate in nation-to-nation relationships. This is essential to the preservation of cultural integrity on the one hand and to the fulfillment of treaty obligations on the other.

The concept or term "tribe" is thus ambiguous and represents a superimposition of European modes of viewing and defining the cultural, social, and political organization of indigenous peoples. It is a term of convenience used to designate all North American Indian peoples even though only about half of them actually had any form of tribal organization. The indigenous peoples of North America lived in a wide spectrum of identity groups, including families, clans, bands, villages, tribes, chiefdoms, and empires. Their social and political systems were diverse and distinctive; they were expressions of each group's unique adaptations to the many geographical and environmental conditions evident in North America from prehistoric times to the present.

See also: American Indian; Amerind; Federally recognized tribes; Indian; Native American.

Michael W. Simpson

Sources for Further Study

Deloria, Vine, Jr., and Clifford M. Lytle. *The Nations Within: The Past and Future of American Indian Sovereignty.* New York: Pantheon Books, 1984. An excellent in-depth study of the development of tribal nationalism and of the political meaning of being an enrolled citizen of a federally recognized Indian tribe.

Drinnon, Richard. *Facing West: The Metaphysics of Indian-Hating and Empire-Building.* Minneapolis: University of Minnesota Press, 1980. The author explores the intellectual process which defines indigenous tribal groups as primitive and leads to violence between nations and tribes. Includes many helpful illustrations and an extensive bibliographic essay.

Fried, Morton H. *The Notion of Tribe.* Menlo Park, Calif.: Cummings, 1975. An exploration of the development and meaning of the concept of tribe.

Gluckman, Max. *Politics, Law, and Ritual in Tribal Society.* 1966. Reprint. New York: Blackwell, 1977. This book studies tribal organization and the ways tribal groups develop and maintain their integrity. Though not focused specifically on American Indian tribes, it provides a comprehensive conceptual basis for investigation of the concept. Illustrated in the original.

Sahlins, Marshall D. *Tribesmen*. Englewood Cliffs, N.J.: Prentice Hall, 1968. This book has illustrations which represent tribal life in all its diversity.

Tuscarora War

Date: September 22, 1711-March 23, 1713
Locale: Fort Neoheroka on Contentnea Creek in North Carolina
Tribes involved: Tuscarora
Categories: Colonial history, Wars and battles
Significance: Decimation of the Tuscaroras dispersed their society and opened the way for westward expansion by European settlers.

When European settlers began arriving in North America, the Tuscarora tribe controlled nearly all the North Carolina coastal plains. The tribe's territory stretched from today's Virginia state line, south to the Cape Fear River, and inland to the Appalachians. Tribal land cut a wedge between the Algonquian tribes of the coast and the Siouan tribes of the piedmont. The Tuscaroras held a trade monopoly throughout the area.

Information about the Tuscaroras and their western holdings was limited, because the tribe denied passage through the area. Contact with settlers was infrequent as a result of the natural protection provided by swamps, sand reefs, and shallow harbors. Conflict between the tribe and the settlers began, however, when the two groups started occupying the same areas and the Indians began raids on settlers' livestock and crops. The Indians saw no problem with their actions, because there was no Tuscarora law or custom that discouraged stealing from an enemy. Settlers were helpless to prevent these attacks, because the tribe had a vicious policy of revenge. In 1705, the Tuscaroras became such a problem for the settlers that Virginia passed a law forbidding natives to hunt on patented land.

Trade agreements were established between the tribe and the settlers, but things did not go smoothly. The Tuscaroras felt the settlers were taking advantage of them and complained about being cheated. Tuscarora tribal leaders approached the Pennsylvania government in 1710. They presented eight wampum belts, signifying various grievances concerning the safety of American Indian families. No agreement was reached. Unscrupulous traders accelerated the Tuscarora discontent by describing the settlers as easy targets with no government backing or protection. Then the Tuscaroras declared war.

Tuscaroras Attack. On September 22, 1711, approximately five hundred Tuscaroras and their allies attacked at widely scattered points along the Neuse, Trent, and Pamlico Rivers. Men, women, and children were butchered and their homes destroyed by fire. The Indians' frenzy was slowed only by fatigue and drunkenness. At the end of the two-day rampage more than 130 whites were dead and nearly 30 women and children had been captured. The frightened survivors scrambled to reach fortified garrisons.

The situation in North Carolina was desperate. Planters west of the river could not help protect those under attack without weakening their own defenses. Quaker settlers refused to fight. Governor Edward Hyde appealed to Virginia and South Carolina for help. Virginia worked to secure the loyalty and assistance of the neutral Tuscaroras who had not participated in the raids, but met with little success. South Carolina responded by sending Colonel John Barnwell and a force of five hundred native allies and thirty white men.

Barnwell's departure was delayed, and his winter march was difficult. He crossed the Neuse River in late January and marched an entire day and night to attack the Tuscarora town of Narhontes. Although the natives knew of his approach, Barnwell's raid was successful. For the next four months, Barnwell led several victorious attacks in Tuscarora territory, but he was displeased by the weak North Carolina support. In April, against orders from North Carolina, he signed a treaty with the Tuscaroras. During Barnwell's return to South Carolina, he broke the treaty by capturing native women and children to sell as slaves, thereby provoking new raids.

The summer of 1712 brought no relief. Settlers and natives were starving; no one could plant crops or hunt in safety. Residents along the Neuse and Pamlico Rivers had their homes burned, their stock stolen, and their plantations destroyed. The North Carolina Assembly held a special session in July and passed a law requiring all men between sixteen and sixty years of age to fight the natives or pay a fine. The law was widely disliked and few men obeyed it. Then a yellow fever epidemic hit the area. North Carolina's governor was one of those who died.

Pollock's Negotiations. Thomas Pollock was chosen as the new governor until the colony could receive instructions from the Lord Proprietors. Pollock appealed to South Carolina for aid but suggested that Colonel

Barnwell would not be suitable. Barnwell went before the South Carolina assembly and advised that it was necessary to prosecute the Tuscarora War to a successful conclusion. South Carolina agreed to help. A force of nine hundred Indians and approximately thirty-three soldiers was placed under the leadership of Colonel James Moore, who was experienced in fighting the American Indians.

Governor Pollock reopened negotiations with King Tom Blunt, the chief ruler of the neutral Tuscaroras in the upper towns. In September, Blunt requested peace with North Carolina. Pollock insisted Blunt's people fight on the side of the settlers and would not accept neutrality. Pollock demanded the capture of King Tom Hancock, the chief who had authorized the massacre in September, 1711. In mid-November, 1712, Hancock was delivered and executed. King Blunt then signed a treaty with North Carolina on behalf of nine Tuscarora towns.

Colonel Moore and his forces arrived in the Neuse River region in late December. Although the people were thankful for the protection, they were angered when the troops consumed all the provisions in the area. It was nearly a month before Moore's forces left for Fort Barnwell to prepare an attack on Fort Neoheroka.

Fort Neoheroka lay within a wide curve of Contentnea Creek and was protected on three sides by deep water and steep river banks. The fourth side was enclosed by an angled palisade, a fence created by pointed stakes. There were bastions, or projections, on the four main corners, and an angled passageway led from the fort to the water. The natives also had access to a network of tunnels and caves within the fort.

Moore instructed his men to create zigzag trenches to within gun range of the fort's east wall. He then built a triangular blockhouse to allow his troops to provide crossfire while men raised a battery against the fort wall. Moore also ordered a mine tunneled under the wall near the blockhouse and lined it with explosives.

Once preparations were completed, Moore placed his forces around the fort. Two captains, a battery of artillery, and more than three hundred Cherokees were assigned to the northwest area of the fort and stream to block off the most likely escape route. East of the fort and in the trenches, Moore's brother, two other captains, ten whites, and fifty Yamasees took their positions. Colonel Moore placed himself, four other commanders, eighty whites, and four hundred members of Siouan nations in the southeast. Mulberry Battery took its place within the southern curve of the creek.

Battle of Fort Neoheroka. The attack began on March 20, 1713, with the blast of a trumpet. The powder in the mine failed, but the attack on the northeast quickly succeeded. Captain Maule went against the southern side of the fort instead of the southeast, as he had been ordered. This caused Maule's troops to be caught in the crossfire, and only twenty of his men escaped unhurt. Colonel Moore erected a low wall and managed to set two of the fort's blockhouses on fire. By the next morning, the fire had destroyed the structures as well as several houses within the fort. Some of the Tuscaroras hid in the caves and created problems for the attackers, but by Sunday, March 23, Moore's forces controlled the fort. Destruction of Fort Neoheroka was complete. Moore had lost fewer than sixty men and had fewer than one hundred wounded. Nearly one thousand Tuscaroras were killed or captured.

As word of the defeat spread, other members of the Tuscarora tribe fled. Many of the refugees headed to Virginia, where they endured great hardships and found little food. Several raiding bands continued guerrilla warfare in North Carolina, but Moore's help was no longer needed. He returned to South Carolina in September, 1713.

See also: Fox Wars; Indian slave trade; Indian-white relations: English colonial; Iroquois Confederacy; Yamasee War.

Suzanne Riffle Boyce

Sources for Further Study

Graymont, Barbara, ed. *Fighting Tuscarora: The Autobiography of Chief Clinton Rickard.* Reprint. Syracuse, N.Y.: Syracuse University Press, 1994. Introduction includes information about Tuscarora history. Main text chronicles the life of Chief Clinton Rickard (1882-1971) and his work for American Indian rights.

Johnson, F. Roy. *The Tuscaroras.* Vols. 1 and 2. Murfreesboro: Johnson, 1967. Discusses history, traditions, culture, mythology, and medicine. Maps, illustrations, index, and many footnotes. Provides listings of numerous original resources.

Snow, Dean R. *The Iroquois.* The Peoples of America series. Cambridge: Blackwell, 1994. Follows the development of the Iroquois Confederacy. Extensive bibliography, index.

Waldman, Carl. *Encyclopedia of Native American Tribes.* New York: Facts On File, 1988. One page summarizes events leading to Fort Neoheroka and gives some details about tribal life.

Wilson, Edmund. *Apologies to the Iroquois.* New York: Farrar, Straus & Cudahy, 1959. Contains a chapter on Tuscarora history. Also discusses land disputes at Niagara Falls in the 1960's.

United States v. Kagama

Date: 1886
Locale: California
Tribes involved: Pantribal in the United States
Categories: Court cases, Nineteenth century history
Significance: A U.S. Supreme Court decision reaffirms that Native American tribes are not sovereign in the same ways as nations or states, but are dependent in many ways upon the U.S. government.

American Indian "Pactah Billy" Kagama was charged with murdering another Indian on the Hoopa Valley Reservation in California in 1885. Indian tribes were regarded as a separate people within the United States having the power to regulate their own social relations within reservations.

Kagama challenged the Indian Appropriation Act of March 3, 1871, which gave jurisdiction to U.S. federal courts for several specific crimes, including murder, committed by Native Americans on another Native American within an Indian reservation created by the U.S. government and set apart for use by an Indian tribe.

On May 10, 1886, the U.S. Supreme Court declared the act constitutional and reaffirmed that Native American tribes were not to be considered sovereign in the same way as nations or states but to be viewed as largely helpless communities dependent upon the U.S. government for their food, protection, and constitutional political rights.

See also: Indian Appropriation Act; Indian-white relations: U.S., 1871-1933.

Steve J. Mazurana

United States v. Washington

Date: 1974
Locale: Washington State
Tribes involved: Quinault, Queet, Muckleshoot, Squaxin Island, Sauk-Suiattle, Skokomish, Stillaguamish, Makah, Lummi, Quileute, Yakima, Hoh, Upper Skagit
Categories: Court cases, Treaties, Twentieth century history
Significance: A U.S. district court rules that Indians may fish at sites not on reservations because this right had been reserved in treaties.

Swinomish Indians displaying a skate caught in a tribal fishing trap in Washington State, 1938. Fishing has always been an important part of tribal economies in the Northwest. (National Archives)

United States v. Washington is commonly referred to as the Boldt decision after the judge who decided it in federal district court. In a series of treaties negotiated between 1854 and 1855, various Washington and Oregon tribes ceded nearly sixty-four million acres of land but retained the right to continue to fish in accustomed areas. The states of Washington and Oregon eventually sought to regulate Indians' rights to fish in off-reservation areas. In response, some Indian people staged fish-ins in the 1960's to assert their treaty rights. Finally, the state of Washington used its regulatory powers to limit Indian fishing, and in 1970, thirteen tribes sued the state in federal court.

After extensive study, Federal District Judge George Boldt ruled in 1974 that Indians had rights to fish at off-reservation sites because this right had been reserved in the treaties. The court understood the treaties involved a grant from the tribes to the United States, and in return, the tribes obtained rights for its members and heirs. The ruling also stated that United States citizens and tribal people had the right to share equally in the salmon catch, and both were directed by the court to develop plans to protect and replenish the salmon population.

This decision caused widespread opposition among state officials, sports fishers, and others, and Indian people complained of harassment and continued problems with exercising their fishing rights. On appeal from the state of Washington, the U.S. Supreme Court reviewed the case in 1979 and essentially upheld Boldt's ruling.

See also: Fish-ins; National Indian Youth Council; *Winters v. United States.*

Carole A. Barrett

Wabash, Battle of the

Date: November 4, 1791
Locale: Mercer County, Ohio
Tribes involved: Miami, Shawnee, Lenni Lenape, Ojibwa, Potawatomi, Huron (Wyandot), Ottawa, Cherokee, Creek
Categories: Eighteenth century history, Wars and battles
Significance: Usually known as St. Clair's defeat, this victory of the Maumee Valley tribes and their confederates from around the Great Lakes and Ohio Valley constitutes perhaps the most dramatic defeat of the U.S. Army at the hands of Native Americans in the history of the Indian wars of 1790-1890.

During the 1780's and 1790's, Indian resistance to American encroachment north of the Ohio River rose to new heights. Led primarily by the Miami, Shawnee, and Lenni Lenape (Delaware), the western Algonquian-speaking peoples felt betrayed by the Treaty of Paris of 1783, which placed their homelands within the United States. They also assumed that the Treaty of Fort Stanwix (1768) was still valid, with its prohibition of white settlement in what became the Northwest Territory. The British encouraged them by stationing soldiers at Fort Detroit and through the blandishments of their Indian Department representatives, who raised Indian expectations.

Many of the militant Indians settled along the upper Wabash and Maumee River Valleys. Under the nominal leadership of the Miami war chief Little Turtle (Michikinikwa), the tribes most associated with him were the Shawnee (led by Blue Jacket, or Wyeapiersenwah) and the Lenni Lenape (led by Buckongahelas). Little Turtle's warriors inflicted a critical defeat on the first United States military incursion into their territory. Brigadier General Josiah Harmar's expedition to the Maumee forks (Fort Wayne, Indiana) was badly mauled in two engagements by a pan-Indian force in October, 1791. This defeat caused President George Washington to name the Northwest Territory's governor, Arthur St. Clair, as a major general commanding a second expedition into the Maumee Valley.

Harmar's defeat raised Little Turtle's reputation and increased Indian unity throughout the region. The Maumee Confederacy's contacts and support stretched from Lake Superior to the Lower Creek villages in modern Alabama. The coalitions of Pontiac and Tecumseh were never as broad or as unified as this one. Miami, Shawnee, and Lenni Lenape warriors would be joined by Ojibwa, Potawatomi, Huron (Wyandot), and Ottawa militants and there was some coordination with the Cherokees and Creeks to the south. With Little Turtle in nominal command, the Indians' consensual and tribal kinship approach to combat proved effective in this campaign.

St. Clair's ill-trained and poorly equipped regulars, plus even less effective and less disciplined militia volunteers, left Cincinnati at the end of September, 1791. St. Clair's regulars constituted almost all the combat troops in the U.S. Army. By November 3 they had advanced only 89 miles, and discipline was so poor that entrenched encampments were no longer maintained. The American encampment near the Wabash River's source (now Fort Recovery, Ohio) was divided between regular and militia units, thereby diluting St. Clair's command authority even more.

The Indians advanced south from the Glaize (modern Defiance County, Ohio), keeping their presence and size hidden from St. Clair. Little Turtle struck at dawn on November 4, and his thousand warriors quickly overran the militia camp, pushing the survivors into an ever smaller killing zone among the regulars. With his forces encircled, St. Clair's attempts to rally his defense failed. Indian marksmanship directed at the officers contributed to the disorganization. Eventually a breakout to the south was successful for about a third of the fourteen hundred American soldiers. The remainder were killed, wounded, or taken prisoner. Never before or since has such a high proportion of the total United States military establishment been defeated. Approximately twenty-one Indians died, and forty were wounded.

It would be three years before Major General Anthony Wayne would lead a third expedition toward the Maumee Valley. In the meantime, Indian unity declined. Wayne's subsequent victory at the Battle of Fallen Timbers opened the Ohio country for American settlement.

See also: Fallen Timbers, Battle of; Indian-white relations: U.S., 1775-1830; Little Turtle's War.

David Curtiss Skaggs

Sources for Further Study

Dowd, Gregory Evans. *A Spirited Resistance: The North American Indian Struggle for Unity, 1745-1815.* Baltimore: Johns Hopkins University Press, 1992.

Eid, Leroy V. "American Indian Military Leadership: St. Clair's 1791 Defeat." *Journal of Military History* 57 (January, 1993): 71-88.

Tanner, Helen Hunt. "The Glaize in 1792: A Composite Indian Community." *Ethnohistory* 25 (Winter, 1978): 15-39.

Walking Purchase

Date: September 19, 1737
Locale: Bucks County, Pennsylvania
Tribes involved: Lenni Lenape, Iroquois Confederacy
Categories: Colonial history
Significance: Pennsylvania's acquisition of Native American land enhances Iroquois dominance over eastern Pennsylvania tribes.

The first half of the eighteenth century was a time of profound population growth in Pennsylvania. Europeans, especially Scotch-Irish and German settlers, came into the colony in unprecedented numbers. The steadily expanding population put considerable pressure on the provincial government to make additional acreage available for settlement. The demand for land also created potentially lucrative opportunities for aggressive speculators, particularly speculators who also served as provincial officials. Such was the case with those who initiated the 1737 Walking Purchase.

The Lenni Lenape, or Delaware as they were also known, were among the first Native American tribes to negotiate with William Penn. At the time that Pennsylvania was founded, the Lenni Lenape occupied much of the land between the Delaware and Susquehanna Rivers. Penn's policies toward the Lenni Lenape were more benevolent than were the tribal policies of most colonial administrators. Penn generally recognized native land rights and usually was tolerant of the native lifestyle.

By the 1730's, Pennsylvania settlers along the Delaware River had moved well north of Philadelphia. This was Lenni Lenape territory, and the natives refused to share possession. Some provincial officials, including William Penn's son Thomas, disputed the Native American claim. The younger Penn maintained that the Lenni Lenape had promised his father that they would surrender a portion of the land. The younger Penn no doubt also had ulterior motives for contesting the Lenni Lenape land. While serving as the colony's governor, he was beset with ever-growing family debts. In an effort to solve his financial woes, he chose to sell some of his family's real estate. Among the most desirable and salable parts of his acreage was the Lenni Lenape land along the Delaware.

Border Disputes. When confronted by Thomas Penn's claim to their land, the Lenni Lenape acknowledged that the Penn family had title to a portion of the land along the Delaware. They agreed that Mechkilikishi, one of their chiefs, had granted to William Penn some acreage north of Philadelphia. According to Nutimus, a Lenni Lenape chief who was present when land was given, the Penn claim ended at the Tohickon Creek, which is about thirty miles north of Philadelphia. James Logan, an influential member of Thomas Penn's council, led several Pennsylvania officials in challenging Nutimus's assessment. He contended that Penn's land extended beyond the Forks of the Delaware, which was more than fifty miles to the north.

To resolve the dispute, Thomas Penn called Nutimus and two other Lenni Lenape chiefs to his home at Pennsbury Manor. Assisted by Logan, Penn showed the Native Americans a copy of a deed dated 1686. The agreement transferred to the Penn family a large tract of land west of the Delaware and extending "back into the woods as far as a man can walk in one day and a half."

Nutimus argued that the walk had been made and ended at the Tohickon. The creek, therefore, was the formal border between Penn land and Lenni Lenape territory. Additionally, since Nutimus's village had for several centuries occupied the Forks area, Mechkilikishi, who was chief of another Lenni Lenape village, had no authority to turn over land at the Forks to William Penn.

Nutimus's arguments were greeted with disdain by several influential Pennsylvania officials who, like Penn, had interests in the Forks area beyond providing more land for settlers. One of the most concerned Pennsylvanians was Logan. A few years earlier, he had begun operating an iron furnace in the region and hoped to expand his facility. Two other interested parties were Andrew Hamilton and his son-in-law, William Allen. Hamilton was mayor of Philadelphia, and Allen was on his way to becoming one of the colony's most successful entrepreneurs and the chief justice of the provincial court. Allen already had begun negotiating quietly for a large tract in what is today Allentown. Once he acquired the land, he hoped to divide it into lots and sell the lots to settlers.

Although the Pennsylvanians passionately argued their claim, the 1686 deed upon which they based their arguments was suspicious in several ways. Among other shortcomings, it lacked signatures and seals. There were also blank spaces in several crucial places, including the spot where the final dimensions of the tract should have appeared. In most cases, such a document would have been voided by the British courts. When questioned about the flaws, Penn and Logan claimed that it was a copy of an original that had been lost. Nevertheless, they continued to uphold the document as valid.

In the months that followed the Pennsbury meeting, Logan quietly expanded his plan of attack. To undermine Nutimus's authority, he appealed to Iroquois representatives for support. The powerful Iroquois nation dominated most tribes throughout Pennsylvania; without their support, the Lenni Lenape had little hope of retaining the disputed land along the Delaware. Assisted by Conrad Weiser, Logan was able to get the Iroquois to confirm the Penn claims. With Iroquois approval secured, it was just a matter of time before the Lenni Lenape conceded to Penn's claims. On August 25, 1737, Nutimus and three other Lenni Lenape chiefs grudgingly endorsed Governor Penn's furtive 1686 treaty. A walk that would determine the extent of Penn's holdings along the Delaware was soon scheduled.

The Walk. The walk began at the Wrightstown Quaker Meeting House at daybreak on September 19. Three local men known for their athletic prowess were hired by provincial authorities to make the hike. Two Native American representatives accompanied the Pennsylvanians. The Lenni Lenape expected that the walk would conform to native customs. The walkers would walk for a while then rest, smoke a peace pipe, and share a meal before resuming their trek. The Lenni Lenape expected that the journey would cover about twenty miles. Pennsylvania officials, however, had much different plans.

It became clear immediately that the walk would not be a leisurely stroll along the Delaware. Instead it proceeded northwest toward the Kittatiny Mountains and followed a path that had been cut through the backcountry to aid the walkers. Additionally, much of the time the walkers did not walk. They ran. The Pennsylvanians also were accompanied by supply horses carrying provisions, and boats that were used to ferry the hikers across streams.

By early afternoon, the unsuspecting Lenni Lenape escorts fell far behind the Pennsylvanians. A few hours later, already well beyond the Tohickon, one Pennsylvanian dropped from exhaustion. A second walker gave up the following morning. The final Pennsylvanian persevered until noon on the second day. In all, he covered sixty-four miles, more than three times what the Lenni Lenape had expected.

Even after the walk had ended, the Penn land grab continued. Rather than draw a straight line from start to finish and then a right angle to the river, surveyors were instructed by Logan to set the borders of the walk in a zigzag course that followed the flow of the Delaware. As a result, another 750,000 acres were acquired from the Lenni Lenape.

During the months that followed, Nutimus and his tribe complained bitterly about the devious tactics employed by provincial officials. However, the Lenni Lenape had few alternatives to accepting the results. With Walking Purchase completed, the new land was soon opened to Pennsylvania settlers and the Lenni Lenape relegated to diminished status among Native American tribes living in the colony.

See also: Iroquois Confederacy; Iroquois Confederacy-U.S. Congress meeting.

Paul E. Doutrich

Sources for Further Study

Jennings, Francis. *The Ambiguous Iroquois Empire*. New York: W. W. Norton, 1984. Offers a detailed explanation of the duplicitous tactics used by Pennsylvania officials to acquire the Walking Purchase acreage.

Kelley, Joseph J., Jr. *Pennsylvania: The Colonial Years, 1681-1776*. Garden City, N.Y.: Doubleday, 1980. Describes the Walking Purchase and many other episodes in Pennsylvania's colonial history.

Thomas, David Hurst, et al. *The Native Americans: An Illustrated History*. Atlanta, Ga.: Turner Publishing, 1993. A colorful history that includes a concise accounting of the purchase.

Tolles, Frederick B. *James Logan and the Culture of Provincial America*. Boston: Little, Brown, 1957. Details the life and career of James Logan, including his role in the Walking Purchase.

Wallace, Paul A. W. *Indians in Pennsylvania*. Harrisburg: Pennsylvania Historical and Museum Commission, 1981. Survey of Native Americans, including a general description of the Walking Purchase.

Walla Walla Council

Date: May 24-June 11, 1855
Locale: Mill Creek, Walla Walla, Washington

Tribes involved: Cayuse, Nez Perce, Umatilla, Walla Walla, Yakima
Categories: National government and legislation, Native government, Nineteenth century history, Treaties
Significance: The resulting treaty drastically reduced the area of Indian lands, marking the end of a centuries-old era and forcing Native Americans to make a radical adjustment to white civilization.

The westward migration of settlers and immigrants reached the Northwest by the mid-1800's. In 1848 about five thousand immigrants and one thousand wagons arrived in Oregon, more than the combined population of the Nez Perce, Cayuse, and Walla Walla tribes.

In 1855 Isaac Stevens, governor and superintendent of Indian affairs of the Washington Territory, took steps to implement treaties with the Indians to acquire their land (to provide room for white settlers) and preclude hostilities with the increasingly anxious and angry Indians. He also sought to clear the way for a northern route for the Pacific Railroad. The resulting council was one of the largest tribal gatherings in the United States. Negotiations were carried on in an atmosphere of suspicion, fear, and mistrust of the white negotiators, acrimony between factions of Indians, and even an aborted plan by the Cayuse to massacre all the whites. It was not until between June 9 and 11 that three treaties were finally agreed upon and signed by the Indians, under considerable duress and pressure as well as recognition of the inevitable.

Under the treaties the Indians ceded about 30,000 square miles of land in eastern Oregon and east-central Washington. In return they were given two reservations and promised up to $200,000 per tribe. Emphasis was placed on "civilizing" the Indians by having the government supply personnel and build mills, shops, schools, and hospitals.

The majority of the Nez Perce remained faithful to the treaty. Other tribes, however, felt coerced and betrayed; moreover, they were convinced that whites would never live up to the terms of the treaty. They refused to accept the end of their traditional way of life. Almost immediately turmoil and war began; strife was to continue for more than twenty years before some tribes were finally subdued.

See also: Cayuse War; Nez Perce War; Prehistory: Plateau.

Laurence Miller

Washita River Massacre

Date: November 27, 1868
Locale: Washita River, Indian Territory
Tribes involved: Cheyenne
Categories: Nineteenth century history, Wars and battles
Significance: A decisive step in opening the Indian Territory to white settlement.

At dawn on November 27, 1868, troops of the Seventh Regiment of the United States Cavalry, led by Lieutenant Colonel George Armstrong Custer, attacked and massacred a Cheyenne village on the banks of the Washita River in the Indian Territory. In this village of fifty-one lodges were some of the survivors of the 1864 Sand Creek Massacre, including the great Cheyenne chieftain Black Kettle. Custer, having set out on an Indian-hunting expedition and following what he thought was the trail of a large war party, had found the village, located on the south side of the river and surrounded by thick woods. Custer divided his force of seven hundred men into four groups; under cover of darkness, on the night of November 26, he positioned them to the north, south, east, and west of the village. All through the bitterly cold and snowy night, the soldiers waited in absolute silence, without fires, for Custer's signal to attack. Troops G, H, and M, under Major Joel Elliott, were deployed to the north, while troops B and F were south of the village. Troops E and I were down the Washita River, to the right of Elliott's command. Custer, with the regimental band, the color guard, a special sharpshooter company, all the scouts, and troops A, C, D, and K, waited in the center.

Just before dawn, the soldiers crept closer to the village and, at first light, swept down upon the sleeping Cheyennes to the accompaniment of the strains of "Garry Owen," the theme song of the Seventh Cavalry. Custer, on his black stallion, charged through the village and onto a knoll south, from where he watched the fighting. As the Cheyennes ran from their lodges, they were cut down by gunfire or saber, with no quarter given and no distinction made between men, women, or children. Chief Black Kettle and his wife were both shot as they attempted to escape on his pony. Caught entirely by surprise and with few weapons other than bows and arrows, the Cheyennes' only hope was flight—but most were killed by the sharpshooters positioned among the trees. Some did escape by plunging into the icy waters and making their way down the river channel to the Arapaho village of Chief Little Raven. Within a short time, the village fell to the soldiers, who set about killing or capturing those Cheyennes who had taken up defensive positions in the woods.

About 10:00 A.M., Custer noticed that warriors were beginning to gather atop the neighboring hills and, looking for an explanation, questioned one of the female captives. He learned that Black Kettle's village was not the only one on the banks of the Washita River, as he had thought, but was one of many Cheyenne, Arapaho, and Kiowa villages in the area. Shortly after, an officer who had been supervising the roundup of Cheyenne ponies reported that he had seen a very large Arapaho village downriver.

Even so, Custer directed his troops to gather up the spoils of war, which included saddles, buffalo robes, bows and arrows, hatchets, spears, a few revolvers and rifles, all the winter supply of food, most of the Cheyennes' clothing, and all of their lodges. After making an inventory and choosing some personal souvenirs, including one of the lodges, Custer had all the rest burned.

Almost nine hundred of the Cheyennes' horses and mules had now been rounded up. Custer gave the best horses to his officers and scouts, provided mounts for the female captives, then ordered four companies of his men to

At dawn on November 27, 1868, U.S. troops led by George Armstrong Custer attacked and massacred a Cheyenne village on the banks of the Washita River in the Indian Territory. Some felt the Washita action was justified because of raids by Cheyenne warriors on white settlements; others insisted that an entire tribe should not be punished for the acts of a few and noted the United States' failure to meet its obligations under the 1867 Medicine Lodge Creek Treaty. In either case, the massacre marked an escalation in violence as a method of removing Indians to clear the way for white settlement of the Great Plains. (Library of Congress)

slaughter the rest of the animals. He had no intention of leaving the horses behind for the warriors and reasoned that taking them along when he left the area would surely provoke attempts by the Cheyennes to recapture them.

In the late afternoon, Custer was informed that Major Elliott, with seventeen men, had chased a small band of fleeing Cheyennes down the river and had not returned. Custer sent out a search party, but no trace of the missing men was found. Custer then called off the search—a decision that added to the growing resentment and anti-Custer sentiments among some of his officers.

As night approached, Custer realized his command was in a precarious position. Besides being burdened with prisoners and their own wounded, his troops were cold and hungry, their mounts were exhausted, and warriors from the other villages had gathered in the surrounding hills. Thus unprepared for further battle, Custer knew that he could not simply retreat toward his supply train, left behind at a safe distance from the fighting, without alerting the warriors to its location and risking that they would reach it first. The stratagem he devised was to convince them that he was advancing downriver to attack again; at the head of his regiment, with band playing, he traveled east until darkness fell. Seeing this, the warriors hurried back to protect their villages, leaving only a few scouts behind. Custer then reversed back to the battlefield and up the Washita Valley, finally stopping at 2:00 A.M. to camp for the night. The next day, the troops rejoined the supply train and two days later reached Camp Supply, the fort from which Custer had started and at which General Philip Sheridan waited for news of the expedition.

Custer's Report. In his official report of the Washita action, Custer stated that 103 Cheyennes had been killed and 53 women and children, some of them wounded, had been taken prisoner. Among the dead were two Cheyenne chieftains, Black Kettle and Little Rock. During the fighting in the village, one officer and three enlisted men of the Seventh Cavalry had been killed. Custer also reported the deaths of Major Elliott and his seventeen men, although at the time he had no actual knowledge of their fate. Their bodies were discovered in the woods by a later expedition.

Opinions differ as to whether Custer's attack upon the Cheyenne was simply another unprovoked massacre such as that at Sand Creek four years earlier. General William T. Sherman, Sheridan, and Custer, among others, believed that the Washita action was justified because of Cheyenne raids on white settlements along the Saline and Solomon Rivers in Kansas in August, 1868. During a three-day rampage, two hundred Cheyenne warriors had committed murder and rape and abducted women and children.

When Black Kettle and two chiefs of the Arapaho had arrived at Fort Cobb in mid-November, seeking sanctuary and subsistence for their people under the terms of the Medicine Lodge Creek Treaty, they had been refused because General Sheridan now considered both tribes to be hostile after the recent raids. They were told to leave the Indian Territory and warned that troops were in the field.

On the other hand, Indian agent Edward Wynkoop and others insisted that an entire tribe should not be punished for the acts of a few. They further argued that the promises made at Medicine Lodge had led the Cheyenne and Arapaho to expect fair treatment at Fort Cobb, which had not been forthcoming. Furthermore, it has since been established that the trail Custer followed, which he later claimed was that of a Cheyenne war party, actually had been made by Kiowas returning from a raid against the Utes in Colorado.

To place the Washita Massacre in historical perspective, scholars point out that the United States Army had failed to subdue the plains tribes in battle on the prairie, and efforts to achieve peace through treaty had been largely unsuccessful. Thus, the invasion of the Indian Territory, of which the Washita Massacre was a decisive first step, represented a change of tactics in the United States government's efforts to achieve its ultimate goal: the removal of the plains tribes as an obstacle to white settlement of the Great Plains.

See also: Indian-white relations: U.S., 1831-1870; Little Bighorn, Battle of the; Medicine Lodge Creek Treaty; Sand Creek Massacre.

LouAnn Faris Culley

Sources for Further Study

Barnitz, Albert Trovillo Siders, and Jennie Barnitz. *Life in Custer's Cavalry, Diaries and Letters of Albert and Jennie Barnitz, 1867-1868.* Edited by Robert M. Utley. New Haven, Conn.: Yale University Press, 1977. An account of the massacre completed from the writings of one of Custer's troop commanders and his wife.

Brady, Cyrus. *Indian Fights and Fighters.* Lincoln: University of Nebraska Press, 1971. A narrative of the Plains wars, including the Washita Massacre. Includes many eyewitness accounts not available elsewhere.

Brill, Charles. *Conquest of the Southern Plains.* Millwood, N.Y.: Kraus Reprint, 1975. A fully illustrated account of all events related to the massacre, with the texts of both Sheridan's and Custer's reports.

Custer, George Armstrong. *My Life on the Plains.* London: The Folio Society, 1963. Contains Custer's account of the events before, during, and after the Washita Massacre.

Hoig, Stan. *The Battle of the Washita*. Garden City, N.Y.: Doubleday, 1976. A thoroughly documented account of the Sheridan-Custer campaign. Maps and photographs.

West Indian uprisings

Date: 1495-c. 1510
Locale: Hispaniola, Greater Antilles
Tribes involved: Taino
Categories: Colonial history, Wars and battles
Significance: Spanish policy of coopting native West Indians ultimately resulted in rebellion.

The island of Hispaniola (today, the two independent states of Haiti and the Dominican Republic) was the key site of the Christopher Columbus's arrival in the New World in 1492. Historians have not only Columbus's own account of contacts with the native inhabitants of the Caribbean islands but also a number of descriptions by other explorers and missionaries who soon came to these early outposts in the Western Hemisphere. These accounts tended from the outset to distinguish two West Indian subgroups: Caribs and Arawaks. This conventional dualistic view gradually was reworked as ethnohistorians came to reserve the ethnolinguistic term "Arawak" for mainland populations, using the term "Taino" to refer to island groupings, including the native population of Hispaniola. The westernmost Tainos on Cuba and Jamaica appear to have been the most peaceful, both in their relations with other Taino groupings and in their reaction to the first Spaniards. Ciguayan and Borinquen Tainos of Hispaniola and Puerto Rico had a pre-Columbian tradition of warring, mainly against aggressive raids from groupings now known archaeologically as Island Caribs (from the Lesser Antilles, mainly Guadeloupe). They were, however, relatively receptive in the first ten years after 1492 to trying to adapt to Spanish colonial presence.

It was among the eastern Tainos on the Virgin Islands that the Spaniards encountered the first signs of open hostility to their presence. After clashes with otherwise unidentifiable natives on St. Croix, whom Columbus called Caribs, a number of negative observations began to enter Spanish accounts, including presumed acts of cannibalism and enslavement of women captives (later identified as a ceremonial bride-capture tradition).

These early violent encounters with eastern Tainos stemmed more from the natives' fear of strangers than from a considered reaction against Spanish plans for colonization. However, by the time Columbus became Hispaniola's first governor, a policy had been defined that called for direct methods of colonial control, including the *encomienda* system. The latter involved forced attachment of native laborers to Spanish colonial economic ventures, both in agriculture and in mining. By 1495, when the first West Indian revolt against the Spaniards broke out, the long-term movement of all of Hispaniola's Tainos toward extinction had entered its first stage.

Historians have noted that the native population of Hispaniola declined most dramatically by the first decade of the sixteenth century, mainly because of a lack of immunological resistance to diseases brought by the Spaniards. Scores of thousands died from infectious diseases, others from the overwork and undernourishment associated with the notorious *encomienda* system. A surprising number, however, fell victim to violent repression of resistance movements led by their tribal chiefs.

First Uprisings. Between 1495 and 1500, there were at least two armed uprisings against Spanish control. Each of these (that of Caonabo, in 1495, and that of Guarionex, in 1498) was headed by a native tribal head, or *cacique*, who had been able to retain his leadership (in Caonabo's case, as head of a chiefdom west and south of the island's central mountains; in Guarionex's case, local leadership in Magua, near the gold fields north of the mountains) by at first agreeing to cooperate with the main lines of Spanish colonial policy, including the *encomienda*. Especially after the appointment of Governor Nicolás de Ovando in 1502, however, the situation became worse, and Spanish excesses were bound to cause an escalation of violence.

A final royal note to Ovando, dated in September, 1501, authorized Spaniards to take natives into labor service "in order to get gold and do . . . other labors that we order to have done," probably presuming that reasonable wages would be paid for work carried out. In fact, this was the beginning of forced labor that reduced many natives to the status of slaves.

The excessive actions of Ovando against any sign of the *caciques'* discontent with Spanish control set a pattern of violent conflict that took a high toll, especially among the native leadership. Much of the discontent after 1502 came from the sudden dramatic increase in the numbers of Spaniards on Hispaniola. Ovando had arrived with a contingent of about twenty-five hundred persons, including not only soldiers, missionaries (among them the later famous author of the *History of the Indies*, Father Bartolomé de Las

Casas), and administrators, but also private settlers, more than tripling the Spanish population of the previous decade. This increased settler population was certain to demand more native forced labor under the *encomienda* system.

The village chiefdom of Higüey, on the eastern tip of Hispaniola, was the first site of what became major clashes between Spanish troops and what seemed to be rebelling elements of the local population. Governor Ovando's decision in 1502 to kill seven hundred Higüey Indians who had reacted violently to the killing of one of their chiefs by a Spanish dog was followed a year later by a wholesale massacre, in the western province of Xaragua (the former territory of Caonabo, the 1495 rebel leader), of some eighty district chiefs. In the 1503 massacre, Caonabo's widow, Anacaona, assembled the chiefs to meet Ovando's party. While the Spanish murdered the subchieftains brutally in a mass slaughter, Ovando's "respect" for Anacaona compelled him to end her life by hanging. The future conquistador of Cuba, Diego Velázquez, at that time Ovando's deputy commander, followed up the massacre by systematic conquest of the entire western half of Hispaniola.

Broken Spanish Promises. From 1503 forward, it became obvious that no previously offered Spanish promises to recognize the local ruling authority of *caciques* in any part of Hispaniola would hold. In 1504, some local chieftains, such as Agüeybana in the Higüey region, began trying to organize serious resistance forces before the Spanish dared to carry out added systematic removals or massacres of the remaining *caciques*. Despite the fact that Agüeybana's revolt was joined by diverse tribal elements, including groups the Spanish called Caribs, from the Lesser Antilles (more likely Eastern Tainos, not the traditional island Carib enemies of Hispaniola's shores), it was brutally repressed. Agüeybana's execution impelled any remaining potential leaders to leave Hispaniola, or at least to take refuge in the more remote eastern Taino region.

Five years after the bloody events in the western region of Xaragua, and shortly after the failure of Agüeybana's abortive efforts in the east, Chief Guarocuya, Anacaona's nephew, tried in 1509 to go into hiding in the island's mountain region of Baonuco. When local troops condemned this act as rebellion, the commanding authorities hunted him down and killed him. More out of fear than in active resistance, the neighboring provinces of Guahaba and Hanyguayaba rebelled, and immediately suffered violent repression by the hand of Diego Velázquez.

With such harsh actions, the short and uneasy period of cooperation between the Spanish and the native West Indians was over. As the native population died off under the overwhelming odds of disease, the process of importing African slave laborers began. They became the ancestors of most of today's West Indian population—the inevitable consequence of this breakdown of the *encomienda* system.

See also: Indian-white relations: Spanish colonial.

Byron D. Cannon

Sources for Further Study

Hulme, Peter. *Colonial Encounters: Europe and the Native Caribbean, 1492-1797.* New York: Methuen, 1986. Covers a longer time period than other listings here. Focuses on literary and anthropological approaches to understanding the psychological distances separating the colonial and colonized populations of the Caribbean.

Keegan, William F., ed. *Earliest Hispanic/Native American Interactions in the Caribbean.* New York: Garland, 1991. A series of specialized studies of both Spanish and native Indian institutions, including methods of agriculture and local administration, before and during the Ovando governorate.

Las Casas, Bartolomé de. *History of the Indies.* Edited and translated by Andrée Collard. New York: Harper & Row, 1971. A partial translation of the massive work (three volumes in the Spanish edition) of the Spanish missionary who, after coming to Hispaniola with Governor Ovando, turned critical of Ovando's repressive policies.

Rouse, Irving. *The Tainos: Rise and Decline of the People Who Greeted Columbus.* New Haven, Conn.: Yale University Press, 1992. Contains the most extensive coverage of the distant past of the native West Indian population, with a concluding chapter on their short history of contacts with Europeans before dying out.

Tyler, S. Lyman. *Two Worlds: The Indian Encounter with the European, 1492-1509.* Salt Lake City: University of Utah Press, 1988. Provides the most concise history of the circumstances of West Indian revolts and repression in this period.

White Paper of Canada

Date: Proposed 1969, withdrawn 1970
Locale: Canada
Tribes involved: Pantribal in Canada

Categories: National government and legislation, Native government, Twentieth century history

Significance: This proposal by the Canadian government to revamp its relationships with, and obligations to, Native Canadians met with the near-unanimous disapproval of native groups.

By the late 1960's, it had long been recognized that Native Canadians had failed to share socially and economically in the general prosperity that followed World War II. They were frequently the victims of discrimination and lacked access to the economic, educational, medical, and social benefits available to the majority of Canadians. These issues were frequently lumped together in the popular media and by government bureaucrats as the "Indian problem." The White Paper of 1969 was a policy statement and plan issued by Prime Minister Pierre Trudeau to resolve the problem.

Running on the campaign slogan "The Just Society," Trudeau led the Liberal Party to victory in the Canadian national elections in June of 1968. The slogan signified a social consciousness that had been growing among the Canadian populace throughout the 1960's. The White Paper was part of a general attempt by Trudeau and his ministers, following that election, to review and reorder all Canadian social and economic policy.

Trudeau and his followers firmly believed that the special status granted to natives by the Indian Act was at least partly to blame for the discrimination against them. According to the White Paper,

> The separate legal status of Indians and the policies which have flowed from it have kept the Indian people apart from and behind other. . . . The treatment resulting from their different status has been often worse, sometimes equal and occasionally better than that accorded to their fellow citizens. What matters is that it has been different.

The White Paper recommended the repeal of the Indian Act, the dissolution of the Indian Division of the Department of Indian Affairs and Northern Development (DIAND), and the transfer to the provinces of all responsibility for the delivery of social services to natives.

In order to gain native approval of its proposals, the government facilitated and funded the formation of a variety of native political organizations. The most prominent of these was the National Indian Brotherhood, which later became the Assembly of First Nations. Much to the surprise of the Trudeau government, these native political organizations were nearly unanimous in their rejection of the White Paper proposal. Their objections were many but hinged primarily on the failure of the Trudeau government to recognize native claims of aboriginal rights and sovereignty. These, they believed, would require the acceptance of long-ignored treaty obligations and the settlement of land claims.

Faced with such outspoken and vocal opposition, the Trudeau government withdrew the White Paper in 1970 but continued in various other says to disavow the notion of distinct rights for natives and other cultural minorities. It was later to acknowledge a measure of "existing aboriginal and treaty rights" via the 1982 Constitution Act. Subsequent governments, while implementing some of the White Paper proposals (specifically the transfer of responsibility for social services to the provinces), have also negotiated land claims and aboriginal rights agreements with a number of native political entities.

See also: Department of Indian Affairs and Northern Development; Indian Act of 1876; Indian Act of 1951; Indian Act of 1989; Indian-white relations: Canadian; Treaties and agreements in Canada.

Pamela R. Stern

Wild west shows

Date: 1883-1914
Locale: United States and Europe
Tribes involved: Sioux, other Plains tribes
Categories: Nineteenth century history, Twentieth century history
Significance: Wild west shows, in re-creating events from the American frontier days, fixed the image of the American Plains Indian in the minds of European Americans and the world.

From 1883 until World War I, hundreds of North American Indians—primarily from the Great Plains—took part in a variety of wild west shows that traveled throughout the United States, Canada, and Europe. Buffalo Bill Cody staged the first one in 1883, and it was immediately joined by many imitators. "Wild wests," usually held outdoors in big arenas, were an entertaining combination of rodeo, circus, and stage play. Their intent was to present "a living picture of life on the frontier," as one poster explained. In addition to trick riders, sharpshooters, and cowboy bands, these shows featured reenactments of famous events from the recent Plains Indian wars, even recruiting as performers some of the Indian people who had

An 1899 poster advertising Buffalo Bill Cody's Wild West Show. (Library of Congress)

participated in the battles and events being portrayed. Many famous Indians of the day who were highly regarded by their own people as warriors, holy men, and wise men took part in these shows. Notable wild west participants included men who not many years before were considered to be "hostiles"—men such as Bull, Red Cloud, American Horse, Chief Joseph, Geronimo, and Rain in the Face.

Many of the Indians who took part in the shows had already begun to gain notoriety as outspoken critics of federal Indian policy and were able to use the shows for public-relations purposes. Government policy of the time sought to assimilate Indians into mainstream society, reduce their land base, and erase many customs and traditions. Humanitarian Christian reformers and others who believed that Indians should shed their past and accept the civilization of whites vehemently opposed Indian participation in these shows, fearing that they glorified the warrior days and would thereby delay acceptance of the federal government's assimilationist policies. Wild west shows, which emphasized Plains Indian lifeways, were thus attractive to many Indians because they placed a value on the older way of life and became a natural forum from which to speak out on Indian issues. Reservation life was difficult in the 1880's and 1890's, and the federal government sought to suppress most traditional cultural and religious expression. Now, suddenly, newspapers were carrying interviews with the Indian performers as they met and spoke with politicians, kings, queens, and presidents. Although Indian policy did not change drastically, an eloquent Indian voice of opposition was heard. The wide popularity of the wild west shows made them influential in more lasting ways, as well. Because most shows recruited their Indian performers from the Sioux reservations, particularly Pine Ridge and Rosebud, the image of the Plains Sioux began to take its place in the popular imagination as the quintessential American Indian.

Even though government officials voiced opposition to wild west shows, the secretary of the interior permitted Indians to tour and enforced a number of regulations to protect the performers, following a number of mishaps. Promoters were compelled to pay performers a fair wage for their time and services, usually fifteen to thirty dollars a month for women and twenty-five to ninety dollars a month for men. Additionally, the shows were required to provide all meals, transportation, and medical expenses. At the end of their contracts, all Indians were to be returned to their reservations at the show's expense. Show owners posted bonds of two to twenty thousand dollars, based on the numbers of Indians employed.

Wild west shows continued until World War I. After the war, films replaced wild wests but for the most part adhered to the image of the Indian the shows had created. The wild west shows were a fascinating chapter in white-Indian relations and contributed many potent symbols that are still prominent in American legend.

See also: Indian-white relations: U.S., 1934-2002; Wounded Knee Massacre.

Carole A. Barrett

Winnebago Uprising

Date: June 26-September 27, 1827
Locale: Prairie du Chien, Wisconsin
Tribes involved: Winnebago
Categories: Nineteenth century history, Wars and battles
Significance: This uprising against white settlers resulted in the death of several whites, imprisonment and death of the warrior leader Red Bird, and seizure of Winnebago land.

A combination of increasing traffic on the Mississippi River and a lead-mining rush in 1821 brought thousands of miners and settlers from the east to Winnebago territory, and hostile incidents and confrontations between whites and Indians began almost immediately. They culminated in June of 1827, when two Winnebagos were arrested for murdering a white family. A false rumor circulated that the two Indians had been turned over to the Chippewa, hated enemies of the Winnebago, and beaten to death by them. Responding to this rumor, Red Bird, a warrior, was asked by tribal leaders to retaliate against the whites. On June 26, 1827, two men and a child were killed. Three days later two crewmen on keelboats were killed, and four wounded.

The government threatened severe reprisals. On September 27, Red Bird surrendered to save his tribe and the Red Bird War or Winnebago Uprising ended. Red Bird died in prison shortly thereafter, and the government used the uprising as a pretext to seize the Winnebagos' lead-mining lands.

See also: Black Hawk War.

Laurence Miller

Winters v. United States

Date: 1908
Locale: Fort Belknap Reservation, Montana
Tribes involved: Gros Ventre, Assiniboine
Categories: Court cases, Nineteenth century history, Reservations and relocation, Twentieth century history
Significance: The Supreme Court established the reserved water rights doctrine through the Winters decision, where it ruled that water bordering and running though reservations belongs to tribes, not states.

In the late nineteenth century, non-Indian farmers in Montana began irrigating farms with water from the Milk River. Twenty years later, Gros Ventre and Assiniboine Indians on the Fort Belknap Reservation began farming operations on its lands near the Milk River. Non-Indian farmers claimed prior appropriation—that they used the water first—so they built dams and reservoirs to prevent tribal use of the water. The tribes appealed to federal court, saying that when they negotiated for their reservation they also had negotiated for rights to the water. Ultimately, the Supreme Court agreed with the tribes and clarified that reservation lands were not given to tribes by the federal government but were lands reserved by the tribes from lands ceded to the United States, and further, that the tribes have rights to water on or near their reservations. Other court cases made it clear that as needs for water change, tribes will continue to have access to adequate water supplies. This reserved water rights doctrine is controversial because it affects western states' access to water and puts tribal needs ahead of the needs of states.

Carole A. Barrett

See also: Reservation system of the United States; *United States v. Washington.*

Wolf Mountains, Battle of

Date: January 1-8, 1877
Locale: Wolf Mountains, Montana
Tribes involved: Cheyenne, Oglala Sioux
Categories: Nineteenth century history, Wars and battles
Significance: This battle, the last fight between the U.S. Army and the Cheyenne and Sioux, ended in stalemate but sufficiently weakened the Indians that they sought peace shortly thereafter.

After the U.S. Army's resounding defeat at the Battle of the Little Bighorn in June, 1876, the United States redoubled its resolve to defeat the Indians. The Powder River expedition, under the command of General George Crook and Colonel Nelson A. Miles, soundly defeated the Cheyenne in the Wolf Mountains on November 6, 1876. The survivors joined the Oglala Sioux camp under Crazy Horse.

In a series of skirmishes and running battles on January 1, 3, and 7, and a five-hour battle on January 8, 1877, in the Wolf Mountains, Miles was able to drive the Indians out. He was then stopped by fatigue and a shortage of supplies, but the damage to the Indians was already done. Their weakened condition, lack of food, and increasing desire for peace led to negotiations. On May 6, 1877, Crazy Horse and his followers surrendered at the Red Cloud Agency, essentially marking the end of the Plains Indians wars.

See also: Fort Laramie Treaty of 1868; Little Bighorn, Battle of the; Rosebud Creek, Battle of; Sioux War.

Laurence Miller

Women of All Red Nations

Date: Established 1978
Locale: United States
Tribes involved: Pantribal in the United States
Categories: Organizations, Twentieth century history
Significance: WARN works for autonomy among Native American individuals and communities in areas of health care, legal issues, and economic matters.

Women of All Red Nations (WARN) exists for the purpose of achieving autonomy for Native Americans, whatever their tribal affiliation. This Rosebud, South Dakota, association works to establish local chapters across the country.

Many issues of importance to Native Americans fall within the focus of WARN activities. Health care, in particular women's health matters and the misuse of sterilization practices on Indian women, is the group's main concern. Other problems that WARN addresses include children's foster care, adoption, political imprisonment, and juvenile justice. Inequities resulting from abuses of energy resources development on Indian-owned land is another concern.

Since WARN is a grassroots organization, its efforts also include community education. Its focus is on self-reliance, whether it be for the individual or the local group affiliation. WARN also encourages Native American women to seek positions of leadership, both in and out of governments. WARN issues publications regarding health problems of Native American women and conducts an annual conference.

See also: American Indian Movement; American Indian Religious Freedom Act; Indian Child Welfare Act; Indian Claims Commission; Longest Walk.

Ruffin Stirling

World wars

Date: 1914-1918, 1939-1945
Locale: Canada, United States
Tribes involved: Pantribal
Categories: Wars and battles

Significance: The world wars, especially World War II, caused many North American Indians to have significant, and generally positive, contact with mainstream society; however, this contact led to national policies in Canada and the United states that sought to dissolve the Indian land base and force assimilation.

World War I. In both Canada and the United States, World War I brought changes in the Indian relationship with their respective governments, and there was pressure in both countries to increase production in agriculture, stock-raising, and timber resources. In the United States, more Indian lands were approved for sale or lease to non-Indians, creating a gradual loss of tribal lands. In Canada, the Indian Act was amended to permit Indian lands to be put into production without band approval, and once this occurred, the band was forced to provide funds to finance the operation. Despite poverty, native people on both sides of the border raised money for the Red Cross, purchased war bonds, and knitted bandages and other items for the war effort. During the war, some Indian people moved to urban areas to work as shipbuilders or in factories.

Indians in both countries were not citizens, so they were not subject to conscription into military service. However, large numbers of native men did join the military. In Canada, Indian men joined at a rate comparable to the non-Indian population, with about 35 percent of the total male Indian population serving in the Canadian Expeditionary Services. In the United States, large numbers enlisted in the military, primarily the Army, and Indians enlisted in greater proportion than any other population. Many Indians on reservations located in the northern United States joined the Canadian military because Canada entered the war against Germany earlier. In both countries, Indian and white soldiers served together in military units, and since the national goal for Indians in Canada and the United States was assimilation, this integration of troops was viewed as an opportunity for Indians to learn the white man's ways. While in the military, Canadian Indians were permitted to vote; however, this right was rescinded at the end of the war as were other rights and veterans' benefits. In the United States, in gratitude for service, any Indian honorably discharged from the military was granted citizenship through an Act of Congress on November 6, 1919. American citizenship in no way abridged rights as a tribal member. In 1924, the United States Congress extended citizenship to all Indians, partially in return for patriotism demonstrated by all Native people during World War I.

World War II. In World War II, Indians in Canada and the United States were subject to military service because they had, by now, become citizens.

Large numbers joined the military voluntarily in any case. Again, some Indians on northern reservations in the United States entered the Canadian military, because that country declared war before the United States. In the United States, over twenty-five thousand men joined the military and over two hundred women joined the WACS or WAVES. Unlike their Japanese and African American counterparts, Indians served in integrated units. There were a few all-Navajo training units for Indians who did not speak English, but once they learned the language, they joined white units. Tribes with strong warrior traditions volunteered in disproportionate numbers, and in the Northern Plains some Indian men brought their own rifles to induction stations. On all the reservations there was a great deal of enthusiasm and pride in the young men and women who volunteered for military service. It was common for family members or the tribal community to honor the new recruits by sponsoring a feast and having old men talk about the tribal traditions of warfare. On some Northern Plains reservations, old men who had participated in battles against the United States military in their youth recounted their deeds as a way to inspire this new generation of warriors. When these young men returned from the war, they were expected to recite their own exploits in order to carry forth the tribal warrior traditions. During the war, the media in both Canada and the United States carried many stories about Indian soldiers in World War II, and almost universally, the men were praised for natural fighting instincts, endurance, and ferocity. Additionally, many articles praised the Indian soldiers for their loyalty and willingness to sacrifice for their countries. More than once, Indians were proclaimed to be the perfect soldier. Partly as a result of these stereotypes, Indians were assigned as scouts, fought on the front lines, and generally saw a good deal of combat action. Comanche, Sac

Three reservists with the U.S. Marine Corps during World War II (left to right): Minnie Spotted Wolf (Blackfoot), Celia Mix (Potawatomi), and Viola Eastman (Chippewa). (National Archives)

and Fox, and most notably Navajo men were pressed into duty as code talkers in the Army and Marine signal corps. They used tribal languages to develop codes and communicate between units, and the enemy could not penetrate their coded messages.

On the reservations, there was a great deal of support for the war effort. More tribal lands were put into production to raise crops for food. Reservation resources were made available to the federal government, and some reservation lands were turned into gunnery or bombing ranges. Tribal councils, as well as individual Indians, purchased war bonds and donated sums of money to the war effort. Indian youth in boarding and day schools contributed money and time to doing projects for the Red Cross. Due to the war and resulting personnel and monetary shortages, the United States government significantly cut back medical, educational, and other services on reservations. Thousands of Indians in Canada and the United States left their reservations for wartime jobs in urban areas. For the first time, large numbers of Indians came into contact with white society.

In 1943 Ira Hayes, a Pima, was a paratrooper with the U.S. Marine Corps. He was one of four Marines who appeared in the famous photograph that shows them raising the U.S. flag over Iwo Jima. (National Archives)

Impact of Wartime. World War II was a significant event in modern American Indian life. Indian servicemen enjoyed respect and freedom of association in the military, a contrast to the discrimination they often faced at home. Also, those Indians who moved to urban areas to work enjoyed a higher standard of living, and for the first time, large numbers of Indian children attended public schools. In urban areas, as in the military, Indian people generally found acceptance. As a result, some Native Americans decided to reside permanently in urban areas. Canadian and American federal policies had always sought the assimilation of Indians as individuals into mainstream society. As a result, after World War II there was much talk of "freeing" or "emancipating" all Indians from the segregated environment of the reservations through the withdrawal or termination of federal obligations. In the United States, there were efforts to settle outstanding land claims through the Indian Claims Commission (1946) and then to terminate the federal relationship with tribes. A good deal of public attention was directed at ways to solve the so-called Indian problems in the United States. Conservatives supported the pullout of federal services as beneficial because it would mean less government regulation and interference, while liberals supported pullouts as a way to promote democratic ideals. Both groups sought to end the reservation system.

From the Indian perspective, their reservations were homelands, not the outdoor prisons politicians described them as being. Tribal people on both sides of the border sought to preserve their aboriginal homelands because they were absolutely necessary to cultural survival and integrity as a people. Nonetheless, assimilationist policies prevailed throughout the 1950's and 1960's, and there was steady erosion of tribal sovereignty, tribal land bases, and continuous attempts to dissolve the reservation system. However, as a result of service in World War II and full participation in the war effort, American Indians increasingly demanded a voice in their own affairs. They began to assert their rights under treaties, organize politically, and take advantage of greater opportunities for higher education, and in the end, they were able to guide development of new national policies of self-determination.

Carole A. Barrett

Sources for Further Study

Bernstein, Alison R. *American Indians and World War II: Toward a New Era in Indian Affairs.* Norman: University of Oklahoma Press, 1991. Documents Indian participation in the war and the ongoing struggle for tribal sovereignty and self-determination.

Dempsey, James. "Problems of Western Canadian Indian War Veterans after World War I." *Native Studies Review* 5, no. 2 (1989): 1-18. Canadian Indian war veterans did not receive the same benefits as non-Indians, lost their right to vote, and were even encouraged to pursue hunting and trapping as a livelihood after the war.

Hauptman, Laurence M. *The Iroquois Struggle for Survival: World War II to Red Power*. Syracuse, N.Y.: Syracuse University Press, 1986. Provides a case study of Iroquois participation in World War II and analyzes the quest for tribal rights after the war.

Nash, Gerald D. *The American West Transformed: The Impact of the Second World War*. Bloomington: University of Indiana Press, 1988. American Indian tribal life, always intimately connected to national trends and policies, underwent profound changes because American life, especially in the West, altered after the war.

See also: Code talkers; Indian Act of 1951; Indian Citizenship Act; Indian Claims Commission; Indian New Deal; Termination Resolution.

Wounded Knee Massacre

Date: December 29, 1890
Locale: Wounded Knee Creek, twenty miles east of Pine Ridge, South Dakota
Tribes involved: Sioux
Categories: Nineteenth century history, Wars and battles
Significance: The last Indian war heralds the close of the American frontier and the end of traditional life for Native Americans.

The Battle of Wounded Knee, on December 29, 1890, was preceded on December 15 by the slaying of Sitting Bull, the last great Sioux warrior chief. His death resulted from an effort to suppress the Ghost Dance religion, which had been begun by Wovoka. Wovoka's admixture of American Indian and Christian beliefs inspired hope in an eventual triumph of the American Indians over the white settlers, who, Wovoka envisioned, would fall through the earth and disappear forever. Although Wovoka preached passivity and patience, some of his zealous disciples carried a slightly more aggressive message, among them a Minneconjou Sioux named Kicking Bear and his brother-in-law, Short Bull. They and other followers of Wovoka introduced the Ghost Dance to the Dakota reservations, including Standing Rock and Pine Ridge.

In an effort to suppress Ghost Dancing, James McLaughlin, the government agent in charge of the Standing Rock reservation, first arrested Kicking Bear, then moved against Sitting Bull, an old adversary and, in McLaughlin's mind, the cynosure of tribal unrest. McLaughlin was convinced that Ghost Dancing could be suppressed only if Sitting Bull were in prison. He called Sitting Bull a fomenter of disturbances, prompting General Nelson A. Miles, U.S. Army Commander of the Missouri Division, to send Buffalo Bill Cody to Standing Rock to persuade the chief to negotiate with Miles. However, McLaughlin complained to Washington and had Cody's mission aborted.

Death of Sitting Bull. What followed was a fiasco. Forty-three American Indian police, commanded by Lieutenant Bull Head, surrounded Sitting Bull's cabin and ordered him outside. Sitting Bull obeyed, but one of the assembled Ghost Dancers, angered at the arrest, wounded Bull Head with a rifle. Attempting to hit his assailant, Bull Head accidentally shot Sitting Bull at the same time that another American Indian policeman fired a lethal shot through the old chief's head.

When news of Sitting Bull's death reached Big Foot, chief of the Minneconjou at Cherry Creek, he decamped his followers and started a journey toward Pine Ridge, hoping to find protection under Chief Red Cloud. His band consisted of 120 men and 230 women and children. Big

The gruesome aftermath of the Wounded Knee Massacre: innocent victims buried in mass graves. (Library of Congress)

Foot himself was ill with pneumonia and had to make the journey in a wagon. On December 28, near Porcupine Creek, the natives encountered troops of the Seventh U.S. Cavalry under the command of Major Samuel Whitside. Although near death, Big Foot arranged a meeting with Whitside, who informed the chief that his orders were to escort the American Indians to Wounded Knee Creek. Big Foot agreed to comply with the major's directions, because Wounded Knee was on the way to Pine Ridge. Whitside then had his men move Big Foot to an Army ambulance to make the trip more comfortable.

The combined trains reached Wounded Knee Creek before nightfall. Whitside saw to their encampment south of his military bivouac. He provided them with rations, some tents, and a surgeon to tend to Big Foot. He also took measures to ensure that none of the American Indians could escape, posting sentinels and setting up rapid-fire Hotchkiss guns in key positions.

During the night, the remaining troops of the Seventh Cavalry arrived, and command of the operation passed from Major Whitside to Colonel James W. Forsyth. The colonel told the junior officer that he had received orders to accompany Big Foot's bands to the Union Pacific Railroad for transport to a military prison in Omaha. The next morning, after issuing hardtack rations to the Indians, Colonel Forsyth ordered them to turn over their weapons. Soldiers stacked up the surrendered arms and ammunition. Not satisfied that all weapons had been turned in, Forsyth sent details to search the tipis. Then the searchers ordered the natives to remove their blankets, which, the soldiers assumed, masked some hidden weapons.

The situation grew tense. The Indians were both humiliated and angry, but they were badly outnumbered and almost all of them had been disarmed. Only the Minneconjou medicine man, Yellow Bird, openly protested. He began Ghost Dance steps and chanted lines from the holy songs that assured the Indians that their Ghost Shirts would not let the soldiers' bullets strike them.

The soldiers found only two rifles during the last search, but one of them belonged to a deaf Sioux brave named Black Coyote, who resisted. Soldiers grabbed him and spun him around, attempting to disarm him, and at that point Black Coyote fired his Winchester, probably by accident. A debacle followed.

The soldiers opened fire on the unarmed Minneconjou at once, slaughtering many of them with repeated volleys from their carbines. Most of the Indians tried to flee, but the Hotchkiss guns opened up on them from their hillside positions. Firing almost a round a second, the soldiers' shots tore into the camp, indiscriminately killing braves, women, and children. The Hotchkiss guns turned the rout into a massacre.

Slaughter of Indians. When it was over, Big Foot and more than half of his followers were either dead or seriously wounded. One hundred fifty-three lay dead on the ground, but many of the fatally wounded had crawled off to die elsewhere. One estimate claimed that there were barely more than fifty native survivors, only those transported after the massacre. Only twenty-five soldiers were killed, most of them having fallen to friendly fire, not to the Indians.

After the wounded troopers were decamped and sent off toward Pine Ridge, a detail of soldiers rounded up the surviving Indians: four men and forty-seven women and children. Placed in wagons, they also set out for Pine Ridge, leaving their dead to a blizzard that prevented their immediate burial and froze them into grotesque, hoary reminders of the debacle.

An inquiry followed the events at Wounded Knee, prompted by General Miles, who brought charges against Forsyth, but the colonel was exonerated and nothing else came of the investigation. The affair traditionally has been viewed as the last resistance of the Indians to reservation resettlement. It and the death of Sitting Bull, both in 1890, although not singled out, were certainly factors in the conclusions of Frederick Jackson Turner, who claimed in his renowned 1893 thesis that the U.S. frontier had closed in the year of the massacre.

For American Indians, however, the infamous day did not die with the victims. On February 27, 1973, more than two hundred members of the American Indian Movement (AIM) took the reservation site at Wounded Knee by force, proclaiming it the Independent Oglala Sioux Nation and demanding that the federal government make amends for past injustices by reviewing all American Indian treaties and policies. Federal marshals immediately surrounded the group and after two months, coaxed them to surrender with promises of an airing of grievances. For American Indians, Wounded Knee has remained an important symbol of the Euro-American injustice and suppression of their people.

See also: Indian-white relations: U.S., 1871-1933; Wounded Knee occupation.

John W. Fiero

Sources for Further Study

Brown, Dee. *Bury My Heart at Wounded Knee: An Indian History of the American West*. New York: Holt, Rinehart & Winston, 1970. A very readable, popular account of the displacement and oppression of the American

Indian nations by European settlers, from the beginning to 1890. Includes a helpful but dated bibliography.

Gonzalez, Mario, and Elizabeth Cook-Lynn. *The Politics of Hallowed Ground: Wounded Knee and the Struggle for Indian Sovereignty.* Urbana: University of Illinois Press, 1999. An account of the Wounded Knee Survivors' Association to obtain formal apology from the U.S. government for the massacre and to name the site a National American Monument.

Jensen, Richard E., R. Eli Paul, and John E. Carter. *Eyewitness at Wounded Knee.* Lincoln: University of Nebraska Press, 1992. Fine collection of photographs from the Wounded Knee battlefield and related sites, with essays on the American Indian perspective, the Army's role, and the distorted media coverage.

Klein, Christina. "'Everything of Interest in the Late Pine Ridge War Are Held by Us for Sale': Popular Culture and Wounded Knee." *Western Historical Quarterly* 25 (Spring, 1994): 45-68. Argues that commercial exploitation of Wounded Knee in Cody's Wild West show, photographs, and the dime novel played as significant a role as the military in defeating the Ghost Dancers' dreams of American Indian autonomy. Includes photographs.

Neihardt, John G. *Black Elk Speaks: Being the Life Story of a Holy Man of the Oglala Sioux.* 1932. Reprint. Lincoln: University of Nebraska Press, 1979. This classic work chronicles the spiritual odyssey of Black Elk, a holy man of the Oglala Sioux. Provides important insight into American Indian beliefs and an account of the Wounded Knee Massacre.

Utley, Robert M. *Last Days of the Sioux Nation.* New Haven, Conn.: Yale University Press, 1963. A highly regarded, sensitive, evenhanded study that documents the events leading up to Wounded Knee. Contains a chapter on sources, making it invaluable for further study.

Voices from Wounded Knee, 1973. Rooseveltown, N.Y.: Akwesasne Notes, 1974. With edited transcripts of interviews, documents the efforts of the Oglala Sioux to gain national sympathy for the plight of the American Indian by their stand at Wounded Knee Creek in 1973. Includes a chronicle of events from 1868 to 1973 and an account of the 1890 massacre.

Wounded Knee occupation

Date: February 27-May 8, 1973
Locale: Pine Ridge Reservation, South Dakota

Tribes involved: Lakota Sioux, Oglala Sioux
Categories: Protest movements, Twentieth century history
Significance: Native Americans highlight their grievances against the
U.S. government by staging an armed occupation at an old battle site.

Internal strife on the Oglala reservation had reached the explosive stage by February, 1973, when the village of Wounded Knee, site of the last massacre of the Indian Wars in 1890, became the focal point for another confrontation between American Indians and U.S. military forces.

Tribal unemployment was at 54 percent, not counting those tribe members who lived in cities. Many of those with jobs worked for the government. One-third of the people were on welfare or similar pensions. Median income was around eight hundred dollars per year. Children were malnourished. Poverty, alcoholism, and suicide were widespread, and the average life span for Oglalas was forty-six years of age.

In February, 1972, an elderly American Indian had died after a public beating by two white men, who were charged with only second-degree manslaughter and released without paying bail. The American Indian Movement (AIM) was called in to support the family, and a full investigation showed evidence of misdealing in this and other incidents. As AIM's popularity increased nationally, the positions of Sioux tribal chairman Richard Wilson and other government-employed American Indians were being threatened.

Wilson Stirs Controversy. The trouble at Wounded Knee began with the controversy over chairman Wilson, who had a heavy drinking habit, had been identified as a bootlegger, and nearly had been indicted on charges of misuse of federal funds. After his extravagantly funded campaign, Wilson awarded positions to more than nine hundred supporters, including his wife and sons, and had given a twenty-five thousand dollar job to his brother. He claimed that nothing was said in tribal law about nepotism.

Wilson used federal highway funds to arm his private police force. Known as the "goon squad" because of their brutality, they called themselves Guardians of the Oglala Nation (GOON) and suppressed with beatings or threats anyone who challenged Wilson. The Bureau of Indian Affairs (BIA), the Federal Bureau of Investigation (FBI), and the Justice Department gave full support to Wilson when he offered his goon squad's services to attack members of AIM.

Several elder Oglala women had spoken out about Wilson's incompetence. "[He] hasn't got the backbone to stand up and protect his Indians," declared Gladys Bissonnette. Grace Black Elk said, "He hates AIM people because they are doing what he should have been doing." Ellen Moves Camp wondered, "Why is it that the government is backing him up so much?"

Wilson had fired the tribal vice president for supporting AIM and had banned AIM leader Russell Means from the reservation, threatening to "personally cut his braids off." Returning to his Pine Ridge home, Means was immediately arrested by BIA tribal police. Dennis Banks, with Means during the BIA takeover in Washington, D.C., was taken into custody upon his arrival. Both were released pending later trials. Citing suspicion of corruption, tribal members and AIM leaders began impeachment proceedings against Wilson, who illegally terminated the action. Attempts to speak out against this were quelled by further intimidation and violence.

AIM Protests. In January, 1973, a young American Indian was stabbed to death by a white man. A riot ensued while AIM leaders were meeting with officials in the courthouse at Calico. In late February, traditional people marched on the Pine Ridge BIA building to protest Wilson's actions and the illegal presence of U.S. marshals on their reservation.

AIM again was summoned by spokesman Chief Fools Crow, and more than six hundred people were at the meeting led by Means and Banks. Lakota mothers pleaded for protection for the children by asking that the fighting spirit return. One by one, the chiefs stood up. The Lakota would gather at the most symbolic spot on the reservation, Wounded Knee, for what was expected to be a two- or three-day stand. A public statement, signed by eight Oglala chiefs and medicine men, demanded treaty hearings and investigation of the BIA.

A poster inviting participation in a demonstration sponsored by the American Indian Movement to support the struggle of Native Americans at Wounded Knee in 1973. (Library of Congress)

The next day, approximately two hundred Oglalas armed with hunting rifles were stationed at Wounded Knee. They were surrounded by the FBI, state police, and U.S. marshals armed with high-powered weapons and riding in armored personnel carriers. They were surrounded by BIA tribal police, while planes and helicopters circled the area. The media soon arrived.

Many separate factions were involved at Wounded Knee II: Wilson, his corrupt government, his GOON, and some older leaders in the tribal council who did not condone Wilson's methods, but were concerned about the possibility of losing federal support; the FBI, the BIA, U.S. marshals, and other government forces—all of whom were waging a war against AIM, the young militants, and the traditional elders who were trying to preserve the old ways.

On the third day, Fools Crow had just begun talks with traditionalists, AIM people, and federal authorities, when shots were exchanged. With military planes flying overhead, there was much confusion and many people were injured.

In the days and weeks that followed, much occurred at Wounded Knee: People hiked in at night to bring supplies and support; two U.S. senators visited; Wilson threatened to attack with nine hundred men; the Independent Oglala Nation (ION) was created; citizenships were granted; government agents were caught inside the compound; negotiations continued; a blizzard inundated the area; firefights continued; food and fuel ran out; airlifts arrived; medicine men Black Elk and Crow Dog led a Ghost Dance and pipe ceremonies; a wedding was performed by Black Elk; an Iroquois Six Nation delegation arrived; a child was born; the trading post burned; a U.S. marshal was disabled; and two American Indian men died.

In spite of ongoing firefights, the leaders had helped to maintain the spiritual bonds of community. Wallace Black Elk or Leonard Crow Dog held prayer ceremonies with the sacred pipe before every meeting. Although Fools Crow went into Wounded Knee thirteen times, he remained neutral and continued to pray for peace throughout the long siege. He guided negotiations and carried in the peace document that finally ended the standoff.

More than two hundred Lakotas had begun the occupation and others had joined. Nearly four hundred American Indians were arrested as a result. According to Peter Matthiessen, author of *In the Spirit of Crazy Horse*, the U.S. Army was involved directly in behind-the-scenes operations as "military intelligence, and perhaps weapons and equipment, were provided to civilian authorities, with unofficial approval reportedly coming all the way from the White House." He also cited reports that the FBI requested two thousand soldiers to seize control of the reservation so arrests could be made, but the request was refused. The eight volunteers who had airlifted food and medical supplies were later charged with conspiracy and interfering with the official duties of federal troops.

Means and Banks were arrested later, but charges were dismissed because of evidence of perjury by government witnesses. In April, 1975, *The New York Times* reported that violence resulting from Wounded Knee II had continued. According to an FBI report, six people had been killed and sixty-seven assaulted on the Pine Ridge Reservation since January 1.

The fighting spirit of the Lakota had returned. As Black Elk declared, "Now, this is a turning point. The hoop, the sacred hoop, was broken here at Wounded Knee, and it will come back again."

See also: American Indian Movement; Pine Ridge shootout and Peltier killings; Wounded Knee Massacre.

Gale M. Thompson

Sources for Further Study
Matthiessen, Peter. *In the Spirit of Crazy Horse*. 2d ed. New York: Viking Press, 1991. Covers Lakota struggles with the United States, including Little Big Horn, Wounded Knee I and II, and the 1975 Pine Lodge shootout that resulted in Leonard Peltier's imprisonment. Personal accounts, trial records, chapter notes, index.

Sayer, John William. *Ghost Dancing the Law: The Wounded Knee Trials*. Cambridge, Mass.: Harvard University Press, 2000. The first book-length study of the trials looks at the influence of media and legal institutions on the way the defendants and their cause were constrained in the presentation of their case.

Smith, Paul Chaat, and Robert Allen Warrior. *Like a Hurricane: The American Indian Movement from Alcatraz to Wounded Knee*. New York: New Press, 1997. A history of AIM focusing on its leadership.

Voices from Wounded Knee, 1973: In the Words of the Participants. Rooseveltown, N.Y.: Akwesasne Notes, 1974. Includes daily events during occupation; logs kept by U.S. marshals; quotations, interviews, diaries, and taped radio conversations from a ten-day battle; negotiations; treaty meetings at Kyle; maps and photographs.

Waldman, Carl. *Atlas of the North American Indian*. New York: Facts on File, 1985. Comprehensive coverage of history and culture; land cessions and wars; and contemporary issues. Maps and illustrations; historical chronology; locations of tribes and reservations; place names; museums and archaeological sites in the United States and Canada.

Zimmerman, Bill. *Airlift to Wounded Knee.* Chicago: Swallow Press, 1976. Chronicle of eight airlift participants who delivered food and medical supplies during the occupation and were subsequently indicted for conspiracy and interfering with official duties of federal troops. Photos, notes, comments by author's attorney.

Yakima War

Date: 1855-1856
Locale: South-central Washington State
Tribes involved: Cayuse, Umatilla, Walla Walla, Yakima
Categories: Nineteenth century history, Wars and battles
Significance: A gold strike in north-central Washington caused a major influx of European gold seekers to encroach on the isolated territories of the Yakima tribe, leading to the Yakima War.

The Yakimas lived in an area that was relatively isolated until the mid-nineteenth century—the Columbia River Valley in south-central Washington. Conditions changed suddenly, however, when a gold strike in north-central Washington created an influx of white gold seekers. In general, relations between Indians and European-descended residents in the Northwest in the 1850's were characterized by mutual suspicion and dislike, and the latest arrivals made things worse as isolated attacks and retaliations increased.

Isaac Stevens, the newly appointed governor of the new Northwest Territory, arrived in Olympia in 1853 to take over his duties. Stevens was determined to persuade all the tribes in the territory to give up their lands and accept being moved to reservations. He ordered his treaty commission secretary, James Doty, to organize a grand treaty council in the Walla Walla area. It was attended by about a thousand Yakimas, including Chief Kamiakin, and members of other area tribes and bands. There was a disagreement among the tribes as to whether to agree to the treaty, but most tribes finally did. Kamiakin was among those leaders who refused. A treaty was signed on June 9, 1855. An Indian agent, Andrew Bolon, was killed by a band of Indians in Yakima country, however, and Major Granville O. Haller was sent to Yakima country from The Dalles. The purpose of his 102-man expedition was to avenge Bolon's death.

The first major battle of the Yakima War occurred at the foot of Eel Trail on Toppenish Creek, where Haller and his forces suffered a substantial defeat. Following this skirmish a full-scale war erupted when several tribes joined with the Yakimas in order to drive the European Americans from their country. Major Gabriel Rains was ordered to avenge Haller's defeat in Yakima country.

Rains's forces pursued the Native Americans to Union Gap (near present-day Yakima). After the Yakimas escaped across the Yakima River, the Union forces proceeded to a nearby Catholic mission and razed it, believing that the mission's Father Pandum had aided and abetted the Yakimas. During the spring of 1856 the fighting resumed with a Yakima attack at a blockade in the Cascades.

Colonel George Wright was in command of the Northwest forces at the time. Wright intensified the campaign against the Yakimas, and a truce was agreed upon in 1856. The volunteers who had participated in the Yakima campaign were dismissed, and with the construction of Fort Simcoe, the U.S. military established control of the Yakima Valley.

By September, 1856, Wright's forces had established control of the area west of the Cascades. Since the original truce was not completely successful, a second Walla Walla Council was organized by Governor Stevens; he demanded unconditional surrender by the Native Americans. In spite of the fact that Chief Kamiakin and other band leaders did not participate, the 1855-1856 Yakima War was essentially terminated at the end of the second Walla Walla Council.

See also: Walla Walla Council.

Bruce M. Mitchell

Yamasee War

Date: 1715-1728
Locale: Florida, Georgia, South Carolina
Tribes involved: Cherokee, Choctaw, Creek, Yamasee
Categories: Colonial history, Wars and battles
Significance: This largest Indian war of the eighteenth century American South destroyed the Yamasee as a tribe and significantly changed English-Indian relations in the South.

Beginning in the 1680's, the Yamasee conducted a large amount of trade with the English in South Carolina, trading deerskins and Indian slaves for English guns and rum. After the Tuscarora War of 1711-1713, however, the ability of the Yamasee to pay for English goods declined. White settlement on Indian lands had ruined the Yamasee deer hunting grounds. The English victory in the Tuscarora War removed most of the tribes from which the Yamasee abducted their slaves. By the 1710's, the Yamasee were heavily indebted to Carolina traders. When they could not pay their debts, Carolina traders started to enslave Yamasee women and children as payment.

The Yamasee made an alliance with the Creeks and Catawbas, who also had trade grievances with the English, and began a war against South Carolina in April of 1715. The Yamasee and their allies attacked Carolina traders and settlements, killing four hundred English and driving the English out of the Port Royal region. The South Carolinians fought back with a hastily constructed army of colonial militia and African slaves, who made up half of the Carolina troops. The English won a decisive advantage after 1717, when they made an alliance with the powerful and abundant Cherokees. The defeated Creeks signed a peace treaty with the Carolinians in November, 1717, and moved westward. The defeated Yamasee retreated to Florida, from which they continued to raid South Carolina for several years, killing whites and stealing black slaves for sale to the Spanish. South Carolina conducted a final expedition against the Yamasee in 1728. The Yamasee were destroyed and subsequently lost their identity as a tribe.

The defeat of the Yamasee and the Creeks opened new lands to white settlement in Georgia and South Carolina. The war induced the Creeks to begin a policy of neutrality toward the English, French, and Spanish, playing the European powers against one another for maximum advantage. The Cherokees realized that the English were dependent upon them for military success, and began to make greater demands on them.

See also: Cherokee War; Indian slave trade; Tuscarora War.

Harold D. Tallant

Zuñi Rebellion

Date: February 22-27, 1632
Locale: Zuñi pueblos, New Mexico
Tribes involved: Zuñi, Pueblo peoples,
Categories: Colonial history, Wars and battles
Significance: A century after the first Spanish inroads into New Mexico, Puebloan peoples resist.

Zuñi Indian contact with Spanish explorers began in violence. The Zuñi lived in six pueblos widely scattered across what is now western New Mexico. They occupied communities of apartment houses built on the sides or tops of mesas. They had no central government, and each pueblo spoke a distinct language.

Spaniards first entered this territory in 1539. They came north from Mexico, hunting for great cities of gold reported to be in the area. The legend of the Seven Cities of Gold, called Cíbola, had spread through Spanish possessions in the New World three years earlier, when Álvar Núñez Cabeza de Vaca—a sailor who had spent eight years wandering through Texas and the Southwest after a shipwreck on the Gulf coast—brought to Mexico City the story he had been told by native peoples. The governor of New Spain sent an expedition led by a Franciscan priest, Marcos de Niza, and a former slave named Estevanico into the region to verify the story. Estevanico reached a Zuñi pueblo a few days before the priest. By the time Fray Marcos arrived, the Zuñi had killed Estevanico reportedly for taking liberties with Zuñi women. The priest returned south and, contrary to all evidence, told the governor what the latter wanted to hear: that the Seven Cities of Cíbola did exist and were as magnificent as legend had held.

In the summer of 1540, the Spanish launched an expedition of more than a hundred men, including several priests, led by Francisco Vásquez de Coronado, the governor of Nueva Galicia, a state in western Mexico. After six months of travel, the explorers reached the Zuñi villages previously visited by Fray Marcos and were greatly disappointed by the poverty they discovered. The Zuñis, fearing that the invaders were looking for slaves, met the Spaniards in front of their village and warned that trying to enter their homes meant death. Coronado explained through an interpreter that he had come on a sacred mission to save souls for Christ. A priest then read the *requerimiento*, a statement read by a priest before all battles, warning the Zuñi that if they did not accept Spain's king, Philip IV, as their ruler, and if they did not embrace Christianity, they would be killed or enslaved.

Zuñi Resistance. The Zuñis responded with arrows, killing several Spaniards, but Spanish muskets and steel swords proved far superior to native weapons, and Coronado's forces quickly destroyed much of the village. The Zuñis fled, leaving behind a large quantity of corn, beans, turkeys, and salt, but no gold. Coronado, who had traveled much of the way in full armor, received several wounds during the battle but survived. He concluded that Cíbola must be somewhere else. Before continuing his search, however, he destroyed the village, called Hawikuh by the Zuñis. Despite the victory, no Spaniard returned to Zuñi territory until 1629.

Zuñi Pueblo, New Mexico, in 1879 as "Mud Head" dancers prepare for a ceremony.
(National Archives)

By 1629, Franciscan missionaries had more than fifty churches in the area of New Mexico. Their headquarters in Santa Fe had been built by Pueblo Indian laborers in 1610. Most of the mission churches had been constructed by native labor, with women building the walls and the men doing the carpentry. The priests decided to reestablish contact with peoples living farther to the west. In 1629, eight priests traveled to Acoma, a village built on top of a four-hundred-foot mesa, where a church was built. The next year, Fray Estevàn de Pereá, sixty-four years of age, was sent to Hawikuh, about sixty miles west of Acoma. He found a village of eight hundred people, who greeted him peacefully. An interpreter told the Zuñis that the expedition had come to free them from slavery and the "darkness of idolatry." This was the same message brought to them a hundred years before by Coronado, and it had led to bloodshed. This time, however, the Zuñi allowed the Spanish to remain and build a church. Three years later it was completed.

Zuñi religious leaders, called sorcerers by the Christian fathers, fought the new religion from the very beginning. In their religion, there were many gods, not just one, who lived on the earth in trees, mountains, plants, and various animals. Zuñis worshiped water gods, according to Coronado, because water made the corn grow and sustained life in a very harsh climate. Water seemed almost as valuable to them as gold did to the Spaniards, something the Spaniards could not understand. Zuñi priests taught that people should live in harmony with the earth and learn to live with nature, not conquer it as Christians seemed to believe. Zuñis sought harmony in every aspect of their lives, which to them meant compromise and getting along with everything. They did fight wars, especially with Apache raiders, but violence and aggression were generally to be avoided. The Spaniards found little of value in these teachings and believed their god had chosen them to conquer the heathen, bring light to those living in darkness—which meant anyone who was not Christianized—and then grow rich, as God meant them to do. Compromise meant weakness to them; conquest, the highest good. These conflicting values would finally lead to rebellion and violence.

Another source of conflict between Zuñis and Spaniards was the system of labor that developed. Zuñis and other native peoples did most of the manual labor on construction projects; they also worked in mines and in the fields. Spanish nobles, government officials, and settlers simply did not work in these types of jobs; hard labor was beneath their dignity. Native Americans were forcibly recruited for this backbreaking labor. Wealthy Spanish landlords supposedly owned the right to the labor of all Indians living on their land under the *encomienda* system. They also received tribute from all families on their extensive properties, usually 1.6 bushels of maize (corn), and a cotton blanket or deer or buffalo hide each year. In times of drought, these payments were especially harsh and deeply resented.

Native peoples also hated the compulsory labor demanded of them by Spanish authorities. Thousands of Pueblo Indians, including Zuñis, had built Santa Fe under this system. They were supposed to be paid for their work, but many were not. In other places, the native peoples were used largely as pack animals to carry logs and heavy mining equipment across the desert. Many mines used slaves captured on frequent slaving expeditions into tribal territory. Slavery and economic exploitation added to Native American resentment of the Europeans.

Killing of Priests. On February 22, 1632, according to Spanish government records, Zuñi warriors killed Fray Francisco Letrado, the missionary at Hawikuh, during a mass he was celebrating to honor the completion of his church. The Zuñis then abandoned the pueblo and did not return for several years. Upon hearing of the killing, Governor Francisco de la Mora Ceballas sent a party of soldiers after the Zuñis. The soldiers found the Zuñi's hiding place and took revenge on the population, killing some and enslaving others.

Five days after the murder of Fray Letrado, Zuñis killed another priest, Fray Martín de Arvide, at a pueblo fifty miles west of Hawikuh. Two soldiers in Fray Martín's party were killed also. The governor sent another military expedition to avenge these deaths. Several Zuñis were killed in battle, and at least one was later executed for participating in the murders. The rebellion spread no further at this time, although Christian missionaries did not return to the Zuñi pueblos until 1660. The missionaries remained in the area until the rebellion of 1680, when violence between Spaniards and Zuñi again broke out and the Zuñi mission churches again were destroyed.

See also: Acoma, Battle of; Indian-white relations: Spanish colonial; Pueblo Revolt.

Leslie V. Tischauser

Sources for Further Study

Crampton, C. Gregory. *The Zuñis of Cíbola*. Provo: University of Utah Press, 1977. A general history of the Zuñi people. Black-and-white photographs illustrate how the Pueblos have changed over time.

Ganner, Van Hastings. "Seventeenth Century New Mexico." *Journal of Mexican American History* 4 (1974): 41-70. Provides a pro-Indian view of tribal relations with the Spanish. Includes a brief description of the events leading up to 1632.

Hodge, Frederick Webb. *History of Hawikah, New Mexico, One of the So-Called Cities of Cíbola*. Los Angeles: Southwest Museum, 1937. Contains translations of Spanish mission records and early histories of Spanish-Zuñi relations. The only detailed history of the revolt.

Scholes, France V. *Church and State in New Mexico, 1610-1650*. Historical Society of New Mexico Publications in History 7. Albuquerque: University of New Mexico Press, 1942. Takes a pro-Spanish point of view, treating Native Americans in a condescending manner. Based on translations of Spanish documents.

Weber, David J. *The Spanish Frontier in North America*. New Haven, Conn.: Yale University Press, 1992. A general overview and detailed history of the Spanish presence in North America, from the early 1500's to the 1830's. A balanced view of relations between Native Americans and the Spanish, with much useful information on religion, social structure, and culture.

Gazetteer of Historic Places

ACOMA PUEBLO, NEW MEXICO
Location: Forty-five miles southwest of Albuquerque, off U.S. Interstate 40 in northwestern New Mexico
Significance: This Native American village at the top of a mesa known as the Rock of Acuco is one of the oldest continuously occupied sites in the continental United States. The first inhabitants probably arrived between 1075 and 1200 C.E.

ALCATRAZ ISLAND, CALIFORNIA
Location: An island one and a half miles from the city of San Francisco
Significance: This was the site of the first U.S. fort on the Pacific Coast. It was used as a federal maximum-security prison between 1934 and 1963, occupied repeatedly by Native American groups between 1964 and 1971, and absorbed into the Golden Gate National Recreation Area, a National Park, in 1972.

ALKALI RIDGE, UTAH
Location: Monticello, San Juan County
Significance: This is a series of thirteen habitation sites along Alkali Mesa. Excavations helped clarify the development of Anasazi culture in the San Juan drainage, by defining the Pueblo II period (c. 900-1100 C.E.). Local development from Basketmaker III (400-700) through Pueblo III (1100-1300) periods was shown to be a continuous growth influenced by neighboring peoples.

ANGEL MOUNDS, INDIANA
Location: Evansville, Vanderburgh County
Significance: Covering a hundred-acre area, this site is the northeastern-most extension of the Mississippian culture, which flourished in the period 1000-1600 C.E. The mounds now form a state park.

AWATOVI RUINS, ARIZONA
Location: Keams Canyon, Navajo County
Significance: Located on the Hopi Indian Reservation, Awatovi Ruins is the site of one of the most important Hopi Indian villages encountered by Francisco Vásquez de Coronado's men in 1540. It contains the remains of a five-hundred-year-old pueblo and a seventeenth

century Spanish mission complex. Excavations were conducted at the site by the Peabody Museum in the 1930s.

AZTALAN, WISCONSIN

Location: Aztalan State Park, near Lake Mills on Wisconsin 89, Jefferson County

Significance: This large, stockaded temple mound site, first discovered in 1836, is the northernmost of the major Mississippian culture archaeological sites. It now forms Aztalan State Park. It represents an important northern extension of the Cahokia phase of the Middle Mississippi culture.

AZTEC RUINS, NEW MEXICO

Location: On the Animas River in northwestern New Mexico, just north of the town of Aztec; fourteen miles northeast of Farmington, New Mexico, or thirty-five miles southwest of Durango, Colorado, on U.S. Interstate 550

Significance: This monument, on twenty-seven acres, is devoted to Anasazi pueblo ruins dating from the twelfth through thirteenth centuries; it includes six major archaeological sites, partially excavated, and the only fully reconstructed Anasazi kiva (ceremonial chamber).

BANDELIER NATIONAL MONUMENT, NEW MEXICO

Location: Nearly fifty square miles on the Pajarito Plateau west of the Rio Grande; the main part of the site is about forty-six miles west of Santa Fe on Route 4, while the separate Tsankawi section of the monument, a large unexcavated Indian ruin on a high mesa, is eleven miles north from Bandelier on Route 4

Significance: The Pajarito Plateau is an elevated area of volcanic rock called tuff (hardened volcanic ash) and basaltic lava thrown out thousands of years ago by a great volcano. The surface of the plateau is crossed by deep gorges cut by streams running east to the Rio Grande valley. One of the largest and most accessible of these valleys is Frijoles Canyon, the site of numerous ruined structures and cliff dwellings built mostly between 1200 and 1400 C.E. by the Anasazi, ancestors of modern-day Pueblo Indians.

BAT CAVE, NEW MEXICO

Location: On the plains of San Agustin in southwestern New Mexico

Significance: The site of Bat Cave has provided some of the most complete evidence for manifestations of the Cochise culture, a regional variant of the more widespread Desert culture of the Archaic period in western North America. Archaeological remains at Bat Cave, excavated by archaeologist Herbert Dick, span a period of almost four thousand years, from 4000-200 B.C.E. The area in which Bat Cave is located was later the homeland of the Mogollon cultural tradition, which corresponds to the establishment of pottery-producing sedentary villages reliant on the rainfall cultivation of maize, squash, and other crops.

BEAR BUTTE, SOUTH DAKOTA

Location: Sturgis, Meade County

Significance: Sacred to the Cheyenne, Bear Butte is the place where Maheo imparted to Sweet Medicine (a mythical hero) the knowledge from which the Cheyenne derive their religious, political, social, and economic customs. The site is in Bear Butte State Park.

BEAR RIVER MASSACRE SITE, IDAHO

Location: Southeastern Idaho

Significance: On January 29, 1863, California Volunteers under the command of Colonel Patrick Edward Conner attacked a band of Northwestern Shoshone. The bloodiest encounter between Native American and white men to take place in the West in the years between 1848 and 1891, Bear River Massacre resulted in the deaths of almost three hundred Shoshone and fourteen soldiers.

BIG AND LITTLE PETROGLYPH CANYONS, CALIFORNIA

Location: China Lake, Inyo County

Significance: First reported in 1938, this site deep within the Coso Mountains is one of the most spectacular petroglyph areas known in the western United States, exhibiting more than twenty thousand designs. It represents at least two cultural phases.

BIG BEAD MESA, NEW MEXICO

Location: Near Ojo del Padre, Sandoval County

Significance: Occupied from about 1745 to 1812, this is an impressive fortified Navajo village site. After moving into the Big Bead Mesa region, the Navajos established a stronghold that menaced the pueblos of Laguna and Acoma and formed an alliance with the Gila Apaches. The site is an important representative of patterns of trade and raiding that characterized Navajo relations with Pueblos, Apache, and Hispanics.

BLOOD RUN SITE, IOWA

Location: Sioux Falls, Lyon County

Significance: Blood Run Site is the only known mound group attributable to the Oneota culture, which is ancestral to many midwestern Native American groups. The archaeological complex consists of the remains of a village that once included more than 158 visible conical burial mounds and an effigy earthwork. Limited archaeological data indicate Native American occupation of this site in the early 1700's extending back perhaps as far as 1300 c.e.

CAHOKIA, ILLINOIS

Location: The Cahokia Mounds State Historic and World Heritage Site is fifteen miles to the northeast, near Collinsville, extending just north of Route 40 and bordered on the east by U.S. Interstates 55 and 70, on the west by U.S. Interstate 255, and on the south by Routes 50 and 64

Significance: The Cahokia Mounds were built between 900 and 1300 by Mississippian Indians, who used the mounds as ceremonial centers. The largest and most famous of these structures is Monks Mound, which rises to a height of one hundred feet and has a base measuring eight thousand square feet. Sixty-eight of the estimated 120 mounds can still be viewed. The nearby town of Cahokia was founded in 1699 by French missionaries. It is the oldest permanent European settlement in Illinois and contains many historic French colonial buildings.

CAMAS MEADOWS BATTLE SITES, IDAHO

Location: Kilgore, Clark County

Significance: On August 19, 1877, the military force led by Major General Oliver Otis Howard which had been pursuing the Nez Perce since their departure from Clearwater was in a position to intercept them in their flight to Canada. Here, on August 20, a predawn raid by Nez Perce warriors succeeded in capturing most of Howard's pack mules, forcing the army to halt until more mules and supplies could be secured, which resulted in a time-consuming detour. The army's delay made it possible for the Nez Perce to escape into Yellowstone Park and Montana. Their remarkable journey toward Canada continued six weeks longer as a result of this raid.

CANYON DE CHELLY, ARIZONA

Location: East of Chinle, on the Navajo reservation, in northeastern Arizona near the New Mexico border; ninety miles north of Interstate 40 on Arizona 191

Significance: This National Monument, currently inhabited by Navajo farmers, includes well-preserved ruins of Anasazi cliff dwellings in sandstone canyons dating from 350-1300 C.E.

CARLISLE INDIAN SCHOOL, PENNSYLVANIA
Location: Carlisle, Cumberland County
Significance: Founded in 1879 by Brigadier General Richard H. Pratt (1840-1924), a Civil War officer and veteran of the Indian campaigns in the West, the school pioneered federal programs for Indian education and was a model for similar schools built elsewhere.

CARRINGTON OSAGE VILLAGE SITES, MISSOURI
Location: Horton vicinity, Vernon County
Significance: Occupied from about 1775 to 1825, this was the last dwelling place of the Big Osage Indians in southwest Missouri, prior to their removal to a reservation in Kansas. The site was visited in 1806 by Zebulon Pike. Because of the large number of trade goods found here, the site illustrates the rapid acculturation of the Big Osage.

CASA GRANDE RUINS, ARIZONA
Location: Approximately forty miles south of Phoenix on Highway 87 or U.S. Interstate 10; the monument is on Highway 87 about one mile north of Coolidge, approximately halfway between Phoenix and Tucson
Significance: This is the site of a large, unusual multistoried structure, the Casa Grande, built by the Hohokam people around 1350 C.E. Now protected by a steel shelter, the thick walls of the Casa Grande are clearly visible in the distance as visitors approach the monument, which for centuries has been used by travelers as a landmark and meeting place. Surrounding the Casa Grande are the ruins of one or more Hohokam villages that are open to visitors. Park rangers are available on the site to answer questions about the monument and the daily lives and culture of the Hohokam.

CASA MALPAIS SITE, ARIZONA
Location: Springerville, Apache County
Significance: Situated on terraces of a fallen basalt cliff along the upper Little Colorado River, the site dates from late Pueblo III to early Pueblo IV (1250-1325 C.E.) times. Casa Malpais appears to incorporate features of both early and late Mogollon culture settlement patterns.

CATALDO MISSION, IDAHO
Location: Cataldo, Kootenai County
Significance: The oldest extant mission church in the Pacific Northwest, Cataldo was used by Jesuit missionaries (1850 or 1853) in their efforts to convert the Coeur d'Alene Indians.

CHACO CANYON, NEW MEXICO
Location: Northwestern New Mexico, about 175 miles northwest of Albuquerque; the southern entrance is located sixty-four miles north of Interstate 40 on Route 57
Significance: This large, prehistoric pueblo community, trading center, and ceremonial site flourished circa 900-1180 C.E. The thirty-four-square-mile park contains one of the largest collections of ancient pueblo ruins in the southwestern United States. Chaco Canyon was the hub of a four-hundred-mile network of roads connecting it with numerous outlying communities, usually called outliers. The size and intricacy of its architecture, the sophistication of its agricultural irrigation system, and evidence of artistic, economic, and astronomical endeavors indicate this was an advanced ancient civilization, sometimes called the "Chaco Phenomenon." Abandoned for unknown reasons in the twelfth century, its existence first became known to the outside world in 1849 when it was discovered by a U.S. Army expedition.

CHIEF JOSEPH BATTLEGROUND OF BEAR'S PAW, MONTANA
Location: Chinook, Blaine County
Significance: This is the site of the battle in which Chief Joseph (c. 1840-1904) and more than four hundred Nez Perce Indians surrendered to the United States Army (1877). The Bear's Paw surrender signaled the close of the Nez Perces' existence as an "independent Indian people." Henceforth, they lived as a group of displaced persons—in the white culture, but certainly not of it.

CHIEF PLENTY COUPS HOME, MONTANA
Location: 0.5 mile west of Pryor, at the intersection of BIA roads #5 and #8 (Edgar Road), Big Horn County
Significance: This was the homestead of Chief Plenty Coups (c. 1849-1932), also called Aleekchea'ahoosh, one of the last and most celebrated traditional chiefs of the Crow Indians. It includes the house of Chief Plenty Coups, an adjacent log store operated by the chief, and the Plenty Coups Spring, a site of historic and cultural significance to

the Crow people. Chief Plenty Coups established the homestead in 1884 and lived there until his death in 1932, making his political career of more than a half a century one of the longest of any chief. One of the most important Native American leaders of the transitional period and an ambassador and negotiator for the Crow, Chief Plenty Coups advocated the adoption of those aspects of American culture necessary to succeed on the reservation while maintaining traditional Crow religious beliefs and cultural values.

CHUCALISSA SITE, TENNESSEE
Location: Memphis, Shelby County
Significance: Chucalissa is a Walls Phase (1400-1500) prehistoric mound and plaza complex, and the best known and preserved of such sites in the Central Mississippi River Valley. The site is known for its excellent preservation of architectural, floral, faunal, and human skeletal materials.

CLOVER SITE, WEST VIRGINIA
Location: Lesage, Cabell County
Significance: These are the extraordinarily well preserved remains of an Indian town dating to about four hundred years ago. The site pertains to the Fort Ancient culture, descendants of the cosmopolitan Hopewell trading societies and related to the other great urbanizing mound builders of the Mississippian period.

CORONADO NATIONAL MEMORIAL, ARIZONA
Location: Twelve miles south of Sierra Vista
Significance: This memorial commemorates Francisco Vásquez de Coronado's exploration of the United States Southwest (1540-1542). The memorial is located near his point of entry into the United States in his search for the Seven Cities of Cíbola. It was established four hundred years later.

COUFAL SITE, NEBRASKA
Location: Cotesfield, Howard County
Significance: Coufal (1130-1350 c.e.) is a major village of the Central Plains tradition. Earth lodges of the prehistoric Indians of the Itskari Phase have been excavated here, bridging the gap between late prehistoric villagers and the origins of the Pawnee.

CREEK NATIONAL CAPITOL, OKLAHOMA

Location: 6th Street and Grand Avenue, Okmulgee, Okmulgee County

Significance: This Victorian-style structure was used by the Creeks from 1878 to 1907, after their adoption of a representative form of government modeled on the United States Congress.

DANCING RABBIT CREEK TREATY SITE, MISSISSIPPI

Location: Macon, Noxubee County

Significance: On September 27, 1830, at Dancing Rabbit Creek, a traditional gathering place of the Choctaw people, an infamous treaty was signed for the removal of the Choctaw people from their homeland. This treaty was the most important of the pacts between the United States and the Choctaw as it resulted in the removal of a large part of the tribe from their traditional Southeastern homeland in present-day Mississippi. The Dancing Rabbit Creek Treaty served as a model for treaties of removal with the Chickasaw, Cherokee, Creek, and Seminole tribes. The treaty led to the extinguishing of all Choctaw title to land east of the Mississippi River owned by the Choctaw nation. It also led to the opening of a vast territory to American settlement.

DANGER CAVE, UTAH

Location: Wendover, Tooele County

Significance: Results of excavations at this site formed the basis for definition of a long-lived Desert culture which existed in the Great Basin area. The earliest cave stratus (c. 9500-9000 B.C.E.) is characterized by crude chipped stone artifacts; Zone II (c. 8000-7000 B.C.E.) by milling stones, basketry, and notched projectile points characteristic of the Desert culture; and Zones III, IV, and V (c. 7000 B.C.E.-500 C.E.) by materials showing an elaboration of the same culture.

EFFIGY MOUNDS NATIONAL MONUMENT, IOWA

Location: In eastern Iowa, along the Mississippi River; Three miles north of Marquette, on Highway 76

Significance: The monument was founded to preserve and protect a representative example of prehistoric American Indian mound-building culture and the wildlife and scenic wildness around the area. While mound building was widespread throughout the eastern half of North America, only in the upper Mississippi Valley was a culture established that specialized in mounds built in the shape of living creatures such as eagles, falcons, bison, deer, turtles, lizards, and especially bears.

EL CUARTELEJO, KANSAS

Location: Scott City, Scott County

Significance: This pueblo ruin is attributed to a group of Picuria Indians who left the Southwest because of friction with the Spanish. El Cuartelejo is a state park.

EL MORRO, NEW MEXICO

Location: Forty-two miles from the Grants exit of U.S. Interstate 40 to the site entrance via New Mexico State Road 53; fifty-six miles from the Gallup exit of U.S. Interstate 40 to the site entrance, also via New Mexico State Road 53

Significance: This natural outcropping or mesa of sandstone carries inscriptions dating from prehistoric times to the early twentieth century by people who have lived there and by those who passed by. It is also called Inscription Rock. One of El Morro's mysteries is the identity of the prehistoric people who carved petroglyphs, or rock art, of mountain sheep, bear claws, and people into the rock some seven hundred years ago. Another mystery is how they built two fortified villages atop the rock. The Zuñi have named the larger mesa-top town A'ts'ina, meaning "writing on the rock." The ruins suggest that the pueblos there rose as high as three stories and enclosed five hundred rooms. Some fifteen hundred people were housed there, and by 1990, sixteen rooms and two kivas, or sunken ceremonial chambers, had been excavated. One of the kivas is unusual because it is square (most extant kivas are round).

EMERALD MOUND, MISSISSIPPI

Location: Stanton

Significance: The Emerald (Selzertown) Mound site is located on Fairchild's Creek in the hardwood-covered löessial hills of southwestern Mississippi about six miles east of the Mississippi River, one mile north of Stanton Station, and nine miles northeast of Natchez. It was the last major ceremonial seat of the prehistoric Natchez Indians immediately before European contact. Emerald was occupied from circa 1300 to 1600 c.e., or during the late Anna or early Foster through the Emerald phases of the Late Mississippian period.

ETOWAH, GEORGIA

Location: Etowah River Valley, near Cartersville and Atlanta

Significance: Etowah Mounds and village site, the largest Indian settlement in the Etowah Valley, occupied between 700 and 1650 c.e., was a political, religious, and trade center for several thousand people of the Mississippian or mound builder culture. Influences from the Adena and Hopewell periods are evident along with possible Meso-american influence.

FALLEN TIMBERS BATTLEFIELD, OHIO

Location: Maumee, Lucas County

Significance: On August 20, 1794, General "Mad Anthony" Wayne's victory here over the Indians at Fallen Timbers asserted American sovereignty in the Old Northwest and made possible the Treaty of Greenville. The battle and treaty insured a period of peaceful settle-ment in the Ohio Country long enough for the new nation to consoli-date its hold on the Northwest Territory.

FOLSOM SITE, NEW MEXICO

Location: Folsom, Colfax County

Significance: The archaeological discoveries at this site confirmed theo-ries of the early advent of humans in America.

FORT ANCIENT, OHIO

Location: Lebanon, Warren County

Significance: This hilltop area with large surrounding earthworks was built and inhabited by people of the Hopewell culture (c. 300 B.C.E.-250 C.E.). Hundreds of years after the site had been abandoned by the Hopewell, the Fort Ancient people (1200-1600 C.E.) settled in the area, establishing villages on the south fort of the earthworks and the An-derson Village site.

FORT BELKNAP, TEXAS

Location: Newcastle, Young County

Significance: Established in 1851 following the Mexican War when the Texas frontier was being ravished by Comanche-Kiowa raids, Fort Belknap was the anchor of a chain of outer border posts stretching from the Red River to the Rio Grande. Until 1865, it was the key post in the protection of the exposed frontier; it bore the brunt of Comanche-Kiowa assault, and during the Civil War it served as a base for campaigns against these raiders.

FORT GIBSON, OKLAHOMA

Location: Lee and Ash Streets, Fort Gibson, Muskogee County

Significance: Cherokee, Creek, and Seminole Indians removed from the

Southeast by the government were brought here between 1824 and 1840. The fort was abandoned in 1857 and turned over to the Cherokee Nation. During the Civil War, it was reoccupied by federal forces consisting of three Cherokee Regiments, four companies of Kansas Cavalry, and Hopkins Battery. After the war, the post was garrisoned intermittently until it was abandoned as a military post in 1890 and reverted to the Cherokee Nation.

FORT OSAGE, MISSOURI

Location: Sibley, Jackson County

Significance: Established in 1808 by General William Clark (1770-1838) for the protection and promotion of trade with the Osage Indians, Fort Osage was one of the most successful of twenty-eight trading houses operated from 1795 to 1822 under the U.S. government's factory system. The fort served as the point from which distances were measured by the Federal Survey of 1825.

FORT PHIL KEARNY AND ASSOCIATED SITES, WYOMING

Location: Story, Johnson County

Significance: Established in 1866 to protect travelers along the Bozeman Trail, the fort was under virtual siege (1866-1868) in the "Red Cloud War" as Sioux groups fought successfully to prevent white invasion of their hunting grounds. This was one of the few times when the Army was forced to abandon a region it had occupied.

FORT RICHARDSON, TEXAS

Location: Jacksboro, Jack County

Significance: Established in 1867 to replace the recently abandoned Fort Belknap as the northernmost fort in the Texas chain of fortifications, the fort played an important role in the protection of American lives and property during the days of the Kiowa-Comanche conflict of the post-Civil War period, particularly the Red River War of 1874.

FORT ROBINSON AND RED CLOUD AGENCY, NEBRASKA

Location: Crawford, Dawes County

Significance: In 1873, the U.S. government moved Chief Red Cloud and his large band of Cheyenne, Arapaho, and Sioux to the White River area; nearby Fort Robinson was established in 1874 to protect government employees and property. The fort served as a base for Army campaigns against several groups of Native Americans, including the 1876 campaign against the Powder River Sioux. After 1919, the fort became a major quartermaster remount depot.

FORT SHANTOK, CONNECTICUT
Location: Montville, New London County
Significance: From 1636 to 1682, this was the site of the main Mohegan town and the home of Uncas, the most prominent and influential Mohegan leader and statesman of his era. Uncas was first noted in European records as the leader of a small Indian community at "Munhicke" in 1636; within a few years of this, Uncas had emerged as the most prominent Indian client of the Connecticut authorities at New Haven and Hartford. Attracted by his success and influential connections, substantial numbers of Connecticut Indian people joined his community.

FORT SILL, OKLAHOMA
Location: Fort Sill, Comanche County
Significance: Troops stationed here were active in campaigns against Southern Plains tribes in the late 1800's. Virtually all the original fort survives; it has expanded and continued to play a significant role for the Army in modern times.

FORT THOMPSON MOUNDS, SOUTH DAKOTA
Location: Fort Thompson, Buffalo County
Significance: This large group of low burial mounds dating from Plains-Woodland times (c. 800 C.E.) contains evidence of the first pottery-making peoples in the area. It is situated on the Crow Creek Indian Reservation.

FORT WASHITA, OKLAHOMA
Location: Nida, Bryan County
Significance: This fort was established in 1842 (reportedly by Zachary Taylor) because of treaty commitments to the Chickasaws and Choctaws and to serve as a way station for travelers on the Southern Overland Trail.

GATLIN SITE, ARIZONA
Location: Gila Bend, Maricopa County
Significance: Probably first occupied sometime before 900 C.E., the Gatlin Site contains one of the few documented Hohokam platform mounds. Associated with the mound are pit houses, ball courts, mid-

dens, and prehistoric canals. The mound is one of the only excavated and documented Sedentary Period platform mounds that is still relatively intact.

GILA CLIFF DWELLINGS, NEW MEXICO

Location: On Route 15, forty-two miles north of Silver City

Significance: These five caves were inhabited by the Mogollon people until the thirteenth century.

GRAHAM CAVE, MISSOURI

Location: Mineola, Montgomery County

Significance: At the time of the 1949 excavations of the site, remains found here, dating to 8000 B.C.E., were among the earliest known for the Archaic Period. The remains from Early and Middle Archaic times give the site its importance and illustrate a merging of Eastern and Plains influence in Missouri.

GRAND CANYON, ARIZONA

Location: Encompasses 178 miles of the Colorado River in northwestern Arizona

Significance: There is evidence of human habitation in and around the Grand Canyon dating back about five thousand years. The early residents, the Anasazi, hunted large and small animals and gathered native plant foods in season. About two thousand years ago, they adopted maize and squash farming. Later Anasazi were known as Pueblo Indians after the communal structures in which they lived. The region's Pueblo Indians made pottery, grew cotton, traded over large distances, and practiced elaborate ceremonies. More than five hundred Pueblo ruins have been found in the vicinity of the Grand Canyon, but none is of the size or complexity of better-known ruins like those at Mesa Verde. The Pueblo Indians abandoned the Grand Canyon about 1200. Since then the canyon has been frequented by the Hopi, who are descended from the Pueblo Indians, and occupied by the Havasupai and Hualipai south of the river and the Paiute to the north. The most recent arrivals on the scene were the Navajo. In the twentieth century, Indian lands in and around the Grand Canyon were reduced to designated reservations.

GRAVE CREEK MOUND, WEST VIRGINIA

Location: Moundsville, Marshall County

Significance: Dating to c. 500 B.C.E., this is one of the largest and oldest

mounds in the United States representative of the burial mound tradition of the Adena culture, which preceded the Hopewell culture.

GUNTHER ISLAND SITE 67, CALIFORNIA

Location: Eureka, Humboldt County
Significance: One of the largest Wiyot villages, this site (900 c.e.) typi-
fies the late prehistoric period and was instrumental in outlining the
prehistory of the Northern California coast. The site is a shell mound
encompassing approximately six acres and attaining depths of up to
fourteen feet.

HARDAWAY SITE, NORTH CAROLINA

Location: Badin, Stanly County
Significance: During the Paleo-Indian to Early Archaic Periods (12,000-
6,000 b.c.e.), prehistoric Indian populations came here to exploit the
lithic resources of the area to manufacture projectile points and stone
tools; these activities created stratified cultural deposits as much as
four feet in depth. This site has played a significant role in the development of archaeological method and theory, by advancing knowledge and understanding of the sequential development of prehistoric cultures in the eastern United States, particularly with regard to
the earliest periods of human occupation.

HASKELL INSTITUTE, KANSAS

Location: Lawrence, Douglas County
Significance: Founded in 1884, this was one of the first large off-reservation boarding schools for Indian students established by the federal government. It served students from the southern Plains and upper Midwest; in 1965, it became Haskell Indian Junior College.

HAWIKUH, NEW MEXICO

Location: Zuñi, Valencia County
Significance: Established in the 1200's and abandoned in 1680, the Zuñi
pueblo of Hawikuh, largest of the "Cities of Cíbola," was the first
pueblo seen by Spanish explorers. In 1539, the black scout Estevan
(also known as Estevanico) became the first non-Indian to reach this
area; he was killed by the people of Hawikuh as he entered their city.
The next year, when the Coronado Expedition reached the fabled
pueblo, they found not gold but a small, crowded, dusty sandstone
village.

HOLLY BLUFF SITE, MISSISSIPPI

Location: Holly Bluff, Yazoo County

Significance: This is the type of site for the Lake George phase of the prehistoric Temple Mound period of the area. The site is important in that it is on the southern margin of the Mississippian cultural advance down the Mississippi River and on the northern edge of that of the Cole's Creek and Plaquemine cultures of the South.

HORNER SITE, WYOMING

Location: Cody, Park County

Significance: This site has yielded evidence that several distinctive weapons and tools found in the Plains region were all part of a single prehistoric flint tool industry of Early Hunter origin. Initial age estimates place occupation of this site at approximately 5000 B.C.E.

HUBBELL TRADING POST, ARIZONA

Location: Ganado, Apache County

Significance: This still-active trading post represents the varied interactions of Navajos and the white traders who ran trading posts on the Navajo Reservation in the late nineteenth and early twentieth centuries.

HUFF ARCHAEOLOGICAL SITE, NORTH DAKOTA

Location: Huff, Morton County

Significance: By 1500 C.E., the Middle Missouri agricultural villages were the principal focus for social organization of the Mandan people, who had developed extensive trading networks over the previous two hundred years. The Huff Village is one of the best-known and best-preserved sites of this period. Its bastioned fortification system, dense and regular arrangement of houses, and wide variety in material culture attest to the extraordinary regional impacts of their way of life. The remains of a large central house facing an open plaza preserve evidence about the ritual space, which corresponds to the complex spiritual and ideological world that the Mandan have maintained since historic times.

JAKETOWN SITE, MISSISSIPPI

Location: Belzoni, Humphreys County

Significance: Located in northwestern Mississippi, Jaketown Site is the remains of a complex regional trade center dating from 2000-600 B.C.E., an era known as the Poverty Point period within the Late Archaic prehistory of the United States. Significant as a settlement important in trade in raw materials and manufacture of finished items distributed throughout the Eastern United States, it consists as deeply stratified archaeological deposits, well-preserved earthen mounds, and hidden features which represent extensive and intensive occupation over a long period.

KATHIO SITE, MINNESOTA

Location: Vineland and vicinity, Mille Lacs County

Significance: Occupied from Archaic to historic times (3000 B.C.E.-1750 C.E.), this was the ancestral homeland of the Dakota Sioux at the beginning of the historic period. In 1679, French explorer Sieur Duluth noted the existence of forty Sioux villages in the vicinity. In the mid-eighteenth century, the Chippewa, pressured by the westward expansion of European settlers, drove the Sioux from this area to the west and south, where the Sioux later figured prominently in the history of the Plains and Rocky Mountain states.

KEY MARCO, FLORIDA

Location: West coast of Florida

Significance: Key Marco (also called Marco Island) is the largest of the group of islands off the southwest coast of Florida called the Ten Thousand Islands; it lies a few miles south of the mainland city of Naples. Beginning in 1895, a site at the north end of the island—a sort of courtyard surrounded by shell mounds—was excavated by Frank Hamilton Cushing and others, and a variety of artifacts were uncovered. The culture reconstructed from the finds at Key Marco was sophisticated and technologically advanced. Radiocarbon dating suggests that the Key Marco site was occupied from about 750 until just before Spanish exploration of the area, about 1500. The Indians of Key Marco were probably part of the Calusa empire that covered south Florida.

KNIFE RIVER INDIAN VILLAGES, NORTH DAKOTA

Location: One-half mile north of Stanton

Significance: An important hub of intertribal and later international trade, the Knife River Indian Villages also played an important role in Plains Indian agricultural and cultural development. Many archaeological sites are preserved at the site. A reconstructed earth lodge re-creates aboriginal life. In addition, the site preserves important native prairie and riverine habitats.

KOSTER, ILLINOIS

Location: Lower Illinois Valley

Significance: Koster is one of the most intensively investigated sites in the midwestern United States. Excavations conducted under the direction of archaeologist Stuart Streuver revealed thirteen sequential strata dating from the Early Archaic through the Mississippian traditions, beginning around 6400 B.C.E. The last occupation was a Mississippian village dating from 900 to 1200 C.E.

LANDERGIN MESA, TEXAS

Location: Vega, Oldham County

Significance: A ruin consisting of a series of buildings atop a steep-sided mesa on the east side of East Alamosa Creek, this is one of the largest, best-stratified, least-damaged, and most spectacularly located ruins of Panhandle culture.

LANGDEAU SITE, SOUTH DAKOTA

Location: Lower Brule, Lyman County

Significance: Possibly the earliest reliably dated village of the Missouri Trench, Langdeau Site represents the full emergence of the Plains Village traditions in the Middle Missouri cultural area. It is also a cultural intrusion of organized village people with highly adaptive strategies, including horticulture, into an area previously occupied by hunter-gatherers.

LEARY SITE, NEBRASKA

Location: Rulo, Richardson County

Significance: This large prehistoric village and burial area of the Oneota Culture was first noted by Meriwether Lewis and William Clark in 1804.

LEHNER, ARIZONA

Location: Southern Arizona

Significance: Lehner is one of the best-documented mammoth kill sites of the Llano complex in the southwestern United States, with Clovis projectile points found in direct association with the bones of extinct animals. Occupied between 10,000-9000 B.C.E., Lehner represents a kill site and butchering locality. Animals were trapped at a watering hole by hunters, who took advantage of the steep and slippery sides of the arroyo to isolate and kill young mammoths. Butchering took place on the spot, and the location was subsequently used for trapping other animals.

LEMHI PASS, TENDOY, IDAHO

Location: On the Idaho-Montana border, twelve miles east of Tendoy, Idaho

Significance: Lemhi Pass was the highest point reached by Meriwether Lewis and William Clark on their epic journey across the American West. At this mountainous site, the Corps of Discovery first glimpsed the headwaters of the Columbia River and realized that a water passage across the continent was impossible. For the Shoshone and Nez Perce, the route was especially important for seasonal migrations between hunting areas, and the Blackfoot frequented the trail and pass so often that it was locally known as the "Blackfoot Road."

LITTLE BIGHORN, MONTANA

Location: Within the Crow Reservation in southeastern Montana, one mile east of Route 1-90 (U.S. 87) and eighteen miles north of Hardin; connected with the Black Hills and Yellowstone National Park on U.S. Route 212

Significance: The Little Bighorn Battlefield National Monument includes the site of the Battle of the Little Bighorn (June 25, 1876), Custer National Cemetery, the Reno-Benteen Battlefield, Medicine Tail Ford, and the site of an Indian village.

LONG ISLAND OF THE HOLSTON, TENNESSEE

Location: Kingsport, Sullivan County

Significance: Located just east of the junction of the North and South Forks of the Holston River, Long Island was a sacred council and treaty ground surrounded by the vast hunting territory of the Cherokee Nation. Starting at Long Island in March, 1775, Daniel Boone (1734-1820) led a team of thirty axmen to open the trail through Cumberland Gap that was to gain fame as the Wilderness Road. Between 1775 and 1795, this trail was used by more than two hundred thousand emigrants.

LOWRY RUIN, COLORADO

Location: Pleasant View, Montezuma County

Significance: This pueblo (c. 1100 C.E.) of fifty rooms is unusual in that it has a great kiva, a large ceremonial structure more commonly found in Arizona and New Mexico.

LUBBOCK LAKE SITE, TEXAS

Location: Lubbock, Lubbock County

Significance: Excavations at the site in Yellow House Canyon, discovered in the 1930's, have revealed a stratified sequence of human habitation spanning eleven thousand to twelve thousand years and providing evidence for occupation during Clovis, Folsom, Plainview, Late Paleo-Indian, Archaic, Ceramic, and historic periods.

MARMES ROCKSHELTER, WASHINGTON

Location: Lyons Ferry, Franklin County

Significance: This is one of the most outstanding archaeological sites yet discovered in the Northwest. Excavations at the site have revealed the earliest burials in the Pacific Northwest (c. 5500-4500 B.C.E.) and possibly the oldest human remains yet encountered in the Western Hemisphere (c. 11,000-9,000 B.C.E.). The eight strata at the site all contain cultural materials.

MASHANTUCKET PEQUOT RESERVATION ARCHAEOLOGICAL DISTRICT, CONNECTICUT

Location: Ledyard, New London County

Significance: The Mashantucket Pequot Reservation Archaeological District comprises nearly 1,638 acres of archaeologically sensitive land in the northern portion of the uplands historically called Wawarramoreke by the Pequots, and within territory first chronicled as Pequot land in the earliest known surviving map (1614) of the region.

MEDICINE LODGE PEACE TREATY SITE, KANSAS

Location: Medicine Lodge, Barber County

Significance: Here, near the confluence of Medicine Lodge and Elm Creeks, members of a Peace Commission created by Congress met with about five thousand Kiowa, Comanche, Plains Apache, Arapaho, and Southern Cheyenne Indians in October, 1867. Under the terms of the Medicine Lodge Treaty, the first to include provisions aimed at "civilizing" the Indian, Plains Indians were to give up nomadic ways and relinquish claims to ancestral lands, in return for federal economic and educational help.

MEDICINE WHEEL, WYOMING

Location: Kane, Big Horn County

Significance: This represents one of the most interesting and mysterious remains of late period aboriginal culture. Its builders and function are unknown. Composed of loose, irregularly shaped, whitish flat stones placed in a circle, it is apparently little modified since its construction (c. 1800); twenty-eight linear spokes, seventy to seventy-five feet in length, radiate from the hub.

MENOKEN INDIAN VILLAGE SITE, NORTH DAKOTA
Location: Menoken, Burleigh County
Significance: This site shows certain structural and artifactual similarities to historic and prehistoric earthlodge villages along the upper Missouri River. Pottery and projectile point styles are indicative of the prehistoric period, and the cultural/temporal affinity is suggested to be Initial Middle Missouri Tradition from about 950 to 1300 c.e.

MESA VERDE, COLORADO
Location: In the high plateau or mesa country of southwestern Colorado, in the Four Corners area where Colorado, Utah, Arizona, and New Mexico meet; the park entrance is midway between Cortez on the west and Mancos on the east on U.S. 160
Significance: The first area in the United States to be declared a national treasure for the preservation of the works of humanity: the ruins of an ancient people referred to as Anasazi (from the Navajo, meaning "ancient ones"). Evidence of a civilization growing in complexity in its toolmaking, agriculture, and architecture is to be found at numerous sites in Mesa Verde.

MINISINK ARCHAEOLOGICAL SITE, PENNSYLVANIA
Location: Bushkill, Pike County
Significance: Minisink was the most important Munsee Indian community for much of the seventeenth and eighteenth centuries. Archaeological resources located here have yielded information on historic contact between Indian and European people in Munsee Country, a region stretching from southern New York across northern New Jersey to northeastern Pennsylvania. Today, Minisink remains one of the most extensive, best-preserved, and most intensively studied archaeological locales in the Northeast.

MISSION SAN GABRIEL ARCANGEL, CALIFORNIA
Location: Two miles north of the San Bernardino Freeway (Interstate 10) on South Mission Drive in the city of San Gabriel
Significance: Heralded as the first European settlement of the Los An-

geles basin, this mission was the most prosperous of the California missions and served as a way station for the colonization of Alta (Upper) California. In addition to its status as one of only two Spanish colonial-era stone churches of Alta California located south of Monterey, the church is singularly unique for its Moorish-inspired architectural characteristics and its unique collection of via cruces paintings crafted by an Indian artisan of Mission San Fernando.

MISSION SANTA INES, CALIFORNIA

Location: South of State Highway 246, Solvang, Santa Barbara County
Significance: Mission Santa Ines is one of the best-preserved Spanish mission complexes in the United States, containing an unrivaled combination of landscape setting, original buildings, extant collections of art and interior furnishings, water-related industrial structures, and archaeological remains. The property is also important as the location of the start of the Chumash Revolt of 1824, one of the largest and most successful revolts of Native American neophytes in the Spanish West, representing indigenous resistance to European colonization. The intact archaeological remains of the two mission wings, a portion of the convent, and the Native American village are rare survivors and have been demonstrated to contain the potential for exceptional information on the critical period of accommodation between native peoples and European colonial powers.

MOCCASIN BEND ARCHAEOLOGICAL DISTRICT, TENNESSEE

Location: Chattanooga, Hamilton County
Significance: This is the best-preserved and most important compact, yet diverse, sample of archaeological remains known in the Tennessee River Valley, indicative of Chattanooga's pivotal status in trade, communications, economics, and political importance in the interior Southeast. The site includes evidence of occupation by Native American groups of the Archaic, Woodland, and Mississippian periods; because of sixteenth century Spanish trade and gift items found there, the site provides significant opportunities to study the early contact period in the Southeast. Also included are Civil War earthworks associated with the Battle of Chattanooga.

MOHAWK UPPER CASTLE HISTORIC DISTRICT, NEW YORK

Location: Danube, Herkimer County
Significance: Archaeological and architectural resources located in this district are associated with Nowadaga, the most westerly part of the

major eighteenth century Mohawk Indian community of Canajoharie. During the eighteenth century, Mohawk people regarded Canajoharie as the most important community in the western half of Kanienke, their name for the Mohawk River Valley heartland. Included in the district is the still-standing Indian Castle Church, a wooden-framed Anglican chapel built in 1769.

MOLSTAD VILLAGE, SOUTH DAKOTA

Location: Mobridge, Dewey County

Significance: A tiny fortified prehistoric village site containing five circular house rings enclosed by a ditch, Molstad appears to represent a period of transition, when Central Plains and Middle Missouri cultural traits were combining to form the basis for Mandan, Hidatsa, and Arikara cultures as they existed at the time of the first contact with Europeans.

MOUNDVILLE SITE, ALABAMA

Location: Moundville, Hale County

Significance: Settled first in the tenth century, Moundville is situated on a level area overlooking the Black Warrior River and consists of thirty-four mounds, the largest of which is over fifty-eight feet high. The site represents a major period of Mississippian culture in the southern portion of its distribution and acted as the center for a southerly diffusion of this culture toward the Gulf Coast.

NATCHEZ, MISSISSIPPI

Location: Southwestern Mississippi, along the banks of the Mississippi River

Significance: This Southern city is rich in history. It was originally occupied by the Natchez Indians and later colonized by France, England, and Spain. The Natchez Indians were a tribe of the Mississippians, who lived all along the river from mouth to source. By 1200 the Mississippians had developed the most advanced Indian civilization located north of Mexico, and by the mid-sixteenth century the Natchez culture had reached its height. The Natchez, like other Mississippian peoples, excelled at agriculture, raising maize, pumpkins, melons, and tobacco. The Natchez also were highly skilled at pottery making. The Natchez had a socially stratified society, with clear distinctions between aristocrats and common people. The Natchez constructed their Grand Village, the ceremonial and religious center of their culture, along the banks of St. Catherine Creek, within the present-day city limits of Natchez. The tribe was very much entrenched in the area when the first Europeans arrived early in the eighteenth century.

NAVAJO NATIONAL MONUMENT, ARIZONA

Location: On the Navajo Reservation in northeastern Arizona, about fifty miles northeast of Tuba City and twenty-two miles southwest of Kayenta, off U.S. Interstate 160, via Route 564, a nine-mile paved road that leads to the visitors' center

Significance: Site of Betatakin, Kiet Seel, and Inscription House, three Anasazi dwellings built between 1250 and 1280 and abandoned around 1300. The sites, in what is today Navajo land, were excavated in the early twentieth century and made a National Monument in 1909. The monument's visitors' center is open year round and offers cultural exhibits about Anasazi life; between late May and mid-September, the staff offers guided tours on foot and horseback (guides must accompany all visitors to the ruins). Because of its extreme fragility, Inscription House is no longer open to tourists.

NEZ PERCE NATIONAL HISTORICAL PARK, IDAHO

Location: Clearwater, Idaho, Lewis, and Nez Perce Counties in north-central Idaho, as well as southeastern Washington, northeastern Oregon, and western Montana

Significance: This National Historical Park does not focus on one location but rather comprises a unique cooperative arrangement of public and private lands administered by the National Park Service, state, tribal, local, or other federal agencies. The complete route of thirty-eight sites in four states includes locations of important encampments, missions, battles, trails, and other areas significant to Nez Perce and related U.S. history; the Idaho route alone comprises about four hundred miles of travel. The park sites' varying topographic and climatic features exemplify the wide diversity of Nez Perce country, which is largely still wilderness.

NORTON MOUND GROUP, MICHIGAN

Location: Grand Rapids, Kent County

Significance: This site contains well-preserved Hopewell mounds of the western Great Lakes region. Norton Mound Group was the center of Hopewellian culture in that area, c. 400 B.C.E. to 400 C.E.

OBSIDIAN CLIFF, WYOMING

Location: Mammoth, Park County

Significance: Obsidian Cliff occupies a unique position in national pre-history as a singularly important source of lithic materials for prehistoric peoples of interior western North America. It is recognized as an exceptionally well preserved, heavily utilized lithic source that served the utilitarian needs and ceremonial requirements or early indigenous peoples over a large area of North America for twelve thousand years.

OCONTO SITE, WISCONSIN

Location: Oconto, Oconto County

Significance: At this prehistoric burial ground, implements of the Old Copper Culture people, who occupied the northern Midwest about 2500 B.C.E., have been found in association with human burials. The site forms the Copper Culture State Park.

OLD ORAIBI, ARIZONA

Location: Oraibi, Navajo County

Significance: Located on the westernmost of the Hopi mesas, this is probably the oldest continuously inhabited pueblo in the Southwest. Old Oraibi documents Hopi culture and history from before European contact to the present day. The village is on the present Hopi Indian Reservation.

OZETTE, WASHINGTON

Location: Olympic Peninsula

Significance: The Ozette site, located on the westernmost point of the Olympic Peninsula on the Pacific coast of Washington, represents the remains of a large, late prehistoric whaling village. Portions of the site that were buried by catastrophic mudslides have provided a large number of organic remains, preserved by their rapid burial and the site's waterlogged condition. Ozette has provided information that is invaluable for the reconstruction of ways of life on the Northwest Coast that predate the arrival of Europeans. The village is believed to have been occupied by ancestors of the Makah Indians, modern indigenous residents of the region who still occupied parts of Ozette as recently as the 1920's.

PEMAQUID ARCHAEOLOGICAL SITE, MAINE

Location: New Harbor, Lincoln County

Significance: Pemaquid contains the remains of a large English town occupied throughout the early period of contact on the Maine Coast along the frontier separating French Acadia from New England. European settlement of the area dates to around 1628, when New England colonists erected their first houses at the site; these first English colonists fished, farmed, and traded food and manufactured goods for furs with their Indian neighbors. As the first and most important early center for intercultural relations between Indian people and English settlers in Maine, the large amounts of artifacts and other materials preserved in Pemaquid's fieldstone foundations, cellar-holes, chimney-bases, hearths, and other features have yielded much valuable information associated with this time period.

PICOTTE MEMORIAL HOSPITAL, NEBRASKA

Location: Walthill, Thurston County

Significance: This hospital was built by Dr. Susan La Flesche Picotte (1865-1915), the first Native American physician, who pioneered in providing health care for Native Americans. Picotte was born on the Omaha Indian Reservation, the youngest child of Chief Joseph La Flesche (Iron Eye), the last recognized chief of his tribe and a strong advocate of integration. Picotte was educated at the Hampton Institute in Virginia and received her medical degree from the Woman's Medical College of Pennsylvania. She returned to the Omaha Reservation in 1890 as physician at the government boarding school, ultimately becoming physician for the entire tribe, serving as well as teacher, social worker, adviser, and interpreter. Picotte was an active advocate for temperance and Omaha Indian rights.

PICTOGRAPH CAVE, MONTANA

Location: Billings, Yellowstone County

Significance: This is one of the key archaeological sites used in determining the sequence of prehistoric occupation on the northwestern Plains. The deposits indicate occupation from 2600 B.C.E. to after 1800 C.E.

PIKE PAWNEE VILLAGE SITE, NEBRASKA

Location: Guide Rock, Webster County

Significance: This is generally accepted as the Pawnee village where Lieutenant Zebulon Pike, on his mission to secure the new territory in the Plains acquired under the Louisiana Purchase, caused the American flag to be raised and the Spanish flag lowered in late September, 1806. Archaeological evidence corroborates the identification.

PIPESTONE QUARRIES, MINNESOTA

Location: Southwest Minnesota

Significance: The quarries, located in southwest Minnesota, were being worked in the seventeenth century with metal tools acquired from European traders. From the beginning, the area was considered a sacred place where peoples from various tribes could quarry stone in peace.The earliest diggers were the Iowa and Oto. By the 1700's, the Dakota Sioux had acquired a monopoly, trading pipestone extensively throughout North America. The stone, prized for its color and softness, was ideal for carving ceremonial pipes, including calumets. Today an interpretive center housing displays of carvings and quarrying techniques is on the site and open to public view.

POVERTY POINT, LOUISIANA

Location: Delhi, West Carroll County

Significance: The largest and most complex ceremonial earthworks of its kind yet found in North America, the site is dominated by the huge Poverty Point Mound, which is 640 feet by 710 feet in base dimension and rises to a height of nearly 70 feet.

PUEBLO GRANDE RUIN AND IRRIGATION SITES, ARIZONA

Location: Pueblo Grande City Park, Phoenix, Maricopa County

Significance: The prehistoric platform mound and associated archaeological remains at Pueblo Grande represent one of the last surviving urban architectural sites of its kind in the southwestern United States. There is evidence that between 1100 and 1400 C.E., Pueblo Grande served as a Hohokam administration center for a major irrigation canal system. Due to its prehistoric significance, preeminent archaeologists have conducted research at Pueblo Grande since the 1880's.

SALINAS PUEBLO MISSIONS, NEW MEXICO

Location: Mountainair, one block west of the U.S. 60 and New Mexico 55 junction; about eighty miles south of Albuquerque

Significance: Administered by the National Park Service, this was once a major trading center and is now the site of mission ruins and Indian pueblo ruins that have survived since the villages were abandoned in the 1600's.

SAN ANTONIO MISSIONS, TEXAS

Location: On the Mission Trail in the south central portion of San Antonio, south of Interstate 35, west of Interstate 37, and north of the south section of Interstate 410

Significance: This site consists of four Spanish missions: Mission Concepción, Mission San José, Mission San Juan, and Mission Espada. All four are prime examples of Spanish Mission architecture as adapted for use in the New World. The construction of these historic missions was a joint effort of skilled craftsmen from Spain and Mexico and the local Coahuiltecan Indians.

SAN XAVIER DEL BAC MISSION, ARIZONA

Location: Tucson, Pima County

Significance: Founded in 1700 by the Jesuits, Bac then formed the extreme northern thrust of Nueva Espana. The present structure is the third, perhaps the fourth, church on the site. Consecrated by Franciscans, it was begun in 1783 and completed in 1797. One of the finest Spanish Colonial churches in the country, it is a synthesis of Baroque design and the desert materials from which it was built by Papago Indian laborers supervised by Spanish-American master craftsmen.

SEQUOYAH'S CABIN, OKLAHOMA

Location: Akins, Sequoyah County

Significance: This frontier house of logs was occupied (1829-1843) by Sequoyah (c. 1770-1843), the teacher who in 1821 invented a syllabary which made it possible to write and read the Cherokee language. The giant California sequoia trees are named for him.

SERPENT MOUND, OHIO

Location: Locust Grove, Adams County

Significance: This giant, earthen snake effigy, the largest and finest in America, probably dates from the Adena period (1000 B.C.E.-200 C.E.). The site is one of the first in the United States to be set aside because of its archaeological value.

SHAWNEE MISSION, KANSAS

Location: Fairway, Johnson County

Significance: From 1839 to 1862, Indian children of many nearby tribes were taught English, manual arts, and agriculture at the school established in 1830 by the Reverend Thomas Johnson. Also, the first territorial governor of Kansas had his executive offices here in 1854, and the first territorial legislature met here in 1855.

SHILOH, TENNESSEE

Location: If traveling on Interstate 40, south at Jackson, Tennessee, on U.S. 45 and then east on Tennessee Route 142; if traveling east from Memphis, approximately eighty miles on Highway 72 to Corinth, Mississippi, then northeast twenty-five miles on U.S. Highway 45

Significance: Shiloh is the site of one of the earliest and most decisive full-scale battles in the western theater of operations during the Civil War. Within the park also are thirty Indian burial mounds, which were excavated by the Smithsonian Institution in 1934.

SITKA, ALASKA

Location: The seaward side of Baranof Island, an extinct volcano in southeast Alaska's island chain; approximately one hundred miles from the coast of North America

Significance: Originally an Alaskan Indian village, Sitka was the center of the northwest international fur trade, the site of the first recorded contact between Eurasians and Alaskan Indians, and the site of several battles between Indians and Russians; the capital of Russian America, the first capital of Alaska under U.S. rule, and the site of transfer for Alaska's sale to the United States by Russia in 1867.

SNAKETOWN, ARIZONA

Location: Near the city of Phoenix in Southern Arizona

Significance: The site of Snaketown, in southern Arizona, was the largest of the early pit house villages. With occupations dating from between 300 and 1150, it remains the best-known center of Hohokam culture. It is situated on an upper river terrace in the Phoenix Basin, near the confluence of the Salt and the Gila rivers. The site was excavated by archaeologist Emil Haury in 1934-1935 and again in 1964-1965. This research provided detailed information on the Southwest's first irrigation farmers.

SPIRO, OKLAHOMA

Location: Eastern Oklahoma

Significance: Spiro was the most important western center of Caddoan culture in the Late Prehistoric period (1200-1350). It is situated within an area of escarpments along the Arkansas River, in a location that was strategic for contacts between the southern Plains and the lowlands of the Mississippi Valley. The site covers an area of 80 acres, although not all of this area was occupied simultaneously. It is best known for its elaborate burials and thousands of art objects of shell and copper. The site was first occupied during the Late Archaic period (circa 2500 to 500 B.C.E.), but its most spectacular features date between 900 and 1350 C.E.

SUNKEN VILLAGE ARCHAEOLOGICAL SITE, OREGON

Location: Portland, Multnomah County

Significance: Sunken Village is the archaeological remains of a Chinook settlement (1250-1750 C.E.) which is extraordinarily well preserved. The Chinooks who lived there were a cosmopolitan people and practiced a successful, complex hunter-gatherer economy that permitted densely occupied villages and extensive trade relations.

SUNWATCH SITE, OHIO

Location: Dayton, Montgomery County

Significance: Sunwatch, formerly known as the Incinerator Site, is located on the west bank of the Great Miami River within the city limits of Dayton. Ceramics, radiocarbon dates, and other evidence indicate that this open village site is a discrete Fort Ancient period, Anderson phase village probably occupied for not more than twenty-five years during the late twelfth and early thirteenth centuries. The site is one of the best preserved and most completely excavated and analyzed archaeological village sites associated with the Post Archaic Eastern Farmers.

SYCAMORE SHOALS, TENNESSEE

Location: Elizabethton, Carter County

Significance: A treaty signed by the Cherokee here in 1775 allowed the United States to purchase twenty million acres of Cherokee land. Also, in 1780, the site served as the rendezvous point for the Overmountain Men on their way to Kings Mountain, where they contributed to the defeat of the British army.

TAHLEQUAH, OKLAHOMA

Location: Cherokee County in the Ozark plateau area of eastern Oklahoma, sixty-seven miles southeast of Tulsa

Significance: This is the site where the Eastern and Western branches of the Cherokees came together to sign the Cherokee Constitution on September 6, 1839. Tahlequah functioned as the Cherokee national capital until the Curtis Act of 1898 abolished tribal authority in the Indian Territory. Following Oklahoma's admission as a state, Tahlequah became the seat of Cherokee County. The town remains the administrative headquarters for the Cherokee tribal government.

TAOS, NEW MEXICO

Location: Northern New Mexico, at the base of the Sangre de Cristo Mountains; seventy miles northeast of Santa Fe

Significance: This artists' and ski resort town in New Mexico was inhabited originally by Native Americans and later by Spanish settlers. The Taos Pueblo has been home to Taos-Tiwa Indians for one thousand years. By 1200 C.E. the Pit House People had started organizing their buildings into pueblos to avert the constant attacks by Plains Indians for food and slaves, and to serve as a site for trading with other tribes. The Taos Pueblo serves as a reminder of those early settlers; it is one of the oldest continually inhabited communities in the United States, one of New Mexico's nineteen Native American pueblos still in existence.

TIPPECANOE BATTLEFIELD, INDIANA

Location: Lafayette, Tippecanoe County

Significance: In response to the efforts of Shawnee chief Tecumseh and his brother, the Prophet, to unite the Indian nations of the northwest and southwest territories to resist American expansion, Indiana Territory governor William Henry Harrison led a force of about one thousand men to the Shawnee settlement at the Great Clearing, where Tippecanoe Creek flows into the Wabash. On November 7, 1811, Harrison's army defeated the Shawnee led by the Prophet and sacked their village, in the process destroying all hope that Tecumseh had for an Indian confederacy. The American victory here was also an important cause of the second war with Britain (1812-1815).

TOBIAS-THOMPSON COMPLEX, KANSAS

Location: Geneseo, Rice County

Significance: The complex is composed of a cluster of eight village sites along the Little Arkansas River, all of which relate to the Little River Focus of the Great Bend Aspect dating from 1500 to 1700. These sites have been related to a historic culture, the Wichita Tribe, and may have been among the villages visited by Francisco Vásquez de Coronado in Quivira in 1542.

TOLTEC MOUNDS SITE, ARKANSAS

Location: Scott, Lonoke County

Significance: A large ceremonial complex and village site, Toltec Mounds represents the northhernmost occupation during the Coles Creek Period (c. 700-1000 C.E.) and may yield information about the interaction between Lower and Central Mississippi Valley cultures. It is part of Toltec Mounds Archaeological State Park.

TOOLESBORO MOUND GROUP, IOWA

Location: Toolesboro, Louisa County

Significance: First excavated in 1875, this is the best-preserved Hopewell site in Iowa, representing an extension of the "classic" Hopewellian mortuary practices of the Illinois River Valley.

UTZ SITE, MISSOURI

Location: Marshall, Saline County

Significance: Located on bluffs overlooking the Missouri River, this site was occupied from c. 1400 C.E. to the late 1700's. Probably the principal village area occupied by the Missouri Indians at the time of their first contact with Europeans, Utz is noted by French explorers, beginning with Píre Jacques Marquette, whose 1673 map placed "Messourit" Indians here.

VANDERBILT ARCHAEOLOGICAL SITE, SOUTH DAKOTA

Location: Pollock, Campbell County

Significance: Archaeological information about the earliest culture history of today's Mandan and Hidatsa peoples is preserved in the Vanderbilt Village Site. They began to transform their environment along the Missouri River floodplain near the Cannonball River around 1000 C.E. by expanding their horticultural economy with permanent villages, substantial houses, and more complex technologies. By 1400, the Vanderbilt Village was a well-established, dynamic community within which its people lived comfortably, traded, hunted, fished, and created a highly developed clan tradition with neighboring villages.

WALLOWA LAKE SITE, OREGON

Location: Joseph, Wallowa County

Significance: This site, commanding an excellent view of a high, glaciated lake and mountain country, preserves a traditional Nez Perce ancestral campground associated with religious and cultural values that have persisted for more than the century that has elapsed since the band of nontreaty Nez Perce led by Young Chief Joseph was driven out.

WASHITA BATTLEFIELD, OKLAHOMA

Location: Cheyenne, Roger Mills County

Significance: This was the scene of an 1868 attack by George Armstrong Custer's troops on the village of Black Kettle, peace chief of the southern Cheyenne. It demonstrated the effectiveness of winter campaigns against Southern Plains Indian groups.

WEIPPE PRAIRIE, IDAHO

Location: Weippe, Clearwater County

Significance: On the morning of September 20, 1805, an advance party of the Lewis and Clark Expedition came out of the Bitterroot Mountains onto the southeastern corner of Weippe Prairie, the western terminus of the Lolo Trail and long a favored source of camas root for the Nez Perce Indians. Here, the expedition first met the Nez Perce, who had never before seen white men. The Nez Perce gave the explorers food as well as much-needed help and directions during the two-and-a-half-week period spent in their territory.

WOUNDED KNEE BATTLEFIELD, SOUTH DAKOTA

Location: Batesland, Shannon County

Significance: On December 29, 1890, this was the scene of the last major clash between Native Americans and U.S. troops in North America. In the period following the introduction of the Ghost Dance among the Lakota and the killing of Sitting Bull, a band of several hundred led by Big Foot left the Cheyenne River Reservation. Intercepted by U.S. troops, they had given themselves up and had been escorted to an army encampment on Pine Ridge Reservation when shooting suddenly started. The ensuing struggle, short but bloody, resulted in seventy-five army casualties and the virtual massacre of Big Foot's band.

WUPATKI NATIONAL MONUMENT, ARIZONA

Location: Thirty-two miles north of Flagstaff, between Flagstaff and Cameron, off U.S. Interstate 89 via a thirty-six-mile driving loop that leads directly to Wupatki as well as to the adjacent Sunset Crater National Monument

Significance: The thirty-six-thousand-acre National Monument is the site of Indian ruins dating from the twelfth and thirteenth centuries.

The most famous ruins are Wukoki, the Citadel, Lomaki, and Wupatki Pueblo. The structures were built after a nearby volcanic eruption blanketed the area with volcanic ash, attracting a variety of Indian groups—the Sinagua, Cohonino, Anasazi, Hohokam, Mogollon, and Cíbola—to the newly arable land. The site was abandoned in the thirteenth century. In the mid-nineteenth century, the site was inhabited by Navajo and Hopi Indians. By the turn of the century, archaeological excavations had begun there.

YELLOWSTONE, WYOMING

Location: Northwestern Wyoming, extending into Montana and Idaho

Significance: Yellowstone National Park, dedicated by Congress on March 1, 1872, was the first national park in the United States and the first step toward the creation of a National Park Service. Cultural sites show human occupation dating back twelve thousand years. The park embraces the area traversed by the fleeing Nez Perce Indians in 1877.

YUMA CROSSING, ARIZONA AND ASSOCIATED SITES

Location: Yuma

Significance: First used by Native Americans, this natural crossing served as a significant transportation gateway on the Colorado River during the Spanish Colonial and U.S. westward expansion periods. The surviving buildings of the Yuma Quartermaster Depot and Arizona Territorial Prison are the key features on the Arizona side of the border; across the river, in California, stand the surviving buildings of Fort Yuma, an Army outpost that guarded the crossing from 1850 to 1885.

ZUÑI-CÍBOLA COMPLEX, NEW MEXICO

Location: Zuñi, Valencia County

Significance: A series of sites on the Zuñi Reservation, containing house ruins, kivas, pictographs, petroglyphs, trash mounds, and a mission church and convent. They have proven to be an important source of material for ethnological studies of the early Zuñi, Mogollon, and Anasazi cultures. They include the Village of the Great Kivas, Yellow House, Hawikuh, and Kechipbowa.

Historic Native Americans

Adams, Hank: Assiniboine-Sioux negotiator during the Trail of Broken Treaties

Agüeybana: chief in the Higüey region during the West Indian uprisings

Alokut (1842-1877): Joseph the Younger's brother, a tribal war leader during the Nez Perce exile

Anacaona: chieftainess in the western provinces during the West Indian uprisings

Arpeika, also known as Sam Jones (c. 1760-1860): Mikasuki shaman during the Seminole Wars

Atotarho: Onondaga chief of the Iroquois Confederacy

Attakullakulla (1714?-1781?): Cherokee diplomat during the Cherokee War

Banks, Dennis (born 1935?): co-founder of the American Indian Movement (AIM)

Barboncito (c. 1820-1871): Navajo war chief during the Long Walk of the Navajos

Bean, Lou: sister of Buddy Lamont at the Wounded Knee Occupation

Big Bear, also known as Mistahimaskwa (1825-1888): Cree chief who sought peace during the second Riel rebellion

Big Foot (c. 1825-1890): chief of the Minneconjou Sioux at the Battle of Wounded Knee

Big Warrior (died 1825): mico of the Upper Creeks, leader of the progressive peace party during the Creek War

Bissonnette, Gladys: tribal elder at the Wounded Knee Occupation

Black Elk, Wallace (born 1921): Oglala medicine man at the Wounded Knee Occupation

Black Kettle (1803?-1868): chief of the Southern Cheyenne during the Sand Creek massacre, Cheyenne chieftain at the Washita River massacre, and leading Cheyenne chief at Medicine Lodge Creek

Blue Jacket, also known as Weyapiersenwah (1764?-1810): Shawnee war chief at the Battle of Fallen Timbers, and led the native troops against General Anthony Wayne during Little Turtle's War

Blunt, King Tom (died 1739?): leader of hostile Tuscarora towns during the Tuscarora War

Boudinot, Elias (Buck Watie, c. 1803-1839): nephew of Major Ridge and editor of the *Cherokee Phoenix*

Bowlegs, Billy, also known as Holatamico (c. 1810-1864): Seminole war leader during the Seminole Wars

Brant, Joseph, also known as Thayendanegea (1742-1807): Mohawk leader who fought with the British during the Revolutionary War

Caonabo: 1495 rebel leader during the West Indian uprisings

Clearwater, Frank (died 1973): Indian casualty of the confrontation at the Wounded Knee Occupation

Coacoochee, also known as Wildcat (c. 1810-1857): Seminole war leader during the Seminole Wars

Cochise, also known as Goci, or His Nose (c. 1812-1874): principal chief of the eastern Chiricahua during the Apache Wars.

Colbert, Levi (1790?-1834): Chickasaw chief who tried to ease the burden of removal during the Trail of Tears

Cornplanter, also known as John O'Bail (c. 1732-1836): principal Seneca chief during the American Revolution, half brother of Handsome Lake

Cornstalk (c. 1720-1777): Shawnee leader who tried to negotiate with Dunmore during Lord Dunmore's War

Crazy Horse (c. 1842-1877): key Sioux strategist in the Fetterman battle during the Bozeman Trail War

Crow Dog, Leonard (born 1942): Oglala medicine man on the Rosebud Reservation at the Wounded Knee Occupation

Deganawida, also known as Peacemaker (c. 1550-c. 1600): Huron or Mohawk prophet or holy man of the Iroquois Confederacy

Drew, John (1796-1865): Confederate Cherokee who led a regiment of full-blooded Cherokees in the Civil War

Elk, John: American Indian who voluntarily separated from his tribe; he sued for the right to vote in *Elk v. Wilkins*

Fools Crow, Frank (born 1890): Teton Sioux ceremonial chief at the Wounded Knee Occupation

Geronimo (c. 1827-1909): shaman and important leader of the western Chiricahua during the Apache Wars

Gray Beard (died 1875): Cheyenne war chief during the Red River War

Guarionex: 1495 rebel leader during the West Indian uprisings

Guarocuya (died 1509): nephew of Anacaona in the West Indian uprisings

Hall, Louis, also known as Karoniaktajeh (c. 1920-1993): Mohawk leader of Warrior Society; twentieth century critic of Handsome Lake

Hancock, King Tom (died 1712): leader of hostile Tuscarora towns during the Tuscarora War

Handsome Lake, also known as Ganeodiyo (c. 1735-1815): Seneca founder of the Code of Handsome Lake

Hendrick (c. 1680-1755): Mohawk leader at the Albany Congress

Hiawatha (c. 1525-c. 1575): Mohawk chief of the Iroquois Confederacy

Iroquet: Algonquian chief during the Beaver Wars

Japasus or Iopassus: king of the Potomacs in the Powhatan Confederacy

Joseph the Elder (1786-1871): chief of the Wallamwatkins during the Nez Perce exile

Joseph the Younger (c. 1832-1904): chief of the Wallamwatkins after his father during the Nez Perce exile

Kekataugh: the ruler of the village of Pamunkey in the Powhatan Confederacy

Kiala: war chief during the most brutal period of repression of Fox tribes fleeing French and other tribes' assaults during the Fox Wars

Kiotsaeton: Mohawk orator who presented wampum belts at peace council during the Beaver Wars

Lamont, Buddy (died 1973): Pine Ridge resident who died in the confrontation at the Wounded Knee Occupation

Lavelle, Jeannette (born 1942): Ojibwa woman who fought the enfranchisement provision of the Indian Act of 1876 (Canada)

Little Crow, also known as Taoyateduta (c. 1820-1863): principal war chief of the Santee Sioux in the Sioux War

Little Six, also known as Shakopee (died 1865): Santee leader of the "blanket" Sioux, hanged at Fort Snelling in the Sioux War

Little Turtle, also known as Michikinikwa (c. 1752-1812): Miami war chief at the Battle of Fallen Timbers

Logan, John, also known as Tachnechdorus, the Great Mingo (c. 1723-1780): Mingo war chief during Lord Dunmore's War

Lone Wolf (c. 1820-c. 1879): Kiowa chief, leader of the Kiowa war faction during the Red River War, and the principal complainant in the Supreme Court case *Lone Wolf v. Hitchcock*

Looking Glass (c. 1823-1877): Nez Perce tribal chief and warrior during the Nez Perce exile

McQueen, Peter (died 1818): mixed-blood planter, mico, and a leader of the Red Stick faction during the Creek War

Main Poc (1760?-1816): Potawatomi shaman and war chief at Prophetstown

Mangas Coloradus, or Red Sleeves (c. 1791-1863): father-in-law to Cochise and an important chief of the eastern Chiricahua during the Apache Wars

Mankato (c. 1830-1862): Santee chief killed at the Battle of Wood Lake in the Sioux War

Manuelito (c. 1818-1894): Navajo resistance leader and war chief during the Long Walk of the Navajos

Massasoit, also known as Ousamequin (c. 1580-1661): one of three paramount Wampanoag sachem during Metacom's War

Means, Russell (born 1939): Lakota cofounder of American Indian Movement (AIM)

Mekaga: minor chief who negotiated the 1738 "pardon" of the remaining tribal groups in the Rock River Valley during the Fox Wars

Menewa (c. 1765-1865): Creek chief who strongly defended his people's rights during the Trail of Tears

Metacom, also known as King Philip (c. 1640-1676): one of three paramount Wampanoag sachem during Metacom's War

Miantonomo (c. 1600-1643): chief of the Narragansetts during the Pequot War

Micanopy (c. 1780-1849): Seminole chief during the Seminole Wars

Moves Camp, Ellen: tribal elder at the Wounded Knee Occupation

Nutimus (c. 1660-c. 1742): chief of the Lenni Lenape in the Walking Purchase

Oconostota (c. 1710-1783): Cherokee military leader during the Cherokee War

Opechancanough (c. 1544-1644): chief of the Pamunkey Indians and a Powhatan successor in the Powhatan Confederacy

Opitchapam: Powhatan's successor in the Powhatan Confederacy

Osceola, also known as Billy Powell (c. 1804-1838): Seminole war leader during the Seminole Wars

Ote-emathla, also known as Jumper: Seminole war leader during the Seminole Wars

Parker, Ely Samuel (1828-1895): Seneca leader and President Grant's commissioner of Indian affairs

Parker, Quanah (c. 1845-1911): Comanche war chief during the Red River War

Peltier, Leonard (born 1944): Ojibwa-Sioux security director during the Trail of Broken Treaties; later accused of murdering two FBI agents in the Pine Ridge shootings

Pocahontas, or Matoaka (c. 1596-1617): daughter of Powhatan, wife of John Rolfe

Pontiac, also known as Obwandiag (c. 1720-1769): Ottawa war chief who organized pan-Indian resistance to the British during the French and Indian War

Popé (died 1688): major instigator of the Pueblo Revolt

Poundmaker (1842-1886): Cree chief who joined in the second Riel rebellion

Powhatan, also known as Wahunsonacock (c. 1550-1618): leader of the Powhatan Confederacy

Pushmataha (1764-1824): principal chief of the Choctaws and an able negotiator during the Trail of Tears

Red Cloud (1822-1909): chief opponent to the Bozeman Trail

Red Jacket, also known as Sagoyewatha (1751?-1830): principal Seneca chief; nephew of Handsome Lake

Reifel, Benjamin (born 1906): South Dakota congressman and member of the Rosebud Sioux tribe

Ridge, John (c. 1803-1839): son of Major Ridge and a Cherokee leader and lobbyist against the Indian Removal Act

Ridge, Major (c. 1770-1839): influential Cherokee leader who signed the removal treaty of the Indian Removal Act after resisting it for years

Riel, Louis-David (1844-1885): leader of the Metis and second president of the government of Assiniboia in the Riel rebellions

Roman Nose (c. 1830-1868): Cheyenne warrior who opposed the agreements of the Medicine Lodge Creek Treaty

Ross, John (1790-1866): elected principal chief of the Cherokees during the debate over the Indian Removal Act

Sacagawea (c. 1788-1812): Shoshoni woman whose presence with the expedition facilitated the Rocky Mountain portage of the Lewis and Clark expedition

Sassacus (c. 1560-1637): sachem of the Pequots during the Pequot War

Satank, also known as Sitting Bear (c. 1801-1871): Kiowa chief and orator at Medicine Lodge Creek

Satanta, also known as White Bear (c. 1830-1878): Kiowa chief and orator at Medicine Lodge Creek

Sequoyah (1770-1843): Cherokee author of the syllabary that made the written language of the Cherokees possible

Sitting Bull (c. 1831-1890): last great Sioux warrior chief at the Battle of Wounded Knee

Spotted Eagle Black Elk, Grace (1919-1987): tribal elder and wife of Wallace Black Elk at the Wounded Knee Occupation

Tandihetsi: Huron chief married to an Algonquian woman during the Beaver Wars

Tecumseh (1768-1813): Shawnee war chief and diplomat, advocate of a Native American alliance to stop the European advance in the Ohio Valley and nearby areas during Little Turtle's War

Ten Bears (1792-1872): Comanche chief and orator who led peace efforts between the Native Americans and the U.S. government that led to the Medicine Lodge Creek Treaty

Tenskwatawa, also known as the Prophet (1768-1837): religious leader who reportedly inspired Pontiac's resistance, founder of Prophetstown

Tomasito: Taos Indian rebel who was believed to have murdered New Mexico governor Charles Bent

Tupatú, Luis: successor to Popé and a principal aid during the Pueblo Revolt

Uncas (c. 1606-c. 1682): relative of Sassacus, who rebelled during the Pequot War

Wamsutta, also known as Alexander (died 1661): one of three paramount Wampanoag sachem during Metacom's War

Ware, Ralph: Kiowa negotiator for the Indians during the Trail of Broken Treaties

Watie, Stand (1806-1871): Confederate general who led a regiment of mixed-blood American Indians in the Civil War

Weatherford, William (c. 1780-1822): mixed-blood son of a Scots trader and a leader of the Red Stick faction during the Creek War

Wilson, Richard: chairman of the Bureau of Indian Affairs tribal council at the Wounded Knee Occupation

Wovoka, also known as Jack Wilson (c. 1858-1932): Paiute messiah of the Ghost Dance religion

Museums, Archives, and Libraries

Select list of museums, archives, and libraries in four parts: museums in the United States; museums in Canada; libraries and archives in the United States; libraries and archives in Canada. Each part is arranged alphabetically, first by state, territory, or province, then by city.

Museums in the United States

ALABAMA

Alabama Museum of Natural History
Smith Hall, University of Alabama
Tuscaloosa, 35487-0340
Resource center of Southeastern Indians; ties with Moundville Archaeological Park.

ALASKA

Alaska State Museum
395 Whittier Street
Juneau, 99801-1718
Alaskan Native Gallery; Subarctic and Northwest Coast items.

Totem Heritage Center
601 Deermount
(mailing address: 629 Dock Street)
Ketchikan, 99901
Programs and artifacts in Northwest Coast arts; index to all Alaska totem poles.

ARIZONA

Arizona State Museum
University of Arizona
Tucson, 85721
Extensive collections from the historic and prehistoric peoples of the area.

Colorado River Indian Tribes Museum
Route 1, Box 23B
Parker, 85344
Artifacts from Mojave, Chemehuevi, Hopi, and Navajo as well as prehistoric cultures.

Gila River Arts and Crafts Center
P.O. Box 457
Sacaton, 85247
Museum and crafts reflect all tribes of the area.

Heard Museum
22 E. Monte Vista Road
Phoenix, 85004-1480
Southwest emphasis; inventory of 8,200 Native American artists. Library of 40,000 volumes includes Fred Harvey Company documents and photo archives.

Museum of Northern Arizona
Fort Valley Road
(mailing address: Route 4, P.O. Box 720)
Flagstaff, 86001
Southwest Anglo and Indian art, with Hopi and Navajo emphasis. Harold S. Colton Memorial Library of 24,000 volumes.

Navajo Tribal Museum
Highway 264
(mailing address: P.O. Box 308)
Window Rock, 86515
Four Corners archaeology and ethnography, including re-creation of 1870-1930 era trading post.

ARKANSAS

Arkansas State Museum
P.O. Box 490
State University, 72467
Emphasizes northeastern Arkansas tribes such as the Osage, Caddo, Chickasaw, and others.

CALIFORNIA

Bowers Museum of Cultural Art
2002 North Main Street
Santa Ana, 92706
Collection of 85,000 items focuses on the fine arts of indigenous peoples, including pre-Columbian and Native American.

Fowler Museum of Cultural History
University of California, Los Angeles
405 Hilgard Avenue
Los Angeles, 90024-1549
   Extensive archaeological and ethnographic collections include Native American materials.

Maturango Museum
100 E. Las Flores
(mailing address: P.O. Box 1776)
Ridgecrest, 93556
   A small regional museum focusing on one of the richest petroglyph areas in the United States at China Lake.

Natural History Museum of Los Angeles County
Times-Mirror Hall of Native American Cultures; Hall of Pre-Columbian
   Cultures
900 Exposition Boulevard
Los Angeles, 90007
   Excellent permanent displays, with changing exhibitions on contemporary issues in art and culture. The Pre-Columbian Hall covers cultures from Mexico to Peru.

Southwest Museum
234 Museum Drive
(mailing address: P.O. Box 558)
Los Angeles, 90065
   Collections range from Alaska to South America, with permanent displays focusing on the Southwest, Great Plains, California, and Northwest Coast. Braun Research Library contains 50,000 volumes, 100,000 photos, 900 recordings, and archival material.

COLORADO

Denver Art Museum
100 W. 14th Avenue Parkway
Denver, 80204
   Art collection includes Indian clothing, Southwest pottery and kachinas, and Northwest Coast carvings. Frederick H. Douglas Library includes 6,000 volumes.

Denver Museum of Natural History
2001 South Colorado Boulevard
Denver, 80205

Strong on Paleo-Indian culture, including the original Folsom spear point; a 24,000-volume library.

Southern Ute Cultural Center and Gallery
Highway 172
(mailing address: P.O. Box 737)
Ignacio, 81137

Early history; contemporary bead and leather work.

CONNECTICUT

American Indian Archaeological Institute (AIAI)
38 Curtis Road
(mailing address: P.O. Box 1260)
Washington Green, 06793-0260

Continental coverage, but focus is on Northeast Woodlands. Reconstructed Indian village, with Indian Habitats Trail; 250,000 artifacts and a 2,000-volume library.

Peabody Museum
Yale University
170 Whitney
New Haven, 06511-8161

Extensive holdings include both archaeological and ethnographic materials of the Americas.

DELAWARE

Delaware State Museum
316 South Governors Avenue
Dover, 19901

Eastern prehistory; 1,000-volume library; State Archaeological Collection.

DISTRICT OF COLUMBIA

U.S. National Museum of Natural History
Smithsonian Institution
Washington, DC 20560

FLORIDA

Ah-Tha-Thi-Ki Museum
3240 North 64th Avenue
Hollywood, 33024
   Artifacts and activities document and preserve Seminole traditions; village, burial site, nature trails.

Florida State Museum
University of Florida
Gainesville, 32601
   Pearsall Collection of ethnographic items ranges from Seminole to Inuit.

GEORGIA

New Echota
Route 3
Calhoun, 30701
   Restoration of Cherokee capital of 1825-1838. Trail of Tears material.

IDAHO

Nez Perce National Historic Park
Highway 95
(mailing address: P.O. Box 93)
Spalding, 83551
   Prehistoric as well as historic regional items. Park notes sites of Indian-U.S. battles. A 600-volume library and archive of 3,000 photos.

ILLINOIS

Field Museum of Natural History
Roosevelt Road at Lake Shore Drive
Chicago, 60605
   Extensive Native American collections, including Pawnee earth lodge replica. Webber Resource Center houses books and audio-visual materials on indigenous cultures.

INDIANA

Eiteljorg Museum of American Indian and Western Art

500 West Washington Street
Indianapolis, 46204

Extensive collection that emphasizes Northeast Woodlands, great Plains, and Southwest culture areas.

IOWA

Putnam Museum of History and Natural Science

1717 West 12th Street
Davenport, 52804

Regional ethnographic collections and important Mississippian materials.

KANSAS

Indian Center Museum

650 North Seneca
Wichita, 67203

Collection reflects Indian art and religion.

KENTUCKY

J. B. Speed Art Museum

2035 South Third Street
(mailing address: P.O. Box 2600)
Louisville, 40201-2600

Collection emphasizes regional materials and the Great Plains, complemented by a 14,000-volume art library that includes the Frederick Weygold Indian Collection.

LOUISIANA

Tunica-Biloxi Regional Indian Center and Museum

Highway 1
(mailing address: P.O. Box 331)
Marksville, 71351

Focuses on descendants of the mound builders. The tribal museum is built in a classic Mississippian style. Collections include colonial Indian-European materials returned to the tribe under the Indian Graves and Repatriation Act.

MAINE

Peary-MacMillan Arctic Museum and Studies Center
Hubbard Hall, Bowdoin College
Brunswick, 04011
   MacMillan collection of Inuit and Subarctic material culture.

MASSACHUSETTS

Peabody Museum of Archaeology and Ethnology
11 Divinity Avenue
Harvard University
Cambridge, 02138
   Worldwide collection of 2,000,000 artifacts has a North and South American focus; 180,000-volume library.

MICHIGAN

Cranbrook Institute of Science
500 Lone Pine Road
(mailing address: P.O. Box 801)
Bloomfield Hills, 48303-0801
   Collection reflects all North American culture areas.

MINNESOTA

Mille Lacs Indian Museum
HCR 67
(mailing address: P.O. Box 95)
Onamia, 56359
   Ojibwa and Dakota artifacts illustrate traditional lifeways.

Minnesota Historical Society's Grand Mound and Interpretive Center
Route 7
(mailing address: P.O. Box 453)
International Falls, 56649
   Burial mounds with extensive exhibits of Woodland, Laurel, and Blackduck cultures.

MISSISSIPPI

Grand Village of the Natchez Indians
400 Jefferson Davis Boulevard
Natchez, 39120

Artifacts explore the culture of the descendants of the Mississippian mound builders.

MISSOURI

St. Louis Science Center
5050 Oakland Avenue
St. Louis, 63110

MONTANA

Museum of the Plains Indian and Crafts Center
U.S. 89
(mailing address: P.O. Box 400)
Browning, 59417

Northern Plains material culture; reconstruction of 1850's Blackfeet camp.

NEBRASKA

Fur Trade Museum
East Highway 20, HC 74
(mailing address: P.O. Box 18)
Chadron, 69337

Museum of Nebraska History
131 Centennial Mall North
Lincoln, 68508

Anthropology and art of the central Plains tribes.

NEVADA

Lost City Museum
721 South Highway 169
Overton, 89040

Reconstructed pueblo and kiva; archaeological museum; 400-volume library.

NEW JERSEY

Montclair Art Museum
3 South Mountain Avenue
Montclair, 07042
   Rand Collection of Native American art. Art history library of 13,000 volumes.

New Jersey State Museum
205 West State Street
Trenton, 08625
   Local material as well as Plains, Arctic, Southwest, and Northeast collections.

NEW MEXICO

Maxwell Museum of Anthropology
University of New Mexico
Roma and University, N.E.
Albuquerque, 87131-1201
   Extensive Southwest collections. Library of 12,500 volumes and photo archives.

Museum of Indian Arts and Culture
708 Camino Lejo
(mailing address: P.O. Box 2087)
Santa Fe, 87504
   Exhibits focus on Pueblo, Apache, and Navajo cultures. A 20,000-volume library on the anthropology of the Southwest.

Western New Mexico University Museum
(mailing address: P.O. Box 43)
Silver City, 88061
   Eisele collection of classic Mimbres pottery.

NEW YORK

American Museum of Natural History
79th Street and Central Park West
New York, 10024-5192
   Exhibitions are especially strong on the cultures of the Arctic and Pacific Northwest.

National Museum of the American Indian
George Gustav Heye Center
Alexander Hamilton Custom House
3753 Broadway at 155th Street
New York, 10032

The first of three planned facilities of the National Museum of the American Indian, part of the Smithsonian Institution, opened in New York in 1994.

Seneca Iroquois National Museum
Broad Street Extension
(mailing address: P.O. Box 442)
Salamanca, 14779

Special wampum belt exhibit; typical nineteenth century elm-bark longhouse reconstruction; contemporary art.

NORTH CAROLINA

Indian Museum of the Carolinas
607 Turnpike Road
Laurinburg, 28352

Exhibits feature Southeast cultures and lifeways.

Native American Resource Center
Pembroke State University
Pembroke, 28372

Eastern Woodlands materials; North and South America.

NORTH DAKOTA

North Dakota Heritage Center
612 East Boulevard
Bismarck, 58505

Plains cultures. A 100,000-volume library on ethnology and history.

Turtle Mountain Chippewa Heritage Center
Highway 5
(mailing address: P.O. Box 257)
Belcourt, 58316

Promotes tribal history and traditions. Contemporary art gallery.

OHIO

Cincinnati Museum of Natural History
1301 Western Avenue
Cincinnati, 45203
Good selection of mound builder artifacts from the Ohio Valley.

Cleveland Museum of Natural History
1 Wade Oval Drive
University Circle
Cleveland, 44106-1767
Research fields include archaeology and physical anthropology. A 50,000-volume natural history library.

OKLAHOMA

Cherokee Heritage Center
Willis Road
(mailing address: P.O. Box 515)
Tahlequah, 74465
Reconstructed village; contemporary arts and crafts.

Museum of the Great Plains
601 Ferris Avenue
Lawton, 73502
Artifacts, library, and photo archives relating to Plains tribes.

The Philbrook Museum of Art, Inc.
2727 South Rockford Road
Tulsa, 74114
Clark Field Basket Collection; Lawson Collection of Indian clothing; Philbrook Collection of American Indian paintings; Lawson Indian library.

Seminole Nation Museum and Library
6th and Wewoka
(mailing address: P.O. Box 1532)
Wewoka, 74884

OREGON

High Desert Museum
59800 South Highway 97
Bend, 97702

Museum of Natural History
University of Oregon
1680 East 15th Avenue
Eugene, 97403-1224
　　Collection includes 13,000-year-old Fort Rock Cave artifacts.

PENNSYLVANIA

Carnegie Museum of Natural History
4400 Forbes Avenue
Pittsburgh, 15213-4080
　　Wide coverage, including Arctic and Northwest Coast collections.

RHODE ISLAND

Haffenreffer Museum of Anthropology
Brown University
Bristol, 02809
　　Arctic and Subarctic materials, including Archaic Period remains of
the Red Paint People of Maine.

SOUTH CAROLINA

McKissick Museum
University of South Carolina
Columbia, 29208
　　Catawba pottery and baskets. Folk Art Resource Center.

SOUTH DAKOTA

Indian Museum of North America
Avenue of the Chiefs, Black Hills
Crazy Horse, 57730

Sioux Indian Museum and Crafts Center
515 West Boulevard
Rapid City, 57709

W. H. Over State Museum
414 East Clark
Vermillion, 57069-2390
　　Plains material culture and contemporary painting.

TENNESSEE

Frank H. McClung Museum
University of Tennessee
1327 Circle Park Drive
Knoxville, 37996-3200

Tennessee State Museum
505 Deaderick Street
Nashville, 37243-1120
Strong in prehistoric Mississippian culture.

TEXAS

Alabama-Coushatta Museum
U.S. Highway 190
Route 3
(mailing address: P.O. Box 540)
Livingston, 77351

Panhandle-Plains Historical Museum
2401 Fourth Avenue
Canyon, 79016
Hall of the Southern Plains. South and Southwest Indian focus; 10,000-volume library.

Texas Memorial Museum
University of Texas
24th and Trinity
Austin, 78705
Broad focus on the anthropology of the American Indian.

Witte Memorial Museum
3801 Broadway
San Antonio, 78209
Samples most North American culture areas.

UTAH

College of Eastern Utah Prehistoric Museum
451 East 400 North
Price, 84501
Focuses on Anasazi and Fremont cultures.

Utah Museum of Natural History
University of Utah
Salt Lake City, 84112
  Regional, Great Basin, and Southwestern materials.

VIRGINIA

Jamestown Settlement
(mailing address: P.O. Box JF)
Williamsburg, 23187
  Reconstruction of Indian village and Powhatan's lodge.

Mattaponi Museum
West Point, 23181
  Important collection of archaeological materials.

Pamunkey Indian Museum
(mailing address: P.O. Box 2050)
King William, 23086
  Contemporary and prehistoric art and artifacts.

WASHINGTON

The Burke Museum
University of Washington, DB-10
Seattle, 98195
  Northwest Coast and Pacific Rim collections.

Makah Cultural and Research Center
(mailing address: P.O. Box 160)
Neah Bay, 98257
  Features remains from the Ozette site, a Late Period pre-contact Makah village buried and preserved in a mudslide. Magnificent Northwest Coast Tradition assemblage of 60,000 artifacts.

Seattle Art Museum
100 University Street
(mailing address: P.O. Box 22000)
Seattle, 98122-9700
  Excellent collection of Northwest Coast art.

Yakima Nation Cultural Heritage Center
Toppenish, 98948

WEST VIRGINIA

Grave Creek Mound State Park
Moundsville, 26041
    Largest mound produced by the Adena ceremonial complex, which flourished around 500 B.C.E. to 100 C.E.

WISCONSIN

Lac du Flambeau Chippewa Museum
(mailing address: P.O. Box 804)
Lac du Flambeau, 54538
    Eighteenth century dugout canoe, artifacts, and seasonal activities displays.

Logan Museum of Anthropology
700 College Street
Beloit College
Beloit, 53511-5595
    Physical and cultural anthropological materials from the Great Lakes, Plains, and Southwest culture areas.

Milwaukee Public Museum
800 West Wells Street
Milwaukee, 53233
    Collections cover North America. A 125,000-volume library.

Neville Public Museum
129 South Jefferson Street
Green Bay, 54301
    Archaic Period materials from the Old Copper and Red Ochre cultures.

WYOMING

Anthropology Museum
University of Wyoming
Laramie, 82071

Museums in Canada

ALBERTA

Glenbow Museum
130 Ninth Avenue, S.E.
Calgary, AB T2G 0P3

Provincial Museum of Alberta
12845 102nd Avenue
Edmonton, AB T5N 0M6
   Regional materials; Inuit; northern Plains.

BRITISH COLUMBIA

Campbell River Museum
1235 Island Highway
Campbell Island, BC V9W 2C7
   Arts of the Indian groups of northern Vancouver Island.

'Ksan Indian Village
(mailing address: P.O. Box 326)
Hazelton, BC B0J 1Y0
   A center for the display, preservation, and promotion of Gitksan arts and crafts skills. Seven traditional buildings.

Museum of Anthropology
University of British Columbia
Vancouver, BC V6T 1Z1
   Major Northwest Coast collections. Center for promotion of traditional arts and customs.

Museum of Northern British Columbia
(mailing address: P.O. Box 669)
Prince Rupert, BC V8J 3S1
   Northwest Coast artifacts. Promotes contemporary carving and craft skills.

Royal British Columbia Museum
675 Belleville Street
Victoria, BC V8V 1X4
   Traditional Kwakiutl dance houses; Thunderbird Park totem pole exhibits; art demonstrations.

MANITOBA

Eskimo Museum
La Verendrye Street
(mailing address: P.O. Box 10)
Churchill, MB R0B 0E0
    Inuit materials include kayaks dating back hundreds of years. Also, Subarctic materials from Chippewa and Cree cultures.

Manitoba Museum of Man and Nature
190 Rupert Avenue
Winnipeg, MB R3B 0N2

NEW BRUNSWICK

New Brunswick Museum
277 Douglas Avenue
Saint John, NB F2K 1E5
    Regional and pre-Algonquian artifacts.

NEWFOUNDLAND

Newfoundland Museum
285 Duckworth Street
St. John's, NF A1C 1G9
    Exhibits cover the six major tribal groups of Labrador and Newfoundland.

NORTHWEST TERRITORIES

Dene Cultural Institute
(mailing address: P.O. Box 207)
Yellowknife, NT X1A 2N2

Northern Life Museum
110 King Street
(mailing address: P.O. Box 420)
Fort Smith, NT X0E 0P0
    Arctic and Subartic tools and artifacts.

NOVA SCOTIA

Nova Scotia Museum
1747 Summer Street
Halifax, NS B3H 3A6
 Artifacts of the Micmac.

ONTARIO

Museum of Indian Archaeology and Lawson Prehistoric Village
1600 Attawandaron Road
London, ON N6G 3M6
 Exhibits cover five phases of culture dating back to Paleo-Indian times. On-site excavation.

North American Indian Travel College
The Living Museum
RR 3
Cornwall Island, ON K6H 5R7

Royal Ontario Museum
100 Queen's Park Crescent
Toronto, ON M5S 2C6
 Ontario prehistory.

Thunder Bay Art Gallery
1080 Keewatin Street
(mailing address: P.O. Box 1193)
Thunder Bay, ON P7C 4X9
 Traditional items as well as contemporary art.

PRINCE EDWARD ISLAND

Micmac Indian Village
(mailing address: P.O. Box 51)
Cornwall, PEI C0A 1H0

QUEBEC

Abenakis Museum
Route 226
Odanak, PQ J0G 1H0
 Displays reflect tribal traditions and lore.

Canadian Museum of Civilization
100 Laurier Street
Hull, PQ J8X 4H2
Spectacular collection of national cultural materials.

McCord Museum
McGill University
690 Sherbrook Street W.
Montreal, PQ H3A 1E9

SASKATCHEWAN

Regina Plains Museum
1801 Scarth Street
Regina, SK S4P 2G9
Metis history and the Riel Rebellions are covered in addition to Plains material.

Saskatchewan Museum of Natural History
Wascana Park
Regina, SK S4P 3V7
Native Peoples Gallery focusing on Subarctic tribes.

YUKON TERRITORY

MacBride Museum
(mailing address: P.O. Box 4037)
Whitehorse, YT Y1A 3S9
Artifacts of the Yukon region.

Libraries and Archives in the United States

ALABAMA

Alabama Department of Archives and History
624 Washington Avenue
Montgomery, 36130

ARIZONA

Navajo Nation Library System
Drawer K
Window Rock, 86515
 Collection has 23,000 books, 1,000 manuscripts, and films and tapes. Files of the *Navajo Times*. Two libraries in Window Rock and one in Navajo, New Mexico.

Smoki People Library
P.O. Box 123
Prescott, 86302
 Library of 600 volumes covers North and South American Indian ceremonials and dances.

Tohono Chul Park, Inc.
7366 North Paseo del Norte
Tucson, 85704
 Nature center, ethnic art exhibitions, and 800-volume library on Southwest culture and environment.

Western Archaeological and Conservation Center
1415 North Sixth Avenue
(mailing address: P.O. Box 41058, Tucson, 85717)
Tucson, 85705
 Focus on Southwest prehistory and ethnography: 17,000-volume library, 100 periodicals, and 160,000-item photo archive.

ARKANSAS

Southwest Arkansas Regional Archives (SARA)
P.O. Box 134
Washington, 71862
 History of Caddo Indians and Southwest Arkansas.

CALIFORNIA

American Indian Resource Center
Public Library of Los Angeles County
6518 Miles Avenue
Huntington Park, 90255
 Special collections on Indians of North America; 9,000 volumes.

Malki Museum Archives
11-795 Fields Road
Banning, 92220
 Oral history project tapes; field notes of J. P. Harrington and others; manuscript and photo archives.

Native American Studies Library
University of California at Berkeley
103 Wheeler
Berkeley, 94720
 Reports of the Bureau of Indian Affairs; Indian Claims Commission materials; special California Indian collection; extensive holdings.

Rupert Costo Library
UCR Library Special Collections
University of California at Riverside
Riverside, 92517
 The 15,000-volume collection is countrywide in scope with a California concentration. Houses the American Indian Historical Society Archives, donated by the Costos. Manuscripts, field notes, and 300 books cover the customs and medicines of the Chinantec Indians of Oaxaca.

Scientific Library
San Diego Museum of Man
Balboa Park
1350 El Prado
San Diego, 92101
 Wide coverage of the Americas, including physical anthropology, archaeology, and ethnology.

COLORADO

Koshare Indian Museum, Inc.
115 West 18th Street
La Junta, 81050
 The 10,000-volume Special Koshare Collection focuses on Native America and Western United States.

National Indian Law Library
Native American Rights Fund
1522 Broadway
Boulder, 80302-6296
 Documents, periodicals, and 7,500 books on U.S.-Indian relations and law.

Taylor Museum Reference Library
Colorado Springs Fine Arts Center
30 West Dale Street
Colorado Springs, 80903
  Art of the Southwest; Hispanic and colonial folk art. Collection houses 30,000 volumes; extensive biographies of folk artists.

Ute Mountain Tribal Research Archive and Library
Tribal Compound
(mailing address: P.O. Box CC)
Towaoc, 81334
  Includes 2,500 books as well as 30,000 archival items, including tribal government documents.

CONNECTICUT

Mashantucket Pequot Research Library
Indiantown Road
Ledyard, 06339

DISTRICT OF COLUMBIA

American Folklife Center
U.S. Library of Congress
Thomas Jefferson Building - G152
Washington, DC 20540
  Biggest collection of early Indian recordings, including the Frances Densmore Collection of 3,600 cylinders and the Helen Heffron Roberts Collection from the Northwest Coast and California.

National Anthropological Archives
Natural History Museum MRC 152
10th and Constitution Avenue
Washington, DC 20560
  Extensive collections of recordings, photographs, field notes, and manuscripts of the Bureau of Ethnology.

Natural Resources Library
U.S. Department of the Interior
Mail Stop 1151
18th and C Streets, N.W.
Washington, DC 20240
  More than 600,000 volumes and extensive periodicals and archival items, including materials on American Indians.

GEORGIA

Hargrett Rare Books and Manuscript Library
University of Georgia
Athens, 30602

ILLINOIS

Newberry Library
D'Arcy McNickle Center for the History of the American Indian
60 West Walton Street
Chicago, 60610
  More than 100,000 volumes, including the E. E. Ayer Collection.

INDIANA

Fulton County Historical Society Library
Route 3
(mailing address: P.O. Box 89)
Rochester, 46975
  Collection houses 4,000 volumes, including coverage of Potawatomi removal to Kansas in 1838 (the Trail of Death).

Lilly Library
Indiana University
Bloomington, 47405
  Collection includes Indian accounts of Custer's defeat at the Battle of the Little Bighorn.

KANSAS

Mennonite Library and Archives
Bethel College
300 East 27th Street
North Newton, 67117-9989
  Includes 26,000 books. Petter Manuscript Collection on the Cheyenne; H. R. Voth Manuscript and Photo Collection on the Hopi.

Mid-America All Indian Center Library
650 North Seneca
Wichita, 67203
  Includes 3,000 books and 200 bound periodical volumes on Indian art, history, and culture. Blackbear Bosin Collection of publications and personal papers.

LOUISIANA

Grindstone Bluff Museum Library
(mailing address: P.O. Box 7965)
Shreveport, 71107

Contains 6,000 books and 2,000 periodical volumes on regional archaeology and ethnology; emphasis on Caddo Indians.

MASSACHUSETTS

Fruitlands Museums and Library
102 Prospect Hill Road
Harvard, 01451

Mashpee Archives Building
Mashpee, 02649

MICHIGAN

Custer Collection
Monroe County Library System
Monroe, 48161

Contains 4,000 books and archival materials on Custer and the West.

MINNESOTA

Minnesota Historical Society
Divison of Archives and Manuscripts
345 Kellogg Boulevard West
St. Paul, 55102-1906

Materials relating to the Ojibwa and Dakota.

MISSOURI

Missouri Historical Society Library
Jefferson Memorial Building
Forest Park
St. Louis, 63112

Northern Plains; papers of William Clark from Lewis and Clark expedition.

MONTANA

Dr. John Woodenlegs Memorial Library
Dull Knife Memorial College
P.O. Box 98
Lame Deer, 59043-0098
Cheyenne history; oral history collection. Contains 10,000 volumes.

NEBRASKA

Joslyn Art Museum
Art Reference Library
2200 Dodge Street
Omaha, 68102
Native American art covered in collection of 25,000 volumes, 3,000 bound periodicals, and 20,000 slides.

Native American Public Broadcasting Consortium Library
P.O. Box 83111
Lincoln, 68501
Special Collection of Native American video programs (171 titles). Audio program "Spirits of the Present." NAPBC quarterly newsletter. Materials available by mail.

Nebraska State Historical Society Library
P.O. Box 82554
Lincoln, 68501
Anderson Collection of Brule Sioux photographs. Library has 70,000 volumes.

NEW JERSEY

Firestone Library Collections of Western Americana
Princeton University
Princeton, 08544

NEW MEXICO

Mary Cabot Wheelwright Research Library
704 Camino Lejo
Santa Fe, 87502
Contains 10,000 volumes; archives on Navajo religion and sand-painting.

Millicent Rogers Museum Library
P.O. Box A
Taos, 87571
　Registry of New Mexico Hispanic artists, including a number of Indian artists.

Museum of New Mexico Photo Archives
P.O. Box 2087
Santa Fe, 87504

NEW YORK

Akwesasne Library
Route 37-RR 1
(mailing address: P.O. Box 14-C)
Hogansburg, 13655

Iroquois Indian Museum Library
P.O. Box 9
Bowes Cave, 12042-0009
　Contains 1,500 volumes; 500 archival items; exhibition catalogs.

Museum of the American Indian Library
9 Westchester Square
Bronx, 10461
　Contains 40,000 volumes; archives.

Seneca Nation Library
Allegany Branch
P.O. Box 231
Salamanca, 14779
Cattaraugus Branch
Irving, 14981

NORTH CAROLINA

State Archives
109 East Jones Street
Raleigh, 27601-2807

OHIO

Ohio Historical Society Archives and Library
1982 Velma Avenue
Columbus, 43211

OKLAHOMA

Chickasaw Nation Library
Arlington and Mississippi Streets
Ada, 74830

Gilcrease Library
1400 Gilcrease Museum Road
Tulsa, 74127
John Ross (Cherokee chief) and Peter Pitchlynn (Choctaw chief) papers; 50,000 volumes.

Oklahoma Historical Society Archives and Manuscript Division
2100 North Lincoln Boulevard
Oklahoma City, 73105
State Indian Agency records; Dawes Commission papers; 125,000 photographs.

OREGON

Siletz Library and Archives
119 East Logsden Road, Building II
Siletz, 97380

PENNSYLVANIA

Free Library of Philadelphia
Logan Square
Philadelphia, 19103

University Museum Library
33rd and Spruce Streets
University of Pennsylvania
Philadelphia, 19104
Brinton Collection on Indian linguistics; Delaware materials.

SOUTH DAKOTA

Center for Western Studies
Augustana College
P.O. Box 727
Sioux Falls, 57197
Great Plains history. Collection has 30,000 volumes, 1,500 linear feet of manuscripts.

TEXAS

Fikes Hall of Special Collections
DeGolyer Library
Southern Methodist University
Dallas, 75275

National Archives
Southwest Region
501 Felix at Hemphill, Building 1
P.O. Box 6216
Fort Worth, 76115
    Bureau of Indian Affairs records for Oklahoma.

UTAH

Ute Tribal Museum, Library, and Audio-Visual Center
Fort Duchesne, 84026

WASHINGTON

Jamestown Klallam Library
Blyn, 98382

Special Collections
University of Washington
Seattle, 98195

WEST VIRGINIA

ERIC Clearinghouse on Rural Education and Small Schools (CRESS) Library
1031 Quarrier Street
(mailing address: P.O. Box 1348)
Charleston, 25325
    Microfiche containing 300,000 documents. Indian/Hispanic issues.

WISCONSIN

Fairlawn Historical Museum
Harvard View Parkway
Superior, 54880
    George Catlin lithographs; David F. Berry Collection of Indian photographs and portraits.

Hoard Historical Museum Library
407 Merchant Avenue
Fort Atkinson, 53538
Rare Black Hawk War materials.

WYOMING

McCracken Research Library
Buffalo Bill Historical Center
P.O. Box 1000
Cody, 82414

Libraries and Archives in Canada

ALBERTA

Canadian Circumpolar Library
University of Alberta
Edmonton, AB T6G 2J8

University of Lethbridge Library
Special Collections
4401 University Drive
Lethbridge, AB T1K 3M4
Native American studies; English literature; education.

BRITISH COLUMBIA

Alert Bay Library and Museum
199 Fir Street
Alert Bay, BC B0N 1A0

Kamloops Museum and Archives
207 Seymour Street
Kamloops, BC V2C 2E7
Interior Salish and Shuswap material.

University of British Columbia Library
1956 Main Hall
Vancouver, BC V6T 1Z1

MANITOBA

Department of Indian Affairs and Northern Development Regional Library
275 Portage Avenue
Winnipeg, MB R3B 3A3

People's Library
Manitoba Indian Cultural Education Centre
119 Sutherland Avenue
Winnipeg, MB R2W 3C9

NEW BRUNSWICK

Education Resource Centre
University of New Brunswick
D'Avray Hall
P.O. Box 7500
Fredericton, NB E3B 5H5

NORTHWEST TERRITORIES

Thebacha Campus Library
Arctic College
Fort Smith, NT X0E 0P0

NOVA SCOTIA

Nova Scotia Human Rights Commission Library
P.O. Box 2221
Halifax, NS B3J 3C4
   Rights of indigenous peoples, women, and others; 4,000 books.

ONTARIO

Department of Indian Affairs and Northern Development Departmental Library
Ottawa, ON K1A 0H4

University of Sudbury Library and Jesuit Archives
Sudbury, ON P3E 2C6

QUEBEC

Canadian Museum of Civilization Library
100 Laurier Street
Hull, PQ J8X 4H2

SASKATCHEWAN

Gabriel Dumont Institute of Native Studies and Applied Research Library
121 Broadway
Regina, SK S4N 0Z6
   Indian History archives; 30,000 volumes.

Indian Federated College Library
University of Regina
Regina, SK S4S 0A2
   Collection has 15,000 volumes. Branch library of 4,000 volumes on Saskatoon campus.

Saskatchewan Provincial Library
1352 Winnipeg Street
Regina, SK S4P 3V7
   Has a 4,000-volume Indian collection. Strong in languages.

Organizations, Agencies, and Societies

All Indian Pueblo Council
Founded: 1958
P.O. Box 3256
Albuquerque, NM 87190

American Indian Council of Architects and Engineers
Founded: 1976
P.O. Box 230685
Tigard, OR 97223

American Indian Culture Research Center
Founded: 1967
Box 98
Blue Cloud Abbey
Marvin, SD 57251

American Indian Graduate Center
Founded: 1969
4520 Montgomery Boulevard NE
Ste. 1-B
Albuquerque, NM 87109

American Indian Health Care Association
Founded: 1975
245 E. 6th Street
Ste. 499
St. Paul, MN 55101

American Indian Heritage Foundation
Founded: 1973
6051 Arlington Boulevard
Falls Church, VA 22044

American Indian Higher Education Consortium
Founded: 1972
513 Capitol Court NE
Ste. 100
Washington, DC 20002

American Indian Horse Registry
Founded: 1961
Route 3, Box 64
Lockhart, TX 78644

American Indian Liberation Crusade
Founded: 1952
4009 S. Halldale Avenue
Los Angeles, CA 90062

American Indian Library Association
Founded: 1979
50 E. Huron Street
Chicago, IL 60611

American Indian Lore Association
Founded: 1957
960 Walhonding Avenue
Logan, OH 43138

American Indian Movement (AIM)
Founded: 1968
710 Clayton Street
Apartment 1
San Francisco, CA 94117

American Indian Registry for the Performing Arts
Founded: 1983
1717 N. Highland Avenue
Ste. 614
Los Angeles, CA 90028

American Indian Research and Development
Founded: 1982
2424 Springer Drive
Ste. 200
Norman, OK 73069

American Indian Science and Engineering Society
Founded: 1977
1630 30th Street
Ste. 301
Boulder, CO 80301

Americans for Indian Opportunity
Founded: 1970
3508 Garfield Street NW
Washington, DC 20007

Arrow, Incorporated (Americans for Restitution and Righting of Old Wrongs)
Founded: 1949
1000 Connecticut Avenue NW
Ste. 1206
Washington, DC 20036

Associated Community of Friends on Indian Affairs
Founded: 1869
Box 1661
Richmond, IN 47375

Association of American Indian Physicians
Founded: 1971
Building D
10015 S. Pennsylvania
Oklahoma City, OK 73159

Association of Community Tribal Schools
Founded: 1982
c/o Dr. Roger Bordeaux
616 4th Avenue W
Sisseton, SD 57262-1349

Association on American Indian Affairs
Founded: 1923
432 Park Ave. S.
New York, NY 10016

Bureau of Catholic Indian Missions
Founded: 1874
2021 H Street NW
Washington, DC 20006

Cherokee National Historical Society
Founded: 1963
P.O. Box 515
Tahlequah, OK 74465

Coalition for Indian Education
Founded: 1987
3620 Wyoming Boulevard NE
Ste. 206
Albuquerque, NM 87111

Concerned American Indian Parents
Founded: 1987
CUHCC Clinic
2016 16th Avenue S
Minneapolis, MN 55404

Continental Confederation of Adopted Indians
Founded: 1950
960 Walhonding Avenue
Logan, OH 43138

Council for Indian Education
Founded: 1970
517 Rimrock Road
Billings, MT 59102

Council for Native American Indians
Founded: 1974
280 Broadway
Ste. 316
New York, NY 10007

Council of Energy Resource Tribes (CERT)
Founded: 1975
1999 Broadway
Ste. 2600
Denver, CO 80202

Crazy Horse Memorial Foundation
Founded: 1948
The Black Hills
Avenue of the Chiefs
Crazy Horse, SD 57730

Creek Indian Memorial Association
Founded: 1923
Creek County House Museum
Town Square
Okmulgee, OK 74447

Dakota Women of All Red Nations (DWARN)
Founded: 1978
c/o Lorelei DeCora
P.O. Box 423
Rosebud, SD 57570

First Nations Development Institute
Founded: 1980
69 Kelley Road
Falmouth, VA 22405

Gathering of Nations
Founded: 1984
P.O. Box 75102
Sta. 14
Albuquerque, NM 87120-1269

Indian Arts and Crafts Association
Founded: 1974
122 La Veta Drive NE
Ste. B
Albuquerque, NM 87108

Indian Heritage Council
Founded: 1988
Henry Street
Box 2302
Morristown, TN 37816

Indian Law Resource Center
Founded: 1978
508 Stuart Street
Helena, MT 59601

Indian Rights Association
Founded: 1882
1801 Market Street
Philadelphia, PA 19103-1675

Indian Youth of America
Founded: 1978
609 Badgerow Building
Sioux City, IA 51101

Institute for American Indian Studies
Founded: 1971
38 Curtis Road
P.O. Box 1260
Washington, CT 06793-0260

Institute for the Development of Indian Law
Founded: 1971
c/o K. Kirke Kickingbird
Oklahoma City University
School of Law
2501 Blackwelder
Oklahoma City, OK 73106

Institute for the Study of American Cultures
Founded: 1983
The Rankin
1004 Broadway
Columbus, GA 31901

Institute for the Study of Traditional American Indian Arts
Founded: 1982
P.O. Box 66124
Portland, OR 97290

Institute of American Indian Arts
Founded: 1962
P.O. Box 20007
Santa Fe, NM 87504

International Indian Treaty
Council
Founded: 1974
710 Clayton Street
Number 1
San Francisco, CA 94117

Inter-Tribal Indian Ceremonial
Association
Founded: 1921
Box 1
Church Rock, NM 87311

Lone Indian Fellowship and Lone
Scout Alumni
Founded: 1926
1104 St. Clair Avenue
Sheboygan, WI 53081

National American Indian Court
Clerks Association
Founded: 1980
1000 Connecticut Avenue NW
Ste. 1206
Washington, DC 20036

National American Indian Court
Judges Association
Founded: 1968
1000 Connecticut Avenue NW
Ste. 401
Washington, DC 20036

National Center for American Indian
Alternative Education
Founded: 1960
941 E. 17th Ave.
Denver, CO 80218

National Center for American Indian
Enterprise Development
Founded: 1969
953 E. Juanita Avenue
Mesa, AZ 85204

National Congress of American
Indians
Founded: 1944
900 Pennsylvania Avenue SE
Washington, DC 20003

National Council of BIA Educators
Founded: 1967
6001 Marble NE
Ste. 10
Albuquerque, NM 87110

National Indian Council on Aging
Founded: 1976
6400 Uptown Boulevard NE
City Centre
Ste. 510-W
Albuquerque, NM 87110

National Indian Counselors
Association
Founded: 1980
Learning Research Center
Institute of American Indian Arts
P.O. Box 20007
Santa Fe, NM 87504

National Indian Education
Association
Founded: 1970
1819 H Street NW
Ste. 800
Washington, DC 20006

National Indian Health Board
Founded: 1969
1385 S. Colorado Boulevard
Ste. A-708
Denver, CO 80222

National Indian Social Workers
Association
Founded: 1970
410 NW 18th Street
Number 101
Portland, OR 97209

**National Indian Training and
Research Center**
Founded: 1969
2121 S. Mill Avenue
Ste. 216
Tempe, AZ 85282

National Indian Youth Council
Founded: 1961
318 Elm Street SE
Albuquerque, NM 87102

**National Native American
Cooperative**
Founded: 1969
P.O. Box 1030
San Carlos, AZ 85550-1000

National Urban Indian Council
Founded: 1977
10068 University Station
Denver, CO 80210

**Native American (Indian) Chamber
of Commerce**
Founded: 1990
c/o Native American Cooperative
P.O. Box 1000
San Carlos, AZ 85550-1000

Native American Community Board
Founded: 1984
P.O. Box 572
Lake Andes, SD 57356-0572

**Native American Educational
Services College**
Founded: 1974
2838 West Peterson
Chicago, IL 60659

**Native American Indian Housing
Council**
Founded: 1974
900 2nd Street NE
Ste. 220
Washington, DC 20002

**Native American Policy
Network**
Founded: 1979
Barry University
11300 2nd Avenue NE
Miami, FL 33161

**Native American Rights Fund
(NARF)**
Founded: 1970
1506 Broadway
Boulder, CO 80302

**North American Indian
Association**
Founded: 1940
22720 Plymouth Road
Detroit, MI 48239

**North American Indian Chamber of
Commerce**
Founded: 1983
P.O. Box 5000
San Carlos, AZ 85550-1000

**North American Indian Museums
Association**
Founded: 1979
c/o George Abrams
260 Prospect Street
Number 669
Hackensack, NJ 07601-2608

**North American Indian Women's
Association**
Founded: 1970
9602 Maestor's Lane
Gaithersburg, MD 20879

**North American Native American
Indian Information and Trade
Center**
Founded: 1991
P.O. Box 1000
San Carlos, AZ 85550-1000

Order of the Indian Wars
Founded: 1979
P.O. Box 7401
Little Rock, AR 72217

**Pan-American Indian
  Association**
Founded: 1984
P.O. Box 244
Nocatee, FL 33864

**Seventh Generation Fund for
  Indian Development**
Founded: 1977
P.O. Box 10
Forestville, CA 95436

Smoki People
Founded: 1921
P.O. Box 123
Prescott, AZ 86302

**Survival of American Indians
  Association**
Founded: 1964
7803-A Samurai Drive SE
Olympia, WA 98503

**Tekakwitha Conference National
  Center**
Founded: 1939
P.O. Box 6768
Great Falls, MT 59406-6768

**Tiyospaya American Indian Student
  Organization**
Founded: 1986
P.O. Box 1954
St. Petersburg, FL 33731

**United Indians of All Tribes
  Foundation**
Founded: 1970
Daybreak Star Arts Center
Discovery Park
P.O. Box 99100
Seattle, WA 98199

United Native Americans
Founded: 1968
2434 Faria Avenue
Pinole, CA 94564

United South and Eastern Tribes
Founded: 1969
1101 Kermit Drive
Ste. 302
Nashville, TN 37217

Time Line

c. 15,000-13,000 B.C.E.	Possible years of migration to the Americas by the ancestors of present-day Native Americans.
c. 12,000 B.C.E.	Estimate of when Paleo-Indians begin to migrate southward through ice-free corridors into the American interior.
c. 11,000 B.C.E.	Clovis Period begins across native North America; centers on hunting mega-fauna, especially the woolly mammoth.
c. 9,000 B.C.E.	Folsom Period emerges, centering on bison hunting.
c. 8,000 B.C.E.	Plano Period replaces Folsom, representing a transitional cultural period culminating in the Archaic.
c. 6,000 B.C.E.	Archaic Period begins, signaling a reliance on a variety of flora and fauna. Cultural innovations such as pottery, the bow and arrow, and the domestication of plants begin to appear across North America.
c. 1,000 B.C.E.	Agriculture appears in the Southwest; it gradually diffuses across North America.
c. 1,000 B.C.E.	Woodland Period emerges in eastern North America.
c. 1-500 C.E.	Complex societies flourish across North America.
c. 825-900	Athapaskan people, ancestors of the Navajo and Apache, invade the Southwest from the north, altering the cultural landscape of the Puebloan people.
c. 1007	Norsemen invade native North America along the eastern seaboard and establish a short-lived colony.
1050-1250	Cahokia, near present-day St. Louis, is established as a great Mississippian trading and ceremonial center. The city may have contained as many as thirty thousand people.
1492	Christopher Columbus lands on Guanahani (the island of San Salvador), launching Europe's exploration and colonization of North America.

c. 1500	European-introduced diseases, warfare, and slavery begin to reduce native populations (from an estimated ten to eighteen million to approximately 250,000 in 1900).
1519-1521	Hernán Cortés conquers the Aztec Empire.
1582-1598	Spanish conquistadores invade and settle in the Southwest.
1585	Roanoke Colony is founded by the British (it lasts only until approximately 1607).
1599	Massacre at Acoma Pueblo. Vincente de Zaldivar attacks Acoma on January 21 because of its resistance to Spanish authority; eight hundred Acomas are killed.
1607	British Virginia Company establishes colony of Jamestown, affecting local indigenous populations.
1609	Henry Hudson opens the fur trade in New Netherlands.
1620	The Pilgrims colonize present-day Massachusetts.
1622-1631	Powhatan Confederacy declares war on the Jamestown colonists.
1629	The Spanish begin establishing missions among the Pueblos, leading to a 1633 revolt at Zuni.
1630	The Puritans colonize New England, carrying with them a religious belief that Native Americans are "children of the Devil."
1636-1637	Pequot War. The Pequot and their allies attempt to defend their homelands against the Puritans.
c. 1640	The Dakota (Sioux), forced in part by hostilities initiated by the fur trade, begin to migrate westward onto the Great Plains.
1642-1685	Beaver Wars. As the supply of beaver is exhausted in the Northeast, the Iroquois Confederacy launches a war against neighboring Native American nations to acquire their hunting territories.

c. 1650	Period of widespread migrations and relocations. Prompted by the diffusion of the gun and the horse, and by the increasing hostility of Europeans, many Native Americans migrate westward.
1655	Timucua Rebellion. Timucuan mission residents rebel against Spanish cruelty in Florida.
1655-1664	Peach Wars. The Dutch launch a war of extermination against the Esophus nation after an Esophus woman is killed for picking peaches.
1670	Hudson's Bay Company is chartered, launching a westward expansion of the fur trade.
1670-1710	South Carolinians in Charleston encourage the development of a Native American slave trade across the Southeast.
1675-1676	King Philip's War. In response to English maltreatment, Metacomet (King Philip) launches a war against the English.
1676-1677	Bacon's Rebellion. Native Americans in Virginia fight a war of resistance but find themselves subject to Virginia rule.
1680	Pueblo (Popé's) Revolt. After decades of Spanish oppression, a Pueblo confederacy expels the Spanish from the Rio Grande region.
1682	Assiniboine and Cree begin to trade at York Factory, initiating European mercantile penetration of the Canadian west as far as the Rocky Mountains.
1689-1763	French and Indian Wars. King William's War initiates conflicts between the French and English that involve Native Americans and disrupt traditional patterns and alliances.
1692	Spanish reconquest of the Southwest (Nueva Mexico).
1695	Pima Uprising. Pimas burn missions in response to Spanish oppression.
c. 1700-1760	The horse diffuses across the Great Plains, prompting massive migrations and a cultural revolution.

1715-1717	Yamasee War. The Yamasee and their allies fight against the English for trading and other abuses.
1729	Natchez Revolt. Resisting French attempts to exact tribute, the Natchez go to war; the tribe is essentially destroyed, and many are sold into slavery.
1730	Articles of Agreement signed between the Cherokee Nation and King George II.
1740	Russia explores the Alaskan coast and begins trading operations.
1755	Some Iroquois settle near the Catholic mission of St. Regis, forming the nucleus of the Akwesasne Reserve.
1763	Proclamation of 1763. The Royal Proclamation of 1763 declares that Native Americans have title to all lands outside established colonies until the Crown legally purchases further land cessions.
1763-1764	Pontiac's War. Ottawa leader Pontiac constructs a multitribal alliance to resist the British.
1765	Paxton Riots (Paxton Boys Massacre). On December 14, 1765, seventy-five Europeans from Paxton, Pennsylvania, massacre and scalp six innocent Conestoga Mission Indians.
1768	Treaty of Fort Stanwix. The Iroquois Confederacy cedes lands south of the Ohio River (a later Fort Stanwix Treaty, 1784, changes the agreement).
1769	The California mission system is established.
1771	Labrador Inuit show missionaries where to build a trading post.
1774	Lord Dunmore's War. Lord Dunmore, the governor of Virginia, leads a fight against Shawnee led by Cornstalk.
1774-1775	The first Continental Congress establishes an Indian Department.
1777-1783	The Iroquois Confederacy is dispersed by the American Revolution.

1787	Northwest Ordinance. The U.S. Congress establishes a legal mechanism to create states from territories.
1789	The Indian Department becomes part of the U.S. Department of War.
1790	First of the Trade and Intercourse Acts enacted; they attempt to regulate trade between Europeans and Native Americans.
1790-1794	Little Turtle's War. Shawnee and their allies under Little Turtle defeat Anthony St. Clair's troops in 1791 but eventually are defeated at the Battle of Fallen Timbers, 1794, by General Anthony Wayne.
1795	Treaty of Fort Greenville. Native Americans of the Old Northwest are forced to treat with the United States after Britain refuses to assist them in their resistance efforts.
1796	Trading Houses Act. On April 18, 1796, the United States establishes government-operated trading houses.
1799	Handsome Lake, the Seneca Prophet, founds the *Gaiwiio*, "the Good Word," also known as the Longhouse religion; it becomes a strong force among the Iroquois.
1803	Louisiana Purchase. The United States acquires 800,000 square miles of new territory.
1804-1806	Lewis and Clark expedition. President Jefferson launches an expedition to collect information of national interest about the Louisiana territory purchased from the French in 1803.
1809	Treaty of Fort Wayne. The Delaware are forced to relinquish approximately 3 million acres.
1809-1811	Tecumseh's Rebellion. Shawnee leader Tecumseh leads a multitribal force to resist United States incursions into their lands.
1811	Battle of Tippecanoe. William Henry Harrison and his forces attack and defeat Tecumseh's forces in Tecumseh's absence.

1812	War of 1812. Tribes of the Old Northwest are drawn into the European conflict.
1812	In August, the Hudson's Bay Company establishes the Red River Colony.
1813-1814	Red Stick civil war. Creeks fight a bloody civil war over disagreements about what their political relations with the United States should be.
1817-1818	First Seminole War. U.S. forces under General Andrew Jackson attack and burn Seminole villages.
1821	Sequoyah creates the Cherokee syllabary, the first system for writing an Indian language.
1823	*Johnson v. M'Intosh.* On February 28, 1823, the U.S. Supreme Court rules that Native American tribes have land rights.
1823	Office of Indian Affairs is created within the War Department.
1827	Cherokee Nation adopts a constitution.
1830	Indian Removal Act. At the urging of President Andrew Jackson, Congress orders the removal of all Native Americans to lands west of the Mississippi River. Removal proceeds from the 1830's to the 1850's.
1830	Treaty of Dancing Rabbit Creek. Choctaws cede more than 10 million acres in Alabama and Mississippi.
1830	Upper Canada establishes a system of reserves for Canadian natives.
1831	*Cherokee Nation v. Georgia.* U.S. Supreme Court rules that Native American tribes are "domestic dependent nations."
1832	Black Hawk War. Black Hawk, the Sauk and Fox leader, leads a war to preserve their land rights.
1832	*Worcester v. Georgia.* U.S. Supreme Court rules that only the federal government has the right to regulate Indian affairs.
1834	Department of Indian Affairs is reorganized.
1835	Texas Rangers begin raids against the Comanche.

1835-1842	Second Seminole War. The Seminole resist removal to Indian Territory.
1838-1839	Forced removal of Cherokees to Indian Territory becomes a "Trail of Tears" marked by thousands of deaths.
1839	Upper Canadian judge James Buchanan submits a report suggesting that Canadian natives should be assimilated into larger Canadian society.
1839	Taos Revolt. Taos Pueblos struggle against U.S. domination.
1848	Treaty of Guadalupe Hidalgo. United States acquires southwestern lands from Mexico.
1848-1849	California Gold Rush. Emigrants cross Native American lands, resulting in ecological destruction and spread of diseases.
1849	Metis Courthouse Rebellion. Metis resist Canadian domination.
1850	Period of genocide against California Indians begins and continues for some thirty years; thousands are killed.
1851	First Treaty of Fort Laramie. Great Plains Native Americans agree to allow emigrants safe passage across their territories.
1853	Gadsden Purchase. U.S. government purchases portions of Arizona, California, and New Mexico from Mexico.
1854-1864	Teton Dakota Resistance. The Teton Dakota and their allies resist U.S. intrusions into their lands.
1855	In the Northwest, Territorial Governor Isaac Stevens holds the Walla Walla Council and negotiates a series of treaties with Native American tribes.
1855-1856	Yakima War. Led by Kamiakin, who refused to sign the 1855 treaty, Yakimas fight U.S. forces after the murder of a government Indian agent initiates hostilities.

1855-1858	Third Seminole War. Seminoles react to the surveying of their lands.
1858	British Columbia Gold Rush precipitates large-scale invasion of Indian lands.
1858	Navajo War. Manuelito leads the Navajo against U.S. forces to fight against whites' grazing their horses on Navajo lands.
1860	The British transfer full responsibility for Canadian Indian affairs to the Province of Canada.
1862	Minnesota Uprising. Little Crow carries out a war of resistance against federal authority because of ill treatment.
1863-1868	Long Walk of the Navajo. In a violent campaign, U.S. forces remove the Navajo from their homeland and take them to Bosque Redondo.
1864	Sand Creek Massacre. Colorado militiamen under John Chivington massacre a peaceful group of Cheyennes at Sand Creek.
1866-1868	Bozeman Trail wars. Teton Dakota and their allies resist the building of army forts in their lands.
1867	U.S. government purchases Alaska.
1867	Canadian Confederation. The Dominion of Canada is created.
1867	Commission Act. Legislation calls for the U.S. president to establish commissions to negotiate peace treaties with Native American nations.
1868	Second Treaty of Fort Laramie pledges the protection of Indian lands.
1868	Canadian government adopts an Indian policy aimed at the assimilation of Indians into Canadian society.
1868	Washita River Massacre. A peaceful Cheyenne camp is massacred by the U.S. Seventh Cavalry.
1869	First Riel Rebellion. Louis Riel leads the Metis in resisting Canadian domination; partly triggered by white surveying of Metis' lands.

1870	Grant's Peace Policy. President Ulysses S. Grant assigns various Christian denominations to various Indian reservation agencies in order to Christianize and pacify the Indians.
1871	Congress passes an act on March 3 that ends treaty negotiations with Native American nations.
1871	*McKay v. Campbell*. U.S. Supreme Court holds that Indian people born with "tribal allegiance" are not U.S. citizens.
1871	Canada begins negotiating the first of eleven "numbered" treaties with Native Canadians.
1871-1890	Wholesale destruction of the bison on the Plains.
1872-1873	Modoc War. The Modoc resist removal to the Klamath Reservation.
1874	Canadian Northwest Mounted Police move to establish order in the Canadian West.
1874-1875	Red River War. Forced by starvation and Indian agent corruption, Kiowa, Plains Apache, Southern Cheyenne, and Arapaho raid European American farms and ranches to feed their families.
1876	First Indian Act of Canada. The act consolidated Canadian policies toward its indigenous people.
1876	Battle of the Little Bighorn. General Custer and the Seventh Cavalry are annihilated by the Sioux, Cheyenne, and Arapaho camped along the Little Bighorn River.
1877	The Nez Perce are exiled from their homeland and pursued by U.S. forces as they unsuccessfully attempt to escape into Canada.
1877	Battle of Wolf Mountain. The last fight between the Cheyenne and the U.S. Army.
1877-1883	The Northern Cheyenne are forcibly removed to Indian Territory but escape north to their homelands.
1878	Bannock War. Because of settler pressures, the Bannock are forced to raid for food.

1879	Carlisle Indian School, a boarding school with the goal of "civilizing" Indian youth, is founded by Captain Richard H. Pratt.
1880	Canadian officials modify the 1876 Indian Act, empowering it to impose elected councils on bands.
1885	Second Riel Rebellion. Louis Riel leads a second protest, then armed revolt, among the Canadian Metis and Cree; defeated, Riel is executed after the rebellion.
1887	General Allotment Act (Dawes Severalty Act). Provides for the dividing of reservation lands into individual parcels to expedite assimilation. (By the early twentieth century, the allotment policy is viewed as disastrous.)
1890	Wounded Knee Massacre. The Seventh Cavalry intercepts a group of Sioux Ghost Dancers being led by Big Foot to the Pine Ridge Reservation. When a Sioux warrior, perhaps accidentally, fires his rifle, the army opens fire; hundreds of Sioux, most unarmed, are massacred.
1897	Education Appropriation Act mandates funding for Indian day schools and technical schools.
1897	Indian Liquor Act bans the sale or distribution of liquor to Native Americans.
1903	*Lone Wolf v. Hitchcock.* U.S. Supreme Court rules that Congress has the authority to dispose of Native American lands.
1906	Burke Act. Congress amends the General Allotment Act to shorten the trust period for individual Native Americans who are proven "competent."
1906	Alaskan Allotment Act. Allows Alaska Natives to file for 160-acre parcels.
1910	Omnibus Act. Establishes procedures to determine Native American heirship of trust lands and other resources.

1912	Classification and Appraisal of Unallotted Indian Lands Act. Permits the Secretary of the Interior to reappraise and reclassify unallotted Indian lands.
1924	General Citizenship Act. As a result of Native American participation in World War I, Congress grants some Native Americans citizenship.
1928	Meriam Report outlines the failure of previous Indian policies and calls for reform.
1932	Alberta Metis Organization is founded by Joseph Dion.
1934	Indian Reorganization Act. Implements the Meriam Report recommendations, reversing many previous policies.
1934	Johnson-O'Malley Act replaces the General Allotment Act.
1936	Oklahoma Indian Welfare Act. Extends many of the rights provided by the Indian Reorganization Act of 1934 to Oklahoma Indian nations.
1944	National Congress of American Indians is founded to guard Native American rights.
1946	Indian Claims Commission Act. Provides a legal forum for tribes to sue the federal government for the loss of lands.
1950	Navajo and Hopi Rehabilitation Act is passed to assist the tribes in developing their natural resources.
1951	Indian Act of 1951. A new Canadian Indian Act reduces the powers of the Indian Affairs Department but retains an assimilationist agenda.
1951	Public Law 280 allows greater state jurisdiction over criminal cases involving Native Americans from California, Wisconsin, Minnesota, and Nebraska (extended to Alaska Natives in 1959).
1953	Termination Resolution. Congress initiates a policy (which continues into the early 1960's) of severing the federal government's relationships with Native American nations.

1955	Indian Health Service is transferred from the Department of the Interior to the Department of Health, Education, and Welfare.
1961	Chicago Indian Conference, organized by anthropologist Sol Tax, mobilizes Indian leaders to reassert their rights.
1961	National Indian Youth Council is founded by Clyde Warrior and others.
1963	State of Washington rules against Native American fishing rights.
1964	American Indian Historical Society is founded to research and teach about Native Americans.
1966	Hawthorn Report examines the conditions of contemporary Canadian natives and recommends that Indians be considered "citizens plus."
1968	American Indian Civil Rights Act guarantees reservation residents many of the civil liberties other citizens have under the U.S. Constitution.
1968	American Indian Movement (AIM) is founded in Minneapolis by Dennis Banks and Russell Means.
1969	Canadian government's White Paper of 1969 rejects the Hawthorn Report's recommendations, arguing that Canadian natives' special status hinders their assimilation and urging the abolition of the Indian Affairs Department and Indian Act.
1969	Occupation of Alcatraz Island by Native American people begins (continues through 1971).
1971	Alaska Native Claims Settlement Act marks the beginning of the self-determination period for Alaska Natives.
1972	Trail of Broken Treaties Caravan proceeds to Washington, D.C., to protest treaty violations.
1972	Native American Rights Fund (NARF) is founded to carry Indian issues to court.

1972	Indian Education Act enacted; it is intended to improve the quality of education for Native Americans (the act is revised in 1978).
1973	Wounded Knee occupation. More than two hundred Native American activists occupy the historic site to demonstrate against oppressive Sioux reservation policies.
1974	Navajo-Hopi Land Settlement Act facilitates negotiation between the two nations over the disputed Joint Use Area.
1975	Indian Self-Determination and Education Assistance Act expands tribal control over tribal governments and education.
1975	Political violence increases on the Pine Ridge Reservation; two FBI agents are killed in a shootout on June 26.
1975	James Bay and Northern Quebec Agreement is signed; Quebec Cree, Inuit, Naskapi, and Montagnais groups cede tribal lands in exchange for money and specified hunting and fishing rights.
1977	American Indian Policy Review Commission Report is released by Congress, recommending that Native American nations be considered sovereign political bodies.
1978	American Indian Freedom of Religion Act protects the rights of Native Americans to follow traditional religious practices.
1978	Federal Acknowledgment Program is initiated to provide guidelines for and assist tribes seeking official recognition by the federal government.
1978	Indian Child Welfare Act proclaims tribal jurisdiction over child custody decisions.
1978	The Longest Walk, a march from Alcatraz Island to Washington, D.C., protests government treatment of Indians.

1980	*United States v. Sioux Nation.* U.S. Supreme Court upholds a $122 million judgment against the United States for illegally taking the Black Hills.
1981	Hopi-Navajo Joint Use Area is partitioned between the Navajo and Hopi nations.
1982	Canada's Constitution Act (Constitution and Charter of Rights and Freedoms) is passed despite the protests of Indian, Metis, and Inuit groups.
1982	Indian Claims Limitation Act limits the time period during which claims can be filed against the U.S. government.
1985	Coolican Report declares that little progress is being made to settle Canadian native land claims.
1988	Indian Gaming Regulatory Act officially legalizes certain types of gambling on reservations and establishes the National Indian Gaming Commission.
1989	U.S. Congress approves construction of the National Museum of the American Indian, to be part of the Smithsonian Institution.
1989	Violence erupts on St. Regis Mohawk Reservation in dispute over whether to allow gambling; under guard by state and federal law enforcement officers, the tribe votes to allow gambling on the reservation.
1990	The U.S. Census finds the Native American population to be 1,959,234.
1990	In *Duro v. Reina*, the U.S. Supreme Court holds that tribes cannot have criminal jurisdiction over non-Indians on reservation lands.
1990	Canada's proposed Meech Lake Accord (amendments to the 1982 Constitution Act) is sent to defeat in Canada by native legislator Elijah Harper; the accord provided no recognition of native rights.
1991	Tribal Self-Governance Act extends the number of tribes involved in the self-governance pilot project.
1992	Native Americans protest the Columbian Quincentenary.

1992	In a plebiscite, residents of Canada's Northwest Territories approve the future creation of Nunavut, a territory to be governed by the Inuit.
1993	The International Year of Indigenous People.
1994	National Museum of the American Indian opens its first facility in New York's Heye Center (a larger museum is planned for the National Mall in Washington, D.C.).
1994	The National Congress of American Indians and the National Black Caucus of State Legislators ally themselves, agreeing that they face similar political and economic forces of oppression.
1998	Canadian minister of Indian Affairs formally apologizes to Indian and Inuit peoples for past government attempts to destroy native cultures.
1999	Eastern portion of Canada's Northwest Territories becomes new territory of Nunavut.
2000	U.S. secretary of the interior Bruce Babbitt announces that the remains of Kennewick Man will be turned over to Washington State Native American tribes under the provisions of the Native American Graves Protection and Repatriation Act.
2001	Native Americans sue Secretary of the Interior Gale Norton over approximately $10 billion they claim was bilked from Native American trust funds of Indian land use royalties, administered by the Department of the Interior since 1887.

Culture Areas of North America

Tribes by Culture Area

Major tribal groups are listed below their geographical culture areas; language groups represented appear after the culture-area heading.

Arctic

Language groups: Eskimo-Aleut (Aleut, Inuit-Iñupiaq, Yupik)

Aleut
Inuit

Yupik

California

Language groups: Athapaskan, Chimariko, Chumashan, Esselen, Karok, Maiduan, Palaihnihan, Pomoan, Salinan, Shastan, Uto-Aztecan, Wintun, Wiyot, Yanan, Yokutsan, Yukian, Yuman, Yurok

Achumawi
Atsugewi
Cahuilla
Chemehuevi
Chumash
Costano
Cupeño
Diegueño
Esselen
Fernandeño
Gabrielino
Hupa
Juaneño
Kamia
Karok
Kato
Luiseño
Maidu
Mattole

Miwok
Patwin
Pomo
Quechan
Salinan
Serrano
Shasta
Tolowa
Tubatulabal
Wailaki
Wappo
Wintun
Wiyot
Yahi
Yana
Yokuts
Yuki
Yurok

Great Basin

Language groups: Hokan, Numic (Shoshonean)

Bannock
Gosiute
Kawaiisu
Mono (Monache)
Numaga (Northern Paiute)

Panamint
Paviotso (Northern Paiute)
Shoshone
Ute
Washoe

Northeast

Language groups: Algonquian, Iroquoian, Siouan

Abenaki
Algonquin
Cayuga
Erie
Fox
Huron
Illinois
Kaskaskia
Kickapoo
Lenni Lenape
Mahican
Maliseet
Massachusett
Menominee
Miami
Micmac
Mohawk
Nanticoke
Narragansett
Neutral
Nottaway

Oneida
Onondaga
Ottawa
Pamlico
Passamaquoddy
Pennacook
Penobscot
Pequot
Petun
Piankashaw
Potawatomi
Sauk
Secotan
Seneca
Shawnee
Susquehannock
Tuscarora
Wampanoag
Wappinger
Winnebago

Northwest Coast

Language groups: Athapaskan, Chinook, Penutian, Salish

Alsea
Bella Bella
Bella Coola
Chehalis
Chinook
Coast Salish
Coos
Eyak
Gitksan
Haida
Klamath

Klikitat
Kwakiutl
Nootka (Nuu-Chah-Nulth)
Quileute
Quinault
Siuslaw
Takelma
Tillamook
Tlingit
Tsimshian
Umpqua

Plains

Language groups: Algonquian, Athapaskan, Caddoan, Kiowa-Tanoan, Siouan, Uto-Aztecan

Apache of Oklahoma
Arapaho
Arikara
Assiniboine
Atsina
Blackfoot (Blood, Piegan, Siksika)
Caddo
Cheyenne
Comanche
Crow
Hidatsa
Iowa
Kansa (Kaw)
Kiowa

Mandan
Missouri
Omaha
Osage
Oto
Pawnee
Ponca
Quapaw
Sarsi
Sioux (Santee, Teton, Yankton)
Tonkawa
Waco
Wichita

Plateau

Language groups: Penutian, Sahaptin, Salishan

Coeur d'Alene
Colville
Flathead
Kalispel
Klamath
Klikitat
Kutenai
Lake
Lillooet
Methow
Mical
Modoc
Molala
Nez Perce

Okanagan
Palouse
Sanpoil
Shuswap
Spokane
Tenino
Thompson
Tyigh
Umatilla
Walla Walla
Wanapam
Wauyukma
Wenatchi
Yakima

Southeast

Language groups: Algonquian, Atakapa, Caddoan, Chitimacha, Iroquoian, Muskogean, Natchez, Siouan, Timucuan, Tunican, Yuchi

Ais
Alabama
Anadarko (Hasinai Confederacy)
Apalachee
Apalachicola
Atakapa
Bayogoula
Biloxi
Calusa
Cape Fear
Catawba
Cheraw
Cherokee
Chiaha
Chickasaw

Chitimacha
Choctaw
Coushatta
Creek
Guale
Guasco (Hasinai Confederacy)
Hitchiti
Houma
Jeaga
Manahoac (Mahock)
Mobile
Nabedache (Hasinai Confederacy)
Natchez
Ocaneechi
Ofo

Pamlico
Pawokti
Powhatan Confederacy
Seminole
Texas (Hasinai Confederacy)
Timucua
Tiou
Tohome

Tunica
Tuscarora
Tuskegee
Tutelo
Waccamaw
Yamasee
Yazoo
Yuchi

Southwest

Language groups: Athapaskan, Keres, Kiowa-Tanoan, Uto-Aztecan, Yuman, Zuni

Acoma
Apache (including Chiricahua,
   Jicarilla, and Mescalero)
Cochiti
Havasupai
Hopi
Isleta
Jemez
Karankawa
Laguna
Nambe
Navajo
Picuris
Pima
Pojoaque

San Felipe
San Ildefonso
San Juan
Sandia
Santa Ana
Santa Clara
Santo Domingo
Taos
Tesuque
Tohono O'odham
Walapai
Yaqui
Yavapai
Zia
Zuñi

Subarctic

Language Groups: Algonquian, Athapaskan, Eskimo-Aleut

Ahtna
Beaver
Carrier
Chilcotin
Chipewyan

Cree
Dogrib
Haida
Han
Hare

Ingalik
Inland Tlingit
Koyukon
Kutchin
Montagnais
Mountain
Naskapi

Saulteaux
Slave
Tagish
Tanaina
Tanana
Tsetsaut
Yellowknife

Bibliography

Acrelius, Israel. *A History of New Sweden*. 1759. Reprint. Translated by William M. Reynolds. Philadelphia: The Historical Society of Pennsylvania, 1874.

Adair, Mary J. *Prehistoric Agriculture in the Central Plains*. University of Kansas Publications in Anthropology 16. Lawrence: University Press of Kansas, 1988.

Adams, Howard. *Prison of Grass: Canada from the Native Point of View*. Toronto: New Press, 1975.

Adkison, Norman B. *Indian Braves and Battles with More Nez Perce Lore*. Grangeville: Idaho County Free Press, 1967.

_____. *Nez Perce Indian War and Original Stories*. Grangeville: Idaho County Free Press, 1966.

Adler, Michael A., ed. *The Prehistoric Pueblo World, A.D. 1150-1350*. Tucson: University of Arizona Press, 1996.

Alden, John R. "The Albany Congress and the Creation of the Indian Superintendencies." *Mississippi Valley Historical Review* 27, no. 2 (September, 1940): 193-210. Describes how the Albany Congress led British officials to create the Indian superintendent system.

Allen, Charles W., and Richard E. Jensen. *From Fort Laramie to Wounded Knee: In the West That Was*. Lincoln: University of Nebraska Press, 1997.

Allen, Robert S. *His Majesty's Indian Allies*. Toronto: Dundurn Press, 1992. Presents material from British sources neglected by U.S. historians.

American Indian Culture and Research Journal 13 (1989). Special issue on contemporary issues in Native American health, edited by Gregory R. Campbell. A collection of articles that focus on issues revolving around American Indians' health in the later 1980's.

American Indian Policy Review Commission Task Force. *Report*. Washington, D.C.: U.S. Government Printing Office, 1977.

Amsden, Charles. "The Navajo Exile at Bosque Redondo." *New Mexico Historical Review* 8 (1933): 31-50. A dated but still significant article concerning the Navajo on the Bosque Redondo reservation.

_____. *Prehistoric Southwesterners from Basketmaker to Pueblo*. Los Angeles: Southwest Museum, 1949.

Anders, Gary C. "Social and Economic Consequences of Federal Indian Policy." *Economic Development and Cultural Change* 37, no. 2 (January, 1989): 285-303. Includes discussion of the effects of the ANCSA on the Alaskan Natives.

Anderson, Fred. *Crucible of War: The Seven Years' War and the Fate of Empire in British North America, 1754-1766.* New York: Alfred A. Knopf, 2000. Presents the French and Indian War as a conflict in and of itself, rather than merely as a prelude to the Revolutionary War.

_____. *A People's Army: Massachusetts Soldiers and Society in the Seven Years' War.* Chapel Hill: University of North Carolina Press, 1984. This illustrated regional study reveals how average colonists experienced and affected the war.

Anderson, Gary Clayton. *Little Crow: Spokesman for the Sioux.* St. Paul: Minnesota Historical Society Press, 1986. A carefully researched and documented biography of the most important Native American war leader; sympathetic to both Little Crow and the Santee Sioux. Provides a detailed description of the war.

Anderson, Gary Clayton, and Alan R. Woolworth, eds. *Through Dakota Eyes: Narrative Accounts of the Minnesota Indian War of 1862.* St. Paul: Minnesota Historical Press, 1988. Carefully edited, readable first-person accounts of the war, some sympathetic to the blanket Sioux, some to the farmer Sioux who opposed the war.

Anderson, Terry Lee. *Sovereign Nations or Reservations? An Economic History of American Indians.* San Francisco: Pacific Research Institute for Public Policy, 1995.

Armstrong, Virginia Irving, comp. *I Have Spoken: American History Through the Voices of the Indians.* Chicago: Swallow Press, 1971. Includes three orations by Red Cloud, including the Powder River exhortation (1866) and the complete Cooper Institute speech (1870).

Arnold, Robert D., et al. *Alaska Native Land Claims.* Anchorage: Alaska Native Foundation, 1978. A comprehensive discussion of the act and its significance.

Auth, Stephen F. *The Ten Years War: Indian-White Relations in Pennsylvania, 1755-1765.* New York: Garland, 1989. Includes Native American perspectives missing in many studies. Final chapter shows the war's implications for later treatment of Native Americans.

Axelrod, Alan. *Chronicle of the Indian Wars: From Colonial Times to Wounded Knee.* New York: Prentice Hall General Reference, 1993. This work provides a useful and detailed overview of the armed struggles of the Indians and the whites.

Axtell, James. *The European and the Indian: Essays in the Ethnohistory of Colonial North America.* New York: Oxford University Press, 1981. Many of the essays in this book were previously published; together they provide a good introduction to the study of ethnohistory and Anglo-Indian relations in the colonial period.

Bachman, Van Cleaf. *Peltries or Plantations: The Economic Policies of the Dutch West India Company in New Netherland, 1623-1639*. Baltimore: The Johns Hopkins University Press, 1969.

Bakeless, John. *Lewis and Clark: Partners in Discovery*. New York: William Morrow, 1947. One of the most reliable sources on Meriwether Lewis and William Clark. Based on both of their journals.

Bamforth, Douglas B. *Ecology and Human Organization on the Great Plains*. New York: Plenum Press, 1988.

Barbour, Philip L. *Pocahontas and Her World*. Boston: Houghton Mifflin, 1970. A good synthesis of seventeenth century accounts of Jamestown's founding, including much information on Powhatan.

Barnitz, Albert Trovillo Siders, and Jennie Barnitz. *Life in Custer's Cavalry: Diaries and Letters of Albert and Jennie Barnitz, 1867-1868*. Edited by Robert M. Utley. New Haven, Conn.: Yale University Press, 1977. An account of the massacre completed from the writings of one of Custer's troop commanders and his wife.

Barrington, Linda, ed. *The Other Side of the Frontier: Economic Explorations into Native American History*. Boulder, Colo.: Westview Press, 1999.

Barsh, Russel. "Indian Land Claims Policy in the United States." *North Dakota Law Review* 58 (1982): 1-82.

Bartlett, Richard H. *Indian Reserves and Aboriginal Lands in Canada*. Saskatoon, Canada: University of Saskatchewan, Native Law Center, 1990.

Beal, Bob, and Rod Macleod. *Prairie Fire: The 1885 North-West Rebellion*. Edmonton: Hurtig, 1984. Emphasizes the Native Canadian perspective.

Beal, Merrill D. *I Will Fight No More Forever: Chief Joseph and the Nez Perce War*. Seattle: University of Washington Press, 1963.

Bemis, Samuel Flagg. *Jay's Treaty*. Rev. ed. New Haven, Conn.: Yale University Press, 1962.

Berger, Thomas R. *Village Journey: The Report of the Alaska Native Review Commission*. New York: Hill & Wang, 1985. A critical account of the effects of the ANCSA on Native Alaskans.

Berkhofer, Robert F., Jr. *Salvation and the Savage: An Analysis of Protestant Missions and American Indian Response 1787-1862*. Lexington: University of Kentucky Press, 1965. This work focuses on how missionaries portrayed white culture to the Indians and on the policy behind these presentations.

Berry, Mary Clay. *The Alaska Pipeline: The Politics of Oil and Native Land Claims*. Bloomington: Indiana University Press, 1975. Describes the influence of the construction of the pipeline on the passage of the ANCSA.

Beverly, Robert. *The History and Present State of Virginia*. Indianapolis: Bobbs-Merrill, 1971. A study of Indian life and customs in the seventeenth century, first published in 1705.

Biddle, Nicholas, and Paul Allen, eds. *History of the Expedition Under the Command of Captains Lewis and Clark*. 2 vols. Philadelphia: J. B. Lippincott, 1961. Prepared by Biddle, a young Philadelphia lawyer, between 1810 and 1814, this work is based on both Lewis's and Clark's journals.

Billington, Ray Allen. *Westward Expansion*. New York: Macmillan, 1949.

Blegen, Theodore C. *Minnesota: A History of the State*. St. Paul: University of Minnesota Press, 1975. The standard history of Minnesota. Its chapter on the Sioux War is solid and balanced.

Borden, Charles E. *Origins and Development of Early Northwest Coast Culture to About 3000 B.C.* Ottawa: National Museums of Canada, 1975.

Boudinet, Elias. *Cherokee Editor: The Writings of Elias Boudinet*. Edited by Theda Perdue. Athens: University of Georgia Press, 1996. Collects nearly all of Boudinet's writings, with a biographical introduction and thorough annotations.

Bourne, Russell. *The Red King's Rebellion: Racial Politics in New England, 1675-1678*. New York: Oxford University Press, 1990. A detailed treatment of the war that is especially critical of the motives and acts of the colonists. Maps, illustrations, and index.

Bowsfield, Hartfield. *Louis Riel: The Rebel and the Hero*. Toronto: Oxford University Press, 1971. A good introductory book.

Brady, Cyrus. *Indian Fights and Fighters*. Lincoln: University of Nebraska Press, 1971. A narrative of the Plains wars, including the Washita Massacre. Includes many eyewitness accounts not available elsewhere.

Brandao, Jose. *Your Fyre Shall Burn No More: Iroquois Policy Toward New France and Its Allies to 1701*. Lincoln: University of Nebraska Press, 1997. Offers a revisionist stance toward the Beaver Wars, arguing that the Iroquois were more interested in taking captives to replenish their disease-ravaged populations than in obtaining beaver skins for trade.

Brandon, William. *The Indian in American Culture*. New York: Harper & Row, 1974. A massive volume covering Indian-white relations since the beginning; includes an interesting discussion of reservation policy. Good index.

Brasser, Ted J. "The Coastal New York Indians in the Early Contact Period." In *Neighbors and Intruders: An Ethnohistorical Exploration of the Indians of Hudson's River*, edited by Laurence M. Hauptman and Jack Campisi. Ottawa: National Museums of Canada, 1978. Argues that the coastal Algonquians were probably in the process of forming a coalition when the Dutch purchased Manhattan.

Braund, Kathryn E. Holland. *Deerskins and Duffels: The Creek Indian Trade with Anglo-America, 1685-1815*. Lincoln: University of Nebraska Press, 1993. Describes the competitors, pricing, credit policies, markets, and distribution of the Muscogee deerskin trade; provides a detailed look at Muscogee life.

Brill, Charles. *Conquest of the Southern Plains*. Millwood, N.Y.: Kraus Reprint, 1975. A fully illustrated account of all events related to the incursion of European Americans into Indian lands of the southern Plains during the second half of the nineteenth century.

Britten, Thomas A. *American Indians in World War I: At Home and at War*. Albuquerque: University of Alabama Press, 1997.

_____. *A Brief History of the Seminole-Negro Indian Scouts*. Lewiston, N.Y.: Edwin Mellen Press, 1999.

Brown, Dee. *Bury My Heart at Wounded Knee: An Indian History of the American West*. New York: Holt, Rinehart & Winston, 1970. A very readable, popular account of the displacement and oppression of the American Indian nations by European settlers, from the beginning to 1890. Includes a helpful but dated bibliography.

Brown, Jennifer S. H. *Strangers in Blood: Fur Trade Company Families in Indian Country*. Vancouver: University of British Columbia Press, 1980. Discusses the development of the Metis people in eastern Canada and the Great Plains from the 1600's to the twentieth century. Illustrations and index.

Brown, Jennifer S. H., and Elizabeth Vibert, eds. *Reading Beyond Words: Contexts for Native History*. Orchard Park, N.Y.: Broadview Press, 1996.

Burt, Larry W. *Tribalism in Crisis: Federal Indian Policy, 1953-1961*. Albuquerque: University of New Mexico Press, 1982.

Calloway, Colin G. *The American Revolution in Indian Country: Crisis and Diversity in Native American Communities*. New York: Cambridge University Press, 1995.

_____. *Crown and Calumet: British-Indian Relations, 1783-1815*. Norman: University of Oklahoma Press, 1987.

_____. *First Peoples: A Documentary Survey of American Indian History*. Boston: Bedford/St. Martin's, 1999.

_____. *New Worlds for All: Indians, Europeans, and the Remaking of Early America*. Baltimore, Md.: Johns Hopkins University Press, 1997.

_____. *The Western Abenakis of Vermont, 1600-1800: War, Migration, and the Survival of an Indian People*. Norman: University of Oklahoma Press, 1990.

_____, ed. *The World Turned Upside Down: Indian Voices from Early America*. Boston: St. Martin's Press, 1994.

Campbell, Gregory R. "The Politics of Counting: Critical Reflections About the Depopulation Question of Native North America." In *Native Voices on the Columbian Quincentenary*, edited by Donald A. Grinde. Los Angeles: American Indian Studies Center, University of California, 1994. An examination of the European manipulation of Native American population counts as justification for continued colonial expansion.

Canada Communication Group. *Looking Forward, Looking Back; Restructuring the Relationship; Gathering Strength; Perspectives and Realities;* and *Renewal: A Twenty Year Commitment*. 5 vols. Ottawa: Author, 1996. The final report of the Royal Commission on Aboriginal Peoples.

Canby, William C. *American Indian Law in a Nutshell*. Minneapolis: West, 1981. Provides simple explanations of complex legal issues that inhere in dealings between the federal government, states, and tribal nations.

Carter, Harvey Lewis. *The Life and Times of Little Turtle: First Sagamore of the Wabash*. Urbana: University of Illinois Press, 1987. Includes a detailed description of the battle with St. Clair's troops from Little Turtle's perspective.

Carter, Sarah. *Lost Harvest: Prairies Indian Reserve Farmers and Government Policy*. Montreal: McGill-Queen's University Press, 1990. Critically exposes the agricultural policies of the Canadian government.

Case, David S. *Alaska Natives and American Laws*. Fairbanks: University of Alaska Press, 1984. A detailed description of the historical interaction of Native Alaskans and U.S. law.

Cave, Alfred A. *The Pequot War*. Amherst: University of Massachusetts Press, 1996. The first in-depth study of the Pequot War, emphasizing the motives behind the hostilities through archaeological, linguistic, and anthropological analysis.

Chalfant, William Y. *Cheyennes at Dark Water Creek: The Last Fight of the Red River War*. Norman: University of Oklahoma Press, 1997. A thorough study of the final encounter of the Red River War and the circumstances leading up to it.

Chalmers, Harvey, II. *The Last Stand of the Nez Perce*. New York: Twayne, 1962.

Chamberlain, Kathleen P. *Under Sacred Ground: A History of Navajo Oil, 1922-1982*. Albuquerque: University of New Mexico Press, 2000. An ethnography and history of the effect of oil production on the formation and expansion of Navajo tribal government.

Chevigny, Hector. *Russian America: The Great Alaskan Venture, 1741-1867*. New York: Viking Press, 1965.

Churchill, Ward, and Jim Vander Wall. *Agents of Repression: The FBI's Secret Wars Against the Black Panther Party and the American Indian Movement.* Boston: South End Press, 1988.

Clark, Blue. *"Lone Wolf v. Hitchcock": Treaty Rights and Indian Law at the End of the Nineteenth Century.* Lincoln: University of Nebraska Press, 1994. A short but comprehensive study of the background and implications of the most significant turn-of-the-century Native American court case.

Clarkin, Thomas. *Federal Indian Policy in the Kennedy and Johnson Administrations, 1961-1969.* Albuquerque: University of New Mexico Press, 2001.

Cleland, Charles E. *Rites of Conquest: The History and Culture of Michigan's Native Americans.* Ann Arbor: University of Michigan Press, 1992. A multiethnic, regional approach to the history of the Ojibwa, Ottawa, and Potawatomi, from precontact to the late twentieth century. Maps, photographs, biographical sketches, chapter notes, bibliography, index.

Cochran, Thomas C. *Pennsylvania: A Bicentennial History.* New York: W. W. Norton, 1978.

Coe, Joffre L., and Thomas D. Burke. *Town Creek Indian Mound: A Native American Legacy.* Chapel Hill: University of North Carolina Press, 1995.

Cohen, Fay G. *Treaties on Trial: The Continuing Controversy over Northwest Indian Fishing Rights.* Seattle: University of Washington Press, 1986. Shows the continuing importance of treaties and the bitterness still evoked by pre-1871 agreements.

Cohen, Felix. *Handbook of Federal Indian Law.* Washington, D.C.: Government Printing Office, 1942. The most complete sourcebook for American Indian legal issues.

Cole, D. C. *The Chiricahua Apache, 1846-1876: From War to Reservation.* Albuquerque: University of New Mexico Press, 1988. A general history of the Chiricahua Apaches with special attention to cultural conflicts with Euro-Americans.

Coleman, Michael C. "Problematic Panacea: Presbyterian Missionaries and the Allotment of Indian Lands in the Late Nineteenth Century." *Pacific Historical Review* 54, no. 2 (1985): 143-159. Shows that the Presbyterians were not united about allotment of tribal lands.

Condon, Thomas J. *New York Beginnings: The Commercial Origins of New Netherland.* New York: New York University Press, 1968. Monograph examining the Dutch purchase decision as part of a wider commercial policy.

Cook, Noble David. *Born to Die: Disease and New World Conquest, 1492-1650.* New York: Cambridge University Press, 1998. Sweeping yet detailed look at the effect of disease in the European colonization of the Americas.

Cook, Noble David, and W. George Lovell, eds. *Secret Judgments of God: Old World Disease in Colonial Spanish America.* Norman: University of Oklahoma Press, 2001. A collection of symposium papers, presented from a wide range of disciplines, assessing the impact of European diseases and epidemics on the Native American population.

Cook, Sherburne F. *The Conflict Between the California Indian and White Civilization.* Berkeley: University of California Press, 1974.

Cordell, Linda S. *Prehistory of the Southwest.* Orlando, Fla.: Academic Press, 1984.

Corkran, David H. *The Cherokee Frontier: Conflict and Survival 1740-1762.* Norman: University of Oklahoma Press, 1962. A detailed account of the complex relations between the Cherokees and English colonists during the mid-1700's.

Costo, Rupert, and Jeannette Henry Costo, eds. *The Missions of California: A Legacy of Genocide.* San Francisco: Indian Historian Press, 1987. A collection that vigorously indicts the evils of the mission system.

Covington, James W. *The Seminoles of Florida.* Gainesville: University Press of Florida, 1993. The most thorough history of the Seminoles in Florida; devotes six chapters to the Seminole Wars.

Coward, John M. *The Newspaper Indian: Native American Identity in the Press, 1820-90.* Urbana: University of Illinois Press, 1999.

Cowger, Thomas W. *The National Congress of American Indians: The Founding Years.* Lincoln: University of Nebraska Press, 1999.

Crampton, C. Gregory. *The Zuñis of Cíbola.* Provo: University of Utah Press, 1977. A general history of the Zuñi people. Black-and-white photographs illustrate how the Pueblos have changed over time.

Crane, Verner. *The Southern Frontier, 1670-1732.* Ann Arbor: University of Michigan Press, 1929. A classic work on relations between European settlers and American Indians in the South.

Cressman, Luther S. *The Sandal and the Cave: The Indians of Oregon.* Corvallis: Oregon State University Press, 1981.

Cronon, William. *Changes in the Land: Indians, Colonists, and the Ecology of New England.* New York: Hill & Wang, 1983.

Crosby, Alfred W. *The Columbian Exchange: Biological and Cultural Consequences of 1492.* Westport, Conn.: Greenwood Press, 1972.

_____. "Virgin Soil Epidemics as a Factor in the Aboriginal Depopulation in America." *William and Mary Quarterly,* 3d ser., 33 (1976): 289-299. This essay is considered a classic examination of the effect of disease on Indian populations in North America.

Crutchfield, James Andrew. *Tragedy at Taos: The Revolt of 1847.* Plano, Tex.: Republic of Texas Press, 1995. First comprehensive narrative of the events at Taos. Contains valuable appendices concerning the participants, a chronology of events, casualty figures, and other items of interest.

Cummings, Byron. *The First Inhabitants of Arizona and the Southwest.* Tucson, Ariz.: Cummings Publication Council, 1953.

Cunningham, Frank. *General Stand Watie's Confederate Indians.* 1959. Reprint. Norman: University of Oklahoma Press, 1998. A full account of Stand Watie's efforts during the Civil War and his political life within the Cherokee Nation. Many photographs of that era.

Curtis, Edward S. *In a Sacred Manner We Live.* Barre, Mass.: Barre Publishers, 1972.

Custer, George Armstrong. *My Life on the Plains.* London: The Folio Society, 1963. Contains Custer's account of the events before, during, and after the Washita Massacre.

Dale, Edward Everett, and Morris L. Wardell. *History of Oklahoma.* New York: Prentice-Hall, 1948. Contains a thorough chapter on the Civil War in Oklahoma by two outstanding Oklahoma historians.

Danky, James P., ed. *Native American Periodicals and Newspapers, 1828-1982.* Westport, Conn.: Greenwood Press, 1984. Overview of the history of Native American newspapers.

Dary, David A. *The Buffalo Book: The Full Saga of the American Animal.* Chicago: Swallow Press, 1974. Detailed account of bison in North America. Black-and-white photos, index, bibliography.

Davidson, Gordon Charles. *The North West Company.* New York: Russell & Russell, 1967. A history of the development and expansion of the second largest fur company in North America. Maps, illustrations, and index.

Deardorff, Merle H. *The Religion of Handsome Lake: Its Origins and Development.* American Bureau of Ethnology Bulletin 149. Washington, D.C.: Smithsonian Institution Press, 1951. Presents a detailed analysis of the Handsome Lake religion from an ethnographic perspective.

Debo, Angie. *A History of the Indians in the United States.* Norman: University of Oklahoma Press, 1989. A comprehensive, in-depth historical survey of Indians of the United States, emphasizing tribal relations with the U.S. government.

——————. *The Rise and Fall of the Choctaw Republic.* 2d ed. Norman: University of Oklahoma Press, 1967.

De Forest, John W. *History of the Indians of Connecticut from the Earliest Known Period to 1850.* Hartford, Conn.: W. J. Hammersley, 1851. Reprint. Hamden, Conn.: Shoestring Press, 1988. A classic study of the native peoples of Connecticut.

Deloria, Vine, Jr. *Behind the Trail of Broken Treaties: An Indian Declaration of Independence.* 2d ed. Norman: University of Oklahoma, 1987. Lawyer-theologian Deloria discusses the doctrine of discovery, treaty-making, civil rights, American Indian activism, sovereignty, and the Trail and Wounded Knee occupations.

_____, ed. *American Indian Policy in the Twentieth Century.* Norman: University of Oklahoma Press, 1985. Several essays deal with the impact of the Indian Civil Rights Act on American Indian tribal governments. Also explores larger constitutional issues and tribal governments.

_____, ed. *The Indian Reorganization Act: Congresses and Bills.* Norman: University of Oklahoma Press, 2002. A collection of primary source documents assembled by the noted Native American legal scholar.

Deloria, Vine, Jr., and Raymond J. DeMallie. *Documents of American Indian Diplomacy: Treaties, Agreements, and Conventions, 1775-1979.* Norman: University of Oklahoma Press, 1999.

Deloria, Vine, Jr., and Clifford M. Lytle. *American Indians, American Justice.* Austin: University of Texas Press, 1983. A clearly written study focusing on the development of the Native American judicial system as it existed in the early 1980's. Explains the complexities of Native American legal and political rights as they are understood by the tribes and by the federal government.

_____. *The Nations Within: The Past and Future of American Indian Sovereignty.* New York: Pantheon Books, 1984. An important discussion of the impact of legal and legislative measures on tribal autonomy and self-rule.

Dempsey, Hugh A. *Big Bear: The End of Freedom.* Vancouver: Douglas & McIntyre, 1984.

DeRosier, Arthur. *The Removal of the Choctaw Indians.* Knoxville: University of Tennessee Press, 1970. Discusses removal circumstances. Includes maps and portraits.

De Voto, Bernard. *The Journals of Lewis and Clark.* Boston: Houghton Mifflin, 1953. A one-volume condensation of the *Original Journals of Lewis and Clark Expedition.* Includes maps.

Dickason, Olive. *Canada's First Nations: A History of Founding Peoples from Earliest Times.* Norman: University of Oklahoma Press, 1992. An unparalleled legal, political, and social history of Canadian Indians.

_____. *The Myth of the Savage and the Beginnings of French Colonialism in the Americas.* Edmonton: University of Alberta Press, 1984.

Dickerson, Mark O. *Whose North? Political Change, Political Development, and Self-Government in the Northwest Territories.* Vancouver: University of

British Columbia Press, 1992. Discusses the contemporary political issues facing the Dene, Metis, Inuit, and non-native residents of northern Canada.

Dillehay, Thomas D. *The Settlement of the Americas: A New Prehistory*. New York: Basic Books, 2001. Offers the archaeological and anthropological evidence for population of the Americas prior to the glaciation 20,000 years ago.

Dillehay, Tom D., and David J. Meltzer. *The First Americans: Search and Research*. Boca Raton, Fla.: Chemical Rubber Company Press, 1991. A set of papers written to explore and encourage exploration of the total context of migrations into North America. Illustrations, reference lists.

Dillon, Richard H. *Meriwether Lewis: A Biography*. New York: Coward-McCann, 1965. A full-length study of Meriwether Lewis's life.

_____. *North American Indian Wars*. New York: Facts on File, 1983.

Dippie, Brian W. *The Vanishing American: White Attitudes and U.S. Indian Policy*. Middletown, Conn.: Wesleyan University Press, 1982.

Dixon, E. James. *Quest for the Origins of the First Americans*. Albuquerque: University of New Mexico Press, 1993. An archaeologist discusses the first Americans in the context of his own research. Illustrations, index, bibliography.

Dobyns, Henry F. *Their Number Became Thinned*. Knoxville: University of Tennessee Press, 1983. A comprehensive volume addressing the population dynamics of eastern North America.

Donck, Adriaen van der. *A Description of the New Netherlands*. Translated by Jeremiah Johnson. 1841. Reprint. Syracuse, N.Y.: Syracuse University Press, 1968.

Douville, Raymond, and Jacques Casanova. *Daily Life in Early Canada*. New York: Macmillan, 1967. Although this carefully documented study concentrates on various conditions affecting French colonial life in Gallia Nova (transportation, religious life, trapping, and trading), each chapter includes useful information on relations with Indian populations.

Dowd, Gregory Evans. *A Spirited Resistance: The North American Indian Struggle for Unity, 1745-1815*. Baltimore: The Johns Hopkins University Press, 1991. A useful short survey of American Indian affairs.

Downes, Randolph C. *Council Fires on the Upper Ohio: A Narrative of Indian Affairs in the Upper Ohio Valley Until 1795*. Pittsburgh: University of Pittsburgh Press, 1940. Discusses the relations between settlers and various tribes in the Ohio Valley, including those at Fort Stanwix.

Drake, Benjamin. *Life of Tecumseh*. 1858. Reprint. New York: Arno Press, 1969. Biography using primary documents and interviews with individuals who knew Tecumseh.

Drinnon, Richard. *Facing West: The Metaphysics of Indian-Hating and Empire-Building*. Minneapolis: University of Minnesota Press, 1980. The author explores the intellectual process which defines indigenous tribal groups as primitive and leads to violence between nations and tribes. Includes many helpful illustrations and an extensive bibliographic essay.

Drucker, Phillip. *Indians of the Northwest Coast*. Garden City, N.Y.: Natural History Press, 1963.

_____. "Sources of Northwest Coast Culture." In *New Interpretations of Aboriginal American Culture History*. Seventy-fifth anniversary volume of the Anthropological Society of Washington. Seattle: Anthropological Society of Washington, 1955.

Echo-Hawk, Walter E. "Loopholes in Religious Liberty: The Need for a Federal Law to Protect Freedom of Worship for Native American People." *NARF Legal Review* 14 (Summer, 1991): 7-14. An important analysis of what AIRFA should provide in the way of legal protection of religious freedoms for American Indian peoples.

Edmunds, R. David. *The Shawnee Prophet*. Lincoln: University of Nebraska Press, 1983. An insightful study of the Shawnee society that produced Tecumseh and his alliance. Argues that Tecumseh's brother, Tenskwatawa, the Prophet, originated the alliance, which Tecumseh took over as Tenskwatawa's influence faded. Maps, illustrations, and index.

_____. *Tecumseh and the Quest for Indian Leadership*. Boston: Little, Brown, 1984. A brief treatment that concentrates on the warrior brother. Map, illustrations, and index.

Edmunds, R. David, and Joseph L. Peyser. *The Fox Wars: The Mesquaki Challenge to New France*. Norman: University of Oklahoma Press, 1993. The most complete study to date of the specific events of the Fox Wars.

Ehle, John. *Trail of Tears: The Rise and Fall of the Cherokee Nation*. New York: Doubleday, 1988. Covers Cherokee history from 1770 to 1840. Details the intratribal conflicts relating to removal policy.

Eid, Leroy V. "American Indian Military Leadership: St. Clair's 1791 Defeat." *Journal of Military History* 57 (January, 1993): 71-88.

Eisler, Kim Isaac. *The Revenge of the Pequots: How a Small Native American Tribe Created the World's Most Profitable Casino*. Lincoln: University of Nebraska Press, 2002. A journalistic account of the effect of IGRA on one tribe.

Ellis, Richard N. *General Pope and U.S. Indian Policy*. Albuquerque: University of New Mexico Press, 1970. Ellis's detailed account provides insight into the policy of punishment and containment that grew out of the war.

_____. *The Western American Indian*. Lincoln: University of Nebraska Press, 1972.

Englehardt, Zephyrin. *The Missions and Missionaries of California*. 4 vols. Santa Barbara, Calif.: Mission Santa Barbara, 1929. The monumental standard reference work on the missions, giving an overall positive evaluation of the system.

Enterline, James Robert. *Viking America: The Norse Crossings and Their Legacy*. Epilogue by Thor Heyerdahl. Garden City, N.Y.: Doubleday, 1972.

Fagan, Brian M. *Ancient North America: The Archaeology of a Continent*. Rev. ed. New York: Thames and Hudson, 1995. A consideration of the first Americans in the context of North American archaeology. Illustrations, index, bibliography.

Falkowski, James E. *Indian Law/Race Law: A Five-Hundred-Year History*. New York: Praeger, 1922. Places the subject of U.S. government policy toward Indians in a wider context both of historical and contemporary international legal models.

Faulk, Odie B. *Crimson Desert: Indian Wars of the American Southwest*. New York: Oxford University Press, 1974. Faulk presents a fine and detailed description of the campaigns of this region.

Fausz, J. Frederick. "Merging and Emerging Worlds: Anglo-Indian Interest Groups and the Development of the Seventeenth-Century Chesapeake." In *Colonial Chesapeake Society*, edited by Lois Green Carr et al. Chapel Hill: University of North Carolina Press, 1988. Details the changing English view of the Native Americans in the Chesapeake from "noble savages" to important trading partners.

Fenton, William Nelson. *The Great Law and the Longhouse: A Political History of the Iroquois Confederacy*. Norman: University of Oklahoma Press, 1998. A massive work—over eight hundred pages—on the history and culture of the Iroquois Confederacy.

Fey, Harold E., and D'Arcy McNickle. *Indians and Other Americans: Two Ways of Life Meet*. Rev. ed. New York: Harper & Row, 1970. Good account of the Collier years from a pro-IRA perspective. McNickle, a Montana Blackfoot, was a BIA employee during this era.

Fisher, Don C. *The Nez Perce War*. Thesis. Moscow: University of Idaho, Department of History, 1925.

Fixico, Donald L. *The Invasion of Indian Country in the Twentieth Century: American Capitalism and Tribal Natural Resources*. Niwot: University Press of Colorado, 1998.

_____. *Termination and Relocation: Federal Indian Policy, 1945-1960*. Albuquerque: University of New Mexico Press, 1986. Detailed discussion, from World War II through 1981. Discusses the Menominee and Klamath, as well as smaller tribes. Useful analysis of Dillon Myer and PL 83-280.

_____. *The Urban Indian Experience in America*. Albuquerque: University of New Mexico Press, 2000. An ethnography of the urban Indian experience, especially in third- and fourth-generation urban dwellers who are increasingly distanced from the reservation experience.

Fladmark, Knut R. "The Feasibility of the Northwest as a Migration Route for Early Man." In *Early Man from a Circum-Pacific Perspective*, edited by Alan Bryan. University of Alberta Department of Anthropology Occasional Papers 1. Edmonton, Alberta: Archaeological Researchers International, 1978.

_____. "Getting One's Berings." *Natural History* 95, no. 11 (November, 1986): 8-19. The first of thirteen articles on the peopling of North America published in *Natural History* between November, 1986, and January, 1988. Illustrations.

_____. "The Patterns of the Culture." In *Indians of the North Pacific Coast*, edited by Tom McFeat. Seattle: University of Washington Press, 1966.

Flanagan, Thomas. *Riel and the Rebellion: 1885 Reconsidered*. 2d ed. Toronto: University of Toronto Press, 2000. Provides a revisionist perspective.

Flanders, Nicholas E. "The ANCSA Amendments of 1987 and Land Management in Alaska." *The Polar Record* 25, no. 155 (October, 1989): 315-322. Discusses the modifications of the ANCSA by the 1991 Amendments.

Font Obrador, Bartolome. *Fr. Junipero Serra: Mallorca, Mexico, Sierra Gorda, Californias*. Palma, Mallorca, Spain: Comissio de Cultura, 1992. A biography of Serra that depends on, but summarizes well, the work of many earlier authors.

Foreman, Grant. *Indian Removal: The Emigration of the Five Civilized Tribes of Indians*. 2d ed. 1953. Reprint. Norman: University of Oklahoma Press, 1985. The classic and most comprehensive history of removal.

Foster, John, ed. *Buffalo*. Edmonton, Canada: University of Alberta Press, 1992. A short collection of papers by specialists in ecology and sociology detailing the relationship between the Plains Indians and the American bison. Illustrations.

Francis, Lee. *A Historical Time Line of Native America*. New York: St. Martin's Griffin, 1996.

Francis, Peter, Jr. "The Beads That Did Not Buy Manhattan Island." *New York History* 67, no. 1 (January, 1986): 4-22. Asserts that the trinkets the Dutch paid for the island were much more valuable than common assumptions hold.

Franco, Jere B. *Crossing the Pond: The Native American Effort in World War II.* Denton: University of North Texas Press, 1999.

Frantz, Klaus. *Indian Reservations in the United States: Territory, Sovereignty, and Socioeconomic Change.* Chicago: University of Chicago Press, 1999. A thorough, detailed cultural-geographic study of life on American Indian reservations.

Franz, George W. *Paxton: A Study of Community Structure and Mobility in the Colonial Pennsylvania Backcountry.* New York: Garland, 1989. Focuses on political and socioeconomic development of the Paxton community.

Frazier, Ian. *On the Rez.* New York: Picador, 2001. A depiction of contemporary Ogalala Sioux life on the Pine Ridge reservation. Written by an Anglo, somewhat controversial among American Indians.

Frideres, James. *Canada's Indians: Contemporary Conflicts.* Scarborough, Ontario: Prentice Hall of Canada, 1974.

Fried, Morton H. *The Notion of Tribe.* Menlo Park, Calif.: Cummings, 1975. An exploration of the development and meaning of the concept of tribe.

Frink, Maurice. *Fort Defiance and the Navajos.* Boulder, Colo.: Pruett, 1968. This text is directed toward a middle school or high school audience. Chapter 7, "Lost Cause, Long Walk," covers the relocations.

Frison, George C. *Prehistoric Hunters of the High Plains.* 2d ed. San Diego: Academic Press, 1991.

Fritz, Henry E. *The Movement for Indian Assimilation, 1860-1890.* Philadelphia: University of Pennsylvania Press, 1963. A comprehensive analysis of government policy in the critical period when assimilation policy was the order of the day.

Gaines, W. Craig. *The Confederate Cherokees: John Drew's Regiment of Mounted Rifles.* Baton Rouge: Louisiana State University Press, 1989. Concentrates on Colonel John Drew's regiment and contrasts it with Stand Watie's more successful regiment.

Gallay, Alan. *The Indian Slave Trade: The Rise of the English Empire in the American South, 1670-1717.* New Haven, Conn.: Yale University Press, 2002. The first book to focus specifically on the Indian slave trade and its effects on the development of the plantation system in the American South.

Ganner, Van Hastings. "Seventeenth Century New Mexico." *Journal of Mexican American History* 4 (1974): 41-70. Provides a pro-Indian view of tribal relations with the Spanish. Includes a brief description of the events leading up to 1632.

Gehring, Charles. "Peter Minuit's Purchase of Manhattan Island: New Evidence." *De Halve Maen* 54 (Spring, 1980): 6ff. Discusses a letter from Minuit suggesting his intention to buy Manhattan Island.

Geiger, Maynard J. *The Life and Times of Fray Junipero Serra, OFM.* 2 vols. Washington, D.C.: Academy of American Franciscan History, 1959. A large, sympathetic biography that relies heavily on original sources.

George, Noah Jackson. *A Memorandum of the Creek Indian War.* Meredith, N.H.: R. Lothrop, 1815. 2d ed. Edited by W. Stanley Hoole. University, Ala.: Confederate Publishing Company, 1986. Based on General Jackson's reports and correspondence, this pamphlet gives a battle-by-battle account of the campaign from the U.S. perspective. Written amid the passions of the War of 1812, it asserts that the Red Sticks were tools of the British.

Getty, Ian, and Antoine Lussier, eds. *As Long as the Sun Shines and Water Flows: A Reader in Canadian Native Studies.* Vancouver: University of British Columbia Press, 1983. Includes essays on issues of self-determination, treaty negotiation, and use of natural resources.

Gibson, Arrell Morgan. "The Centennial Legacy of the General Allotment Act." *Chronicles of Oklahoma* 65, no. 3 (1987): 228-251. Examines the long-range effects of the Dawes Act on Native Americans.

_____. *The Chickasaws.* Norman: University of Oklahoma Press, 1971. Puts removal in context with Chickasaw history from the eighteenth century to 1907.

Gibson, James R. *Imperial Russia in Frontier America: The Changing Geography of Supply of Russian America, 1784-1867.* New York: Oxford University Press, 1976.

Gilpin, Alec R. *The War of 1812 in the Old Northwest.* East Lansing: Michigan State University Press, 1958. A scholarly, well-written study that puts Harrison's 1813 campaign and the Battle of the Thames into context of the entire war in the Northwestern theater. Maps, illustrations, and index.

Gipson, Lawrence Henry. "The Drafting of the Albany Plan of Union: The Problem of Semantics." *Pennsylvania History* 26, no. 4 (October, 1959): 291-316. Argues that Thomas Hutchinson was responsible for writing the Albany Plan of Union.

Giraud, Marcel. *The Metis in the Canadian West.* Translated by George Woodcock. 2 vols. Lincoln: University of Nebraska Press, 1986. A primary source on the Metis, originally published in French in 1945. Volume 2 deals with the period of the rebellion. Some of the language suggests racial determinism.

Gleach, Frederic W. *Powhatan's World and Colonial Virginia: A Conflict of Cultures.* Lincoln: University of Nebraska Press, 1997.

Gluckman, Max. *Politics, Law, and Ritual in Tribal Society.* 1966. Reprint. New York: Blackwell, 1977. This book studies tribal organization and the ways tribal groups develop and maintain their integrity. Though not focused specifically on American Indian tribes, it provides a comprehensive conceptual basis for investigation of the concept. Illustrated in the original.

Gonzalez, Mario, and Elizabeth Cook-Lynn. *The Politics of Hallowed Ground: Wounded Knee and the Struggle for Indian Sovereignty.* Urbana: University of Illinois Press, 1999. An account of the Wounded Knee Survivors' Association attempt to obtain a formal apology from the U.S. government for the massacre and to name the site a National American Monument.

Grant, John Webster. *Moon of Wintertime: Missionaries and the Indians of Canada in Encounter Since 1543.* Toronto: University of Toronto Press, 1984. Examines Indian-white contact through the eyes of missionaries and through their cultural legacy.

Gray, John S. *Centennial Campaign.* Ft. Collins, Colo.: Old Army Press, 1976.

Graymont, Barbara. *The Iroquois.* New York: Chelsea House Press, 1988. Graymont is an expert on the Haudenosaunee or Iroquois; this precise, concise text is essential for scholars of the Longhouse culture.

_____. *The Iroquois in the American Revolution.* Syracuse, N.Y.: Syracuse University Press, 1972. An excellent, highly detailed account of the Iroquois during the American Revolution.

_____, ed. *Fighting Tuscarora: The Autobiography of Chief Clinton Rickard.* Reprint. Syracuse, N.Y.: Syracuse University Press, 1994. Introduction includes information about Tuscarora history. Main text chronicles the life of Chief Clinton Rickard (1882-1971) and his work for American Indian rights.

Green, Michael D. *The Politics of Indian Removal: Creek Government in Crisis.* Lincoln: University of Nebraska Press, 1982. Well-researched history of removal as it affected the Creek nation.

Greene, Jerome A. *Lakota and Cheyenne: Indian Views of the Great Sioux War, 1876-1877.* Norman: University of Oklahoma Press, 1994. Collects firsthand accounts from Indians at the Battle of Little Big Horn.

_____, ed. *Battles and Skirmishes of the Great Sioux War, 1876-1877: The Military View.* Norman: University of Oklahoma Press, 1993.

Greenwald, Emily. *Reconfiguring the Reservation: The Nez Perces, the Jicarilla Apache, and the Dawes Act.* Albuquerque: University of New Mexico Press, 2002.

Griffen, William B. *Apaches at War and Peace: The Janos Presidio, 1750-1858.* Albuquerque: University of New Mexico Press, 1988. Details the emergence of the Mexican presidio system and the subsequent relocation and resettlement of various Apache groups in southern New Mexico, Arizona, and northern Mexico.

_____. *Utmost Good Faith: Patterns of Apache-Mexican Hostilities in Northern Chihuahua Border Warfare, 1821-1848*. Albuquerque: University of New Mexico Press, 1989. Summarizes historical accounts of hostilities between the Chiricahua Apache and Mexican military forces in Northern Mexico.

Griffith, Benjamin W., Jr. *McIntosh and Weatherford, Creek Indian Leaders*. Tuscaloosa: University of Alabama Press, 1988. A highly readable account of the war. Argues that Weatherford was a most reluctant Red Stick, knowing from the outset that the movement was doomed.

Grinde, Donald A., Jr. *The Iroquois and the Founding of the American Nation*. San Francisco: Indian Historian Press, 1977. Provides cultural and historical background; discusses Iroquois relationships with colonists before and after the American Revolution. Photographs, maps, illustrations, references, sources. Constitution of the Five Nations and Albany Plan of Union are included as appendices.

Grinnell, George Bird. *The Fighting Cheyennes*. 1915. Reprint. Norman: University of Oklahoma Press, 1956. An author who observed the Cheyenne at first hand presents their history up to 1890.

Gummerman, George J., ed. *Exploring the Hohokam: Prehistoric Desert Peoples of the American Southwest*. Dragoon, Ariz.: Amerind Foundation, 1991.

Gurko, Miriam. *Indian America: The Black Hawk War*. New York: Thomas Y. Crowell, 1970.

Guttmann, Allen. *States' Rights and Indian Removal: "The Cherokee Nation v. the State of Georgia."* Boston: D. C. Heath, 1965. Brief documentary history of the Cherokees' legal struggle to keep their land.

Hackett, Charles W. *Revolt of the Pueblo Indians of New Mexico and Otermín's Attempted Reconquest, 1680-1682*. Translated by Charmion Shelby. 2 vols. Albuquerque: University of New Mexico Press, 1942. The definitive report on the subject to date.

Hafen, LeRoy, and Francis Young. *Fort Laramie and the Pageant of the West, 1834-1890*. Glendale, Calif.: Arthur H. Clark, 1938.

Hagan, William T. *American Indians*. Rev. ed. Chicago: University of Chicago Press, 1979.

_____. *The Indian Rights Association: The Herbert Welsh Years, 1882-1904*. Tucson: University of Arizona Press, 1985. An account of the organization that participated in the litigation of the *Lone Wolf* case.

_____. *The Sac and Fox Indians*. 2d ed. Norman: University of Oklahoma Press, 1980. A general history, including cultural and religious topics.

_____. *United States-Comanche Relations*. New Haven, Conn.: Yale University Press, 1976. The most complete coverage of the council and treaty at Medicine Lodge Creek.

Hait, Pam. "The Hopi Tricentennial: The Great Pueblo Revolt Revisited." *Arizona Highways* 56, no. 9 (September, 1980): 2-6. The entire issue is a beautifully illustrated exploration of Hopi culture, the persistence of which is a tribute to the Pueblo Revolt.

Halbert, Henry Sale, and T. H. Ball. *The Creek War of 1813 and 1814*. Chicago: Donohue and Henneberry, 1895. Reprint with introduction and annotation by Frank L. Owsley, Jr. University: University of Alabama Press, 1969. Provides a lengthy discussion of the causes of the war, presenting it as an intertribal difference that would have been resolved had whites not interfered.

Haley, James L. *The Buffalo War: The History of the Red River Indian Uprising of 1874*. Garden City, N.Y.: Doubleday, 1976. Provides substantial background information and military analysis. Maps, illustrations, notes, bibliography, and index.

Hamilton, Charles, ed. *Cry of the Thunderbird*. Norman: University of Oklahoma Press, 1972. Extensive quotations from some of Little Turtle's speeches.

Hamilton, Edward P. *The French and Indian Wars: The Story of Battles and Forts in the Wilderness*. Garden City, N.Y.: Doubleday, 1962. The first chapters of this narrative history discuss the role played by George Washington.

Hamilton, Raphael N. *Marquette's Explorations: The Narratives Reexamined*. Madison: University of Wisconsin Press, 1970. This scholarly monograph not only describes the experiences of Father Marquette before and during his famous exploration of the 1670's but also provides a critical analysis of the authenticity of manuscript sources ascribed to Marquette.

Handsome Lake. *The Code of Handsome Lake, the Seneca Prophet*. New York State Museum Bulletin 163. Albany: University of the State of New York, 1913. Outlines the Handsome Lake religion and discusses the historical circumstances of its creation.

Hanke, Lewis. *Aristotle and the American Indians*. Chicago: Henry Regnery, 1959.

_____. *The Spanish Struggle for Justice in the Conquest of America*. Boston: Little, Brown, 1965. Historical study of the Spanish debate concerning the treatment of Indians, with emphasis on the work of Bartolomé de Las Casas.

Hann, John. *Apalachee: The Land Between the Rivers*. Gainesville: University Presses of Florida, 1988. An in-depth synthesis of a crucial area in Indian-Spanish relations based on thorough research and thoughtful analysis.

Hardorff, Richard G. *Hokahey! A Good Day to Die! The Indian Casualties of the Custer Fight*. Spokane, Wash.: Arthur H. Clark, 1993.

Harvey, Karen D., and Lisa D. Harjo. *Indian Country: A History of Native People in America*. Golden, Colo.: North American Press, 1994. Written and illustrated by American Indians. Presents ten culture areas, historical perspectives, contemporary issues, major ceremonies, and time lines from 50,000 B.C.E. to the twentieth century. Summaries, lesson plans, resources, and index; appendices include "Threats to Religious Freedom," the text of the Fort Laramie Treaty of 1868, and a list of Indian activist organizations and events.

Hatley, Tom. *The Dividing Paths: Cherokees and South Carolinians Through the Era of Revolution*. New York: Oxford University Press, 1993. Focuses on the multicultural aspects of the Cherokee War, including a discussion of the roles of women and African slaves.

Hawke, David. *The Colonial Experience*. Indianapolis: Bobbs-Merrill, 1966. Chapter 13 brilliantly places Pontiac's resistance in the context of Great Britain's halting steps toward imperial reorganization.

Hawley, Donna L. *The Annotated 1990 Indian Act*. 3d ed. Toronto: Carswell, 1990.

Hays, Robert G. *A Race at Bay: New York Times Editorials on "the Indian Problem," 1860-1900*. Carbondale, Ill.: Southern Illinois University Press, 1997.

Hedren, Paul. *Fort Laramie and the Great Sioux War*. Norman: University of Oklahoma Press, 1998. Focuses on the events of 1876 at Fort Laramie.

_____. *Fort Laramie in 1876*. Lincoln: University of Nebraska Press, 1988.

Heizer, Robert F. *The Destruction of California Indians*. Lincoln: University of Nebraska Press, 1993.

_____. "Treaties." In *California*. Vol. 8 in *Handbook of North American Indians*. Washington, D.C.: Smithsonian Institution Press, 1978. A brief description of treaty making before 1871.

Henry, Thomas R. *Wilderness Messiah: The Story of Hiawatha and the Iroquois*. New York: W. Sloane, 1955. Defines the line between legend and history in the founding of the Iroquois league, and in the stories of Hiawatha, Deganawida, and Atotarho.

Highsaw, Robert B. *Edward Douglass White: Defender of the Conservative*

Faith. Baton Rouge: Louisiana State University Press, 1981. An analysis of the judicial record of the writer of the Supreme Court opinion in *Lone Wolf v. Hitchcock*.

Hilger, M. Inez. *Chippewa Families: A Social Study of White Earth Reservation, 1938*. St, Paul, Minn.: Minnesota Historical Society Press, 1998.

Hill, Joseph. "The Pueblo Revolt." *New Mexico Magazine* 58 (June, 1980): 38. An overview of the subject, with nine illustrations.

Hindle, Brooke. "The March of the Paxton Boys." *William and Mary Quarterly*, 3d ser., 3 (October, 1946): 461-486. Still one of the best narrative accounts of the massacres.

Hodge, Frederick Webb. *History of Hawikah, New Mexico, One of the So-Called Cities of Cíbola*. Los Angeles: Southwest Museum, 1937. Contains translations of Spanish mission records and early histories of Spanish-Zuñi relations. The only detailed history of the revolt.

Hoig, Stan. *The Battle of the Washita*. Garden City, N.Y.: Doubleday, 1976. A thoroughly documented account of the Sheridan-Custer campaign. Maps and photographs.

──────────. *Night of the Cruel Moon: Cherokee Removal and the Trail of Tears*. New York: Facts on File, 1996. An account of Cherokee removal relying on first-person accounts.

──────────. *The Peace Chiefs of the Cheyennes*. Norman: University of Oklahoma Press, 1980. This short work paints the Cheyenne in general, and Black Kettle in particular, as men of peace. Includes many interesting photographs.

Hopkins, Stephen. *A True Representation of the Plan Formed at Albany*. Providence, R.I.: Sidney S. Rider, 1880. Hopkins, who represented Rhode Island at the Albany Congress, details the issues that delegates discussed concerning Indian affairs.

Horn, James. *Adapting to a New World: English Society in the Seventeenth-Century Chesapeake*. Chapel Hill: University of North Carolina Press, 1994. A scholarly but lively study of the extent to which English colonists in the Chesapeake were influenced by their homeland in their attitudes about race, authority, and other matters.

Horsman, Reginald. *Expansion and American Indian Policy, 1783-1812*. East Lansing: Michigan State University Press, 1967.

Hoxie, Frederick E. *A Final Promise: The Campaign to Assimilate the Indians, 1880-1920*. Lincoln: University of Nebraska Press, 1984.

Hoxie, Frederick E., and Peter Iverson. *Indians in American History: An Introduction*. 2d ed. Wheeling, Ill.: Harlan Davidson, 1998.

Hoxie, Frederick E., Ronald Hoffman, and Peter J. Albert. *Native Americans and the Early Republic*. Charlottesville: University Press of Virginia, 1999.

Hoxie, Frederick E., James Merrell, and Peter C. Mancall, eds. *American Nations: Encounters in Indian Country, 1850-Present.* New York: Routledge, 2001. A series of essays on aspects of Indian-U.S. relations and cultural encounters.

Huddleston, Lee Eldridge. *Origins of the American Indians: European Concepts, 1492-1729.* Austin: University of Texas Press, 1967.

Hudson, Charles M. *The Southeastern Indians.* Knoxville: University of Tennessee Press, 1976. Places the Muscogee within the larger framework of the native population of the area. One of several excellent volumes on Southeastern American Indians by ethnologist Hudson.

Hulme, Peter. *Colonial Encounters: Europe and the Native Caribbean, 1492-1797.* New York: Methuen, 1986. Covers a longer time period than other listings here. Focuses on literary and anthropological approaches to understanding the psychological distances separating the colonial and colonized populations of the Caribbean.

Hutton, Paul Andrew. *Phil Sheridan and His Army.* Lincoln: University of Nebraska Press, 1985. An expansive study of Sheridan's post-Civil War career, including his role as the Red River War's chief architect. Maps, illustrations, notes, bibliography, and index.

Hyde, George E. "Red Cloud's War." In *Red Cloud's Folk: A History of the Oglala Sioux Indians.* Rev. ed. Norman: University of Oklahoma Press, 1976. Originally published in 1937 and revised in 1957, this is considered to be a definitive history of the Oglala Sioux. Includes extensive background for the events on the Bozeman Trail. Thirteen illustrations, two maps.

Indian-Eskimo Association of Canada. *Native Rights in Canada.* Calgary: Author, 1970.

Isenberg, Andrew C. *The Destruction of the Bison: An Environmental History, 1750-1920.* New York: Cambridge University Press, 2001. A study of the human and ecological factors leading to the near-extinction of the bison.

Jackson, Donald, ed. *Black Hawk.* Urbana: University of Illinois Press, 1964.

Jackson, Helen Hunt. *A Century of Dishonor: A Sketch of the United States Government's Dealings with Some of the Indian Tribes.* 1880. Reprint. New York: Barnes & Noble, 1993. This volume is a reprint of an 1880 history of Indian-white relations from earliest colonial times through 1871, with many excellent quotations from official documents.

_____. *The Indian Reform Letters of Helen Hunt Jackson, 1879-1885.* Norman: University of Oklahoma Press, 1998.

Jackson, Robert H., and Edward Castillo. *Indians, Franciscans, and Spanish Colonization: The Impact of the Mission System on California Indians.* Albuquerque: University of New Mexico Press, 1995. An ethnohistory of Indian life under the mission system.

Jacob, John J. *A Biographical Sketch of the Life of the Late Captain Michael Cresap.* Cincinnati: J. F. Uhlhorn, 1866. John Jacob worked for Michael Cresap and later married Cresap's widow. His book challenges the notion that Cresap was responsible for the Yellow Creek Massacre.

Jacobs, Wilbur R. "British Indian Policies to 1783." In *History of Indian-White Relations,* edited by Wilcomb E. Washburn. Vol. 4 in *Handbook of North American Indians,* edited by William C. Sturtevant. Washington, D.C.: Smithsonian Institution Press, 1988. As the title indicates, this essay details British policy toward the Indians. It covers the formal relations between Indians and colonists and is particularly good at examining the role of land in the Indian-English experience.

_____. *Dispossessing the American Indian: Indians and Whites on the Colonial Frontier.* New York: Charles Scribner's Sons, 1972.

_____. *The Paxton Riots and the Frontier Theory.* Chicago: Rand McNally, 1967. A brief booklet that includes many primary documents produced during the episode.

Jaenen, Cornelius J. *Friend and Foe: Aspects of French-Amerindian Cultural Contact in the Sixteenth and Seventeenth Centuries.* New York: Columbia University Press, 1976.

Jennings, Francis. *The Ambiguous Iroquois Empire.* New York: W. W. Norton, 1984. Offers a detailed explanation of the duplicitous tactics used by Pennsylvania officials to acquire the Walking Purchase acreage.

_____. *Empire of Fortune: Crowns, Colonies, and Tribes in the Seven Years War in America.* New York: W. W. Norton, 1988. A comprehensive study by a major scholar; offers easily accessible information on all aspects of the war. Illustrations, maps, and indices.

_____. *The Founders of America.* New York: W. W. Norton, 1993. An excellent general history of the Indian population of all regions of North America from precolonial to contemporary times. The colonial section contains essential facts of French and Indian relations.

_____. *The Invasion of America.* New York: W. W. Norton, 1975.

_____, ed. *The History and Culture of Iroquois Diplomacy: An Interdisciplinary Guide to the Treaties of the Six Nations and Their League.* Syracuse, N.Y.: Syracuse University Press, 1985. Extensive discussion of treaty negotiations, terms, and results.

Jennings, Jesse D. *Prehistory of North America.* New York: McGraw-Hill, 1968.

Jensen, Richard E., R. Eli Paul, and John E. Carter. *Eyewitness at Wounded Knee.* Lincoln: University of Nebraska Press, 1992. Fine collection of photographs from the Wounded Knee battlefield and related sites, with essays on the American Indian perspective, the Army's role, and the distorted media coverage.

Johansen, Bruce E. *Life and Death in Mohawk Country.* Golden, Colo.: North American Press, 1993. Details conflicts involving followers of Handsome Lake's code and Louis Hall's Warriors at Akwesasne in the late twentieth century.

Johansen, Bruce, and Roberto Maestas. *Wasi'chu: The Continuing Indian Wars.* New York: Monthly Review Press, 1979.

John, Elizabeth A. H. *Storms Brewed in Other Men's Worlds: The Confrontation of the Indians, Spanish, and French in the Southwest, 1540-1795.* College Station: Texas A&M University Press, 1975. Readable overview of the confrontations involving the Indians, Spanish, and French in the American Southwest from 1540 to 1795. Heavy emphasis on the Native Americans' responses.

Johnson, F. Roy. *The Tuscaroras.* Vols. 1 and 2. Murfreesboro: Johnson, 1967. Discusses history, traditions, culture, mythology, and medicine. Maps, illustrations, index, and many footnotes. Provides listings of numerous original resources.

Johnson, Paul C., et al., eds. *The California Missions: A Pictorial History.* Menlo Park, Calif.: Lane, 1985. A colorful, popular, accessible, and reliable work.

Jones, Dorothy V. *License for Empire: Colonialism by Treaty in Early America.* Chicago: University of Chicago Press, 1982. Discusses abuses of the system and how native peoples failed to understand the process.

Josephy, Alvin M., Jr. *Civil War in the American West.* New York: Alfred A. Knopf, 1991. Discusses the Civil War battles that were fought west of the Mississippi River.

_____. *Five Hundred Nations: An Illustrated History of North American Indians.* New York: Alfred A. Knopf, 1994. A well-illustrated history of North America from its original inhabitants' viewpoint; pages 371-374 cover the treaty, including direct quotations from Indian leaders.

_____. *The Indian Heritage of America.* Rev. ed. Boston: Houghton Mifflin, 1991. Examines the clash of cultures in words and illustrations.

_____. *Now That the Buffalo's Gone: A Study of Today's American Indians.* Norman: University of Oklahoma Press, 1984. Contains a chapter on American Indian efforts to retain their spirituality and provides American Indian perspective on this issue.

_____. *The Patriot Chiefs: A Chronicle of American Indian Resistance.* Rev. ed. New York: Penguin Books, 1993. Gives an account of the precursors to the revolt, but presents no consideration of the aftermath.

Kan, Sergei. *Memory Eternal: Tlingit Culture and Russian Orthodox Christianity Through Two Centuries.* Seattle: University of Washington Press, 1999.

Kappler, Charles, ed. *Indian Treaties, 1778-1883.* New York: Interland, 1972. Provides the texts of most of the actual treaties.

Keegan, William F., ed. *Earliest Hispanic/Native American Interactions in the Caribbean.* New York: Garland, 1991. A series of specialized studies of both Spanish and native Indian institutions, including methods of agriculture and local administration, before and during the Ovando governorate.

Keenan, Jerry. *The Wagon Box Fight: An Episode of Red Cloud's War.* Conshohocken, Pa.: Savas, 2000. A thorough account of this encounter, with detailed appendices of the official army reports and results of recent archaeological excavation at the site.

Keleher, William A. *Turmoil in New Mexico, 1846-1868.* Santa Fe, N.Mex.: Rydal Press, 1952. Details the events leading up to the U.S. invasion of New Mexico and the subsequent occupation of the province.

Keller, Robert H. *American Protestantism and United States Indian Policy, 1869-82.* Lincoln: University of Nebraska Press, 1983.

Kelley, Joseph J., Jr. *Pennsylvania: The Colonial Years, 1681-1776.* Garden City, N.Y.: Doubleday, 1980. Describes the Walking Purchase and many other episodes in Pennsylvania's colonial history.

Kelley, Robert. *American Protestantism and United States Indian Policy.* Lincoln: University of Nebraska Press, 1983. Discusses how Protestant reformers influenced Indian policy and Indian-white relations.

Kelly, Lawrence C. "The Indian Reorganization Act: The Dream and the Reality." *Pacific Historical Review* 44 (August, 1975): 291-312. Balanced look at what the IRA failed to achieve in contrast to the claims of some proponents. Discusses Collier's strong points and shortcomings as American Indian commissioner during the New Deal era.

_____. *Navajo Roundup: Selected Correspondence of Kit Carson's Expedition Against the Navajo, 1863-1865.* Boulder, Colo.: Pruett, 1970. A collection of personal letters and U.S. Army general orders, especially those of General E. R. S. Canby, Brigadier General James Carleton, and Colonel Kit Carson.

Kelly, William H., ed. *Indian Affairs and the Indian Reorganization Act: The Twenty Year Record.* Tucson: University of Arizona Press, 1954. A collection of scholarly essays on this subject.

Kennedy, John H. *Jesuit and Savage in New France*. New Haven, Conn.: Yale University Press, 1950.

Kessler, Donna J. *The Making of Sacagawea: A Euro-American Legend*. Tuscaloosa: University of Alabama Press, 1996.

Kinney, J. P. *A Continent Lost, a Civilization Won: Indian Land Tenure in America*. 1937. Reprint. Baltimore: The Johns Hopkins University Press, 1991.

Klein, Christina. "'Everything of Interest in the Late Pine Ridge War Are Held by Us for Sale': Popular Culture and Wounded Knee." *Western Historical Quarterly* 25 (Spring, 1994): 45-68. Argues that commercial exploitation of Wounded Knee in Cody's Wild West show, photographs, and the dime novel played as significant a role as the military in defeating the Ghost Dancers' dreams of American Indian autonomy. Includes photographs.

Knaut, Andrew L. *The Pueblo Revolt of 1680: Conquest and Resistance in Seventeenth-Century New Mexico*. Norman: University of Oklahoma Press, 1995.

Kohn, Richard H. *Eagle and Sword*. New York: Free Press, 1975.

Kraft, Louis. *Gatewood and Geronimo*. Albuquerque: University of New Mexico Press, 2000. Focuses on the events leading up to Geronimo's surrender.

Krech, Shepard, III. *The Ecological Indian: Myth and History*. New York: W. W. Norton, 1999.

Kroeber, Alfred Louis. *Handbook of the Indians of California*. New York: Dover, 1976. A large anthropological tome.

Kupperman, Karen Ordahl. *Indians and English: Facing Off in Early America*. Ithaca, N.Y.: Cornell University Press, 2000. A highly readable account of the evolutions of Indian-English relations along the East Coast of North America.

Kvasnicka, Robert M. "United States Indian Treaties and Agreements." In *History of Indian-White Relations*, edited by Wilcomb E. Washburn. Vol. 4 in *Handbook of North American Indians*. Washington, D.C.: Smithsonian Institution Press, 1988. A short discussion of the debate over treaties and how the process was ended.

La Farge, Oliver. "Termination of Federal Supervision: Disintegration and the American Indians." *Annals of the American Academy of Political and Social Science* 311 (May, 1957): 41-46. Summarizes arguments against termination, except when tribes request it and members are ready to handle their own affairs.

Las Casas, Bartolomé de. *History of the Indies*. Edited and translated by Andrée Collard. New York: Harper & Row, 1971. A partial translation of the massive work (three volumes in the Spanish edition) of the Spanish missionary who, after coming to Hispaniola with Governor Ovando, turned critical of Ovando's repressive policies.

Lass, William E. *Minnesota: A History.* New York: W. W. Norton, 1977. Chapter 5 is a concise but insightful statement of the war's effect on Minnesota.

Lavender, David. *The Great West.* Boston: Houghton Mifflin, 1985. Suggests that Black Kettle may have been more interested in handouts than in peace.

Lazarus, Edward. *Black Hills, White Justice: The Sioux Nation Versus the United States, 1775 to the Present.* New York: HarperCollins, 1991. Includes the full text of the Fort Laramie Treaty of 1868.

Leach, Douglas E. *Arms for Empire: A Military History of the British Colonies in North America, 1607-1763.* New York: Macmillan, 1973. A formidable study that details the increasingly impossible task Great Britain faced in trying to devise an effective military defense for a vast colonial empire against France and Spain, British colonists, and Native Americans. The latter chapters provide excellent background on Pontiac's resistance.

_____. "Colonial Indian Wars." In *History of Indian-White Relations,* edited by Wilcomb B. Washburn. Vol. 4 in *Handbook of North American Indians.* Washington, D.C.: Smithsonian Institution Press, 1988. More specific in its focus than the Leach study, this article combines British and American Indian politics and perspectives in the context of colonial wars.

_____. *Flintlock and Tomahawk: New England in King Philip's War.* New York: Norton Library Edition, 1966. This elegantly written study, long considered the standard modern account of the war, indicts English land hunger as a cause of the war. Maps, illustrations, and index.

Leckie, William H. *The Buffalo Soldiers: A Narrative of the Negro Cavalry in the West.* Norman: University of Oklahoma Press, 1967. Discusses the considerable role played by African Americans in the frontier Army, devoting an entire chapter to the Red River War. Maps, illustrations, notes, bibliography, and index.

Legters, Lyman, and Fremont J. Lyden, eds. *American Indian Policy: Self-Governance and Economic Development.* Westport, Conn.: Greenwood Press, 1994. A series of articles detailing current trends in Native American life and law.

Lepore, Jill. *The Name of War: King Philip's War and the Origins of American Identity.* New York: Random House, 1998. A very well-received history of Metacom's war, arguing that the conflict between Europeans and Indians served to crystallize a sense of American self-identity on the part of the colonists.

Liebersohn, Harry. *Aristocratic Encounters: European Travelers and North American Indians.* New York: Cambridge University Press, 1998.

Lincoln, Charles A., ed. *Narratives of the Indian Wars, 1675-1699.* New York: Scribner's, 1913. Reprint. New York: Barnes & Noble Books, 1941. Contains a number of contemporaneous accounts of the war, including *The Soveraignty & Goodness of God . . . the Captivity and Restoration of Mrs. Mary Rowlandson,* Rowlandson's account of her capture in the attack on Lancaster, Massachusetts, in 1676. Her often reprinted classic is the earliest American captivity narrative. Rowlandson reports firsthand exchanges with Metacom, who at times traveled with the mixed band that held her prisoner.

Little Bear, Leroy, and Menno Boldt, eds. *Pathways to Self-Determination.* Toronto: University of Toronto Press, 1984.

Long, Carolyn N. *Religious Freedom and Indian Rights: The Case of "Oregon v. Smith."* Lawrence: University Press of Kansas, 2000. Part of the Landmark Law Cases and American Society series, this is the first book-length study of *Oregon v. Smith,* focusing on the case's sharp differences from previous opinions on First Amendment freedom of religion rights.

Long, J. Anthony, and Menno Boldt, eds., in association with Leroy Little Bear. *Governments in Conflict? Provinces and Indian Nations in Canada.* Toronto: University of Toronto Press, 1988. Addresses aboriginal-provincial relations focusing on self-government, provincial jurisdiction, land claims, and financial responsibility.

_____. *The Quest for Justice: Aboriginal Peoples and Aboriginal Rights.* Toronto: University of Toronto Press, 1985. Presents a broad cross section of tribal, geographic, and organizational perspectives. The authors discuss constitutional questions such as land rights, concerns of Metis, nonstatus Indians and Inuit, and historical, legal/constitutional, political, regional, and international rights issues.

Longhena, Maria. *Ancient Mexico: The History and Culture of the Maya, Aztecs, and Other Pre-Columbian Peoples.* New York: Tabori & Chang, 1998.

Luebke, Barbara P. "Elias Boudinot, Indian Editor: Editorial Columns from the *Cherokee Phoenix.*" *Journalism History* 6 (1979): 48-51. Discusses Boudinot's conflicts as editor of the *Cherokee Phoenix.*

Lyons, Oren, et al. *Exiled in the Land of the Free.* Santa Fe, N.Mex.: Clear Light Publishers, 1992. Lyons, faithkeeper of the Six Nations Confederacy, is distinctive in his understanding of the role of the American Indian in U.S. history.

McAlister, Lyle. *Spain and Portugal in the New World, 1492-1700.* Minneapolis: University of Minnesota Press, 1984. Includes a clearly written account of Spain's general imperial policies such as the *encomienda* and the *repartimiento*.

McCary, Ben C. *Indians in Seventeenth Century Virginia*. Williamsburg: Virginia 350th Anniversary Celebration Corporation, 1957. Reviews the history of seventeenth century Native Americans in Virginia.

McConnell, Michael N. *A Country Between: The Upper Ohio Valley and Its Peoples, 1724-1774*. Lincoln: University of Nebraska Press, 1992. Discusses colonial expansion from the eighteenth century Native American perspective. McConnell sees the Treaty of Fort Stanwix as a deciding factor in the coming of Lord Dunmore's War.

McCormick, Anita L. *Native Americans and the Reservation in American History*. Springfield, N.J.: Enslow, 1996.

McCutchen, David, ed. *The Red Record: The Wallam Olum, the Oldest Native North American History*. Garden City Park, N.Y.: Avery, 1993.

McDermott, John D. "Price of Arrogance: The Short and Controversial Life of William Judd Fetterman." *Annals of Wyoming* 63, no. 2 (Spring, 1991): 42-53. A look at Fetterman's character and its fatal consequences.

_____, ed. "Wyoming Scrapbook: Documents Relating to the Fetterman Fight." *Annals of Wyoming* 63, no. 2 (Spring, 1991): 68-72. Gives details of the most significant Army loss in the war.

McDonnell, Janet A. *The Dispossession of the American Indian, 1887-1934*. Bloomington: Indiana University Press, 1991.

McDougall, John. *In the Days of the Red River Rebellion*. Edmonton: University of Alberta Press, 1983. Memoir of a Methodist missionary during the time of the rebellion.

MacFarlan, Allan A. *Book of American Indian Games*. New York: Associated Press, 1958. Discusses and describes various games, including gambling games, played by a variety of North American tribes.

McGrath, Patrick. *The Lewis and Clark Expedition*. Morristown, N.J.: Silver Burdett, 1985. A simple but complete telling of the Lewis and Clark adventure for younger readers.

McHugh, Tom. *The Time of the Buffalo*. New York: Alfred A. Knopf, 1972. A factual, readable revision of a professional wildlife biologist's dissertation. Illustrations, index, and detailed bibliography.

McLoughlin, William G. *Cherokee Renascence in the New Republic*. Princeton, N.J.: Princeton University Press, 1983. Cherokee history up through the removal crisis.

_____. *Cherokees and Missionaries, 1789-1839*. New Haven, Conn.: Yale University Press, 1984. Discusses missionary support for the Cherokees.

McMillan, Alan D. *Native Peoples and Cultures of Canada: An Anthropological Overview*. Vancouver: Douglas & McIntyre, 1988. Chapter 12 discusses both the Indian Act and issues related to the status of Canadian Indians.

McMurtry, Larry. *Crazy Horse*. New York: Viking Press, 1999.

McPherson, Robert S. *The Northern Navajo Frontier, 1860-1900: Expansion Through Adversity*. Albuquerque: University of New Mexico Press, 1988. A well-documented study of the clash of cultures in the Four Corners area.

Magnusson, Magnus, and Hermann Palsson, eds. and trans. *The Vinland Sagas: The Norse Discovery of America*. New York: Penguin Books, 1980.

Mahon, John K. *History of the Second Seminole War, 1835-1842*. Rev. ed. Gainesville: University Presses of Florida, 1985. Describes the battles and leaders, the problems of military organization and ordnance, and Seminole culture and history in the period of the Second Seminole War.

Mails, Thomas E. "Transformation of a Culture." In *The Cherokee People: The Story of the Cherokees from Earliest Origins to Contemporary Times*. Tulsa, Okla.: Council Oak Books, 1992. Describes the history of relations between Cherokees and Europeans up to the Trail of Tears.

Malone, Patrick M. *The Skulking Way of War: Technology and Tactics Among the New England Indians*. Baltimore: The Johns Hopkins University Press, 1991. Study of Native American military tactics and their evolution under the influence of European weapons and methods. Argues that New England's natives adopted the more ruthless methods of total war through English influence and example. Map, illustrations, and index.

Mancall, Peter C., and James H. Merrell. *American Encounters: Natives and Newcomers from European Contact to Indian Removal*. New York: Routledge, 1999.

Mangusso, Mary Childers, and Stephen W. Haycox, eds. *Interpreting Alaska's History: An Anthology*. Anchorage: Alaska Pacific University Press, 1989.

Marshall, Samuel L. A. *Crimsoned Prairie*. New York: Charles Scribner's Sons, 1972. Details the Indian campaigns of the West. The author is an excellent military historian, although slightly biased in the direction of preserving the honor of the military.

Martin, James Kirby. *In the Course of Human Events: An Interpretive Exploration of the American Revolution*. Arlington Heights, Ill.: Harlan Davidson, 1979. Links the Proclamation of 1763 with other British decisions to control the colonies, such as stationing ships in American waters.

Martin, Joel. *Sacred Revolt: The Muscogees' Struggle for a New World*. Boston: Beacon Press, 1991. Emphasizes the importance of spirituality in Muscogee life, in the evolution of the Red Sticks' back-to-our-culture campaign, and in their war making.

Matthews, Anne. *Where the Buffalo Roam*. New York: Grove Weidenfeld, 1992. Describes a plan to restore the Great Plains to their natural condition and the bison to their former numbers. Illustrations and index.

Matthiessen, Peter. *In the Spirit of Crazy Horse*. 2d ed. New York: Viking Press, 1991.

Mayer, Brantz. *Tah-Gah-Jute, or Logan and Cresap, an Historical Essay*. Albany: Munsell, 1867. The most famous study of the Cresap-Logan controversy written in the nineteenth century.

Merwick, Donna. *Possessing Albany, 1630-1710: The Dutch and English Experiences*. Cambridge, England: Cambridge University Press, 1990.

Middlekauff, Robert. *Bacon's Rebellion*. Chicago: Rand McNally, 1964. A good collection of the primary documents associated with the uprising, beginning with Berkeley's American Indian policy and concluding with the official report submitted to London.

Milanich, Jerald T., and Susan Milbruth, eds. *First Encounters: Spanish Explorations in the Caribbean and the United States, 1492-1570*. Gainesville: University of Florida Press, 1989.

Miller, J. R. *Skyscrapers Hide the Heavens: A History of Indian-White Relations in Canada*. 3d ed. Toronto: University of Toronto Press, 2000. An excellent study of Indians as politicians and cultural survivors.

_____. *Sweet Promises: A Reader on Indian-White Relations in Canada*. Toronto: University of Toronto Press, 1991. Contains key, previously published articles concerned with regional developments from the days of New France to the present.

Miller, Jay, Colin G. Calloway, and Richard A. Sattler. *Writings in Indian History, 1985-1990*. Norman: University of Oklahoma Press, 1995.

Milling, Chapman J. "The Cherokee War." In *Red Carolinians*. Chapel Hill: University of North Carolina Press, 1940. A detailed, carefully documented account of the war. An important reference despite its age.

Mintz, Steven, ed. *Native American Voices*. St. James, N.Y.: Brandywine Press, 1995. Contains part of the Dawes Act and a complaint by a Cherokee farmer in 1906.

Mitchell, Donald Craig. *Take My Land, Take My Life: The Story of Congress's Historic Settlement of Alaska Native Land Claims, 1960-1971*. Fairbanks: University of Alaska Press, 2000. Discusses the legal and regulatory history of ANCSA.

Moeller, Bill, and Jan Moeller. *Chief Joseph and the Nez Perces: A Photographic History*. Missoula, Mont.: Mountain Press, 1995.

Mooney, James. *Calendar History of the Kiowa Indians*. 1898. Reprint. Washington, D.C.: Smithsonian Institution Press, 1979. Provides a chronology of the tribe.

_____. *The Ghost-Dance Religion and the Sioux Outbreak of 1890*. 1896. Reprint. Lincoln: University of Nebraska Press, 1991.

_____. *Historical Sketch of the Cherokee*. Chicago: Aldine, 1975. Valuable study by a contemporary who interviewed people involved.

Morris, Alexander. *The Treaties of Canada with the Indians of Manitoba and the North-west Territories*. Toronto: Belfords, Clark & Co., 1880. Reprint. Toronto: Coles, 1971. An account by one of the negotiators of Treaties 3 through 6.

Morris, Glenn T., and Ward Churchill. "Between a Rock and a Hard Place: Left-Wing Revolution, Right-Wing Reaction, and the Destruction of Indigenous People." *Cultural Survival Quarterly* 11, no. 3 (1987): 17-24.

Morrison, Andrea P., with Irwin Cotler, eds. *Justice for Natives Searching for Common Ground*. Montreal: McGill-Queen's University Press, 1997. A volume that came together around the Oka crisis between aboriginal people in Quebec and the government. Its thirty-five essays and stories provide helpful discussions on native women and the struggle for justice, self-determination, title and land claims, the Oka crisis, and legal relations and models for change.

Morrison, Kenneth M. *The Embattled Northeast: The Elusive Ideal of Alliance in Abenaki-Euramerican Relations*. Berkeley: University of California Press, 1984.

Morse, Bradford W. *Aboriginal Peoples and the Law: Indian, Metis, and Inuit Rights in Canada*. Rev. ed. Ottawa: Carleton University Press, 1989. Provides a basic resource for cases and materials on the original inhabitants of Canada.

Morton, W. L. *Manitoba: A History*. Toronto: University of Toronto Press, 1967. One chapter is devoted to the importance of the Red River colony. Presents a decidedly old-fashioned view of the métis, referring to them as "halfbreeds" and "savages." Maps, illustrations, and index.

Moses, L. G. *Wild West Shows and the Images of American Indians, 1883-1933*. Albuquerque: University of New Mexico Press, 1996.

Moulton, Gary E. *John Ross, Cherokee Chief*. Athens: University of Georgia Press, 1978. Biography of the Cherokee leader at the time of removal.

Mowat, Farley. *Westviking: The Ancient Norse in Greenland and North America*. Boston: Little, Brown, 1965.

Muench, David. *Anasazi, Ancient People of the Rock*. Palo Alto, Calif.: American West, 1975.

Mullin, Michael J. "The Albany Congress and Colonial Confederation."

Mid-America 72, no. 2 (April-July, 1990): 93-105. Discusses the role of Indian affairs at the Congress.

Munroe, John A. *History of Delaware*. 2d ed. Newark: University of Delaware Press, 1984.

Murphy, James E., and Sharon M. Murphy. *Let My People Know: American Indian Journalism, 1828-1978*. Norman: University of Oklahoma Press, 1981. A history of Native American journalism, with some discussion of the *Cherokee Phoenix*.

Nagler, Mark. *Natives Without a Home*. Don Mills, Ontario, Canada: Longman, 1975.

Nash, Gary B. *Red, White, and Black: The Peoples of Early America*. Englewood Cliffs, N.J.: Prentice-Hall, 1974.

Native American Rights Fund. *Annual Report*. Boulder, Colo.: Author, 1993.
_____. *Legal Review* 19, no. 1 (Winter/Spring, 1994).

Neihardt, John G. *Black Elk Speaks: Being the Life Story of a Holy Man of the Oglala Sioux*. 1932. Reprint. Lincoln: University of Nebraska Press, 1979. This classic work chronicles the spiritual odyssey of Black Elk, a holy man of the Oglala Sioux. Provides important insight into American Indian beliefs and an account of the Wounded Knee Massacre.

Nelson, Paul D. *Anthony Wayne: Soldier of the Early Republic*. Bloomington: Indiana University Press, 1985. The best biography of Wayne to date.
_____. "Anthony Wayne's Indian War in the Old Northwest, 1792-1795." *Northwest Ohio Quarterly* 56 (1984): 115-140. An excellent short account of this war.

Nester, William R. *Haughty Conquerors: Amherst and the Great Indian Uprising of 1763*. Greenwood, Conn.: Praeger, 2000. An up-to-date history of Pontiac's resistance.

Newbold, Robert C. *The Albany Congress and Plan of Union of 1754*. New York: Vantage Press, 1955. A summation of the scholarship on Albany at the time.

Newcomb, William. *North American Indians: An Anthropological Perspective*. Pacific Palisades, Calif.: Goodyear, 1974.

Nichols, Roger L. *Black Hawk and the Warrior's Path*. Arlington Heights, Ill.: Harlan Davidson, 1992.

Noble, David G., ed. *The Hohokam: Ancient People of the Desert*. Santa Fe, N.Mex.: School of American Research Press, 1991.

Oberg, Michael Leroy. *Dominion and Civility: English Imperialism and Native America, 1585-1685*. Ithaca, N.Y.: Cornell University Press, 1999. Focuses on English interactions with Algonquian groups in the Chesapeake Bay area.

O'Donnell, James H. *Southern Indians in the American Revolution*. Knoxville: University of Tennessee Press, 1973. Focusing on the Cherokees, Chickasaws, Creeks, and Choctaws, O'Donnell describes the attitudes of both the British and the Americans toward their Indian allies and Indian enemies. Indexed, annotated, with bibliography.

Oliphant, John. *Peace and War on the Anglo-Cherokee Frontier, 1756-1763*. Baton Rouge: Louisiana State University Press, 2001. Focuses on the clashes of individual personalities that fomented the war.

Olson, James S., and Raymond Wilson. *Native Americans in the Twentieth Century*. Chicago: University of Illinois Press, 1984. A good text for interpreting major trends, events, and attitudes affecting American Indian peoples, including the myriad issues involved in the citizenship debate.

Orr, Charles, ed. *History of the Pequot War: The Contemporary Accounts of Mason, Underhill, Vincent, and Gardener*. Cleveland, Ohio: Helman-Taylor, 1897. A valuable anthology of eyewitness reporting on the Pequot War from the Puritan perspective, drawing on the recollections of major English participants.

Oswalt, Wendell H. *Mission of Change in Alaska*. San Marino, Calif.: Huntington Library, 1963.

Otis, Delos S. *The Dawes Act and the Allotment of Indian Lands*. Edited by Francis Paul Prucha. Norman: University of Oklahoma Press, 1973.

Owram, Doug. *Promise of Eden: The Canadian Expansionist Movement and the Idea of the West, 1856-1900*. Toronto: University of Toronto Press, 1980. Chapter 4 discusses the politics of the Canadian response to the rebellion.

Owsley, Frank Lawrence, Jr. *Struggle for the Borderlands: The Creek War and the Battle of New Orleans, 1812-1815*. Tuscaloosa: University of Alabama Press, 2000. Considers the Creek War in the larger context of the War of 1812.

Page, James K., Jr. "Rebellious Pueblos Outwitted Spain Three Centuries Ago." *Smithsonian* 11 (October, 1980): 221. Tells the story through Padre Pio's last day. Good observations on the revolt's modern significance.

Palmer, Dave R. *1794. America, Its Army, and the Birth of the Nation*. Novato, Calif.: Presidio Press, 1994. A helpful study of early U.S. military policy.

Parker, Arthur. *Parker on the Iroquois*. Edited by William Fenton. Syracuse, N.Y.: Syracuse University Press, 1968. A detailed description of the Handsome Lake religion by a noted Seneca ethnologist.

Parker, Arthur C. *Red Jacket: Seneca Chief.* Lincoln: University of Nebraska Press, 1998.

Parkman, Francis. *The Conspiracy of Pontiac and the Indian War After the Conquest of Canada.* 1874. Reprint. 2 vols. Lincoln: University of Nebraska Press, 1994. Despite minor inaccuracies, this remains the classic study of the subject. Based on original documents and written by one of the greatest of American historians.

_____. *Count Frontenac and New France Under Louis XIV.* 1877. Reprint. New York: Library of America, 1983. A pioneering work providing background on French interests in the Great Lakes area just before dealings with the Foxes became focal.

Parman, Donald L. *The Navajos and the New Deal.* New Haven, Conn.: Yale University Press, 1976. A study of the troubled relations between the American Indian policy reformers in the Roosevelt administration and the nation's largest tribe.

Peale, Arthur L. *Memorials and Pilgrimages in the Mohegan Country.* Norwich, Conn.: Bulletin Company, 1930. Peale, author of a groundbreaking study of Uncas, was celebrated for his knowledge of the Mohegans and the Pequots. Remarkably readable reflections.

Peckham, Howard. *Pontiac and the Indian Uprising.* Princeton, N.J.: Princeton University Press, 1947. Corrects Parkman's inaccuracies, updates the subject, and provides fresh insights into American Indian attitudes.

Perdue, Theda, ed. *Cherokee Editor: The Writings of Elias Boudinot.* Knoxville: University of Tennessee Press, 1983. Brief biographical introduction to Boudinot, with reproductions of important documents in the history of the *Cherokee Phoenix* and Boudinot's fund-raising.

Peroff, Nicholas C. *Menominee Drums.* Norman: University of Oklahoma Press, 1982. A case study of one of the most important examples of tribal termination actions.

Philbrick, Francis S. *The Rise of the West, 1754-1830.* New York: Harper & Row, 1965.

Philp, Kenneth R. *John Collier's Crusade for Indian Reform, 1920-1954.* Tucson: University of Arizona Press, 1977. A detailed, objective account of Collier's achievements and shortcomings as a policy critic, activist, reformer, and administrator.

_____. *Termination Revisited: American Indians on the Trail to Self-Determination, 1933-1953.* Lincoln: University of Nebraska Press, 1999. A history of termination policy, with useful emphasis on the ambivalent attitudes of Native Americans themselves toward U.S. policy.

Pommersheim, Frank. "Economic Development in Indian Country: What Are the Questions?" *American Indian Law Review* 12 (1987): 195-217. Explains the need for revenue in American Indian country and the possibilities gaming provides tribes.

Porter, C. Fayne. *Our Indian Heritage: Profiles of Twelve Great Leaders.* Philadelphia: Chilton Books, 1964. Little Turtle is one of the twelve leaders discussed.

Preucel, Robert, ed. *Archaeologies of the Pueblo Revolt: Identity, Meaning, and Renewal in the Pueblo World.* Albuquerque: University of New Mexico Press, 2002. A collection of essays exploring the light archaeology and material culture can shed on the historical understanding of the Pueblo Revolt.

Priest, Loring Benson. *Uncle Sam's Stepchildren: The Reformation of United States Indian Policy, 1865-1887.* New Brunswick, N.J.: Rutgers University Press, 1942.

Pritchett, John Perry. *Red River Valley, 1811-1849: A Regional Study.* New Haven, Conn.: Yale University Press, 1942. Contains an almost minute-by-minute account of the Seven Oaks Massacre.

"Proclamation of 1763: Governor Henry Ellis' Plan May 5, 1763." In *The American Revolution, 1763-1783: A Bicentennial Collection,* edited by Richard B. Morris. Columbia: University of South Carolina Press, 1970. Demonstrates the thinking by one colonial official that prompted the Proclamation of 1763.

Prucha, Francis Paul. *American Indian Treaties: The History of a Political Anomaly.* Berkeley: University of California Press, 1994. The full story of treaty making and how it was ended in 1871. Index and list of treaties.

_____. "Andrew Jackson's Indian Policy: A Reassessment." *Journal of American History* 56, no. 3 (1969): 527-539. A discussion of Jackson's Indian policy from a sympathetic viewpoint, describing the pressures leading to Indian removal.

_____. *The Great Father: The United States Government and the American Indians.* 2 vols. Lincoln: University of Nebraska Press, 1984. An extensive, fully annotated, indexed, and illustrated history of Indian-white relations from the founding of the United States to the 1980's by one of the premier authorities on Indian-white relations.

_____. *The Sword of the Republic.* New York: Macmillan, 1969.

_____, ed. *Americanizing the American Indians: Writings of the "Friends of the Indian" 1880-1900.* Lincoln: University of Nebraska Press, 1973. Section 2 provides a representative sampling of primary source writings about the Dawes Act.

_____, ed. *Documents of United States Indian Policy.* 3d ed. Lincoln: University of Nebraska Press, 2000. General policy and issues for specific tribes.

Purich, Donald J. *The Inuit and Their Land: The Story of Nunavut.* Toronto: James Lorimer, 1992. Contains a thorough discussion of each of the Inuit land claims agreements, paying special attention to the Eastern Arctic Agreement and the preparations for native self-government in the proposed New Nunavut Territory.

_____. *The Metis.* Toronto: James Lorimer, 1988. Highly readable treatment of the Metis. Chapters 3, 4, and 5 deal with the 1869 and 1885 rebellions and their outcomes.

Rawls, James J. *Chief Red Fox Is Dead: A History of Native America Since 1945.* Fort Worth, Tex.: Harcourt Brace College Publishers, 1996.

Ray, Arthur J. *Indians in the Fur Trade: Their Role as Trappers, Hunters, and Middlemen in the Lands Southwest of Hudson Bay, 1660-1870.* Toronto: University of Toronto Press, 1974.

Ray, Dorothy Jean. *The Eskimos of Bering Strait, 1650-1898.* Seattle: University of Washington Press, 1975.

Redmond, Elsa M., ed. *Chiefdoms and Chieftaincy in the Americas.* Gainesville: University Press of Florida, 1998.

Reman, Edward. *The Norse Discoveries and Explorations in America.* Berkeley: University of California Press, 1949.

Remini, Robert V. *Andrew Jackson and His Indian Wars.* New York: Viking, 2001. An acclaimed biography of Jackson in the context of his ideas about and policies toward Indians. Attempts to show the underlying motives for Indian removal.

_____. *The Legacy of Andrew Jackson: Essays on Democracy, Indian Removal, and Slavery.* Reprint. Baton Rouge: Louisiana State University Press, 1990. The leading biographer of Andrew Jackson reflects on his significance to these issues.

Richter, Daniel K. *Facing East from Indian Country: A Native History of Early America.* Cambridge, Mass.: Harvard University Press, 2002. Presents early American history from an Indian perspective, focusing on the figures of Pocohontas, Blessed Catherine Tekawitha, and Metacom, a.k.a. King Philip.

_____. *The Ordeal of the Longhouse: The Peoples of the Iroquois League in the Era of European Colonization.* Chapel Hill: University of North Carolina Press, 1992. Published for the Institute of Early American History and Culture, this study of the Iroquois League demonstrates the influence of factionalism on an Indian people as they dealt with the Europeans. It synthesizes much scholarship on the Six Nations and their relationship with the French, Dutch, and English. It is particularly strong on seventeenth century relations.

Riel, Louis. *The Collected Writings of Louis Riel*. Edited by George F. G. Stanley. Edmonton: University of Alberta Press, 1985. Shows that Riel was a thinker as well as a political leader.

Riley, Carroll L. *Rio Del Norte: People of the Upper Rio Grande from Earliest Times to the Pueblo Revolt*. Salt Lake City: University of Utah Press, 1995.

Riley, Sam G. "The *Cherokee Phoenix:* The Short, Unhappy Life of the First American Indian Newspaper." *Journalism Quarterly* 53, no. 4 (Winter, 1976): 666-671. Discusses Boudinot's editorial dilemmas and political pressure.

Rink, Oliver A. *Holland on the Hudson: An Economic and Social History of Dutch New York*. Ithaca, N.Y.: Cornell University Press, 1986.

Robbins, Rebecca L. "Self-Determination and Subordination: The Past, Present, and Future of American Indian Governance." In *The State of Native America*, edited by M. A. Jaimes. Boston: South End Press, 1992.

Robinson, Charles M. *Bad Hand: A Biography of General Ranald S. Mackenzie*. Austin, Tex.: State House Press, 1993. A comprehensive study that treats Mackenzie's pivotal role in the Red River War in suitable detail. Maps, illustrations, notes, bibliography, and index.

Rollings, Willard H. *The Comanche*. New York: Chelsea House, 1989. Describes the change in Comanche life after the Medicine Lodge Creek Treaty.

Ronda, James P. *Lewis and Clark Among the Indians*. Bicentennial edition. Lincoln: University of Nebraska Press, 2002. A detailed look at the Indian cultures encountered by the Lewis and Clark expedition.

Rosenberg, Bruce A. *Custer and the Epic of Defeat*. University Park: Pennsylvania State University Press, 1974.

Ross, Norman A., ed. *Index to the Expert Testimony Before the Indian Claims Commission: The Written Reports*. Washington, D.C.: Congressional Information Service, 2001.

Rountree, Helen C. *Pocahontas's People: The Powhatan Indians of Virginia Through Four Centuries*. Norman: University of Oklahoma Press, 1990. Written by an ethnohistorian and anthropologist, this is one of the best studies of Jamestown and the settlement's relationship to the Powhatan Confederacy.

_____. *The Powhatan Indians of Virginia: Their Traditional Culture*. Norman: University of Oklahoma Press, 1989. A comprehensive study of all aspects of life among the Powhatan Confederacy tribes.

_____, ed. *Powhatan Foreign Relations, 1500-1722*. Charlottesville: University Press of Virginia, 1993.

Rouse, Irving. *The Tainos: Rise and Decline of the People Who Greeted Columbus*. New Haven, Conn.: Yale University Press, 1992. Contains the most extensive coverage of the distant past of the native West Indian population, with a concluding chapter on their short history of contacts with Europeans before dying out.

Rozema, Vicki. *Footsteps of the Cherokees: A Guide to the Eastern Homelands of the Cherokee Nations.* Winston-Salem, N.C.: John F. Blair, 1995. Devotes several pages to American Indian slavery, helping to correct the previously small amount of attention given to this topic.

Russell, Don. *Custer's Last.* Fort Worth, Tex.: Amon Carter Museum of Western Art, 1968.

_____. *The Lives and Legends of Buffalo Bill.* Norman: University of Oklahoma Press, 1960. A detailed examination of the Army scout and bison hunter. Footnotes, extensive bibliography, index, illustrations.

Rutledge, Joseph Lister. *Century of Conflict.* Garden City, N.Y.: Doubleday, 1956. A comprehensive account of American Indian relations with both French and British colonial regimes from the early to the late eighteenth century, including the key Seven Years' War period.

Sachese, Julius F. *History of the German Role in the Discovery, Exploration, and Settlement of the New World.* Reprint. *Germany and America, 1450-1700.* Edited by Don H. Tolzman. New York: Heritage Books, 1991.

Sagard, Gabriel. *The Long Journey to the Country of the Hurons.* Translated by Hugh H. Langton. Toronto: Champlain Society, 1939. This is a translation of the French explorer's original travel logs, published in 1632.

Sahlins, Marshall D. *Tribesmen.* Englewood Cliffs, N.J.: Prentice Hall, 1968. This book has illustrations which represent tribal life in all its diversity.

St. Germain, Jill. *Indian Treaty-Making Policy in the United States and Canada, 1867-1877.* Lincoln: University of Nebraska Press, 2001. Explores and contrasts the "civilizing" efforts of the United States and Canada through their Indian treaty policies.

Salisbury, Albert, and Jane Salisbury. *Two Captains West.* Seattle: Superior Publishing, 1950. Descriptions of the Lewis and Clark trail, with maps and photographs. Designed for the lay reader.

Salisbury, Neal. *Manitou and Providence: Indians, Europeans, and the Making of New England.* New York: Oxford University Press, 1982.

Sando, Joe S. *Pueblo Nations: Eight Centuries of Pueblo Indian History.* Santa Fe, N.Mex.: Clear Light, 1992.

_____. "The Pueblo Revolt." In *Handbook of North American Indians.* Vol. 9, edited by Alfonso Ortiz. Washington, D.C.: Government Printing Office, 1979. A brief article that gives details on the planning of the revolt.

Sandos, James. "Junípero Serra's Canonization and the Historical Record." *American Historical Review* 93 (December, 1988): 1253-1269. An important article on the controversies surrounding the early California missions.

Sandos, James A., and Larry E. Burgess. *The Hunt for Willie Boy: Indian-Hating and Popular Culture*. Norman: University of Oklahoma Press, 1994.

Santoni, Roland J. "The Indian Gaming Regulatory Act: How Did We Get Here? Where Are We Going?" *Creighton Law Review* 26 (1993): 387-447. Provides a comprehensive chronology of the legislation, pertinent legal cases, suggested amendments, and a table of tribal-state compacts.

Satz, Ronald N. *American Indian Policy in the Jacksonian Era*. Lincoln: University of Nebraska Press, 1974. Excellent coverage of the Cherokee cases; also clarifies the complex political climate in which the cases developed around conflicts between the Jackson administration, Georgia, and the Cherokees.

_____. *Indian Treaty Rights*. Madison, Wis.: Wisconsin Academy, 1991. Provides a fascinating pro-Indian account of the fishing-rights controversy in Wisconsin and elsewhere.

Satzewich, Vic, and Terry Wotherspoon. *First Nations: Race, Class, and Gender Relations*. Scarborough, Ont.: Nelson Canada, 1993. Contains a thoughtful discussion of the impact of the Indian Act on native women in Canada.

Sayer, John William. *Ghost Dancing the Law: The Wounded Knee Trials*. Cambridge, Mass.: Harvard University Press, 2000. The first book-length study of the trials looks at the influence of media and legal institutions on the way the defendants and their cause were constrained in the presentation of their case.

Scholes, France V. *Church and State in New Mexico, 1610-1650*. Historical Society of New Mexico Publications in History 7. Albuquerque: University of New Mexico Press, 1942. Takes a pro-Spanish point of view, treating Native Americans in a condescending manner. Based on translations of Spanish documents.

Schulz, Eric, and Michael Tougias. *King Philip's War: The History and Legacy of America's Forgotten Conflict*. Woodstock, Vt.: Countryman, 1999. A detailed history of Metacom's war, as well as a guide to the sites of conflict.

Schwartz, Sally. *"A Mixed Multitude": The Struggle for Toleration in Colonial Pennsylvania*. New York: New York University Press, 1987. A general history that describes the various tensions within colonial Pennsylvania and how the colony dealt with them.

Schwartz, Seymour. *The French and Indian War, 1754-1763: The Imperial*

Struggle for North America. New York: Simon & Schuster, 1994. A concise, well-illustrated study that provides a thoughtful, readable overview.

Shannon, Timothy J. *Indians and Colonists at the Crossroads of Empire: The Albany Congress of 1754.* Ithaca, N.Y.: Cornell University Press, 2000. Argues that the Albany congress was actually the moment of shifting European-Indian relationships from independent commerce to an imperialist model, based on hierarchy and governed by a distant authority rather than face-to-face.

Shattuck, Petra T., and Jill Norgren. *Partial Justice: Federal Indian Law in a Liberal Constitutional System.* New York: Berg, 1991. This study carefully analyzes the relationship of U.S. Indian law and policy to the U.S. constitutional order and governmental administrative policy.

Sheehan, Bernard W. *Savagism and Civility: Indians and Englishmen in Colonial Virginia.* New York: Cambridge University Press, 1980.

_____. *Seeds of Extinction: Jeffersonian Philanthropy and the American Indian.* Chapel Hill: University of North Carolina Press, 1973.

Sherrow, Victoria. *"Cherokee Nation v. Georgia": Native American Rights.* Springfield, N.J.: Enslow, 1997.

Sherwood, Morgan B., ed. *Alaska and Its History.* Seattle: University of Washington Press, 1967.

_____. *Exploration of Alaska, 1865-1900.* New Haven, Conn.: Yale University Press, 1965.

Siggins, Maggie. *Riel: A Life of Revolution.* Toronto: HarperCollins, 1994. Readable, lively narrative account.

Silverberg, Robert. *The Pueblo Revolt.* Introduction by Marc Simmons. Lincoln: University of Nebraska Press, 1994. An account based mainly on Hackett's earlier work. Introduction considers the revolt's legacy three centuries later.

Simmons, Marc. *New Mexico: An Interpretive History.* Albuquerque: University of New Mexico Press, 1988. Chapter 4 covers the events of the occupation of New Mexico and briefly discusses the Taos Rebellion.

Skimin, Robert. *Apache Autumn.* New York: St. Martin's Press, 1993. A historical novel that describes the Apache Wars.

Sleeper-Smith, Susan. *Indian Women and French Men: Rethinking Cultural Encounter in the Western Great Lakes.* Amherst: University of Massachusetts Press, 2001. Considers the effect of Indian women married to French men upon the early colonial fur trade.

Slotkin, Richard, and James K. Folsom, eds. *So Dreadful a Judgment: Puritan Responses to King Philip's War, 1676-1677.* Middletown, Conn.: Wesleyan University Press, 1978. Six contemporaneous accounts, including Rowlandson's narrative and the liveliest, best contemporary description of the fighting, Thomas Church's *Entertaining Passages Relating to Philip's War* (1716), based on the recollections of his father, Captain Benjamin Church.

Smith, Dwight L. "Wayne and the Treaty of Green Ville." *Ohio State Archaeological and Historical Quarterly* 63 (January, 1954): 1-7. Careful analysis of the treaty.

Smith, John. *The General History of Virginia, New England, and the Summer Isles*. Philadelphia: Kimber and Conrad, 1812. An account of life in Virginia by the first Englishman to meet Chief Powhatan.

Smith, Michael T. "The History of Indian Citizenship." In *The American Indian Past and Present*. 2d ed. New York: John Wiley & Sons, 1981. Traces the major factors that made it difficult for American Indians to obtain citizenship.

Smith, Paul Chaat, and Robert Allen Warrior. *Like a Hurricane: The American Indian Movement from Alcatraz to Wounded Knee*. New York: New Press, 1997.

Snow, Dean R. *The Iroquois*. The Peoples of America series. Cambridge: Blackwell, 1994. Follows the development of the Iroquois Confederacy. Extensive bibliography, index.

Sosin, Jack M. *Whitehall and the Wilderness: The Middle West in British Colonial Policy, 1760-1775*. Lincoln: University of Nebraska Press, 1961. Detailed examination of royal decisions leading to the Proclamation of 1763.

Spicer, Edward H. *Cycles of Conquest: The Impact of Spain, Mexico, and the United States on the Indians of the Southwest, 1553-1960*. Tucson: University of Arizona Press, 1962. Broad study of the impact of several generations of outside cultural, economic, and military invasions on the Indian peoples. Somewhat dated by more recent research but contains much useful material.

Stagg, Jack. *Anglo-Indian Relations in North America to 1763 and an Analysis of the Royal Proclamation of 7 October 1763*. Ottawa: Research Branch, Indian and Northern Affairs Canada, 1981. Provides a detailed interpretation of the text of the Proclamation of 1763 and the Crown's motives.

Stanley, George F. G. *The Birth of Western Canada: History of the Riel Rebellions*. Toronto: University of Toronto Press, 1960. Argues that the rebellions were the defining event in western Canadian history.

Stannard, David E. *American Holocaust: The Conquest of the New World*. New York: Oxford University Press, 1992.

Starkey, Armstrong. *European and Native American Warfare, 1675-1815*. Norman: University of Oklahoma Press, 1998.

Steele, Ian K. *Warpaths: Invasions of North America*. New York: Oxford University Press, 1994. Places the decisions for the Proclamation of 1763 within the context of the military actions of the recent war and earlier treaties.

Stefon, Frederick J. "The Irony of Termination: 1943-1958." *The Indian Historian* 11, no. 3 (Summer, 1978): 3-14. A thorough chronological review that begins with 1887 and ends in 1968. Copiously documented, with many quotations from congressional documents and policymakers.

Stern, Theodore. *Chiefs and Change in the Oregon Country: Indian Relations at Fort Nez Perces, 1818-1855.* Corvallis: Oregon State University Press, 1996.

Stockel, Henrietta H. *Survival of the Spirit: Chiricahua Apaches in Captivity.* Las Vegas: University of Nevada Press, c. 1993. Describes the history of Chiricahua captivity.

Stone, William L. *Life of Joseph Brant.* Albany, N.Y.: J. Munsell, 1864. A source for quotations of early colonial documents. Contains some historical inaccuracies; for example, this is the source of the erroneous information that Brant was in North America at the time of the Philadelphia meeting.

Stoutenburgh, John L., Jr. *Dictionary of the American Indian.* New York: Philosophical Library, 1960. A concise resource with excellent brief biographies and summary descriptions of key events in Native American history.

Strachey, William. *The Historie of Travell into Virginia Britania (1612).* Edited by Louis Wright and Virginia Freund. 1953. Reprint. Nendeln, Liechtenstein: Kraus Reprint, 1967. A contemporaneous account of Virginia's Native Americans.

Strohmeyer, John. *Extreme Conditions: Big Oil and the Transformation of Alaska.* New York: Simon & Schuster, 1993. Illustrates the impact of the petroleum industry and law on native peoples.

Sugden, John. *Blue Jacket: Warrior of the Shawnees.* Lincoln: University of Nebraska Press, 1997. A biography of one of the main Indian leaders in the conflict.

_____. *Tecumseh: A Life.* New York: Henry Holt, 1998.

_____. *Tecumseh's Last Stand.* Norman: University of Oklahoma Press, 1985. Detailed analysis of the battle and the campaign that preceded it. Examines the question of who killed Tecumseh. Maps, illustrations, and index.

Sword, Wiley. *President Washington's Indian War: The Struggle for the Old Northwest, 1790-1795.* Norman: University of Oklahoma Press, 1985. Discusses the struggle for the northwest frontier.

Szasz, Margaret C. *Education and the American Indian: The Road to Self-Determination Since 1928.* 3d ed. Albuquerque: University of New Mexico Press, 1999.

_____. *Indian Education in the American Colonies, 1607-1783.* Albuquerque: University of New Mexico Press, 1988.

Tanner, Helen Hornbeck, ed. *Atlas of Great Lakes Indian History.* Norman: University of Oklahoma Press, 1987. This monograph traces Shawnee history through cartographic evidence. Contains a discussion of Lord Dunmore's War.

Tanner, Helen Hunt. "The Glaize in 1792: A Composite Indian Community." *Ethnohistory* 25 (Winter, 1978): 15-39.

Tate, Thad W., and David L. Ammerman. *The Chesapeake in the Seventeenth Century: Essays on the Anglo-American Society.* Chapel Hill: University of North Carolina Press, 1979. An essential collection of articles addressing race relations, class structure, and the demographics of the seventeenth century Chesapeake. Includes a historiographic discussion of Bacon's Rebellion.

Taylor, Colin F., ed. *The Native Americans: The Indigenous People of North America.* New York: Smithmark, 1991. Companion book to a 1990's televised series on Native Americans.

Taylor, Graham D. *The New Deal and American Indian Tribalism: The Administration of the Indian Reorganization Act, 1934-1945.* Lincoln: University of Nebraska Press, 1980. Argues that the IRA, although enlightened compared to previous policies, was weakened by its emphasis on tribal reorganization and its mistaken assumptions about contemporary American Indian societies.

Tebbel, John W. *The Battle of Fallen Timbers, August 20, 1794.* New York: Franklin Watts, 1972. Useful history of the battle.

Tebeau, Charlton W. "The Wars of Indian Removal." In *A History of Florida.* Rev. ed. Coral Gables, Fla.: University of Miami Press, 1980. This chapter in a standard Florida history covers the Seminole Wars.

Tennant, Paul. *Aboriginal Peoples and Politics: The Indian Land Question in British Columbia, 1849-1989.* Vancouver: University of British Columbia Press, 1990. A thorough discussion of the history of Canadian Indian policy and relations between Canadian Indians and whites in the province of British Columbia. Several sections deal specifically with the Indian Act.

Thomas, David Hurst. *Exploring Ancient Native America: An Archaeological Guide.* New York: Macmillan, 1994. An outline of Native American prehistory and a guide to accessible sites. Illustrations, index, appendix of sites to visit, bibliography.

Thomas, David Hurst, et al. *The Native Americans: An Illustrated History.* Atlanta, Ga.: Turner Publishing, 1993. A colorful history that includes a concise accounting of the purchase.

Thompson, Scott. *I Will Tell My Story: A Pictorial Account of the Nez Perce War*. Seattle: University of Washington Press, 2000.

Thornton, Russell. *American Indian Holocaust and Survival: A Population History Since 1492*. Norman: University of Oklahoma Press, 1987. Provides an overview of Native American population and recovery from European contact to 1980.

Tobias, John L. "Protection, Civilization, Assimilation: An Outline History of Canada's Indian Policy." In *Sweet Promises: A Reader on Indian-White Relations in Canada*, edited by J. R. Miller. Toronto: University of Toronto Press, 1991. This article, reprinted from the *Western Canadian Journal of Anthropology*, provides a critical overview of legislation and policy making with regard to Canadian Indians.

Todorov, Tzvetan. *The Conquest of America: The Question of the Other*. Translated by Richard Howard. Norman: University of Oklahoma Press, 1999. Investigates the cultural clash between Spanish and Native American mentalities and explores the European conquest of North America as a semiotic process.

Tolles, Frederick B. *James Logan and the Culture of Provincial America*. Boston: Little, Brown, 1957. Details the life and career of James Logan, including his role in the Walking Purchase.

Tourtelott, Jonathan B., ed. "Meriwether Lewis/William Clark." In *Into the Unknown: The Story of Exploration*. Washington, D.C.: National Geographic Society, 1987. A thirty-four-page chapter devoted to the Lewis and Clark expedition.

Trafzer, Clifford. *The Kit Carson Campaign: The Last Great Navajo War*. Norman: University of Oklahoma Press, 1982. The definitive text on the Long Walk of the Navajos. Well researched and thoroughly annotated, although with some turgid language, especially when describing landscape. Three maps and sixty-eight illustrations.

Trail of Broken Treaties: BIA, I'm Not Your Indian Anymore. Rooseveltown, N.Y.: Akwesasne Notes, 1973. Contains articles published during and after the Trail events; text of the Twenty Points; the White House response; replies suggested by Trail leadership; and an update on the BIA one year later.

Trelease, Allen W. *Indian Affairs in Colonial New York: The Seventeenth Century*. Ithaca, N.Y.: Cornell University Press, 1960.

Trennert, Robert A., Jr. *Alternative to Extinction: Federal Indian Policy and the Beginnings of the Reservation System, 1846-51*. Philadelphia: University of Pennsylvania Press, 1975.

Trigger, Bruce G. *Natives and Newcomers: Canada's "Heroic Age" Reconsidered*. Montreal: McGill-Queen's University Press, 1985.

_____, ed. *Northeast*. Vol. 15 in *Handbook of North American Indians*, edited by William C. Sturtevant. Washington, D.C.: Smithsonian Institution, 1978. Discusses Native Americans from the Northeast in considerable detail, including language, history, customs, culture, and religion.

Tucker, Glenn. *Tecumseh: Vision of Glory*. Indianapolis: Bobbs-Merrill, 1956.

Turner, Allen C. "Evolution, Assimilation, and State Control of Gambling in Indian Country: Is *Cabazon v. California* an Assimilationist Wolf in Preemptive Clothing?" *Idaho Law Review* 24, no. 2 (1987-1988): 317-338. Explores the seminal case that influenced involvement of states in the compacting process.

Twitchell, Ralph Emerson. *The History of the Military Occupation of the Territory of New Mexico from 1846 to 1851 by the Government of the United States*. 1909. Reprint. Chicago: Rio Grande Press, 1963. Quotes extensively from government documents; provides biographical sketches of the principal participants.

Tyler, S. Lyman. *A History of Indian Policy*. Washington, D.C.: Government Printing Office, 1973. A brief chronological guide to Indian policy. Illustrated, containing maps, time lines, and bibliography.

_____. *Two Worlds: The Indian Encounter with the European, 1492-1509*. Salt Lake City: University of Utah Press, 1988. Provides the most concise history of the circumstances of West Indian revolts and repression in this period.

U.S. Indian Claims Commission. *Indian Claims Commission, August 13, 1946-September 30, 1978: Final Report*. Washington, D.C.: Government Printing Office, 1978.

Utley, Robert M. *Frontier Regulars: The United States Army and the Indian, 1866-1891*. Lincoln: University of Nebraska Press, 1984. An essential study of the frontier Army and the Indian Wars. Includes a chapter on the Red River War and a wealth of other pertinent information. Maps, illustrations, notes, bibliography, and index.

_____. *The Indian Frontier of the American West, 1846-1890*. Albuquerque: University of New Mexico Press, 1984. Chapter 3 includes a good partial discussion of the events leading to the Long Walk.

_____. *Last Days of the Sioux Nation*. New Haven, Conn.: Yale University Press, 1963. A highly regarded, sensitive, evenhanded study that documents the events leading up to Wounded Knee. Contains a chapter on sources, making it invaluable for further study.

Utley, Robert Marshall, and Wilcomb E. Washburn. *Indian Wars*. Boston: Houghton Mifflin, 2002. A comprehensive survey of the wars, battles, and conflicts between European Americans and Indians, written by two well-respected historians.

Vance, John T. "The Congressional Mandate and the Indian Claims Commission." *North Dakota Law Review* 45 (1969): 325-336.

Van Kirk, Sylvia. *Many Tender Ties: Women in Fur-Trade Society, 1670-1870.* Norman: University of Oklahoma Press, 1983. Examines relations between white traders and Indian/ Metis women.

Vaughan, Alden T. *New England Frontier: Puritans and Indians, 1620-1675.* Boston: Little, Brown, 1965. This helpful study of a half-century of relationships between Native Americans and European settlers is a fine starting point for research.

Vaughn, Jesse W. *Indian Fights.* Norman: University of Oklahoma Press, 1966.

Verano, John W., and Douglas H. Ubelaker, eds. *Disease and Demography in the Americas.* Washington, D.C.: Smithsonian Institution Press, 1992. A collection of articles assessing the health and demography of precontact and post-contact Native American populations.

Viola, Herman J. *Diplomats in Buckskin: A History of the Indian Delegations in Washington City.* Washington, D.C.: Smithsonian Institution Press, 1981.

_____. *Thomas L. McKenney: Architect of America's Early Indian Policy, 1816-1830.* Chicago: Sage Books, 1974. Informative biography of McKenney, superintendent of Indian trade and the first director of the Bureau of Indian Affairs, and description of his Indian policy under the administrations of presidents James Madison, James Monroe, John Quincy Adams, and Andrew Jackson. Illustrated and indexed. Bibliography.

Voices from Wounded Knee, 1973: In the Words of the Participants. Rooseveltown, N.Y.: Akwesasne Notes, 1974. Includes daily events during occupation; logs kept by U.S. marshals; quotations, interviews, diaries, and taped radio conversations from a ten-day battle; negotiations; treaty meetings at Kyle; maps and photographs.

Waddell, Gene. *Indians of the South Carolina Lowcountry, 1562-1751.* Spartanburg, S.C.: Reprint Company, 1980. Describes how enslavement was one of several major factors in the extinction of South Carolina's lowcountry tribes.

Wahlgren, Erik. *The Vikings and America.* London: Thames & Hudson, 1986.

Walch, Michael C. "Terminating the Indian Termination Policy." *Stanford Law Review* 35, no. 6 (July, 1983): 1181-1215. Well-documented survey of the rise of termination, its effects, and the impact of the fact that Congress did not repeal the termination acts.

Waldman, Carl. *Atlas of the North American Indian*. New York: Facts on File, 1985. Comprehensive coverage of history and culture, land cessions, wars, and contemporary issues. Maps, illustrations, and appendices.

_____. *Encyclopedia of Native American Tribes*. New York: Facts On File, 1988. One page summarizes events leading to Fort Neoheroka and gives some details about tribal life.

Wallace, Anthony F. C. *The Death and Rebirth of the Seneca*. New York: Alfred A. Knopf, 1970. A classic work on the history of the Seneca at the time of Handsome Lake.

_____. *Jefferson and the Indians: The Tragic Fate of the First Americans*. Cambridge, Mass.: Belknap Press of Harvard University Press, 1999.

_____. *The Long, Bitter Trail: Andrew Jackson and the Indians*. New York: Hill & Wang, 1993. Brief overview of the removal policies, the Trail of Tears, and the implications of both for U.S. history.

Wallace, Paul A. W. *Indians in Pennsylvania*. Harrisburg: Pennsylvania Historical and Museum Commission, 1981. Survey of Native Americans, including a general description of the Walking Purchase.

Washburn, Wilcomb E. *The Assault on Indian Tribalism: The General Allotment Law (Dawes Act) of 1887*. Philadelphia: J. B. Lippincott, 1975.

_____. *The Governor and the Rebel*. Chapel Hill: University of North Carolina Press, 1957. A classic study of the small details of the uprising; generous in its forgiveness of Governor Berkeley.

_____. *Red Man's Land/White Man's Law*. New York: Charles Scribner's Sons, 1971. An older but still useful account.

_____, ed. *History of Indian-White Relations*. Vol. 4 in *Handbook of North American Indians*, edited by William C. Sturtevant. Washington, D.C.: Smithsonian Institution Press, 1988. Extensive coverage of relations between American Indians and whites across the United States, from first contact to 1987.

_____, ed. *The Indian in America*. New York: Harper & Row, 1975. Arguably the best one-volume survey of the Indian experience in North America, with many useful insights and comments concerning the reservation system. Contains an extensive bibliography and comprehensive index.

_____, ed. *Indian-White Relations*. Vol. 4 in *Handbook of North American Indians*. Washington, D.C.: Smithsonian Institution Press, 1988. Discusses the American Indian in the complex federal-tribal context and contains information on citizenship.

Waters, Frank. *Brave Are My People: Indian Heroes Not Forgotten*. Santa Fe, N.Mex.: Clear Light Publishers, 1992.

Weatherford, Jack. *Native Roots: How the Indians Enriched America*. New York: Fawcett Columbine, 1991. One chapter is devoted to American Indian slaves, with a section describing the important part played by Charleston merchants in Indian slavery.

Weaver, Sally M. *Making Canadian Indian Policy: The Hidden Agenda, 1968-70*. Toronto: University of Toronto Press, 1981.

Webb, Stephen Saunders. *1676: The End of American Independence*. Cambridge, Mass.: Harvard University Press, 1985. Places the rebellion in a larger context, as a prerevolutionary condition, while providing a detailed study of the events of 1676-1677.

Weber, David J. *The Mexican Frontier, 1821-1846: The American Southwest Under Mexico*. Albuquerque: University of New Mexico Press, 1982. A comprehensive overview of the Mexican borderlands before the Mexican War. Discusses the economic impact of the Santa Fe Trade, American Indian relations, the church, society, and culture.

_____. *The Spanish Frontier in North America*. New Haven, Conn.: Yale University Press, 1992. A general overview and detailed history of the Spanish presence in North America, from the early 1500's to the 1830's. A balanced view of relations between Native Americans and the Spanish, with much useful information on religion, social structure, and culture.

_____. *What Caused the Pueblo Revolt of 1680?* Boston: Bedford/St. Martin's Press, 1999.

Wedel, Waldo C. *Central Plains Prehistory: Holocene Environments and Culture Change in the Republican River Basin*. Lincoln: University of Nebraska Press, 1986.

_____. "The Prehistoric Plains." In *Ancient North Americans*, edited by Jesse D. Jennings. San Francisco: W. H. Freeman, 1983.

Weslager, C. A. *Delaware's Buried Past: A Study of Archaeological Adventure*. Rev. ed. New Brunswick, N.J.: Rutgers University Press, 1968.

_____. "Did Minuit Buy Manhattan Island from the Indians?" *De Halve Maen* 43 (October, 1968): 5-6. Questions whether Minuit actually purchased the island and suggests that Verhulst did instead.

Weyler, Rex. *Blood of the Land: The U.S. Government and Corporate War Against the First Nations*. 2d ed. Philadelphia: New Society Publishers, 1992.

White, Richard. *The Middle Ground: Indians, Empires, and Republics in the Great Lakes Region, 1650-1815*. New York: Cambridge University Press, 1991. Discusses how both Europeans and American Indians sought accommodation and common meaning. Places Lord Dunmore's War within this context in his analysis of the event.

_____. *The Roots of Dependency: Subsistence, Environment, and Social Change Among the Choctaws, Paw-nees, and Navajos*. Lincoln: University of Nebraska Press, 1983.

Wickman, Patricia R. *Osceola's Legacy*. Tuscaloosa: University of Alabama Press, 1991. A study of the life and myth of Osceola, based on a survey of artifacts and documents.

Wilkins, David E. *American Indian Sovereignty and the U.S. Supreme Court: The Masking of Justice*. Austin: University of Texas Press, 1997. Close analysis of legal cases that Wilkins argues "mask questionable federal and administrative activities against tribes and individual Indians."

Wilkins, Thurman. *Cherokee Tragedy: The Ridge Family and the Decimation of a People*. Rev. ed. Norman: University of Oklahoma Press, 1986. Discusses the prominent family of Cherokee leaders.

Wilkinson, Charles F. *American Indians, Time, and the Law: Native Societies in a Modern Constitutional Democracy*. New Haven, Conn.: Yale University Press, 1987. Discusses tribal sovereignty as a preconstitutional right and how this inherent right can be diminished.

Williams, Jeanne. "The Cherokees." In *Trails of Tears: American Indians Driven from Their Lands*. Dallas: Hendrick-Long, 1992. Puts Cherokee removal in the context of the similar experiences of the Comanche, Cheyenne, Apache, and Navajo.

Williams, Robert A. *Linking Arms Together: American Indian Treaty Visions of Law and Peace, 1600-1800*. New York: Oxford University Press, 1997.

_____. *The American Indian in Western Legal Thought: The Discourses of Conquest*. New York: Oxford University Press, 1990. This book deals with earlier times in white-Indian relations but is vital reading for anyone who wishes to understand the philosophical and traditional bases of American Indian law.

Wilson, Edmund. *Apologies to the Iroquois*. New York: Farrar, Straus & Cudahy, 1959. Contains a chapter on Tuscarora history. Also discusses land disputes at Niagara Falls in the 1960's.

Wilson, Frazer. *The Treaty of Greenville*. Pigua, Ohio: Correspondent Press, 1894. The only work specifically devoted to the treaty ending the campaign.

Wilson, James. *The Earth Shall Weep: A History of Native America*. New York: Atlantic Monthly Press, 1999.

Winger, Otho. *Last of the Miamis: Little Turtle*. North Manchester, Ind.: O. Winger, 1935. Concise sketch of Little Turtle's life and his attempts to forge a Native American confederation in the Ohio Valley.

Wise, Jennings C. *The Red Man in the New World Drama*, edited by Vine Deloria, Jr. New York: Macmillan, 1971. The key words "new world drama" provide a clue to the American Indian perspective of this author and editor.

Woodward, Grace Steele. "'The King, Our Father.'" In *The Cherokees*. Norman: University of Oklahoma Press, 1963. A history of the Cherokee people from the start of the Yamasee War until the end of the Cherokee War.

Woodward, Thomas S. *Woodward's Reminiscences of the Creek, or Muscogee Indians, Contained in Letters to Friends in Georgia and Alabama*. Tuscaloosa: Alabama Book Store, 1859. Reprint. Mobile, Ala.: Southern University Press, 1965. A veteran of the war, Woodward knew many Muscogee leaders and their culture. Although written with the wisdom and common sense of later years, this entertaining little volume has its errors and must be read with a critical eye.

Woodworth, S. E. *Jefferson Davis and His Generals: The Failure of Confederate Command in the West*. Lawrence: University Press of Kansas, 1990. Discusses Jefferson's top military men and their leadership on the Western front during the Civil War.

Wooster, Robert. *Nelson A. Miles and the Twilight of the Frontier Army*. Lincoln: University of Nebraska Press, 1993. Includes a chapter on the controversial soldier's extensive Red River War operations.

Wright, J. Leitch, Jr. "Brands and Slave Cords." In *The Only Land They Knew: The Tragic Story of the American Indians in the Old South*. New York: Free Press, 1981. Gives details on the Carolina slave trade in American Indians, with emphasis on historical details.

_____. *Creeks and Seminoles: The Destruction and Regeneration of the Muscogulge People*. Lincoln: University of Nebraska Press, 1986. An examination of the culture of the Creeks and Seminoles, and their Spanish, British, and African connections.

Wright, J. Leitch, Jr., and James H. Merrell. *The Only Land They Knew: American Indians in the Old South*. Lincoln: University of Nebraska Press, 1999.

Wright, Ronald. *Stolen Continents*. Boston: Houghton Mifflin, 1992. A wide-ranging study of North America since the voyages of Columbus. Contains extensive treatment of the Iroquois Confederacy; describes Handsome Lake and his religion in the general context of the subjugation of the confederacy after the Revolutionary War.

Wunder, John R. *"Retained by the People": A History of American Indians and the Bill of Rights*. New York: Oxford University Press, 1994. Chronicles the history of the relationship between American Indians and the Bill of Rights. Presents a detailed assessment of the 1968 Indian Civil Rights Act.

Wuorinen, John H. *The Finns on the Delaware, 1638-1655: An Essay in Colonial American History*. Philadelphia: University of Pennsylvania Press, 1938.

Young, Calvin M. *Little Turtle*. 1917. Reprint. Fort Wayne, Ind.: Public Library of Fort Wayne and Allen County, 1956. A sketch of Little Turtle's life, including the St. Clair battle.

Zimmerman, Bill. *Airlift to Wounded Knee*. Chicago: Swallow Press, 1976. Chronicle of eight airlift participants who delivered food and medical supplies during the occupation and were subsequently indicted for conspiracy and interfering with official duties of federal troops. Photos, notes, comments by author's attorney.

Web Resources

AcademicInfo
http://academicinfo.net/index.html
An invaluable resource for all academic online research. Offers guides to
Internet resources on just about every discipline, from all perspectives.

American Indian History and Related Issues
http://www.csulb.edu/projects/ais/
A wide-ranging list of links to sites dealing with mostly modern American
Indian history. Contains links to tribal home pages, federal depart-
ments, image banks, cultural resources, and much more.

American Indian History as Told by American Indians
http://www.manataka.org/page10.html
Links to over one hundred U.S. and Canadian Native American sites with
information on American Indian history from a native perspective.

American Indian Resources
http://jupiter.lang.osaka-u.ac.jp/~krkvls/naindex.html
A collection of links for academic research in Native American studies. Includes links to oral and written tribal histories, primary source documents, maps, and bibliographies.

American Indian Tribal Directory
http://www.indians.org/tribes/tribes.html
Site of the American Indian Heritage Foundation, with a useful directory to
all federally recognized tribes and resource library.

Black-Indian History Resources
http://anpa.ualr.edu/f_black_indian.htm
A very interesting site on the intermixing of African Americans and the
Five Civilized Tribes.

CodeTalk
http://www.codetalk.fed.us/
A federal web site that covers subjects of interest to Native American communities, with links to most federal government offices dealing with Indian Affairs.

Diversity and Ethnic Studies: Recommended American Indian Web Sites

http://www.public.iastate.edu/~savega/amer_ind.htm

A list of academically reliable web sites, including links to a number of on-line journals and newspapers.

First Nation Information Project

http://www.johnco.com/firstnat/index.html

A very thorough resource for information on all aspects of life among the Canadian First Nations.

First Nations Histories

http://www.tolatsga.org/Compacts.html

Provides short histories of all Canadian First Nations, along with bibliographies and maps.

Index of Native American Resources on the Internet

http://www.hanksville.org/NAresources/

A comprehensive index to Internet resources, frequently updated.

Indian Affairs: Laws and Treaties

http://digital.library.okstate.edu/kappler/index.htm

A digitized edition of Charles J. Kappler's 1904 work on the relations between the U.S. government and Native American tribes.

Indian Peoples of the Northern Great Plains

http://libmuse.msu.montana.edu:4000/NAD/nad.home

A searchable photographic database.

Indian Trusts Assets Management

http://www.doi.gov/indiantrust/index.html

The U.S. Department of the Interior's web site covering issues regarding Indian Trusts, with updates on the ongoing legal disputes.

Internet Law Library: Indian Nations and Tribes

http://www.nsulaw.nova.edu/library/ushouse/31.htm

Links to numerous sites with information on legal relations between the U.S. government and Native American tribes. Includes a number of links dealing with treaties.

Library of Congress: American Indians of the Pacific Northwest
http://memory.loc.gov/ammem/award98/wauhtml/aipnhome.html
A virtual museum of photographs and archive of texts relating to the history of the Plateau and Northwest Coast Native Americans. May be browsed by keyword, subject, and geographic location.

Native American Documents Project
http://www.csusm.edu/nadp/
Provides primary source documentation of the allotment system, published reports of the Bureau of Indian Affairs in the 1870's, and information on the Rogue River War and the Silitz reservation.

Native American History and Studies
http://www.tntech.edu/www/acad/hist/nativam.html
A collection of historical links hosted by the history department at Tennessee Technological University.

Native American Research Page
http://maple.lemoyne.edu/~bucko/indian.html
A collection of links to resources on all aspects of Native American culture and life.

Native American Sites
http://www.nativeculture.com/lisamitten/indians.html
A web site maintained by a Native American librarian and editor, dedicated to providing academically sounds links to the web sites of Native American organizations and nations.

NativeWeb History Resources
http://www.nativeweb.org/resources/history/
A page on the larger NativeWeb site offers links to pages on many events in Native American history, with each link identified for the tribe and geographic location it covers.

Office of Tribal Justice
http://www.usdoj.gov/otj/
The web site of the division of the U.S. Department of Justice that deals with Native American issues. Includes a statement of the Department of Justice's sovereignty policy.

On This Date in North American Indian History
http://americanindian.net/
A site dedicated to timelines of Native American historical events.

Smithsonian Institution: Native American History and Culture
http://www.si.edu/resource/faq/nmai/start.htm
Links to Native American resources at the Smithsonian, including a number of online museum exhibits. The "Native American Portraits from the National Portrait Gallery" exhibit features many historically important Native Americans.

Treaty Negotiations Office of the Attorney General of British Columbia
http://www.gov.bc.ca/tno/
Contains information about treaties between Canada and First Nations, with updates on current legislation and negotiations.

Tribal Law and Policy Institute
http://www.tribal-institute.org/lists/tlpi.htm
The site of a Native American nonprofit institute dedicated to increasing resources for tribal judicial systems and operations.

Leslie Ellen Jones

American Indian History

Categorized Index

Geographical Index

Personages Index

Tribes Index

Subject Index

Please refer to the Tribes Index, which precedes this Subject Index, for names of bands, nations, and other Native American groups. Names of historical figures will be found in the Personages Index, which precedes the Tribes Index.

DRUMS. *See* Determination of Rights and Unity for Menominee Shareholders *and* Determined Residents United for Mohawk Sovereignty

Duro v. Reina (1984-1990), 122-123, 298

Dutch colonialism, 234-236, 270; Manhattan Island purchase, 353-356

Earth lodges, 443

Eastern seaboard. *See* Geographical Index

Economic development, 205

Education, 482; boarding schools, 64-68; early twentieth century, 204; higher, 23-24, 296; Indian Act of 1989, 183; Iroquois comments, 239; nineteenth century, 80-81, 289

Edwardsville, Treaty of (1819), 323

Effigy Mounds National Monument, Iowa, 622

El Cuartelejo, Kansas, 623

El Morro, New Mexico, 623

Eleventh Amendment, 202

Elk v. Wilkins (1884), 123, 190, 289

Emerald Mound, Mississippi, 623

Empire (term), 562

Employment Division, Department of Human Resources of Oregon et al. v. Smith (1990), 32, 124-125

Encomienda system, 261, 466, 584, 612

Endangered Species Act (1973), 558

Enfranchisement Acts (1869), 231

English colonialism, 237-244; Canada, 226-233; vs. Spanish, 263

Epidemics, 125-129, 240, 418, 466; Aleuts, 259; California, 266; Canada, 229. *See also* Diseases

Etowah, Georgia, 623

Ex parte Crow Dog (1883), 130-131, 289, 352

Factory system of trade regulation (1796), 275

Fallen Timbers, Battle of (1794), 131-135, 144, 274, 333, 573

Fallen Timbers Battlefield, Ohio, 624

Federal Acknowledgment Program, 136

Federally recognized tribes, 136, 564

Fifteen Principles (1983), 137

Finn colonists, 270

First Nations. *See* Aboriginal Canadians

Fish-ins, 138-140, 381, 571

Five Civilized Tribes, 98, 290; during Civil War, 282

Florida; Franciscans, 262. *See also* Geographical Index

Folsom points, 439

Folsom Site, New Mexico, 624

Folsom tradition, 447

Fort Ancient, Ohio, 624

Fort Atkinson Treaty (1853), 140

Fort Belknap, Texas, 624

Fort Gibson, Oklahoma, 624

Fort Greenville Treaty (1795), 135, 140-144, 155, 274, 398, 525

Fort Harmar Treaty (1789), 154

Fort Harrison, Treaty of (1819), 323

Fort Industry, Treaty of (1805), 334

Fort Jackson, Treaty of. *See* Horseshoe Bend Treaty

Fort Laramie Treaty of 1851, 69, 140, 145-146

Fort Laramie Treaty of 1868, 147-149, 330

Fort Mims, Battle of (1813), 149-151

Fort Neoheroka, Battle of (1713), 568

Fort Osage, Missouri, 625

Fort Phil Kearny, Wyoming, 625

Fort Richardson, Texas, 625

Fort Robinson and Red Cloud Agency, Nebraska, 625

Fort Shantok, Connecticut, 626

Fort Sill, Oklahoma, 626

Fort Stanwix Treaty (1768), 347, 419, 459, 572

Fort Stanwix Treaty (1784), 141, 151-154, 397

Fort Thompson Mounds, South Dakota, 626

Fort Washita, Oklahoma, 626

Fort Wayne Treaty (1809), 155-156, 463, 527, 537